The Manliest Man

The Manliest Man

SAMUEL G. HOWE

AND THE CONTOURS OF

NINETEENTH-CENTURY

AMERICAN REFORM

James W. Trent Jr.

University of Massachusetts Press
Amherst & Boston

LC 2012008132
ISBN 978-1-55849-959-1 (paper); 958-4 (library cloth)
Designed by Jack Harrison
Set in Adobe Garamond Pro
Printed and bound by Thomson-Shore

Library of Congress Cataloging-in-Publication Data
Trent, James W.
The manliest man : Samuel G. Howe and the contours of
nineteenth-century American reform / James W. Trent Jr.
p. cm.
Includes bibliographical references and index.
ISBN 978-1-55849-959-1 (pbk. : alk. paper) —
ISBN 978-1-55849-958-4 (library cloth : alk. paper)
1. Howe, S. G. (Samuel Gridley), 1801-1876.
2. Philanthropists—United States—Biography.
3. Social reformers—United States—Biography.
4. Physicians—United States—Biography.
5. United States—History—19th century.   I. Title.
HV1624.H7T74 2012
371.9'11092—dc23
[B]
2012008132

British Library Cataloguing in Publication data are available.

Frontispiece:
S. G. Howe (ca. 1850). Courtesy Boyd B. Stutler Collection,
West Virginia State Archives.

CONTENTS

ILLUSTRATIONS

ACKNOWLEDGMENTS

I first became acquainted with Samuel G. Howe while working on my book *Inventing the Feeble Mind: A History of Mental Retardation in the United States.* I found in his perspectives on the integration of disabled people into the ordinary patterns of community life an unexpectedly progressive voice. I was struck by his criticisms of the very institutions he had helped to develop and promote. As I read in the vast primary source materials available, I grew to admire Howe as a man of principle, of optimism, and of faith in individual and social change.

A Longfellow House fellowship I received while living in St. Louis, Missouri, allowed me to launch my study of Howe. In 2003 I moved to the Boston area in convenient proximity to the major repositories of Howe correspondence and other Howe-related documentation. In 2005 I began a nearly three-year journey into the historical records of the Hayes Research Library at the Perkins School for the Blind in Watertown, Massachusetts. This rich collection was always made accessible by the efforts of the Hayes librarian Jan Seymour-Ford. I also thank the librarians and staff members of the John Carter Brown Library at Brown University, the Chapin Library at Williams College, the library of the Massachusetts Historical Society, the Boston Public Library, the Houghton and Schlesinger Libraries of Harvard University, and the library of the Maine Historical Society. Finally, I acknowledge a faculty initiative grant and a sabbatical leave from Gordon College that allowed me to sustain the study and writing of the book.

Several people have read portions of the book in the various stages of its development. I am especially grateful for the comments and criticisms of the following readers: Douglas Baynton, Darryl Rehr, Jan Seymour-Ford, Gregory Walter, and Parnel Wickham. For excellent editorial assistance I thank Carol Betsch, Clark Dougan, and Debby Smith. I also enjoyed the support of colleagues at Gordon College: Sybil Coleman, Margie Deweese-Boyd, Ivy George, Lawrence Holcomb, Daniel Johnson, Judith Oleson, and Dan Russ. Finally, I remain most grateful for the support and many discussions held with Sue Trent, Mary Trent, Andrew Clark, and Rachel Trent. Friends, colleagues, and family made all the difference.

INTRODUCTION

With the exception of Garibaldi, I have always considered Samuel G.
Howe as the manliest man it was my fortune to meet in this world.
HENRY I. BOWDITCH

By the time she arrived at the Boston Music Hall on 8 February 1876, Laura
Bridgman, blind and deaf since before her second birthday, had already
attended two memorial services for her beloved teacher, Samuel G. Howe.
At age forty-six, Bridgman, Howe's most famous pupil, had been a student
and then a resident of the Perkins Institution and Massachusetts School for
the Blind since 1837. The first service for Howe was held Thursday morning,
13 January, in the chapel of the Perkins Institution in South Boston. For that
occasion, the chapel was "appropriately dressed in mourning emblems and
flowers," and Howe's body lay enclosed in a plain casket covered with dark
cloth and trimmed with silver lining. On its lid was a cross. A crown of flowers rested at the head of the casket and a floral helmet at the foot. Earlier that
morning, Bridgman had helped place the ornaments on the casket. Howe's
minister, the Reverend James Freeman Clarke, began the simple service with
a reading of Henry Wadsworth Longfellow's poem "Psalm of Life." Between
hymns sung by a choir of blind students of the Perkins Institution, the Reverend George A. Thayer read from scripture. Clarke ended the service with
a prayer and a benediction. In attendance were the students and the faculty
of the Perkins Institution along with Howe family members. The pall bearers
included Charles Francis Adams, Francis Bird, Samuel Downer, Henry I.
Bowditch, former Massachusetts governor Emory Washburn, Estes Howe,
John S. Dwight, and Franklin B. Sanborn. This first service was small and
intimate, and Bridgman, caught up in the solemnity of the moment, had
wept.[1]

A second service began the same day at 12:30 at the Church of the Disciples, where the Howe family often worshipped. Clarke had been the senior
minister of the church since he founded it as a "free" Unitarian church in

1841.[2] The family, but especially Julia Ward Howe, Samuel's widow, was close to Clarke. Samuel Howe had always respected Clarke's antislavery activities and especially his antislavery preaching. But Howe had been an irregular churchgoer; as he often claimed, "I pray with my feet." The service at the church was far more elaborate than the service at the institution. The Massachusetts State Senate and House had appointed a committee of its members to attend the ceremony. The church choir sang Bach's *Passion,* and Clarke read John Greenleaf Whittier's poem "The Hero," written several decades earlier to commemorate Howe's Romantic exploits in Greece and his humanitarian work among the disabled. The Perkins Institution's choir sang the hymn "Nearer My God to Thee," and as he had at the morning's event, Clarke ended the service with a prayer and a benediction. By late afternoon Howe's remains were buried on Spruce Street in Mount Auburn Cemetery in Cambridge near the grave of his deceased son, Sammy. Bridgman, along with several other students at the Perkins Institution, attended the interment.[3]

The ceremony three weeks later, on 8 February, in the ornate Boston Music Hall was the largest of the three gatherings to memorialize the Boston philanthropist. Less than two years earlier, a similar event at the Music Hall had memorialized Massachusetts senator Charles Sumner, one of Howe's dearest and oldest friends. The hall's large auditorium was filled to capacity with "an audience representing the best culture of Boston, and the platform was occupied by her most prominent citizens." Several guests had come from other cities and even from other states to pay their respects. This was not to be a subdued, intimate service as the earlier two in January had been. Indeed, this service was the one for all the people who had known and been touched by a man who most in attendance regarded as a great humanitarian.[4]

At 2:40 the service began with an organ voluntary, followed by a few words of tribute by Frank Bird, Howe's young friend and one of his pallbearers, and a 'brief" and "fervent" prayer by Clarke The first of many speakers on that cold February afternoon was Massachusetts governor Alexander Hamilton Rice, who described Howe as the greatest philanthropist in Massachusetts history. Howe, he said, "sought the amelioration of every form of human suffering and the elevation of society by means at once comprehensive, philosophical, and humane." Rice ended his remarks with a typically Victorian sentiment: "Death can bring to him no change but from the toils of earth to the fruitions of hope, and to the gratification of his aspiring soul in the higher intelligence and the ever unfolding glories of immortality."

Alexander Hamilton Bullock, a former Massachusetts governor, spoke next, reminding the audience that though Howe had served only one term in the Massachusetts House of Representatives, he was influential in persuading elected officials to enact legislation that assisted the most needy and most helpless citizens of the commonwealth. Alexis Caswell, a former president of Brown University and classmate of Howe's, then drew laughter from the otherwise solemn audience with stories about Howe's undergraduate pranks at Brown.

Another former Massachusetts governor, William Gaston, praised Howe's humanity, his honesty, and his quiet courage. Gaston was followed by Oliver Wendell Holmes Sr., who recited a poem he had written especially for the occasion. Like Howe, Holmes was a physician, and he had known Howe for many years. The two men had long since come to terms with Holmes's signature to a petition favoring Daniel Webster's support for the Compromise of 1850. The recitation left many in the hall in tears. One stanza of the poem reads:

> *He touches the eyelids of the blind,*
> *And lo! The veil withdrawn,*
> *As o'er the midnight of the mind,*
> *Haled the light of dawn.*

The Reverend Frederick H. Hedge spoke about Howe's courage, generosity, and tolerance of difference. Frank Bird spoke about his "love for home, wife, and children, his simple tastes, and his remarkable modesty." Edward Everett Hale and E. M. Gallaudet both recalled Howe's work to educate Laura Bridgman, and Thomas Wentworth Higginson, who had been a friend of Howe's since their days supporting John Brown, spoke about Howe's antislavery activities. Prayers and hymns were presented at intervals between the speakers, among them a hymn written by the Reverend William Ellery Channing and sung "very sweetly" by the choir of the Perkins Institution.

In his remarks during the service, Gallaudet, who could communicate with Bridgman through finger spelling, recounted a conversation he had had with her. These remarks were published in several Boston newspapers. Bridgman told Gallaudet, "I have lost my best friend." When Gallaudet expressed his sympathy, she responded with the Biblical phrase "God is a present help in time of need."

A week earlier Bridgman had described her feelings more intimately in a letter to her former teacher and companion Mary Swift Lamson. "Your letter came to me with much welcome & joy," she wrote. "There is a good comfort [and] in it much sunshine, though it tries my feelings in [the] thought of never meeting & grasping my best & noble friend Dr. Howe on earth. The path seems so desolate & void without sight of him to us all. . . . I think much of Dr. H. day & night with sorrow & gratitude & love & sincerity."[5]

Bridgman's words and those spoken by the many luminaries at the memorial services for Samuel G. Howe in January and February 1876 attest to the love and admiration Howe had inspired. Even among those who felt neither love nor admiration for him, Howe had earned respect. Shortly after his death, Julia Ward Howe published an appreciative biography of her husband. Later his friends and his daughter Laura Howe Richards published equally admiring portraits and sketches of his life.[6] In 1936, to commemorate the tercentenary of Harvard University, a committee under the direction of the historian Dumas Malone ranked the university's "fifty greatest sons" among its deceased graduates. The committee placed Howe at number twenty, ahead of Oliver Wendell Holmes, father and son, Henry Adams, Ralph Waldo Emerson, Francis Parkman, Henry David Thoreau, Wendell Phillips, and Theodore Roosevelt.[7] As late as 1952, Hedda Hopper, the Hollywood gossip columnist, reported that the producer Darryl Zanuck was planning a motion picture (presumably never made) about Howe's exploits in Greece. Gregory Peck, she noted, wanted to play the part of Howe.[8] Whether portraying him as a champion of Greek freedom against Turkish domination, the benevolent teacher of blind and intellectually disabled children, or the friend of the prisoner and the slave, Howe's associates and earliest biographers remembered him fondly. For nearly a hundred years after his death, Howe's legacy remained honored.

In recent decades, however, Howe has lost much of his earlier acclaim. Critics from different disciplines and various perspectives have questioned Howe's character, his philanthropic motives, his treatment of his spouse, and his guidance of Laura Bridgman. By the beginning of the twentieth-first century, Howe's heroic, humanitarian, even manly persona, so firmly held before the mid-1950s, had come under serious doubt.[9]

The biographer of Samuel G. Howe must resist the temptation to venerate or to vilify. Like most human beings, Howe lived a life of good deeds and bad, of heroism and fear, of seriousness and of good humor, and of kindness and sensitivity as well as impatience and cruelty. He participated in extraordinary social, economic, and political changes that shaped, and were shaped by, his life. Having studied Howe for over a decade, like Laura Bridgman, I consider Howe a beloved friend, though a friend with flaws and failings.

In this biography I explore these flaws and failings, along with the idealism and strength of character that became Samuel G. Howe. I do so in the context of three interrelated themes that emerged from my study of the man: Howe's embodiment of the nineteenth-century concept of manliness, his participation in the contemporary reform movement, and his belief in the "perfectibility of man." The words I use in the book's title, "the manliest man," are words Henry I. Bowditch used to describe Howe, his recently deceased friend, fellow physician, and longtime comrade in the free-soil anti-slavery movement. To New Englanders in the antebellum period, manliness included intelligence, physical strength, and moral rectitude. As the book shows, Howe's manliness was embodied in his activities in Greece, which his contemporaries regarded as Romantic and heroic, and his trips to "Bleeding Kansas" but also in his efforts to educate blind and "idiotic" children and in his defense of the fugitive slave Anthony Burns. His close friendships with Horace Mann, Charles Sumner, Henry Wadsworth Longfellow, Theodore Parker, and Francis Bird and his membership in the "Secret Six" backers of John Brown were aspects of his manliness, as were his tender words of solace to the parents of a recently deceased blind pupil, the sentimental letters he sent to Laura Bridgman on his many trips away from the Perkins Institution, and his fatherly relationship with his own children.

Manliness before the Civil War entailed strength of character and a willingness to risk one's life on behalf of noble causes but also deep idealism in a commitment to employ reason and restraint of self-interest to stand for a humane ideal, for the perfect, and for the just and right. John G. Palfrey describes Howe's manliness in a private letter he sent to Frank Bird just days after Howe's death: "It was the heroic character in rare perfection. As brave as the most daring soldier, he was as tender as the gentlest woman. Immovably well-poised in his uprightness, he asked himself what in any case was the course of duty, & that course ascertained, he took it & pursued it without apprehension, without perturbation, without distraction, without passion."[10] We will discover that Howe did not always live up to the manly ideal. On one occasion, for example, he allowed self-preservation to undermine his loyalty to John Brown and to his noble (if misguided) cause; on another occasion, he substituted the ideal of equality by drifting into the "realism" of pseudo-scientific racism.[11]

In following the second theme, this book looks at Howe's place in the contours of early republican, antebellum, and postwar reforms in the United States, especially those that pertained to the education of people with disabilities and to the emancipation of slaves. And in doing so, the book also looks at Howe's private life and at the ways that his private life meshed with his public activities. Just as Howe's character emerges as a mixture of the heroic and the flawed, so too his contributions to nineteenth-century reform emerge as a combination of benevolence and open-mindedness with arrogance and insistence on social regulation. Howe expressed his idealism in a note he wrote in July 1849 to his close friend Henry Wadsworth Longfellow, praising Longfellow for his recently published book *Kavanagh:* "It seems to me that what you most especially deserve the thanks of all us common mortals for, is showing that the great elements of moral beauty and happiness, like the great elements of physical life and well-being, abound everywhere, and lie within the reach of the poorest and humblest of our race. . . . The true nectar of life is not, like the Johannesburg wine, to be squeezed only from the rare fruit that is guarded in the vineyard of princes, but also from the common clusters that hang about the porch of the poorest hut! Oh! When will men and women, especially the young, learn that the true poetry and beauty of life consist, not in rare adventure, in wild excitement, and intense passion, but in the earnest, honest, untiring pursuit of *good,* which is inspired by unselfish love of *autrui* [others]."[12]

Howe was a Jeffersonian who always referred to himself as a liberal, a champion of human rights, a defender of the graduated income tax, and a believer, in the best sense, of American exceptionalism. He believed also in an essential goodness in human beings that came from a Providential source, and he believed that human beings in their social arrangements could do the right thing. Yet, as we shall see, he also opposed the ten-hour workday for America's increasingly wage-dependent working class, and he despised public assistance for the poor, so-called outdoor relief. At times arrogant and righteous as a reformer, Howe could also be extremely self-critical (he once referred to himself as an abortion) and on several occasions begged the for-giveness of people he had offended. Throughout his marriage, his wife, Julia, described her marital frustrations in letters to her sisters; yet, just as regularly she wrote about the great affection and admiration she felt for her husband and for his reformist activities. Though at times harsh, their letters to each other continued throughout their marriage also to be tender, with the tender seeming always to follow the harsh. Howe built institutional structures in Boston and advocated for their construction throughout the nation; yet, he came to deplore those institutions and in the three decades before his death tried to undo much of his earlier work. Through this effort he became an advocate for decentralized, community-based social services.

Howe hated slavery and championed the cause of the slave; yet, he absorbed many of the racist assumptions of his time. He worked with black people such as Louis Hayden, Frederick Douglass, and Charlotte Forten, all of whom he admired, but his experiences remained in tension with his racist ideology. Howe emerges in my biography as a man of interesting contradic-tions that speak to the inconsistencies between care and control that shaped nineteenth-century American reform. Despite these inconsistencies, Howe's mature views of reform were progressive for his own time and for our own time.

The third theme, Howe's unwavering belief in the perfectibility of man, undergirded his assumptions about human nature and about human social relations. This belief was probably kindled in his undergraduate days at Brown University but certainly developed by the time of his medical school experiences at Harvard University. Rejecting the Calvinism of his Puritan ancestors, Howe, like other members of eastern Massachusetts society in the 1830s, 1840s, and 1850s, was caught up in what Robert D. Richardson has called the fervency of individual and social perfection. Though he was never favorably disposed to Emersonian individualistic Transcendentalism, throughout his adult life Howe used the language of human perfection and often associated with Transcendentalism, incorporating that language into his advocacy for groups that had been traditionally devalued (the blind, the intellectually disabled, and the slave). For these groups especially, perfectionism was inextricably linked to Howe's faith in the power of education to transform people into rational, hard-working, law-abiding citizens. Education brought out for Howe the fundamental goodness that God had placed in each human being. As his perspective matured (and he saw that education alone could not guarantee full citizenship for socially devalued people), he increasingly linked perfectibility to the social integration of these groups into the mainstream of American life. Ahead of his time by more than a century, Howe argued that educated blind and intellectually disabled people should engage in activities that were like the normal, everyday activities that all citizens participated in and enjoyed. For Howe, citizenship for people with disabilities was an aspiration that had implications for the well-being of the individual—disabled or not—as well as for the social fabric. Howe advocated for the freedman's participation in the army to defend his newly won freedom and to demonstrate to the skeptical his bravery, his manliness. In both instances, Howe saw that the perfectibility of man was linked to citizenship and that citizenship required the full integration and participation of traditionally devalued people into society. Yet, for the deaf, Howe's insistence on community integration through lip reading and vocalization ensured that many deaf citizens were deprived of the common deaf culture that manual communication provided.[13]

In 1876, when Bowditch referred to Howe as "the manliest man it was my fortune to meet in this world," he was describing a friend whose manliness was influenced by an antebellum perspective that associated manliness with humanitarian and philanthropic activities.[14] Manly adventure in a just cause and philanthropic service reflected a view of reform that emphasized the perfectibility of human beings. As a result of the carnage of the Civil War, these themes would not survive in the postwar years, especially among the younger generation of New England intelligentsia. Although Howe remained the ever adventuring Romantic committed to righting wrongs after the war, much of this younger generation would be committed neither to Romantic, humanistic reform nor to a view of manliness that included idealistic perfectibility. Realism—the touchstone of the postwar years—was a perspective that Howe could not adopt or even understand. To the end, despite his flaws and failures, he remained a man committed to a vision of manhood that embodied idealistic reform and the perfectibility of man.

CHAPTER ONE

"A Respectable, If Ordinary Boyhood"

On 22 November 1801, a Sabbath day at the Brattle Street Church in Boston, the Reverend Peter Thacher baptized the third son and fourth child of Joseph Neals How and Martha Gridley How. Named for his maternal grandfather, Samuel Gridley, the twelve-day-old boy born in his family's Pleasant Street home had the dark black hair and blue eyes of his mother's side of the family. In 1806, eight months before the boy's fifth birthday, Joseph How petitioned a Massachusetts court to add an *e* to the end of the family name, changing its spelling to Howe. Among the ten children born to the Howes, seven lived to be adults. Some, like the oldest child, Joseph Neals Howe Jr., had the light reddish hair of their father, but most, like Samuel, had their mother's dark hair. Besides his parents, the child's paternal grandfather, Edward Compton How, and his second wife, Abigail Harris How, attended the service, as did his maternal grandmother, Elizabeth Harris Gridley. His grandfather Samuel Gridley had died only a week before the boy's birth. Likely also present on that Sabbath were some of the Brattle Street congregation's prominent families. Nathan Hale, a nephew of the Revolutionary War hero, was a member, as were Amos and Abbott Lawrence, the textile manufacturers and their extended family and the families of the China trader Thomas H. Perkins and the businessman and politician Harrison Gray Otis.[1]

Congregational since its founding in 1699, the Church in Brattle Street was known, even in 1801, as a theologically liberal church where reason and control blended with confidence in human nature. Thacher had led the congregation since 1784. In the early days of his ministry, he was known as "rigidly Calvinistic," but he "gradually became more and more Arminian." At Thacher's funeral service in December 1802, the Reverend William Emerson, the father of Ralph Waldo and pastor of the First Church Boston, said of Thacher: "In the state he was the uniform and influential supporter of rational liberty. Equally a foe of licentiousness and oppression, he employed his talents as opportunity presented in defeating the machinations of the wicked, and supporting the measures of upright and consistent rulers."[2]

The Reverend Joseph S. Buckminster, "the melodious preacher . . . who had read his Greek Testament at five," assumed the congregation's pastorate in 1804. Over the next decade, under Buckminster's leadership the congregation moved toward Unitarianism. A gifted scholar and an able speaker, Buckminster died from epilepsy in 1812 at the age of twenty-eight. In that year his successor, the twenty-year-old Edward Everett—future Massachusetts governor, U.S. representative and senator, minister to Great Britain, and the "other" speaker at Gettysburg in 1863—guided the church just long enough to solidify its liberal direction before he sailed to Europe in 1815 to prepare for his appointment as professor of Greek at Harvard University. In Europe he met English and German Romantics and studied the classics at the University of Göttingen. The same day, 12 June 1815, that Everett and his traveling companion, George Ticknor, met with Lord Byron, the English Parliament heard Lord Elgin's request for the purchase of (some would later claim, the theft of) the Greco-Roman statuary that would eventually bear Elgin's name. Everett was a gifted preacher and orator; it was said that on more than one Sunday morning young Ralph Waldo Emerson would slip away from his father's church to hear Everett preach at the Brattle Street Church. Everett, Samuel Howe's pastor in his early adolescence, likely planted the seeds of classical Romanticism during Howe's young life, and he would continue to influence Howe—sometimes in ways that led to contention—for the next forty years.[3]

Everett's successor in 1818 was the twenty-one-year-old John Gorham Palfrey. Palfrey assumed his pastorate shortly after his graduation from Harvard Divinity School and, after 1825, took the Brattle Street Church, like many other Congregational churches in Boston, into formal Unitarianism. Like Everett, he influenced Howe in his adolescence. But because Palfrey and Howe later shared antislavery, free-soil loyalties, that influence never had contentious results. Palfrey's face, according to Frank Gatell, "suggested his character, with blunt features and close-set eyes, indicating a forceful man of action (he would later be elected to Congress) and a high, broad forehead, indicating intellect and cultivation (he edited the *North American Review*)." Palfrey remained with the congregation until 1831 when, like Everett before him, he took an endowed chair at Harvard and eventually became the dean of the Harvard Divinity School. He was later elected to the U.S. Congress.[4]

The Brattle Street Church might have been known for its liberal theology, but the social standing of its membership hardly reflected broadmindedness. John Adams once quipped that the church was "the politest congregation in

Boston." It was polite because its membership was homogeneous in class and status. At the beginning of the nineteenth century, the congregation claimed many of Boston's wealthiest families and several of its most influential politicians. The theology, wealth, and influence, however, were not incompatible. Drawing on their Puritan ancestry, the members integrated their Calvinism with what they regarded as their Yankee ingenuity. They saw themselves as chosen, elect, and blessed but also rational, scientific, and self-confident. Their wealth reflected God's affirmation not only of their salvation but also of their ingenuity. Even by 1801, the congregation's Yankee initiative was displacing its Puritan traditions. So by the time that the Brattle Street Church formally identified itself with Unitarianism around 1826, it had rejected Calvinistic notions of predestination, original sin, and eternal damnation for the fallen. By rejecting this long-accepted wisdom, the church substituted the image of a loving and benevolent God who rewarded prudent people like the well-to-do members of the Brattle Street congregation. Nearly four decades later and long after his youthful enchantment with Edward Everett had ended, Ralph Waldo Emerson called their theology "the best diagonal line that can be drawn between Jesus Christ and Abbott Lawrence."[5]

Samuel Howe's father, Joseph Neals Howe, was unlike most of his Brattle Street Church contemporaries in that he was not a Federalist but a "Democratic Republican" who supported Thomas Jefferson, James Madison, and President Madison's War of 1812. Joseph's father, Edward Compton How, had shown his revolutionary proclivities by participating in the Boston Tea Party as one of the "Indians." And family legend held that the Howe radicalism went back to a distant relative, Elizabeth How of Ipswich, who had been hanged as a witch in 1692.

During James Madison's second term of office, Joseph had become one of the vice presidents of the Boston Jeffersonian party, a position he would hold for a decade. On the day of Madison's second inauguration, 4 March 1813, he celebrated the party's victory at a public dinner at Boston's Concert Hall with other prominent Democratic Republicans who raised their glasses in patriotic toasts and showed "rational conviviality, hilarity and glee . . . untarnished by the slightest infringement of decency or decorum."[6] That same year, Joseph Howe became a director of the Boston State Bank and a trustee of the Massachusetts Charitable Society and the Boston Humane Society—all institutions supported by Boston Jeffersonians. In January 1814, after a fire destroyed large sections of Portsmouth, New Hampshire, he contributed two hundred dollars—a generous sum at that time—for the city's relief. In 1819, when Samuel was seventeen years old, Joseph ran unsuccessfully for the Massachusetts legislature as a Jeffersonian anti-Federalist, and during the same year, he served as vice president of the Republican Institution, a group of Boston Jeffersonians who purchased a building to use as a political-social enclave for Democratic Republicans in Federalist Boston.[7]

The second decade of the nineteenth century was not a propitious time to be a Jeffersonian Republican in Boston. Although Massachusetts Republicans had secured the governorship and controlled the General Court in 1806, the embargo placed on shipping as a result of the war had incurred the wrath of Boston's business interests, especially those associated with shipping. The ensuing economic downturn had caused a resurgence of the Federalist Party. By 1814 these frustrated Federalists were threatening state succession. Being an adolescent during much of this decade proved to be difficult for Samuel Howe. His children recalled Howe's recounting stories about the abuse he received from his peers because of his family's loyalty to the party of Jefferson and Madison.[8]

Though his politics were unusual for a man of his social standing in Boston, Joseph Howe's occupation was ordinary. Like many other members of the Church in Brattle Street, he was a successful businessman. Following the trade of his father, Howe during his lifetime owned various rope-making businesses. Crucial to the shipping and trading ventures of early nineteenth-century New England, these businesses, known as rope walks, involved trade in hemp (the principal component of rope) and the manufacture of large and long ropes that secured and stabilized much of the nation's merchant and military sailing vessels. The shipping business had always had its ups and downs, and since the years after the American Revolution, the rope-making businesses of Edward and Joseph Howe had experienced good and bad times. But the first decade of the new century had been a time of growth in commerce, in trade, and hence in rope making. By 1810, Joseph Howe controlled one of the largest cordage businesses in Boston. Nearly a decade later, he could boast the manufacturing of the USS *Columbia*'s twenty-four-inch cable of one hundred fathoms in nine hours, and its successful laying up in ten minutes. With sales offices extending from Mouton Street to the Mystic River on the long wharf and manufacturing not far from the Howe home on Pleasant Street, the business made the Howe family not rich but certainly well-to-do.[9]

In an 1857 letter to Horace Mann, who at the time was the president of Antioch College, Samuel Howe described his boyhood. Mann, one of Howe's closest and oldest friends, had asked Howe for biographical information for the New York educator Henry Bernard, who planned to do a piece about Howe for his *American Journal of Education,* and for Mann himself, who hoped to deliver a chapel sermon about Howe to his students at the new Ohio college. Howe had avoided the request for over a year, but Mann had persisted. In the letter, Howe says of his father: "He was wealthy during my childhood and boyhood, & I lacked that inestimable advantage which children in indigent families have of habits of prudence and economy. My father had a large and luxurious home, with servants, horses, etc., at command."[10]

A member of one of Boston's most prominent churches, a supporter of civic and philanthropic associations, and a successful businessman, Joseph Howe had also married prominently. Martha Gridley was nineteen years old when she married the twenty-two-year-old Joseph on 11 September 1794 at the Federal Street Church. The presiding minister was the socially prominent pastor and historian Jeremy Belknap. Her parents, Samuel and Elizabeth Harris Gridley, were delighted to have their daughter, whom they called Patty, married into the How family, whose revolutionary loyalties and business successes paralleled those of the Gridley family. Samuel Gridley had been a captain and an artillery commander with the Massachusetts colonial militia in its 16–17 June 1775 battle at Bunker Hill, and his brother Richard was an engineer who helped to fortify the colonists' position in the same battle. A generation before the American Revolution, their ancestor Jeremy Gridley had been the attorney general of the royal province of Massachusetts Bay. As superintendent of the Boston Glass Manufactory, Martha's paternal grandfather had prospered supplying window panes for Boston's postwar housing boom.[11]

Martha Gridley Howe died on 26 March 1819 at the age of forty-four, giving birth to her tenth child, who would die unnamed. Samuel Howe was then a junior at Brown University. Later, in an 1831 diary entry, he referred to his mother as "our sainted and ever beloved and lamented mother."[12] When his father married Rebecca Thayer Calef of Milton in 1825, Samuel, in Greece at the time, resented the marriage as much for what he expressed as his father's disloyalty to his mother's memory as for what he saw as the bad treatment his stepmother was giving his younger sisters. What little information about Martha Gridley Howe survives suggests that her son Samuel grew to be more a Gridley than a Howe.[13] Ironically, Samuel Howe disliked his middle name and never used it when signing his name. He became known as Samuel Gridley Howe only after his death when his widow, Julia Ward Howe, began the tradition of identifying him by all three names.

"I was an ordinary boy," Howe says in his 1857 letter to Mann, "bashful to the last degree, fond of approbation, fond of adventure, given to fighting as the champion of smaller boys, though I think now, quite as much from the glory to myself, as the good of them." He had, he says, "many mishaps, & hair breadth escapes from drowning, and from fire-arms," adding, "I do not think I have any more than ordinary courage, though love of adventure carried me into many dangers. [I] have been habitually, and never-ceasingly aware of the presence of danger, & circumspect. I always have in mind the safest place . . . and am wary about getting into danger; though able to appear decently cool when it comes."[14] Even as a young man, Howe seems to have regarded manliness as a matter of reason and restraint of passions, as well as of daring and adventure.

Long after Howe's death, Julia and the children recalled the stories Howe would tell about his youth. No doubt because they complemented his children's image of a father who teased and "horsed around," these tales of youthful adventure became family legend. Yet because they showed a different side of their "benevolent" father, the stories also became a source of contrast for the image of a serious philanthropist that much of his adult contemporaries insisted on making him. One story that his daughter Laura remembered his telling was of young Sam "running tiddledies," a spring game that involved jumping among the loose ice sheets on Boston's Back Bay (when it was still a bay). Boys would dare each other to exceed the number of "ice cakes" traversed by the previous contender. Determined to outdo the other boys, Sam Howe eventually slipped and landed in the cold water. Arriving at his father's rope walk dripping wet and chilled from top to bottom, the boy got no sympathy from his father. The adult Samuel Howe would chuckle, inspiring great laughter in his children, as he repeated his father's words, "Go home and tell your mother to whip you." The story always ended with the statement, "I went home, but my mother never whipped me."[15]

Howe felt that his early education had been poor. His father valued learning but beyond basic reading, writing, and ciphering had received little formal education. Howe wrote Mann about attending the Boston Latin School, where a cruel headmaster once threw him down steps onto School Street and where his family's Jeffersonian sympathies left him a lone Republican among Federalists. In an address to the American Institute of Instruction at its 1842 annual meeting, Howe referred to his time at the Boston Latin School as "the period of my school imprisonment" and criticized the school's teaching methods. He described a composition exercise to which, he said, "I looked forward in those days with fear and trembling, and upon which I now look back with mortification and regret." And he recalled "standing up in a row" to read in unison words whose meaning was often unknown to him or to any other boy.[16] Despite these memories, there is no indication in the records of the Boston Latin School that Howe ever attended the school. Perhaps, because of the intimidation and harsh treatment he describes, he attended for so short a time that that no record was made of his attendance.[17]

Howe spent a longer, more pleasant time at a college preparatory school run by the Reverend Joseph Richardson and his wife, Anne Bowers Richardson, in their home in Hingham, Massachusetts, south of Boston. In 1806, Joseph Richardson had succeeded the Reverend Henry Ware as pastor of the

First Parish Church of Hingham. The previous year Ware had accepted the first Hollis Chair of Divinity at Harvard University. Richardson served the Hingham church until 1855 and died in 1871 at the age of ninety-three. He was a member of the Massachusetts General Court between 1821 and 1826, when he was elected to the U.S. House of Representatives, where he served two terms. His contemporaries described him as "of a sanguine temperament, frank and decided in expression of his opinion." Like many other clergymen of the time, Richardson supplemented his income by opening the school in his home. He and his wife had no children of their own, and so they took a keen interest in their pupils. Though not easily accessible, especially when heavy rains turned roads to mud, the Hingham school nevertheless attracted several Boston boys. Samuel attended the school with his younger brother Edward and about fifteen other boys.

Besides Latin and rudimentary algebra and geometry, the instruction Howe received at the school came from Richardson's publication *The American Reader,* which first appeared in 1810, retailing for $3.50 for a dozen copies. One of the earliest textbooks for school boys that included only selections from North American writers, Richardson's reader combined history, biography, and natural philosophy (or science) with lessons in virtue, proper grammar, and useful knowledge, along with examples of adventure and heroism. Before he left Richardson's school, Howe had read selections of the works of John Adams, John Quincy Adams, Benjamin Franklin, Thomas Jefferson, John Marshall, Benjamin Rush, George Washington, and other American exemplars. These readings, selected by Richardson, had in common an anti-Calvinism that looked toward individual responsibility and capability, personal freedom, and social progress—all values that young Howe absorbed and retained throughout his life.[18]

To Providence and Back Again to Boston

In 1818, at the age of seventeen, Howe left Richardson's Hingham school to enter Brown University, or Providence College as he continued to call it throughout his life. Richardson was a Brown graduate and may have influenced Howe's choice. The Howe family claimed that Joseph Howe, because he was a staunch Jeffersonian, did not want his son to attend Federalist Harvard University, and so he sent him to the more tolerant Baptists in Providence. Samuel's classmate Alexis Caswell years later while president of Brown University remembered Howe during his undergraduate years:

> He was a mere stripling, but nature had been generous in giving him an attractive physique. He was of middling height, slender in form, erect, agile, and elastic in movement. With fine features, a fresh, pink complexion, a keen

blue eye, full of purpose and meaning, and of mirth as well, with open, frank, and genial manners, he could not fail to win the kind regard of his youthful companions. He showed mental capabilities which would naturally fit him for fine scholarship. His mind was quick, versatile, and inventive. I do not think he was deficient in logical power, but the severer studies did not seem to be congenial to him. In all practical matters he saw intuitively and at a glance what was the best thing to be done.[19]

Howe's first year at Brown by his own admission was one of mischief making and pranks. As he recounted to Mann in his 1857 letter, "At College I did nothing worthy. My approbationess led me to seek excellence in roguish scrapes, though I had no malice against any one." Another classmate remembered him as "wild and daring" and a "restless spirit," but like Caswell, he also remembered Howe's generosity.[20]

Three events the next year, about which history provides only limited information, would indelibly change Samuel Howe's life. Eighteen years old during most of the year, he was a junior, having, despite his claims of poor educational preparation, entered the university as a sophomore. On 12 March, Brown University's president, Asa Messer, wrote Joseph Howe to inform him that he had decided to rusticate his son to the Reverend Josephus Wheaton, pastor of the First Congregational Church of Holliston, Massachusetts, and, indeed, had sent Samuel that day to Wheaton. Rustication, a method of punishment and reform the administrators of virtually all colleges and universities during the colonial and New Republic years used to control recalcitrant behavior among their undergraduates, was usually reserved for students who were only a short distance from expulsion. These students would be placed with a Protestant minister usually for an academic term. During this time away from the temptations of the college, the student was expected to mend his ways under the guidance of a minister, who was likely chosen because he had had experience with such students. Messer informed Joseph Howe: "Your son since his return has thrown a stone through the window of one of the Tutors, and has put into his bed a shovel of ashes; though the Tutor had given him no Provocation; nor did even know him." Normally his actions would be grounds for expulsion, Messer added, and only "the confession and promises of your son could have forced us from the necessity of inflicting on him this collegial capital punishment." Samuel would remain in Holliston until August. Although Messer did not note other misbehaviors, Howe later in life confessed to endless "monkey shines," including leading Messer's horse up to the top floor of University Hall, and squirting ink through a key hole at an unsuspecting tutor. Several of his Brown contemporaries would remember him—mostly with affection—as the quintessential class prankster.[21]

Two weeks after the start of his rustication, Howe learned that his mother had died. No record exists of the impact this news had on Howe. What the limited evidence suggests is that a profound transformation likely occurred. After the funeral and brief visit home, he returned to the Reverend Wheaton and to a new, solitary community, cut off from his friends at Brown. Wheaton, a dedicated but kindly Calvinist who even in 1819 was a prominent opponent of slavery, must have appeared peculiar to Howe. The pastor's theology and his politics, and both in small-town Holliston, were likely sources of reflection, introspection, even doubt for the young Howe.

A third blow struck Howe shortly after he returned to Brown in August 1819: his father's rope-making business nearly failed, in the midst of a national shipping embargo begun during the War of 1812 and the economic depression exacerbated by the aftermath of the war. The previous spring and summer, in an effort to raise cash, Joseph had sold off much of the contents of his home on Peasant Street and twenty-four acres of land that he owned near Great Barrington, Massachusetts.[22] But the funds from these divestitures did not relieve him from impending liability. While he was trying to refinance his business, the rope manufactory sustained fire damage on 15 November 1819. Fire insurance reimbursement and his successful petition to Congress for payment of wartime notes issued for cordage, as well as the destruction of his five major competitors' rope walks in the same fire, put Joseph back in business in a few months. But the near bankruptcy and a contentious postwar naval investigation of the Boston Navy Yard in 1822 left Joseph Howe with notoriety from which he never fully recovered.[23] Samuel, who was back in Boston in 1821 to study medicine, felt the family embarrassment. In his 1857 letter to Mann, he says of his father: "He manufactured cordage very largely for the Government, & was flattered & fooled by certain compliments from men high in office, to go on with his contract & to take treasury notes in payment—hoping that the sacrifice he was obligated to make in disposing of them would be remembered by a 'grateful country'! & all that sort of nonsense." Howe added, "These losses finally ruined him, though I believe he paid all his creditors, & finally rescued enough from the ruins to keep him from want, in his old age."

The events of 1819 transformed Samuel Howe from a student prankster to a serious young man. He had entered the university in 1818 as a seventeen-year-old sophomore. The university had required him, like every other entering undergraduate, to have an interview with President Messer, who determined his class standing. Handsome, bright, and tutored by the Brown alumnus Joseph Richardson, Howe probably made a good impression on Messer, who, at fifty years old, had been president of Brown University since 1802. A Baptist clergyman with a subtle sense of humor and a reputation for thoughtful but frank opinions, Messer was well liked by students and most alumni. He was not a traditional classicist, caring more for science and engineering than for the classics. In 1826, the theologian Edwards Amasa Park described Messer using almost phrenological language.

> No one who has ever seen him can ever forget him. His individuality was made unmistakable by his physical frame. This, while it was above the average height, was also in breadth an emblem of the expansiveness of his mental capacity. A "long head" was vulgarly ascribed to him, but it was breadth that marked his forehead; there was an expressive breadth in his maxillary bones; his broad shoulders were a sign of the weight which he was able to bear; his manner of walking was a noticeable symbol of the reach of his mind; he swung his cane far and wide as he walked, and no observer would doubt that he was an independent man; he gesticulated broadly as he preached; his enunciation was forcible, and now and then overwhelming, sometimes shrill, but was characterized by a breadth of tone and a prolonged emphasis which added to its momentum, and made an indelible impress on the memory. His pupils, when they had been unfaithful, trembled before his expansive frown, as it portended a rebuke which would well-nigh devour them; and they felt a dilating of the whole soul, when they were greeted with his good and honest and broad smile.

He had survived an investigation into his speaking engagements at liberal Congregational churches (that later became Unitarian) and the receipt in 1820 of an honorary Doctor of Divinity degree from the theologically liberal Harvard University. Yet five years after Howe graduated from Brown, Messer resigned his presidency. After twenty-four years of service, his views had become too liberal and too nonsectarian, his tongue too ironic for some of the university's board of trustees, and in his last years the undergraduate population had become too disruptive. More socially liberal than Harvard, Brown University under Messer was a good place for a Jeffersonian anti-Federalist Boston family, like the Howes, to send their son.[24]

At Brown, some of Howe's classmates were older than twenty and others were as young as fifteen. All the undergraduates lived together in University Hall, a Georgian structure with a widow's walk and eight chimneys that also housed most of the university's classrooms, its library, and its chapel. Messer had introduced natural philosophy and applied mathematics into the standard classical curriculum, which required each undergraduate class to follow the same courses over the same academic years. Most of the faculty members were, like Messer, in or past their fifties, but few were as liberal as he. The classes Howe attended were usually traditional recitations. Professors expected students to be able to recite passages from prescribed readings. By the time Howe was a student, Messer had publicly called for students to think more freely and more creatively, but with the exception of teachers like the relatively young Tristam Burgess, professor of oratory and belles lettres, most faculty members had resisted. The relationship between the professors and students extended beyond the classroom. Except for the medical faculty, most professors at Brown were expected to live in University Hall to monitor student behavior. Rules that governed the classroom also governed the dormitory. During Howe's years at Brown, students were subject to rules that covered almost every situation and most contingencies.[25]

In 1804 the school had received the endowment of Nicholas Brown Jr., the wealthy Rhode Island merchant whose gift had started the transformation of Rhode Island College into the university that bore his family's name. In 1817, the year before Samuel Howe matriculated, the university received the large library of William Richards, an English clergyman who had come to admire what he saw as the university's Christian orthodoxy without Baptist sectarianism.

Societies that emphasized elocution, with "exhibitions" of speaking ability and literary public readings, dominated the official student organizations. It was common for students and the Providence public to attend these contests of public speaking. Topics that the student speakers addressed were many of the subjects that interested Brown, Messer, and Richards: religious liberty, personal responsibility, and human improvement. In short, under Messer, the Rhode Island Baptist university had become concerned with the same enlightened topics that interested its sister institution, Harvard. By the time Howe left Brown, he had been drawn to what even then were known as liberal, "perfectionistic" issues and attitudes.

During his college years, Howe was a member of the Philendean Society, a group of students who collected textbooks for the use of poor students. A classmate at Brown remembered Howe as "quick and bright and talented." Yet with a reputation as "the wildest and most inveterately mischievous man ever connected with the institution," Howe was not expected to amount to much after his graduation on 5 September 1821.[26] During the Brown commencement ceremony in the meeting house of the First Baptist Society of Providence, Howe had no special role to play. Others gave Latin addresses and read poems and compositions, but Howe, near the bottom of his class, would merely graduate.[27] When soon thereafter he began his study of medicine at Harvard, only those Brown University classmates who knew him well were not surprised. Samuel Howe had changed. The transformation was clear even a year earlier in a letter to his classmate and friend Elijah J. Hamlin, the future Maine businessman and older brother of the future U.S. vice president Hannibal Hamlin. Using the blunt, confident diction characteristic of his later writings, Howe tackled the timeless issues of freedom, faith, and truth.

Men may be trained in infancy to belief of the most absurd doctrines, and
there is not one in a hundred who at maturer age will have strength of mind
enough to burst the shackles of superstition, and dare to exercise that *right,*
which the God of nature has given him, freedom of thought.

There are certain principles of truth, implanted in the mind of man, to
which he gives implicit belief, and by mingling *Errors,* with these truths,
they become, as it were, interwoven with his very nature, so that it is next to
impossible to eradicate them. Upon these, and some other principles, have
been reared those structures of religion, which have stood the test of ages;
vain is the attempt to overthrow them, their foundation is laid deep in the
human heart, and intimately connected with those principles dearest to man.
Christian or Mohammedan, it is the same; their religion is dearer to them
than life, and they will resign the one, rather than deny the other. Knowledge,
alone, can free men from error.[28]

Like other graduates of the class of 1821, Samuel Howe might well have
enrolled in the medical school at Brown University. Instead, he headed home
to study medicine with the Harvard University medical faculty. Perhaps the
move back to the seat of Federalism (Federalism that his father so despised)
was an attempt to put his Brown reputation behind him. Perhaps he was
ready to challenge his father, whose Republican loyalties during President
Madison's War of 1812, Samuel felt, had surely betrayed his father. Or perhaps he wanted to be closer to his three young sisters who were now living
at home without a mother. Whatever his motives may have been for leaving
Brown for Harvard, during his three years at Harvard Medical School, he
developed skills and views that would remain with him throughout his life.
In his 1857 letter to Mann, he recalled about his return to Boston, "I was
there very industrious & chose to make up for time lost in College."

At the time of Howe's return to Boston, its population was slightly over
forty thousand. In 1821, Boston still operated as a town meeting with nine
selectmen. Since the second national census in 1800, the town's population
had grown by 30 percent in each of the new century's two decades. Because of
that rapid growth, in 1822 Boston voters agreed to petition the Massachusetts
legislature to incorporate the town as a city with a mayor, an elected board
of alderman made up of eight at-large members, and a common council
consisting of forty-eight members, four from each of the city's twelve wards.
Boston's first mayor was John Phillips, the father of the future abolitionist
Wendell Phillips. Everywhere that Howe walked in 1821 there seemed to be
new construction. Boston hills were continuing to be leveled to fill in tidal
flats, and new neighborhoods were emerging, with new housing erected
quickly to complete the new neighborhoods.[29]

Howe's education over the next three years was typical of medical studies of the early decades of the nineteenth century. He first apprenticed with William Ingalls, a graduate of Harvard whose offices on Mason Street placed him among the most respected Boston physicians. Ingalls had lectured first at Brown Medical School and after 1816 at Harvard.

Howe also studied with George Parkman. Known during these years both for his anatomical museum and his interest in the humane treatment of the insane, Parkman is remembered today more for the gruesome details of his murder in November 1849 at the hands of another physician and Harvard professor of chemistry and geology, John White Webster. After completing his medical degree at Harvard in 1813, where he had been inspired by the lectures and writings of Benjamin Rush, Parkman went to Paris to observe Phillipe Pinel's work with insane patients. There he observed a radical new treatment technique known as "moral treatment."

Back home at the end of the year, Parkman immediately advocated for the use of "moral treatment" methods at the Asylum for the Insane (later known as McLean Asylum) associated with the recently opened Massachusetts General Hospital. To support his advocacy, he published three pamphlets calling for the compassionate treatment of people living with mental illness, *Proposals for Establishing a Retreat for the Insane* (1814), *The Management of Lunatics with Illustrations of Insanity* (1817), and *Remarks of Insanity* (1818). Working with Parkman, Howe was caught up in a new medical-scientific way of observing and treating insanity. The condition, Howe learned, could well come under the purview of the physician, because insanity is an illness. According to the tenets of "moral treatment," insanity is not an essential deviation; rather, as Pinel had observed and his successful treatment method had shown, insanity is merely a deviation from an essentially sane state. As such, insanity is a faulty condition of the mind, and like other faulty conditions, can be treated and cured. Howe learned from Parkman that cure was most likely achieved when insane people could rest and retreat from the stresses of life in an institution under medical supervision. Like other medical conditions, according to Parkman, insanity requires rest and time for cure, but unlike other conditions, insanity with its accompanying idiosyncrasies requires rest and cure away from family, friends, and responsibilities.[30] Later Howe would depart from Parkman's faith in curative segregation, finding instead the value of community integration of people with all sorts of disabilities.

A third faculty member of the Harvard Medical School whose anatomy lectures and dissections Howe attended from time to time was the surgeon John Collins Warren Jr. In 1845 and 1846 Warren became the first U.S. surgeon to use anesthesia in surgery. Never particularly interested in surgery, Howe did less study with Warren than with Ingalls and Parkman, but he gained from Warren an interest in anatomy and phrenology and an appreciation of the purposes of the temperance movement. "I became as expert dissector & pretty good anatomist—that is for that day," he told Mann in the 1857 letter about his youth, though attaining a cadaver required some unorthodox methods. Howe and some of his fellow medical students ventured one evening to the grave of a recently buried convict but were frightened away by jailhouse guards. Not to be deterred, Howe returned alone after midnight to exhume the body, and, as he explained to Mann: "I got the poor devil out & into a chaise & carried him to the [dissection] room. Then I had bodily strength enough to do it. I do not now see [how], but I did it."[31]

In 1823 while Howe was his student, Warren was elected president of the Massachusetts Society for the Suppression of Intemperance. Along with several other physicians, he worked with Boston mayor Josiah Quincy to restrict and eventually prohibit the sale of alcoholic beverages in theaters and other public houses. He also worked with his colleagues to reduce the use of alcohol as a prescriptive medication. During the 1820s and the 1830s leading Boston physicians, politicians, and clergy were calling for the restriction of alcohol.[32] Their efforts and Warren's example influenced Howe, who would remain a lifelong, if imperfect, abstainer from alcoholic beverages.

Harvard University's medical college first offered the M.D. degree in 1788. In 1810, the college moved from Cambridge to Boston. In 1816, five years before Howe entered it, the college moved to a newly constructed building on Mason Street, where it remained until 1846. Because the new facility had come in part from public funds, it was called the Massachusetts Medical College of Harvard University. When Howe attended the school, its location in Boston allowed students and faculty to be within walking distance of the college, of the faculty physicians' private offices, and of the Massachusetts General Hospital. A typical day for students like Howe began in a mentor's office or at the hospital seeing patients or riding with the teacher to a sick patient's home. On some afternoons, or just as likely in the evenings, faculty physicians or other practicing doctors gave lectures and demonstrations at the college. These presentations might be only pedagogical with just students in attendance, or they might be exhibitions of new procedures or new findings open to the entire Boston medical community. At some of these exhibitions, students watched their teachers spar over contentious medical questions, medical procedures, and medical assumptions.[33]

Howe's medical education ended on 25 August 1824 at Harvard University's commencement ceremonies. A warm but clear summer morning greeted the graduates and their families, the university's faculty, board of trustees, and alumni. Although important to the participants, the commencement events were ordinary except for the day's special honoree. Visiting the nation that year was one of the last living embodiments of the American Revolution, the sixty-seven-year-old Marquis de Lafayette, who had arrived in New York only nine days earlier. Word of his participation in the Harvard ceremonies had already spread throughout Boston and Cambridge, and the crowds of admirers had overwhelmed the graduation planners. Arriving two hours late from Cambridgeport, where crowds had delayed him, Lafayette entered the platform in front of University Hall to near unrestrained applause. After an introduction by the Reverend John T. Kirkland, president of the university, Lafayette spoke to the assembled crowd, among whom was the young school teacher Mary Peabody, who almost two decades later would marry Howe's college friend Horace Mann. It had been forty years since Lafayette had last visited Harvard, and he commended the university for its many improvements. He reminded graduates of the aspirations and sacrifices of the revolutionary generation. In a message he would repeat from town to town throughout his 1824–25 visit to the United States, Lafayette spoke with passion and affection for the cause of Greek independence. The struggle was generated by the recent armed insurrection of Greek partisans against their Turkish occupiers. At the end of his address he drifted into Latin, inspiring the *Salem Gazette* to observe, "[Lafayette] proves that the variety of his active pursuits has not withdrawn his attention from study, and which has done great honor to his literary tastes."[34]

Later the ceremonies moved into the university's church, where students presented their literary addresses. The *Salem Gazette* reported that the class's valedictory baccalaureate and master's students, Charles Bliss Emerson and a student identified only as Upham, had "accidentally selected the same subject," the "perfectibility of man." Their choice reflected the optimistic, Romantic, reformist, anti-Calvinistic mood of the time, which Howe was no doubt absorbing.[35] Charles Emerson, the younger brother of the 1821 Harvard graduate Ralph Waldo Emerson, would become an attorney and be engaged to marry Elizabeth Hoar, the daughter of the Concord attorney and U.S. representative Samuel R Hoar, before succumbing in 1836 to tuberculosis, the great killer of young adults throughout the nineteenth century. Inspired by the works of European Romantics and the sermons of the Reverend William Ellery Channing that refute the orthodox Calvinist doctrine of human depravity, Emerson spoke on what the *Gazette* reporter called "the doctrine of perfectibility." Reflecting on Emerson's address, the reporter concluded:

> The unexampled progress of our country in power and in wealth and in all arts of social life has at last changed the current opinion. We cannot help believing, when we daily have the facts before our eyes, that men and nations only require the aid of liberal institutions to make the most rapid advances in civilization—advance that may well be called *indefinite* since no limit in

reason can be assigned to them, excepting always the great barriers of nature. When we speak of the perfectibility of man . . . [we mean] that he will attain under favorable circumstances the degree of perfection that his nature is capable, that no good and sufficient reason can be given for a future form of society that may not exist in Europe or America as much superior to the present one as the present one is to that of the Hottentots of Africa, or the Kansas or Omawhaws of our own continent.

As Emerson, Upham, and the other graduates spoke that day, the audience saw Lafayette wipe tears from his eyes.[36]

At the dinner following the day's activities, Boston mayor Josiah Quincy, U.S. senator Daniel Webster, and the marquis's son, George Washington Lafayette, who had accompanied his father, received honorary degrees. (The senior Lafayette had received an honorary degree from Harvard during his previous visit to the university.) The university awarded sixty-seven A.B., thirty-three A.M., and five M.D. degrees. The only medical school graduate that year who had not been a Harvard undergraduate was Samuel Gridley Howe. It was a rare occurrence in which his middle name appeared in print.[37]

"He Looked More Like a Doll than a Soldier"

Lafayette's plea for Greek independence on that 1824 commencement day was a call for U.S. support for the beleaguered Greek people, who had begun their uprisings against Ottoman rule in 1821. Greece at the time was a collection of city and regional states weakly linked by a common religion, language, and culture. Many Muslim Turks lived in these regions, just as many Orthodox Greeks lived in Muslim Turkish regions. Because the Greek people shared their orthodox faith with Russians, and Russia had a long-held antipathy for the Ottoman Empire, English, French, and Prussian leaders were concerned about Russian influence in Greece and Russian conflict with Constantinople. Once the revolt began, these nations maintained public neutrality as they tolerated support for Hellenic causes among their citizenry. By 1824, support for the liberation of Greece was widespread in Europe and North America. In the United States, Greek committees were organized from New England to Georgia and from Kentucky to Missouri. Lord Byron's trip to Greece in 1823 and the publication of his rhapsodic verse *Childe Harold's Pilgrimage,* which tells of the glories of an archetypal Romantic land that Byron had first visited 1809, renewed American interest in Greece. The nation's passion for all things Greek reached its summit with Byron's untimely death on 19 April 1824. In 1822, President James Monroe, with the backing of Secretary of War John C. Calhoun, had expressed sympathy for the Greek people, but his insistence on European noninterference in American affairs, affirmed in the doctrine he presented to Congress a year later, meant that the nation would remain neutral in the Greek people's war. Also in 1822, Representative Henry W. Dwight of Massachusetts presented a memorial to Congress asking for aid to the Greek cause, and on 8 December 1823, Senator Daniel Webster filed a resolution of support for the Greek cause of independence and for authorization to send an agent to Greece to represent the nation's interests there. On 23 January 1824, General William Henry Harrison spoke for the Greek cause at a Hellenic benefit concert in Cincinnati.[38]

By 1824 committees in support of the Greek revolutionaries had sprung up throughout the United States, and these committees raised money totaling nearly a hundred thousand dollars for the aid of Greece. In some communities there were parades and talk of American men going to Greece to assist the brave revolutionaries. In other communities, as Howe explained to a friend years later, "the religious feeling was awakened, & prayers went up from thousands of churches, & from tens of thousands of closets to God for his blessing upon the Greeks."[39]

In May 1821 Edward Everett, Howe's former minister at the Brattle Street Church who had recently returned from study in Germany and an extended visit to Greece, published *Greek Appeal to America,* in which he called on Americans to aid the cause of Greek liberation. Shortly after his appeal, the Greek revolutionary government produced "Appeal of the Messenian Senate to the American People," a document translated and published in most Boston and national newspapers. At Roulstone's Circus, just a few doors from the Massachusetts Medical College on Mason Street, the "Panorama of Athens" had been on display since 1820. The large drawing had attracted people from Boston and surrounding communities and had been a source of a traveling lecture tour arranged by Everett for the Greek cause.[40] On 19 December 1823, citizens under the leadership of Everett and the Boston blueblood politician Thomas L. Winthrop formed the Boston Committee for the Aid of Greece. Within a month, the committee had representatives in each of the city's twelve wards collecting money for Greek relief and signatures for a petition to Congress for the Greek cause. Howe's medical school professor William Ingalls served as a committee representative in Ward Seven, and Howe's father was one of four representatives in Ward Twelve.[41] In this period later referred to as the "Era of Good Feeling," members of the Boston Greek Committee comprised both Jeffersonian Republicans like Joseph Howe and Federalists like Everett.

In Boston, as in other American communities, neo-classical architecture assumed a new importance as the philhellenic enthusiasm flourished. The popularity of neo-classical architecture among Boston's elite from 1815 through the 1820s, accompanied by a burgeoning population and a return to economic good times in 1821, brought about a frenzy of new construction influenced by all things classical. In 1824 the young William Lloyd Garrison, the future abolitionist and practitioner of nonviolent resistance, whose formal education had been minimal, was, like much of his generation, taken by the writings of Lord Byron. So enchanted was he by Byron's version of Romantic Greece, that he considered joining the armed effort to liberate the country.[42]

From 1822 to 1824 much of what Americans learned about the Greek revolution they read in letters from George Jarvis that were published in local newspapers. Born in New York, the son of a merchant who had moved with his family to Denmark, Jarvis arrived in Greece with several European adventurers on 3 April 1822. Like many philhellenes before and after him, he arrived in Greece expecting to find a land of classical simplicity and refined sensibilities. Instead, he encountered deprivation, hard economic times, and ambiguous values. Among the many European "Franks," as the Greeks called them, Jarvis came to loathe most of the so-called traveling adventurers. Seeking cheap glory and unwilling to endure hardships, these so-called friends of Greece were better at traveling to sights and observing artifacts than they were at fighting. Jarvis's letters painted a heroic but realistic picture of the conflicts. Howe read these letters with interest and envy.[43]

A second American to join the philhellenes in Greece was Jonathan Peckham Miller, a Vermont farmer who went to Greece to serve in the revolution in the summer of 1824, shortly before Howe's graduation from medical school. Six years older than Howe but just as wide-eyed about prospects of adventure in Greece, Miller remembered meeting Howe that summer in the upper rooms of a Boston tavern while he was packing his trunk for his long journey. In a description of the meeting he wrote almost twenty years later, Miller reports, when a knock came at his door, "I opened it and saw before me a fine looking youth of about 20 years of age. He was of good hight [sic] slender, but uncommonly handsom [sic] in his person." The young man announced himself to be Samuel Howe and explained that he had grown up in the city, had graduated from Brown University, and was about to receive a diploma from the medical school in Boston. Miller continues: "He said he had heard of my determination of entering the Greek army & was determined to do so likewise. I was astonished. He looked more like a doll than a soldier." Howe's hands, Miller noticed, were not rough and damaged like his own farm-worn hands, nor were his limbs particularly strong. Miller's tilling of the "genial soil of Vermont" and his two-year service in the regular army had well prepared him for Greek action, and he thought Howe city-like and learned but most of all naïve in his expectations for war. Howe revealed that he had told only a few people about his plans. But, he assured Miller, he had been taking fencing lessons, and he now owned a sword, masks, gloves, and cudgels. Sensing that Miller had his doubts about his readiness for Greek action, Howe invited Miller to his father's house to do some fencing with him.

Miller took up the challenge and soon appeared at the Howe residence on Pleasant Street, where he met Howe's younger sisters, Lizzie, Jennette, and Maria. They had assumed that their brother was merely taking up a new sport and took little notice when he and Miller began practicing their fencing moves. Miller proved to be too strong for Howe in attack and defense, except in the foil when Miller finally yielded. After dinner, the two adventurers "talked of war, the ocean and foreign dangers," Before the evening ended, Jennette, overhearing them, rushed into the room and exclaimed tearfully, "Why Samuel you don't think of seriously going, do you?"[44]

Samuel Howe had, indeed, decided to become part of the Greek revolution. His father, though a public supporter of the Greek cause, thought him foolish to depart for a strange land rather than follow the usual route of a newly graduated doctor and develop a new practice with an established physician. Miller remembered that Samuel's sisters, too, were concerned about him. Their older sister, Martha, had died two years earlier at the age of twenty-one, and two of their brothers had already left home.

One of those brothers, Joseph N. Howe Jr., whose niece Laura Howe Richards described as "steady, intelligent, [and] plodding," had taken up the glass-making trade of his maternal grandfather and in 1822 had married Elizabeth Kneeland Harris, with whom he now had a baby daughter. In 1827, he would become treasurer of the newly founded Third Congregational Church (Unitarian) in Cambridge, and by 1842 he would be the principal owner of the New England Glass Company. A decade later the company would claim to be the largest manufacturer of fancy glass in the world, employing 450 workers, and Howe would be a director of the Lexington and West Cambridge Railroad with an elegant home on Ashburton Place.[45]

A second brother, the youngest Howe brother, Edward Compton, who was only fifteen months younger than Samuel, had joined the crew of a merchant ship rather than go to college. On 18 September 1827, after Samuel had been in Greece for three years, Edward returned home and married Elizabeth Barker of Abington, Massachusetts. Not long thereafter he left again and was lost at sea.[46] The three unmarried sisters, like their father, resisted what they believed were Samuel's wild-eyed plans.

He was set on his course, however, and could not be dissuaded. In November, just after Andrew Jackson won the presidential popular vote only to lose a deciding vote in the House of Representatives a month later to John Quincy Adams, Howe left Boston on the *Triton* for the long journey first to Malta and then on to Greece. He left behind him the hint of an unrequited romance with Sophia Hyatt, a young woman whom he remembered fondly in his Greek diary and in a letter to his college friend William Sampson and regretted not marrying.[47] He carried with him a trunk of personal belongings, a letter of introduction from Edward Everett, a copy of the cantos of Byron's *Childe Harold's Pilgrimage,* a limited knowledge of classical Greek and a passing fluency in French, and a little money, which he had received from his father, from Everett, and from the painter Gilbert Stuart. Except for Jonathan Miller, he knew no one in Greece. On 20 December 1824, just five days before he arrived to celebrate Christmas on Malta, Howe wrote Sampson: "Shall I toil away my best days in amassing a fortune? Are the lists worth entering, when the only goal is gold? I know I shall never be rich, for I do not set sufficient value upon money, and it puzzles me much to account for the ardour, the enthusiasm, with which young and apparently noble spirits enter into the race for this bauble."[48] Imbued with the Romantic spirit of perfectionism, tempered by the self-doubt he would feel throughout his life, Samuel Howe was ready to become in Greece what he had no idea he would become: a hero, a chevalier, a philanthropist, even "the manliest man."

CHAPTER TWO

"Greece! Greece! . . . I thought no land . . . could ever look more sweetly"

In 1821, clusters of Greeks began to revolt against what had been nearly 370 years of Turkish rule. At the time, Greece lacked political unity. With its complex terrain of mountains, plains, bays, and islands and its mixture of ethnic groups, Greece was ill prepared to rebel against an empire that remained strong despite having lost much of its former glory. Complicating matters, Christian Greece had a sizable Muslim Turkish population that had been a part of the nation for generations. Although the Greeks had a merchant class and some highly educated residents, the greater part of the Greek population was illiterate, living as subsistence farmers and paying burdensome taxes to their Turkish overlords. Uniting the Greeks, however, was their language, the Eastern Orthodox faith, and what many perceived to be a common oppressor.

In 1814 at Odessa in what is today Ukraine, a small group of men formed a secret Greek brotherhood, the Philiki Eteria, that involved covert rituals and practices. Its purpose was to overthrow Ottoman rule, and its leadership looked to Russia as a source of its eventual liberation. The members were primarily merchants, landowners, sea captains, orthodox bishops, and other men from Greece's bourgeois class. In 1820, Alexandros Ypsilantis, a Greek phanariote (a member of an elite group of Greeks with diplomatic influence in the Ottoman Empire) who had served in the Russian army, assumed leadership of the brotherhood. On 6 March 1821 he led an army of forty-five hundred troops across the Prut River from Russia south into Turkish-controlled Moldavia. Although Ypsilantis's forces were defeated by the Turks and he died a year later, his invasion precipitated uprisings throughout the Morea and Roumeli, as well as on several of the Greek islands. These uprisings followed Turkish massacres of Greek citizenry in Constantinople. In January

1822, the rebelling Greeks declared their independence. By March, Greek forces controlled most of the Peloponnese, where the Greek population was much larger than that of the Danubian region where Ypsilantis's rebellion had begun.

Despite the Greek rebels' early successes, civil strife broke out first in 1823 and again in 1824 among three groups: forces loyal to the Greek guerilla fighter Theodoros Kolokotronis, those loyal to President Alexandros Mavrokordatos, and those backing the merchant and later president Georgios Kountouriotis. By the end of 1824, the civil wars had concluded with Kolokotronis's defeat and imprisonment on the island of Hydra. But the Greeks soon faced a new threat. The Egyptian Pasha Ibrahim led forces of Egyptian soldiers into the Morea, where they joined with Turkish fighters, catching the Greek forces, already depleted from civil war, off their guard. By the end of May, Navarino and then Tripolitza had fallen to Ibrahim, and in June he laid siege to Nauplion. With the Greek military in defeat and disarray, the government released Kolokotronis from prison to give him command over the Greek forces.[1]

Samuel Howe landed at Navarino in January 1825 in the midst of civil strife and intrigue among the Greeks. Within a month he would experience firsthand the most intense land and naval action of the war.

A few weeks after his arrival, Howe met George Jarvis and Jonathan P. Miller. Miller had been there only since November, but Jarvis, dressing in native attire and speaking Greek fluently, was a seasoned and respected fighter who, unlike many of the European philhellenes Howe met, had become fully involved in the daily workings of the independence movement. That March in Nauplion, Howe wrote letters full of news about Greece to his father, to his college friend William Sampson, and to his benefactor Edward Everett. His letters to his father and to Sampson appeared the following September in the *Independent Chronicle and Boston Patriot* and in the *Boston Courier*, beginning a pattern by his father, Sampson, and eventually by Everett of publishing Howe's letters in local newspapers. Boston readers longed for information about happenings in Greece, and soon newspapers throughout New England and even as far away as Illinois and Virginia were regularly publishing Howe's letters.[2]

Howe also left several journals covering the years 1825 through 1830, which, like his letters, detailed his involvement in the struggle for Greek independence. During his first nine months in the Morea, Howe traveled with Greek guerilla fighters on the mainland and to Hydra. A second period of activities began in September 1825 when he was appointed physician to the Greek fleet at Crete. He later took charge of the military hospital at Nauplion and then became surgeon on the military ship *Karteria*. This period concluded with the fall of Athens in June 1827. Between July and November 1827, Howe distributed food and clothing to refugees, principally on the island of Poros. He then returned to the United States and spent the months between November 1827 and September 1828 soliciting relief for displaced and often starving Greeks. Continuing his efforts on behalf of the Greeks, he went back to Greece in September 1828 and to Paris in June 1830. During this final period, he provided assistance by employing refugees to repair the harbor at Egina. He also started a farm colony, sometimes called Columbia, but eventually identified as Washingtonia, at Hexamilia near Corinth.

Ground War in the Morea

As Ibrahim moved across the Morea capturing Navarino and Tripolitiza and laying siege to Nauplion, Howe followed Jarvis and his guerilla fighters among the besieged populations. Along the way, he absorbed the sights, sounds, smells, and tastes of a new culture that offered a radical change from the New England traditions that had been his only previous experience. "Alas!" he exclaimed in April, describing a "natural bath" he had recently seen, "where are now the nymphs and swains, so beautifully sung by poets of old, transformed into ugly, silly girls, and dirty, lazy loons." Jarvis and Miller were among the few people with whom Howe could speak English. He spoke French with most of the continental Europeans and some of the Greeks he met; it would be another year or more before he could speak Greek with any fluency. The first modern Greek phrase that he later recalled understanding was a remark made about him by an old Greek chieftain, "Ti eumorphon paidi!" (What a handsome youth!).[3] Although he had only a limited official role as a physician in his first months in the country, he attended many of the wounded. Before long, he began to form opinions about the Greek leadership. Mavrocordatos he saw as a cultured man but not competent to lead the nation in its present danger and Kolokotrones he saw as "a dangerous man" who, though "a better general than Mavrocordatos," was "not a friend to the true interests of Greece." His greatest threat was to constitutional government. President Kountouriotis, whom Howe met in June, was, he said, "hardly fit for a constable."[4]

Howe's impressions of the Greek soldiers were mixed and would change over the course of the years. He took some time to fully appreciate their guerilla warfare, and early on he was astonished that the ordinary Greek soldiers fled in the face of Turkish-Egyptian forces, especially if they saw themselves as outnumbered or out-gunned. Early on also a Greek doctor stole many of Howe's medical supplies, and throughout his time in Greece, Howe remained astonished at what he saw as the Greeks' tendency to steal and lie.

In May he recorded an unexpected encounter with a young Turkish woman whom he referred to as the *chère amie* of a Greek captain. His diary entry reads: "I was called today by a young Greek captain to see a patient at his quarters. . . . I went into the upper story of one of the huts, and found there, lying upon one of their mattresses, a most beautiful young girl. . . . Here in this camp where I thought there was not a female. . . . I suddenly came across a most elegant young creature, with as much natural and unaffected grace as I have almost ever seen. Her confusion and partial undress made her the more interesting, and entirely destroyed my equilibrium."[5]

Howe was frustrated by what he saw as the superstitious ignorance of Greek physicians. After the Greeks held off the Egyptian-Turkish forces at Nauplion, one of his patients was taken out of his care and given to a local doctor. Not long thereafter the young man died. "It is painful," Howe wrote in his journal, "to feel the fullest confidence that a scientific treatment affords these men much the best chance of life, and yet not to be able to pursue it." Another "country surgeon" he identified as Nikoli appeared to resent Howe's skills and worry about the business that Howe might be taking from him. The two men came to blows over what began as Nikoli's refusal to give Howe space for his patients. When Howe moved one of his mortally wounded patients near a window where he could get fresh air, Nikoli objected. "I could not endure [him] any longer," Howe wrote. "I lost command of myself, and with one blow sent him staggering across the room." But, he concluded, "Nikoli gradually grew cool, and in two hours was as polite to me as possible."[6]

By mid-June, Howe had moved to Hydra, where he continued to record his reactions to the new culture. Of the women, he wrote: "Their dresses, so tasteless and uncouth, disfigure them. They wear no stays, and their clothes are cut exactly in the same style which we see in the pictures of our grandmothers in their bloom. When they go out, they wrap a shawl round the head, which covers forehead and chin." He was appalled by the way the women were treated.

> Among the common people the women work like jackasses. They bring in the water from fountains in barrels, which they lash over their backs; they go into the country to collect and bring in wood; in fact, do all the labour. The burdens which they carry on their backs are enormous, and I have sometimes met a woman with a child in her arms, and carrying a load of wood on her back which I could not carry myself.
>
> They receive no education, it being a rare thing to find a woman who can read and write. . . . They often, before they are married, wear a string of money round the neck, or in the hair. The pieces are of gold, and as rich as they can afford. . . . A girl never will part with one of these pieces, which go as

her marriage portion. Nothing short of absolute starvation would induce her to spend one of them."[7]

Back at Nauplion for a few days, he witnessed atrocities brought about by the Greek guerillas. He had come to Greece with the assumption that brutality was an attribute of the infidel Ottomans but at Nauplion he learned that the Greeks were equally capable of brutality. They had successfully held Nauplion and had for the first time since Ibrahim's invasion rendered significant casualties to the Egyptian-Turkish forces. On Hydra a few days later, he learned that in his absence, 250 Turkish prisoners who were being kept as slaves on a Greek vessel had been murdered in retaliation for the burning of another Greek vessel by the Turkish navy. On board the Greek ship fifty-five of their friends and relatives had perished in the fire. Howe observed the unburied bodies of the beheaded, savagely beaten soldiers of Ibrahim's army. His diary account reads: "The work of death went on for three hours. The agonizing shrieks of two hundred mangled victims reached the ears of the old Primates, who sat in their balconies smoking their pipes, and who, knocking out their ashes, merely said, 'It is a bad thing,' and let the work of murder go on."[8]

By the end of July Howe was involved in another altercation—this time with an English traveler named Wright. Wright, though not a military man, had assumed the title of colonel and was accustomed to delivering exaggerated claims about himself and others. At dinner with Howe and other fighters for the Greek cause, Wright made the assertion that all Greeks are scoundrels. The assertion along with the Englishman's braggadocio was more than Howe could tolerate, and he responded to the charge by declaring that Wright's statement was too broad and, therefore, simply not true. Wright immediately took offence, and more words of opprobrium were exchanged. Howe ended the dispute when he referred to Wright as "Colonel" to the amusement of the dinner party and to the shame of the Englishman. He left the evening wondering whether Wright would challenge him to a duel.

A duel never materialized. But Howe soon faced a more formidable opponent. After the Greeks on the island of Crete revolted in July, Howe returned to Nauplion. "After a passage of nine hours," he wrote, "we arrived here safely and lodged in a locanda (a sort of tavern), fatigued enough to sleep soundly on rocks. . . . [B]ut after a nap of ten minutes, I was aroused by a tremendous attack of insects of all kinds." At first there were fleas, "who acted as cavalry; then came the main body of lice, followed by the light infantry of bedbugs to the number of forty thousand." In vain he rolled from side to side, but, he wrote, "they pursued and goaded me to intense wakefulness; or if for an instant my eyelids began to drop, a rat running across my face, or a mouse gnawing my boot, [it] would again make me start up to defend myself."[9] In a letter to the Harvard scholar Charles Follen in 1835, Howe recalled that the only way to rid one's self from such vermin was through a smoke bath. Clean linen would only encourage the pests "on an active emigration from their own premises" to "an immigration" to the bodies of other men.[10]

In one of the earliest letters published in Boston newspapers, Howe described the swift movement of Ibrahim's army and the superiority of the Egyptian navy as Ibrahim and the Egyptian-Turkish forces took the towns of Navrino, Tripolitza, and Astros. He told his readers about the necessity of holding Nauplion, injecting a note of hope that Hydra, an island that stood in the way of Nauplion from the sea, would likely block the Egyptian-Turkish force's ability to take Nauplion. Although he continued to champion the cause of the Greeks, he gave a balanced account of the massacre at Nauplion, describing it in the letters published in newspapers in even greater detail than he had in his journal. Back in the city, on 23 August 1825 he received a message from the Greek naval command appointing him surgeon and physician to the naval forces assigned to help Cretan rebels that had just begun a revolt against the Ottomans.[11]

Surgeon and Physician to the Greek Fleet

Samuel Howe arrived in Crete on 1 September 1825 filled with optimism but aware that matters on the island were unsettled. The commander was Kallerges, with whom he spoke French. Miller was there too, the only companion with whom Howe could speak freely. By the end of the week, his optimism had weakened. "It becomes every day more plain to me," he wrote in his journal, "that the chance of doing anything in Crete is small. The inhabitants are divided, a part only wishing a revolution." By the end of the month, his optimism had turned to despair, "Matters in Crete are rapidly going to the deuce," he wrote. A few days later he added, "Affairs are now, I consider, finished in Candia [Crete]; the expedition has shown itself to be incompetent to resist the enemy, and it will require a great deal to inspire the inhabitants with any confidence for future attempts to revolutionize the island."[12]

Despite his waning optimism, Howe was pleased about the medical experience he was gaining. "During this time," he wrote, "I have dressed more difficult wounds than I should have an opportunity of seeing in Boston in years, and performed more operations than might have fallen to my lot during my life had I stayed at home." He cited this experience in letters to his father to justify his leaving Boston and joining the Greek revolutionaries. In his letters and journals he speaks about the trust and respect he received from his patients and from the concerned friends of the wounded fighters. "Poor boy!" he says of a young man of twenty, "a beautiful, modest boy," who sat silently waiting to be attended to. "He has met his doom early, but in the best of causes. Just as he was leveling his musquet at the enemy, he received the shot that which felled him to the ground, which, I fear, will be the passport to another world. Where does the soul go? Say men, but what is the soul? Does it, can it exist independent of the body? Who knows![13] Well into October he remained busy with the wounded from the warfare in Crete, though he saw that the fighting was not going well for the island's forces. As he had on Hydra and at Nauplion, he complained about local doctors whom he found uniformly incompetent, conceited, and stubborn.

Howe reveals his New England upbringing and education in his descriptions of the Greek people he met. He was amused by the curiosity his removable false tooth aroused among people who had never seen one and who assumed that he must have some sort of supernatural powers.[14] And he was struck by the Greeks' seemingly obsessive attentiveness. Greeks welcome you, he observed, when you enter a house, and they bless you to the Holy Virgin when you raise a glass to drink, when you sneeze, when you wash or shave. "If you talk with a Greek in the forenoon," he noted, "at parting he wishes you a good appetite for your dinner; if you meet him after some absence, he kisses you three times on the lips. An inferior kisses your hand and puts it to his forehead, and many kneel in doing it."[15]

The Greek soldier, as Howe characterized him, was "quite a man at ease, a gentleman . . . who does and says what he will, and goes where he wants," and "when in the village, he lives on the villagers." "A soldier," he said, "carries with him his bed, his table, his chair, his all in his capote. His knife is to him dagger, fork, and spoon. He carries no change of clothes, nor will he lay off his dress, perhaps, once in three months. At night he never thinks of getting more than a dry place and a smooth stone for a pillow." Howe acknowledged that he too had not taken his clothes off in two months, that his only bed for months had been his blanket, and his pillow had been a flat stone.[16] Years later, recalling Howe in Greece, Jonathan Miller wrote: "I have known him to stand dressing the wounded until exhausted, then throwing himself down upon the ground & resting. [In a] few moments he would again resume his labour. He shared his crust with the famishing & would often times give all & fast himself knowing that his chances of getting relief were far better than theirs."[17]

Unlike many of the Europeans, who found the Greek people uncouth and primitive, Howe developed a genuine fondness for the Greeks. His 1857 letter to Mann Howe suggests that he felt pride in his assimilation. "I had donned the dress of the country," he wrote,

learned to speak the language, & in the course of the year became quite a Pal-
licavi. I was naturally very handy, active, and tough, and soon became equal
to any of the mountain soldiery in capacity for endurance of fatigue, hunger,
and watchfulness. I could carry my gun and heavy belt with yataghan and
pistols all day long, clamoring among the mountain passes, could eat sorrel
and snails, or go without anything, and at night lie down on the ground with
only my shaggy capote. And sleep like a log.

His willingness to share in the hardships of the ordinary Greek soldier and to
learn their language made him a favorite among the soldiers and the Greek
peasantry. Most foreigners, in contrast—mainly German, French, Swiss, and
English—whom the Greeks did not admire, were not willing to bear the
privation "of poor fare, the exposures, the poverty, but above all, the lack
of glory." "I had many friends in humble life," he told Mann, "God bless
them, & can say sincerely that I found the Greeks kindly, affectionate, trust-
ful, grateful & as then my intercourse with them went, honest people. They
always treated me as well as I wished to be treated."[18]

On 5 November 1825 Howe left Crete and, after traveling first to Hydra
and then to Nauplion on the mainland, he arrived in Athens at the end of the
month. With Ibrahim's attention on the city of Missolonghi, Howe was able
to spend three weeks touring Athens. Jonathan Miller traveled with him.
Howe summed up the glories of the ancient city: "Magnificent columns,
half-ruined temples, rich sculpture, and cyclopean remains are scattered
about with such profusion, meet one at every corner in such a way that at
first only a confused idea remains upon the mind, which is rather filled with
astonishment than admiration."[19] Back in Nauplion by the end of December,
Howe wrote his father that the Greek command had appointed him physician and surgeon at the city's hospital, adding that he had now become fluent
in Greek. At the end of April 1826, Howe learned that Missolonghi, on the
southwestern shores of the Roumeli, besieged for months by the Egyptian
navy and the Turkish-Egyptian armed forces, had fallen and that Ibrahim
was ready to move on to Athens.

Howe remained at the hospital at Nauplion for the next ten months, caring for the sick and wounded. For two months, beginning in April, he too
was bedridden, probably with typhus. "[The experience] brought me once so
low," he told his friend William Sampson, "that I had some idea of what kind
of a process dying was, and I have no appetite for lying on my back fifty days
upon the stretch again!"[20]

Feeling better, on 8 July 1826 he again wrote Sampson, describing the
efforts of the Greek school master Gennadios to rally the people of Nauplion. The letter was published in the *Boston Courier* and then in several other
papers throughout the United States. With the defeat at Missolonghi, he

explained, the Greek populace was discouraged and had started to lose hope. To his dismay, some Greeks were expressing a longing for the days of stability under the Turks. Money for supplies to maintain the struggle was seemingly nonexistent, and the European powers continued to show no interest in interfering. Against this background, Gennadios exhorted his fellow citizens to sacrifice their money and goods for the service of their country and to put aside their differences and their family and regional loyalties. Moved to tears, the people rushed forward to contribute what they could, some giving their jewels or their horses. Because many Americans who had been enthusiastic about Greek independence had grown weary of supporting what increasingly looked like a lost cause, Howe hoped his letter would reinvigorate their interest. "But I say," Howe wrote, "that the modern Greek, notwithstanding his life of slavish oppression, is a more virtuous pleasing character than the Sicilian, the Italian, the Spaniard, or the Russian, and that he has more shrewdness and quickness and as much talent as the native of any other part of Europe."[21] To further inspire American interest, Howe also began to contemplate writing a history of the Greek Revolution for an American audience. In the autumn he wrote Edward Everett to ask whether he thought the plan might be feasible, and in December Everett assured Howe of his support. Between autumn 1826 and spring 1827, one of the lowest points of the Greek War of Independence, Howe continued to send letters, especially to Everett, that were published in Boston and then in other cities. In these letters Howe was able to articulate the very great peril the Greek forces were in without ever showing a lack of confidence in the glorious outcome that he seemed never to doubt.[22]

In autumn 1826 Howe also joined the Greek fleet as ship's doctor on the steam frigate *Karteria*. The constant need to stop the vessel, however, to make repairs because of failures in the vessel's new but untested steam technology left Howe with little to do, and he was bored. With so much free time, he worried continually about the potential fall of Athens, which was under siege by Ibrahim Pasha and his forces. He wondered whether the European powers would intervene. By February 1827, however, the ship began to encounter enemy fire and eventually saw its first battle. For the first time in the war, Howe wrote in his journal about killing a Turk: "The Turks would only poke out their heads [from behind a custom-house], fire their musquets, and retire. But one of them held his head out long enough for me to take aim at it and level him with a rifle-ball; he fell sprawling upon his face, and I hardly know whether pleasure or pain predominated in my mind as I witnessed his fall. Said I, 'A moment more and I may fall in the same way.'"[23]

Three events in spring 1827 changed the course of the Greek revolution. In March, Lord Alexander Cochrane, the British admiral who had gained fame during the Napoleonic Wars, joined the forces of the Greek navy. The Greek leadership had longed for his presence, and for many in Greece it brought promise of the support of the British navy. In April, the Council of Troezene elected John Capodistrias to a seven-year term as president of Greece, renewing hope that the Greek warring parties might finally be united in the face of their common enemy. The third event that spring was the fall of Athens on 5 June. More than Missolonghi, Athens was the symbol of all that was great and glorious about Greece. The loss of modern Athens symbolized the loss of a centuries-old heritage that was fundamental to Romantic notions of what it meant to be European (and even what it meant to be American). Finally the leadership in London, Paris, and St. Petersburg took notice.

For the Starving Many

In July 1827 Howe began serving as a relief worker for thousands of desperate refugees and citizens. "Famine stared them in the face," he told Mann in his 1857 letter. "The great danger seemed to be that the people would be literally starved to death or into submission." Of special concern to Howe were women and children who had suffered years of warfare and social and economic displacement. On the islands of Astros and Poros, the situation was aggravated by the influx of refugees from Athens. Howe took provisions to these islands that had been sent from the United States on the ship *Six Brothers.* Among his concerns was the risk that his supplies might be stolen by pirates who roamed among the Greek islands or taken by Greek officials who might expropriate the provisions for their own use.

While on Astros, Howe wrote in his journal: "[I] commenced at daylight this morning visiting the huts & holes of the poor, and giving orders for flour to those whom I found in misery." There were 400 families "all poor enough, but [I] found 120 in a state of misery almost beyond conception or endurance. Half naked, without shoes, lying under a miserable hut made of the branches of trees was a poor widow with three or four children, without clothes, without food, except the grass and herbs they could pick up around the houses." Metaxa, a local chieftain, arrived in the village and tried to take over Howe's distribution for his own greedy purposes. But despite the interference, Howe continued to distribute relief.[24] He also commented on the curious adulterous affair that Metaxa had with the wife of another local leader, Nakos:

> Nakos, the imbecile & fool, has been led away by the intrigues of Metaxa and made a tool of by Colocotroni [Kolokotronis]. What indeed can be expected from a man who consents to live in the house of another who is in open

adultery with his wife. Every one knows & Nakos knows better than others that Metaxa has his wife as his mistress and this he not only suffers but goes and lives in his house & sleeps quietly in the chamber next that in which his wife & the Count are in their criminal intercourse."[25]

Back at Nauplion in late July he bought a "Negro slave" from a Greek priest and then freed her. For the next several weeks he traveled by mule among the Greek villages distributing food and clothing. Contemplating the cruelty he had been witnessing, Howe concluded, in his journal, that what led men who were ordinarily good to do appalling things was often grief from loss.[26] He described in graphic detail an act of brutality by Turkish forces he encountered in one village:

> There was also brought to me a pretty little girl of ten years but whose pale face announced some disorder. I inquired and found that she had been taken by the Turks and one of them finding that his brutal attempts to ravish her were in vain from her extreme youth & smallness took a knife and slit her so as to lay the vagina & rectum into one & thus effected his purpose. And now that I have broached subjects indelicate let me go on to others whose horrid unnaturalness must shock even by their mention any but those whose long residence in the east have familiarized their ears: and these are the unnatural crimes which the Turks and particularly the Arabs perpetrate upon women, men & beasts: not content with serving women in the way God meant, they search for men & boys and even the jackasses and sheep do not escape. Nor is this a matter of shame or concealment with them: as soon as they take any Greeks prisoners they abuse the men in this way and then kill them or keep them as slaves; unless someone is very young and beautiful, then he is kept for the embraces of some high officer.[27]

As he moved around the eastern Morea, Howe continued to express outrage at the ongoing conflicts between Greek factions, even in the midst of Turkish-Egyptian threats. "A Moriote hates, absolutely hates, a Roumeliote as he does a Turk," he wrote in his journal, "and the latter returns the compliment with the addition of scorn." He also bemoaned the fact that among some of the populace there was now a longing for "the advantages and comforts they once enjoyed under Turkish despotism."[28]

In August and September 1827, another two ships, the *Levant,* sponsored by from the Philadelphia Greek Committee, and the *Statesman,* sponsored by the Boston Committee, arrived from the United States bringing provisions and letters from home. The Boston Committee had also sent five hundred dollars and sponsored the passage of John D. Russ, an 1825 graduate of the Yale Medical College, who would team with Howe. For the next two months Howe spent most of his time distributing the relief supplies on the island of Poros. Every day, men, women, and children flocked to Howe's relief headquarters to receive sacks of flour and grain, along with clothing and other supplies provided by the American people. Howe later remembered "a woman [to] whose lot so many petticoats had fallen that after supplying her own numerous brood, she had a dozen left which she tacked together to make one good coat for herself. They were party-colored & made rather a grotesque appearance, but she declared they made a very warm covering."[29] He also told his wife, Julia, a story she later repeated in his biography. When a European agent came to Howe's headquarters wearing some of the clothing sent from the United States, Howe was so incensed by the fellow's behavior, that he stripped the clothes from him and "turned him naked into the street."[30] Howe hoped to use the funds from the Boston Committee and the proceeds from the sale of some of the provisions to open a hospital on the island with Russ.

On 20 October 1827, after nearly six years of fighting, the war of independence came to an abrupt end as the combined forces of the British, French, and Russian navies destroyed the Egyptian navy at the Battle of Navarino. Howe had anticipated the intervention of the European forces, and he knew that without their involvement the Greek struggle was likely to end in defeat. Before 2 November Howe had heard rumors about a sea battle, but on that date, his journal records, the "glorious news of the destruction of the Turkish fleet" was confirmed. Howe sent letters home announcing that Greek independence had at long last been assured.[31]

On 13 November 1827, with the defeat of Ottoman Empire in Greece, Howe left Poros to return to the United States, leaving John Russ in charge of the hospital that would open there a few days later. Nearly six months earlier the Greek command had ordered him to return home to obtain American supplies and provisions for the Greek cause. At the time it was uncertain whether the Greeks would need arms in addition to food and clothing. Now that the Turkish-Egyptian threat was over, Howe could concentrate his relief efforts in the United States on the latter. What Greece would need in the years ahead were daily provisions and capital to rebuild what in 1827 were the utterly destroyed towns, villages, and cities that had not for centuries functioned as a nation. Howe feared that Americans had become complacent about the fate of Greece now that the revolution had appeared to succeed, and he knew that he must convince them that the Greeks were still in desperate need of help. To achieve his purpose he planned to make speeches across Massachusetts, Connecticut, and New York and to write a book that would tell the Greeks' story to Americans. When he left Poros, he had with him John R. Stuyvesant of the New York Greek Committee and two Greek children whose mothers had given them to Howe to take to the United States.

To Rally American Support

On 5 February 1828 Howe arrived in New York aboard the *Jane*. He had with him one of Lord Byron's helmets and one of the poet's swords, and letters ready to be sent to Greek committees in New York, Philadelphia, and Boston. Within a few days of his arrival, these cities had printed and distributed circulars throughout their neighborhoods announcing his arrival and describing the dire circumstances of the otherwise victorious Greeks. In the three northeastern cities the committees went to work using Howe's celebrity presence and his first- hand accounts of the war and its aftermath to generate money and supplies for Greek relief. Soon newspapers throughout the country were announcing Howe's mission, and plans were made to have him speak in as many places as he could attend in the nine months he was to be in the country. In many of the letters and circulars, the American public was reminded that Howe had with him Lord Byron's helmet and sword and two Greek children.[32]

In an early letter to the New York Greek Committee, Howe stressed the need for medical assistance for the still thousands of soldiers and sailors whose wounds and injuries needed attention. In later letters to committees in all three cities, he spoke about the needs of the civilian populations. After seven years of fierce fighting, sieges, and social and economic dislocation, the Greek people were in desperate circumstances. Almost no village, town or city was unaffected. Destruction was everywhere. Widows were unable to care for their children. Hundreds of orphaned children throughout the countryside and in the towns there were begging for the little food that was available to them. During the years of fighting, Howe told his readers, Europeans had sent provisions that had almost all gone to the fighting soldiers, but the Americans had always given to poor civilians: "Your provisions were distributed among thousands and tens of thousands of miserable women and children, and made glad the hearts of many who had not tasted bread for several days." He reminded them that he had "attended to the distribution of a large portion personally." And he emphasized that the generosity of the citizens of the United States must not now cease. Greece, after all, was as much the cultural ancestor of Americans as of Europeans.[33]

By the end of February, Howe had moved on to Boston. There he wrote the writer-historian W. L. Stone that he worried about the decline of interest in Greece among Americans. In March, the women's magazine *Bower of Taste* noted that Howe had given a speech to a group of Boston woman and that his sister-in-law Elizabeth Harris Howe, Joseph's wife, was head of a committee that was collecting funds and clothing for the Greek cause. At Salem, he worked with Thomas Pickering, a Federalist and the author of the eight-page essay "The Suffering Greeks: To the Inhabitants of the County of Essex," to collect money and supplies from residents of the area north of Boston. Howe spent much of April speaking to audiences in upstate New York. By the end of May, he proudly wrote his friend William Sampson that he had raised fifty thousand dollars for Greek relief. By the time he left for Greece in September, he had raised another ten thousand dollars. He had also persuaded women's groups to donate clothing and shoes and farmers to donate grain and other food provisions. To help reenergize the American public to the cause of Greek independence, Howe's mentor Edward Everett gave a Fourth of July speech at Charlestown entitled, "The History of Liberty" in which he linked the Greek War of Independence to the American Revolution and called on Americans to continue their support for the Greeks in their newly won freedom.[34]

In August 1828, about a month before he returned to Greece, Howe published *An Historical Sketch of the Greek Revolution*. Dedicated to Matthew Carey of the Philadelphia Greek Committee and to Edward Everett chair of the Boston Committee, the book at over 450 pages was more than a sketch. It covered the period from the beginning of the conflicts in 1821 to the Battle of Navarino in 1827. Written in haste and hardly edited, the book contained some inaccuracies, and later in life Howe attempted to buy copies of the book to destroy them. Some of his displeasure with the book may have had less to do with the inaccuracies than with some of the harsh criticism he leveled at the Greek leadership of the period. As the years went on, Howe had second thoughts about some of his claims, feeling, for example, that he had judged Alexandros Ypsilantis too harshly.

The first part of his history covers a period Howe did not personally experience. Most of the information about the years between 1821 and his arrival in the country in 1825 he learned from George Jarvis and his British friend George Finlay. In keeping with comments in his journals, in the book he expresses greater respect for the constitutionally elected Mavrocadatos than for the guerilla fighter Kolokotronis. His descriptions of the Greek leadership show a phrenological bias. Almost always when he introduces a leader into his narrative he describes the man's head and physiognomy and ends by associating the physical description of the leader with his character. Of the Greek admiral Andreas Miaulis, for example, he writes:

> Miaulis was born at Hydra, and was educated on the water. He is about sixty years of age; his frame, large, and rather corpulent, is well made and full of vigour. His countenance is one of those most difficult to describe, yet most strongly impressive; it inspires with affection; and though there are no marks of greatness about it, yet you see there the kind heart, the firm mind. You know not why or wherefore, but you see in his face enough to convince you

that it is the face of an *honest man.* His complexion is light and rather florid; his features strongly marked; the nose particularly large and his eyes of a mild hazel colour. Strangers are always struck with his patriarchal appearance, and after ever so short an interview go away satisfied that there is at least one honest, pure patriot in Greece.[35]

The book sold well in the United States and the positive review it received from Edward Everett in the *North American Review,* along with other similarly positive reviews, ensured that Howe's evaluation of the Greek War of Independence would affect American understanding of the event for another century.[36]

Building a Harbor and a Farm Colony

Howe enjoyed his six-week journey back to Greece on the *Suffolk* and filled his journal with his observations. One day he went fishing and caught a dolphin and a shark. Of the dolphin, he wrote, "The painter could never catch the brilliant and varying hues which play upon its scales as it struggles and dies on the deck." A few days later he described seeing the Aurora Borealis: "I stood for a moment unable to speak, or think, or breathe. I felt my soul swell, as it were within me till it burst forth in the words, 'Good God, how glorious are Thy works!" On 18 October the British quarantined the *Suffolk* at Gibraltar, where yellow fever raged. But after five days of ship-bound boredom, Howe set out, despite the epidemic, to explore the city. There he encountered the occasional Scotsman, dressed, he wrote, "in the beautiful costume of his regiment, the kilt, the knee and leg bare, the ribboned gaiters and red coat, and the black cap, over-hung and flowing with the thick, rich plumb. There is, however," he went on, "in spite of what Scotsmen may say something repugnant to modesty in this dress. They wear no drawers, and the kilt only coming as low as the knee, sometimes shorter, gives an indecent appearance." The Spanish women he found "decidedly fine looking" with sparkling eyes "through which flashed the soul and lit up the whole countenance with spirit and intelligence." They were at ease with themselves, displaying a freedom in their movement that pleased him, whereas the men of Gibraltar seemed to him an "idle, listless looking race without enterprise or persevering industry."[37]

Howe's journal entries for the continuation of the voyage are uncharacteristically personal and contemplative, revealing a certain moodiness that would remain a part of him throughout his life. He describes 2 November 1828 as "one of those few delightful days when I feel happy."

> It is one of those few days when I feel almost unalloyed pleasure at the thought of being alive and existing to the enjoyment of this world—all pleasure

which springs not entirely from external circumstances, not from the consciousness of possessing youth and health and bodily perfection, nor from
any advantages of fortune, nor from the beauties of the day, the balmy air and
clear sunshine. Not these alone (though these should be enough) put me in a
train of pleasing thought and make me happy, but a certain inward elasticity,
a bounding of the heart which I cannot explain and which I sometimes seek
for in vain when every external circumstance would seem to give rise to it.
How is this? How is that I am sometimes happy from the contemplations,
which at other times make me so gloomy? But I will not stop to inquire, or
the inquiry will make me melancholy if I conclude my spirits are merely like a
barometer. So let go; they are now up, let me enjoy the hour.

He concluded the entry by sounding almost like a proto-Transcendental-
ist. Given his later disparagement for what he regarded as the flighty Con-
cordians, it was ironic that he allowed himself in youth to sound so much
like them.

The wide spread of waters around us seems not a solitude now. There is life
and spirit in every swell of the billows, and though it is the Sabbath of the
Lord, the devotee could wish no better temple to worship in. How feeble
the feeling of adoration must be in those who are this day enclosed in walls
built with men's hands, to what they would have were they now here in this
splendid temple with the wide, wide waters beneath, the loft roof of blue
which God's hand hath reared over it, the bright sun rising in silent majesty
and the whole scene in voiceless adoration speaking the praise in the power
and the magnificence of the Creator.[38]

On 3 November he arrived in Malta, where he left three hundred dollars in
deposit for what he knew would eventually be his trip back home. On the
island also he observed what he found were the unusual beliefs of the local
priests. One such priest claimed to have preserved in alcohol the very viper
that bit Saint Paul on his visit to the island. Another monk practiced the
strange practice of flagellation. About these extraordinary happenings Howe
wrote back home where ever-eager readers around the nation learned about
his encounters with a different world.[39]

On 5 November, Howe at long last landed in Greece with his relief supplies. In his diary he exclaimed, "This morning at daylight we discovered
land—Greece! Greece! Welcome again to my eyes, welcome land of science
and song, welcome ancient seat of liberty and light, welcome cradle of new
born freedom. . . . I thought no land, not even my own, could ever look more
sweetly."[40] Within a week he was at his final destination, the island of Egina.
At Nauplion before he had returned to the United States, he had distributed
relief supplies directly to needy families. On Egina, observing the people
there, whose circumstances were not dire, Howe concluded that work for

relief was better than direct relief. He saw that several hundred people who had been building an orphanage before he arrived would soon be finished and in need of new employment. Howe saw also that the harbor of Egina had become a marsh so filled with silt and sediment that it was no longer fit for merchant shipping. He devised a plan to rebuild the harbor by employing stone masons to construct a shoreline retaining wall and common laborers to drain and clean out the sediment and debris. Knowing that the project had little chance of success without the approval of both local island authorities and of the new president, Capodistrias, he spent most of the month of November successfully persuading them to go along with his plan and in December began hiring the necessary labor. Many of the men and women he employed were refugees from fighting around Athens. Without land and implements, these people had been at risk of starvation because the island's inhabitants were for the most part unable to employ them. Because so many of the refugees were women, Howe found that they were suffering even more than the men.[41]

On 19 December 1828 work began with one hundred men and two hundred women. First, they gathered stones at a temple of Venus that was in ruin. Howe noted in his journal that only loose stones were taken, that no ancient artifacts were removed from the site.[42] Workers deposited the stones near the harbor, then drained the water and began removing sediment. For this work Howe hired only men and older, married women. He feared that if he hired young, unmarried women to do public work, they would likely be led into prostitution, and so, he said, "for the unmarried women who have no father or brother, I shall endeavour to find some occupation indoors."[43]

The next day, Howe hired another hundred women to remove sediment. With all of the work done with hands and baskets, the going was slow. And the water in December and January was cold, so, Howe began giving a little wine to workers who were exposed to water. He made clear in his journal that he remained in charge of every detail in the harbor repairs: "Not a stone do I allow to be laid without being present or giving directions. . . . I am obligated to invent everything, to inspect the execution of everything, to instruct the workmen."[44] He noted that he rose in the morning at three or four, and until daylight he wrote letters or handled necessary paperwork. At daybreak he assembled the harbor workers, and at nine ate breakfast. He remained at the harbor until dinner at six and was in bed by ten. This pattern of rising early to do paper work would continue for the remainder of his life.

On 24 March 1828 Howe announced in his journal that the work was almost complete. He felt proud that through nearly four months of the most "rigorous weather of the year" he had kept nearly seven hundred people employed. Even more important, Egina now had a functioning port. Around this time the new Greek government awarded Howe the Chevalier of the Greek Legion of Honor, the Order of Saint Savior. (The nickname "Chev" that his close Boston friends gave him and that his wife called him throughout their marriage came from this award.) When the work on the harbor was completed, Howe moved his sights to another part of the country where relief was needed.

On the Isthmus of Corinth near the town of Hexamilia were people whose houses had been destroyed during the war. Howe had toured the area with George Finlay and determined that a farm colony might well extend his notion of offering relief by providing employment rather than direct relief. He petitioned the Greek government for two thousand acres of land on the isthmus. In late March he received permission to use the acreage for the proposed farm colony. But because the government was slow to respond, he had already begun to assign land to the colonists. In his journal, Howe wrote: "I took the families down to the river and assigned each one stremma of land, and they commenced preparing it for seed, and it gave me a thrill of pleasure to see with what alacrity and joy they went to work. It was the first time, said they, for seven years that they had felt anything like a sure prospect of future good."[45]

He called the farm colony alternatively Columbia and Washingtonia to remind its inhabitants that the source of the seeds for their farm and the other supplies they received was the American relief committees. As Howe told Mann in his 1857 letter, his months at the Hexamilia farm colony were some of the happiest of his life. He was in total charge and control of his surroundings, and the people who were dependent on his aid were grateful for it. His pleasure was intensified by occasional adventures, such as the day in mid-March when John Russ helped him track down some cattle thieves. "[We] started at dawn from Kineta on foot," Howe recounted with glee,

> and followed the path southwest toward the narrow part of the Isthmus and soon out-stripped all our Greeks. We fell in with four soldiers who were in pursuit of some robbers who had just driven off some cattle from Megara, and as we found fresh bullock tracks in the sand, we joined heartily in the chase, right glad of an adventure. The Pallicaris or soldiers who all pride themselves upon their speed at walking endeavored to distance us to show their superiority over Europeans, and as long as they were skipping over the stony ground we were sadly tasked to keep up with them. But as soon as we came out upon the level plain, we began to show our length of leg, both of us being rapid walkers. The soldiers soon began to sweat and puff, one by one lagged behind until a single one only kept by our side in a half walk, half trot, but it soon became too much for him and begging us to stop the robbers if we should see them. He soon lagged behind and we jogged on. I was armed only with my double-barreled fowling piece. Russ had nothing, so we began to think that it

might be as well for us not to catch the Tartars, when suddenly I got a glimpse of two men ahead driving cattle. The soldiers saw them at the same time and as I heard their shouts in the rear I rushed forward with gun cocked, forgetting everything but the chase and the probability of a scuffle, but as soon as the rearmost thief saw me coming towards him upon the full run, he fell to crossing himself in terror and despair and stood still as a post. I passing him, knowing the others would overtake him and made for another robber, whom I saw through the bushes with the cattle. He also yielded in terror.

During his days at Washingtonia Howe continued to record his observations, describing a local Greek merchant, for example, as "a good specimen of a Greek traveling merchant, shrewd, quick and hawk-eyed, careless of his appearance, or rather striving to look poor and shabby, living on little and yet with thousands of dollars in his belt."[46]

On 2 and 3 April at Hexamilia, he wrote about the projected building of houses for poor peasants who were now living in caves. He planned to advance money for the building projects to be paid back over five years from the farmer's proceeds from crops or as rents. A few days later, he bought some slates to start a makeshift school for some of the children. He showed his pride in the accomplishment of the colonists as he commented on their hard work. With matters progressing so well, he sent his clerk to Egina to arrange for more poor families to join the colony. The farm now had implements and oxen to prepare crops for the planting season. To help the colonists, some of whom had never been farmers, he permitted Captain Nostich, a Swiss soldier and commander at Corinth who was skilled at farming, to cultivate land close to Washingtonia as an example to the colonists. He reported that houses were going up rapidly in the colony, and that despite the prediction of some for the colony's failure, the project was thriving. On 15 April he recorded that two houses were at last completed. He continued to envision that after their crops came in there would be common proceeds to start a permanent school and even a hospital.[47]

Between Wednesday 22 April and Sunday 26 April 1829, Howe traveled from Vostitza to the fortress of Lepanto to Patrass. On Sunday in Patrass he celebrated Orthodox Easter with the Greeks. It was a celebration like nothing he had ever seen, certainly not like the somber commemoration back home in Boston. "My ears are stunned with ringing of pistol shots," he wrote,

shouts of boys, the laugh and roar of merry, mellow men and a concatenation of all the various sounds which man by natural or artificial means can produce to express joy. 'Christ is risen' is the salutation given and returned by every man, and everyone kissing every other one three times on the cheeks. . . . Now all are in their gala dresses. They have come out from the churches, and the rising sun looks upon a scene of blood and slaughter unheard of in any other land. At every house the right arm of a man is bare, a knife glitters in his hand, the lamb or sheep lies panting at his feet, now it is weltering in blood, [and] now its skin is off. . . . A boys stands beside and pours out wine in a tumbler, first for one and then for another. They begin to grow mellow. They shout out a toast every time they drink. They begin to vociferate, to sing. They can eat no longer. They roar with unmeaning laughter. Some fire their pistols into the air and shout louder than with reports. Others jump up and joining hands dance to the sound of voices or the lyre. They recruit their spirits now and then with wine. Their faces are flushed, they tire and drop off, one by one, and lying down on the grass, are soon snoring.[48]

During March and April, Howe became sick with what he called "swamp fever." It was almost certainly malaria and it affected him for the remainder of his life. Quinine treated the condition successfully; yet, even before he left Greece he experienced reoccurring symptoms of the condition—fever, head-aches, chills, and nausea. Despite his illness, he could report that as of 13 May there were 150 women and 75 men working the land, and that there were fifteen houses at the colony. He acknowledged, however, that the houses, though newly constructed, would not be suitable even for the poorest Americans. "Its four walls," he wrote, "are built of stones put together with mud and unplastered inside or out. It has three windows and wooded shutters but not a pane of glass. Its two doors move on wooden hinges, the floor is the earth trod hard. Its covering is branches or trees, twigs, etc. overlaid with clay and beat in air and water tight." But they were houses, and far better than the caves where the new inhabitants had formerly been forced to live.[49]

On 21 May, using funds from the American Greek committees, Howe established a Lancastrian school and hired a Greek teacher, Aivali, who had been educated under the Lancastrian system and who desperately needed work. For his wages, Aivali received a new change of clothes, an allowance of food, ten stremmata of land to cultivate, and one dollar a month.[50] Back on Egina in early June Howe hired a French wheelwright to build a cart on wheels, to the delight of the colonists, most of whom had never seen a wheel. By July, he was sick again with swamp fever. This time the ailment would linger for a month. On 11 August for the first and only time in his life, doctors bled Howe. So sick was he with the fever that quinine alone did not seem to treat his condition effectively. Finally, by the end of the month he was feeling better.

Despite the growth of the colony and the enthusiasm of the colonists, Howe remained surprised by what he characterized as the people's superstitions. In early July, for example, one of the colonists had died and needed to be buried. Howe wanted to bury the man near the colony's projected, but not yet built, church. The colonists objected, and at first Howe thought it was from "the fear of smell." Soon, however, he learned that there was "a strong prejudice against burying within any village and a dread of it not [being] sanctified ground." He noted that some colonist had claimed to see a light at midnight coming from the grave. Many of the people were alarmed. He concluded in his journal, "But I will keep a bright lookout tonight, and if I catch anyone with a light, then be it man, ghost or devil, he shall have as much tar as will stick to his hide."[51]

Through the late summer and into the fall the farm colony's crops came in successfully. The only major setback during the time was sickness among some of the colony's cattle. Despite the colony's success, Howe began to encounter bureaucratic problems from the governmental headquarters of Capodistrias. Throughout the spring and summer, he waited, not at all patiently, for supplies promised by the government that never arrived from Egina. By the end of November it had become clear to Howe that the president had no intention of following through on several of his promises. Of special concern to Howe were the issues of land ownership and of the government's commitment to provide the colonists with a five-year exemption from property taxes. Meetings with Capodistrias at Nauplion seemed to produce only polite indifference from governmental officials. When at the beginning of December the president firmly refused to give the colonists the land they had been cultivating, Howe decided that it was time to return home. He had planned to spend only about a year in the country if he could not find a permanent position. When he ran into difficulty with the government, he knew it was best to leave. Finlay, who planned to remain in Greece for longer, agreed to take over leadership of the colony.

Edward Everett placed Howe's name before President Andrew Jackson for a ministry to the new nation, assuring the Jackson administration that Howe's father, Joseph, was a loyal Jeffersonian. But the United States was not yet ready to become entangled in what to most leaders seemed to be an unstable Greece, so Howe would see no appointment from the Jackson White House.[52]

In the meantime, Howe was lonely. In August he wrote to his sister-in-law, Elizabeth Harris Howe, about the beauty of the Corinthian isthmus, where the land was "abounding with the wildest and most romantic scenery, under a sky whose almost perpetual brightness and cleanness is unsullied by a single cloud for months & months together." "Still," he confessed, "we want some one to gaze on his beauties with us—the brilliant sky—the romantic landscape, the ever varying diversity of towering rocky crags & sloping valleys—the abrupt mountains and the level plain—the precipice & the deep abyss—senses which Greece presents at every step—may for awhile interest one alone. He may gaze in solitude and admire & be happy, but after a while he tires and looks round for a friend to whom to communicate his feelings."[53] There was no small irony that he shared his loneliness with his sister-in-law, who died before she received this letter, leaving her husband and Howe's brother Joseph with a young motherless daughter.

To Revolutions in Paris and Brussels

Howe left Greece in June 1830 and traveled first to Geneva and then to Paris, where he arrived shortly before the three days of revolution that put Louis-Philippe at the head of the French government. According to what Howe later told his wife and children and recounted to Horace Mann, he was with a group of young revolutionaries who accompanied Lafayette from his home to the Hôtel de Ville. Lafayette soon came to admire the young American, at whose graduation ceremonies in 1824 he had been a special guest. "I knew it was none of my business," he told Mann in his 1857 letter, "but I could not help joining in & cheering on the revolters."[54] By late August, Howe had gained some perspective. "To hear them talk, you would think there was *no* courage, *no* patriotism, among any people but the French."[55] At the same time, he acknowledged that the lectures he was attending at the Col-lege de France from the world's most celebrated physicians were excellent and informative. In his journal, however, he confessed to boredom, relieved temporarily by a visit to Brussels on 21 September 1830 during the Belgians' month-long rebellion against the Dutch: "The same uninteresting, unprof-itable life which makes me shudder at the loss of time, and which I have so long spent, I shrink involuntarily from the thought of sitting down and drudging at study. But most interesting and cheering news from Belgium keeps up some interest however, and the hope of seeing the progress of liberty and the rights of man in rapid strides toward his amelioration and perfection, adds a lot to the little interest a residence in Paris gives, and which I would not continue were it not that I feel the necessity of reviewing my medical studies."[56] It was clear to Samuel Howe that he was ready to return home "after six months of pleasure and pain in Paris"; he had been away long enough. On 16 April 1831 he was back again in Boston.[57] Some people, even then, were calling him "the Lafayette of Boston."

CHAPTER THREE
"The Cadmus of the Blind"

For Samuel Howe neither the lectures at Parisian hospitals nor demonstrations in the city's clinics matched the radical fervor of France and Belgium during the summer and fall of 1830, both of which had ended in a rapid change of government. In Paris he had been with Lafayette and James Fenimore Cooper at revolutionary meetings and in the streets with liberals seeking to overthrow despots. He had not liked everything he had witnessed, he had complained of arrogant rhetoric, but he had been there and been part of genuine change. Despite having studied with the world's most respected physicians, Howe left Paris for Boston with little interest in using his newly acquired learning to open a Mason Street medical practice and begin making money. His time in revolutionary Paris and Brussels, like his time in revolutionary Greece, had been devoted to "making the self," for "perfecting mankind," but not for making money.[1]

The quandary over his waning interest in his chosen profession was soon resolved. When he arrived in Boston on 16 April 1831, Howe had waiting for him an offer to become the editor of a newspaper in Philadelphia. Hardly pausing to unpack, he set off for Philadelphia. The newspaper was projected by a group of men with loyalties to Henry Clay who were opposed to what they saw as the growing power of President Andrew Jackson. Not yet calling themselves Whigs—that would not occur until 1834—these leaders saw in Jackson's policies and style of leadership a threat to their economic interests and political influence, along with a threat to a stable social order controlled by elites like themselves. They supported a strong national bank, publicly funded means of transportation and communications, and a new tariff in 1824 to protect the nation's emerging industrial manufacturing. In Andrew Jackson they found little presidential support for any of these matters. The Tennessean had been in the White House for only two years, but leaders in Philadelphia were losing no more time. In Henry Clay they saw a bulwark against Jackson's usurpation of their interests. The principal backers of the newspaper were Edward Ingersoll and Nicholas Biddle, and Howe's conduit to the Philadelphia group was his former pastor and ever-present mentor, Edward Everett, now in his third term in the U.S. House of Representatives. Ingersoll was a scion of one of the city's oldest and wealthiest families. Biddle, who shared Ingersoll's status, had supported Howe's 1828 efforts to raise funds for Greek relief. A former magazine editor, he was president of the Second Bank of the United States when Jackson campaigned against it.

Howe spent about a month in Philadelphia. He was drawn to the idea of the paper and, as a single man, felt he could live for a few years on the projected annual salary of one thousand dollars. In late May, Everett wrote to the Philadelphia attorney and principal counsel for the national bank John Sargeant recommending Howe: "I have entire dependence on his probity," he said. "He is bold & high spirited. . . . On arriving in a new city & planting himself among strangers in a profession compelling him to speak on all sorts of subjects he will probably make some mistakes in pointing his pen *á tort et á travers,* but I believe he is a man who is worth the trouble of advising. He had character & feelings far above the mercenary drudges by whom the public press is too inclusively conducted."[2] In short, Everett saw in Howe the makings of a manly man—one with feelings (even revolutionary feelings) who, nevertheless, could control his passions.

Matters seemed to move along during the spring of 1831. Howe's attraction to what he called "literary work" was not merely a way to avoid the drudgery of a medical practice. In Greece, he had become a revolutionary and a philanthropist, in Paris and Brussels, he had witnessed fast-moving revolutions, and in the United States he had emerged a hero and a humanitarian. But in the process he had also become a writer. His letters, some the length of articles, had through the efforts of Everett appeared in newspapers first in Boston and from there across the nation. His book on the Greek War of Independence, which Everett also supported and arranged to have published, had been well received and well reviewed, including by Everett. The editorship would allow him to sustain the recognition he had received from the publication of his writings.[3]

Howe's trip to Philadelphia also showed that, with the nation's "era of good feelings" having passed into history, his political loyalties were with the backers of Clay, not Jackson. Like his father, Howe remained sympathetic to Jeffersonian republicanism. This sympathy, no doubt, had only been reinforced by his participation in the European revolutions of the previous years. Throughout his life, Howe remained loyal to republican values. Yet like some other anti-Federalists, Howe would not become one of the followers of Old

Hickory, who, he remarked in his diary, "I think from my soul have disgraced the country" and who were soon calling themselves Democrats. In short, his Jeffersonian loyalties would not transfer to Jacksonian loyalties. As a National Republican or "Jeffersonian Whig," Howe would begin his uneasy relationship with the emerging party of Clay, Everett, and Daniel Webster.[4]

Sitting in his room in Philadelphia in May 1831, Howe confided in his journal his aspirations for the future. "My views in taking the paper business are disinclination to enter now into the practices of my profession and perhaps above this, a desire to attack the Powers that be, . . . [a] desire for the excitement of an active life, hope of rendering myself of use to the country and known to its best and most powerful citizens, and some idea that it may facilitate my ulterior plans with Greece. For there I wish to go and spend my days, there I am sure I can be of great use, fill a wide field of some kind, probably live respected and die remembered." In 1831, the "powers that be" that Howe wrote about were Jackson and his followers. But the "powers that be" would become the focus of Howe's life as he fought for education of the blind and of people with intellectual disabilities and for prison and public school reforms and the abolition of slavery. The statement also reflects an affection for Greece that would linger, and at times be frustrated, throughout Howe's life.[5]

It is not clear why the newspaper editorship in Philadelphia never worked out. Perhaps the sponsors failed to raise the necessary capital, or perhaps they were uneasy about Howe's inexperience at operating a paper. Even more likely, Howe decided after his return to Boston from Philadelphia in early June 1831 that his sisters needed his protection. His youngest sister, Maria, was engaged to marry Edwin Babcock on 14 July, but his older sisters, Lizzie and Jennette, now in their middle twenties, remained unmarried.[6] Since their father's marriage to Rebecca Thayer Calef, the family had moved south to a newly built home on land she owned in Milton, and the sisters disliked living with their stepmother and missed the familiar environs of Boston.[7]

Howe also had found a Boston outlet for his literary interests in the *New England Magazine,* which in 1831 had published five of his articles in the July through November issues. The articles described Howe's journeys to sights of Greek and Roman antiquity and told stories about Greek and European revolutionaries Howe had encountered: the dying young nobleman Captain Nicolo, the brave but contradictory Greek fighter Francesco whose life Howe had saved (and whose story John Greenleaf Whittier would memorialize two decades later in his poem about Howe, "The Hero"), and the rash and troubled English philhellene William Whitcombe. Howe's articles spoke to the Romantic impulses of Americans whose interest in all things classical had never been greater. He pointed out that the low state of contemporary Greeks could be accounted for by centuries of Ottoman oppression. Freed from domination and with the renewal of learning in the arts and sciences, Greece, Howe had no doubt, would regain its once glorious civilization.[8]

Talks Howe had in July 1831 with John D. Fisher and an offer that came from Fisher at the end of that month set the direction for the remainder of Howe's life. Fisher, a Boston physician, had been an undergraduate with Howe at Brown University and had graduated from Harvard's medical school a year after Howe. After Harvard, Fisher had gone to Paris, where he became interested in techniques first developed by the Abbé Valentin Haüy for teaching blind people to read and write, do mathematics, and acquire musical and foreign-language skills. In 1826 he returned to Boston and began a three-year effort to persuade Massachusetts legislators to fund a school for educating blind young people. A supporter of Fisher's effort was another Brown University contemporary, Horace Mann, now an attorney and recently elected to the state legislature, known in Massachusetts as the General Court.

In March 1829, while Howe was organizing the Greek refugee colony at Washingtonia, the Massachusetts legislature, under Mann's guidance, passed measures to establish the New England Institution for the Education of the Blind. Although it founded the institution, the legislature provided ambiguous funding for its operation—surplus left over from unspent funds appropriated for Massachusetts deaf students at the American Asylum for the Deaf at Hartford, Connecticut. With incorporation from the General Court, Fisher looked for a person to direct the school, still without a building, without teachers, without equipment, and, most important, without secure funding. Fisher approached Thomas Gallaudet, founder in 1817 of the Hartford Deaf Asylum. Because of ill health, however, Gallaudet, though only forty-three years old, was ready to retire from the deaf school and consequently unable to take on the work of establishing a new school in Boston. Gallaudet suggested other candidates for the position, but Fisher failed to develop interest among them. In July, while riding and talking with his college friend Howe, Fisher discussed the prospective blind school. To his surprise, Howe showed interest in leading it. Before the horses were settled in Fisher's barn, the two men were making plans to secure Howe's appointment.[9]

By mid-August, the directors of the blind institution had approved Howe as their first superintendent and arranged for him to sail to Europe to prepare for his new position. There were no American schools for the blind. Knowledge about teaching blind pupils lay with the English, Scottish, Prussian, and especially French specialists. Few Americans knew European authorities better than Edward Everett, and so once again Howe turned to Everett to secure the invitations he needed to visit European institutions that taught blind people. On 30 August, while the papers were full of news about the 21–22 August insurrection by the slave Nat Turner in Southampton County, Virginia, the *Boston Advertiser,* the principal newspaper of the city's emerging Whig elite, announced that Howe was a proper selection for the blind asylum. By that time, Howe was in New York meeting with New York supporters of Polish revolutionaries, a group of men whose efforts he had most likely first linked himself to the preceding May.[10]

Back in May, Howe had spent several days in New York City. On the twenty-sixth, he had created a minor sensation when he visited the twenty-year-old conjoined brothers Chang and Eng, later famously known as "Siamese twins." Howe had insisted that their agent, James W. Hale, who was charging fifty cents for the privilege of viewing the twins, allow him to examine them. When Hale refused, Howe, who had with him a reporter from the *New York Commercial-Advertiser,* suggested that Hale's exhibit was a fraud. Soon that paper and others made Howe's claim headlines, and Hale not long thereafter sued Howe for slander.[11] Objecting to the display of "freaks," Howe was aroused just as much by the possibility of fraud as by Hale's refusal to allow him, a medical man and a now prominent revolutionary and humanitarian, to examine the twins. Hale's refusal, too, only doubled Howe's determination to denounce the exhibiter and his display. When a New York jury found Howe and the *Commercial-Advertiser* not guilty of slander in May 1832, Howe's confidence in his ability to affirm justice only increased.[12]

In May 1831 Howe also had met with the American Polish Committee, which was supporting Polish revolutionaries in the midst of a rebellion begun in Warsaw on 29 November 1830 against Russian domination. Encouraged by communications from Lafayette and James Fenimore Cooper in Paris, the committee met again at Clinton Hall on Monday evening, 5 September 1831. Quite familiar with Howe's exploits in Greece, Paris, and Brussels, the committee entrusted Howe with funds they had raised for Polish national forces in Warsaw. Thus, Howe left for Europe with two humanitarian missions: to study educational methods for the blind in preparation for his new position in Boston and to deliver American funds to the Polish Committee in Paris for distribution in Poland. What neither he nor the American Polish Committee knew as he sailed for Europe was that Polish revolutionary forces were about to surrender to Russian authorities.[13]

Around mid-October Howe arrived in Paris, where he began his observations of blind schools, with the help of introductory letters from Everett and Lafayette.[14] His Parisian roommate, Nathaniel P. Willis, a foreign correspondent for the *New York Mirror,* described Howe as a "slight person, [with]

delicate and beautiful features and a soft voice." With Willis, Howe visited
Versailles in December and through Willis met the Polish scholar and patriot
Joachim Lelewel, who had only recently fled to Paris.[15]

During the four months between October 1831 and February 1832 that
Howe spent observing French teaching methods at the National Institute for
the Blind, Nat Turner went to the gallows in Virginia; John Quincy Adams
took over the seat of Howe's old teacher, Joseph Richardson, in the U.S.
House of Representatives; Charles Darwin left for his trip on the *HMS Bea-
gle;* and William Lloyd Garrison, David Lee Child, and others founded the
New England Anti-Slavery Society in Boston. Much of what Howe found
were techniques that he had anticipated from his talks with Fisher. Blind
pupils, most of whom were typical school-aged children, learned to read by
touch, using books with pages of raised letters. These letters resembled the
lettering of the Roman alphabet that sighted French students learned to read.
(Louis Braille had published his system of embossed points in 1829, but it
was not yet employed at the French Institute.) Thus, rather than using their
eyes, blind pupils employed their fingers to achieve tactile recognition of the
raised letters. Howe also examined techniques and devices to teach penman-
ship, geography, and mathematics to blind students.

In the Parisian and provincial asylums Howe visited, he saw methods,
activities, and attitudes he approved of and that confirmed assumptions he
held about human nature and education, and others that he found objec-
tionable. He admired, for example, the facilities that taught blind pupils to
learn a trade, such as basket weaving, mattress building, and broom making,
and gave them music lessons for their enjoyment and potential employment.
In Paris, he admired the schools that allowed time for physical activities,
encouraged games, and expected their pupils to identify with objects in
nature by taking them for park walks. That some students could identify
trees and flowers from touch and smell impressed him greatly. Howe was
disappointed, however, that some schools seemed to have no desire to teach
their pupils useful trades for self-sufficiency. He found offensive the practice
in some schools of displaying their students to arouse public sympathy and
criticized schools for allowing their pupils to retain mannerisms, such as
repetitive rocking and light staring, that called attention to their disability.
To Howe, the failure to teach pupils proper social manners and to train them
to avoid atypical mannerisms was a failure to consider the social purpose of
their education. Education, as Thomas Jefferson, Lafayette, and the revolutionaries of 1830 knew, was a process that instilled the social graces necessary
for citizenship in free republics, for blind and sighted students alike.[16]

In February 1832 Howe visited schools for the blind in Belgium and Prussia, where he began carrying out his second European mission, bringing

aid to Polish revolutionaries. Earlier in January, Howe had met with several Polish radicals in Paris, whom Willis described as "distinguished men who had shared in that desperate battle [and who] were literally houseless in the streets."[17] After their surrender to Russian forces the previous September, most of the Polish fighters had taken refuge in northeastern Prussia. Prussian authorities had conflicting opinions about their presence in the country. After the revolutions of 1830, Russian plans to invade France through Prussia, drawing Prussia no doubt into the conflict, had been thwarted by the revolutionary Poles. Yet, the Prussian leader, Friedrich Wilhelm III, like his supposedly more liberal counterpart in France, Louis-Philippe, saw little advantage in appearing too supportive of the November rebels. The Poles had prevented Russia from invading Prussia and France, but overt support for the revolutionaries might encourage Russian authorities to renew their original plans.

During the last two weeks of February, Howe traveled between Elbing and Marienburg in eastern Prussia visiting schools for the blind and distributing the funds he had received from the Polish Committee. At first Prussian authorities tolerated his efforts. But in Marienburg a Prussian police officer escorted him out of the town. In Berlin his welcome was no warmer as he toured the city's famous school for the blind and began making contacts for more distribution of American funds to the Polish refugees. When he returned to his hotel room on the night of 3 March, Prussian police were waiting to arrest him. Howe spoke only a little German, and so, relying on the policemen's limited knowledge of French, he stalled them and finally persuaded them to come back in the morning. With only a few hours to spare before morning, when he had agreed to turn himself in, he destroyed papers from the American Polish Committee by swallowing some and tearing others into small pieces and soaking them in the room's water basin. The few documents that he wanted to preserve he hid in the hollow plaster statue of Friedrich Wilhelm that decorated his chamber. In the morning the police authorities arrested him and immediately placed him in prison in a stone cell eight by six feet, without light or fresh air. Never charged with a crime, Howe was at first allowed neither to receive visitors nor to communicate by letter to friends. Guards were instructed not to speak to him, and he was prohibited from having reading material. There he remained in solitary confinement for nearly four weeks.[18]

Had Howe not met Albert Brisbane a few hours before his arrest his prison stay might well have been longer. Brisbane, a twenty-three-year-old New Yorker and future proponent of the French utopian socialist Charles Fourier, was traveling in Germany and had arranged a meeting with Howe for the next day to discuss the Polish refugee cause. When he failed to find

Howe in his hotel room, Brisbane suspected the worst and, in the absence of an American delegate in Berlin, wrote to William C. Rives, the U.S. minister to France, about what he suspected was Howe's plight. By mid-March, Rives was able to confirm Brisbane's suspicions.[19]

In the meantime, Howe persuaded a prison guard to provide him with paper and pencil. Soon, he sent letters to Rives in Paris and to John Fisher and his father in Boston. With the word out about his imprisonment, French and American newspapers began to speculate about what lay ahead for young doctor. Back in Boston, Theodore Parker, a school teacher who would later be an influential theologian and close friend of Howe's, delivered his first lyceum lecture on the Polish revolution, in which he mentioned Howe's imprisonment. In Washington, Representative Everett persuaded Congress to pass a resolution calling for an inquiry into Howe's imprisonment, and communications between the State Department and Paris began. Rives, a Virginia appointee of Andrew Jackson's and former law student of Thomas Jefferson's, who had known Howe in Paris and was in sympathy with what he considered Howe's humanitarian efforts for the Poles, brokered Howe's release. Soon thereafter Prussian authorities took him (cooped up in a wagon with little food and water) from Berlin across Prussia and Hanover to the border of France. At the border the Prussians insisted to the French and American officials: Samuel Howe was never to return to Prussia.[20]

More than eleven years later, on his honeymoon with his German-speaking wife, Julia Ward Howe, Samuel discovered the long memory of the Prussian authorities when, despite his world fame as the teacher of Laura Bridgman, they denied the couple entry into the country. The prison experience, in solitary confinement, had a lasting effect on Howe's views about incarceration, shaping Howe's involvement in the Boston Prison Discipline Society debates a decade later, and his reaction to his culpability in John Brown's action nearly two decades after that.

With his release from prison and his return to Paris, Howe spent April 1832 first in France and then in England and Scotland accumulating books, apparatuses, and two teachers—Emile Trencheri from Paris and John Pringle from Edinburgh—for his prospective school for the blind. While in England, he suffered a bout of night sweats and high fever, almost certainly the result of the "swamp fever" or malaria that had nearly killed him in Greece in 1829. With great expectations driven by his perfectionistic zeal, despite his illness, on 5 July 1832 Howe arrived in New York (on the same boat with Martin Van Buren, who was returning from England to help Andrew Jackson kill off the Second Bank of the United States) and immediately sailed onto Boston.

Having spent all the funds for the blind school on his European travels, Howe faced the prospect of setting up the new blind school while raising resources for its operation. He lost little time. With his father and stepmother now living in Milton, the new site for the asylum (as it was then often called) would be his father's unoccupied house at 140 Pleasant Street. The asylum's housekeepers would be his two unmarried sisters, Lizzie and Jennette, both of whom were eager to return to Boston. The asylum's matron was a woman identified only as Mrs. Brush. Besides himself, the Europeans who had returned with him and with a local music teacher, Lowell Mason, would be the asylum's teachers. Several leading men of Massachusetts, including John D. Fisher, John Homans, William H. Gardiner, and Horace Mann, were appointed by Governor Levi Lincoln to serve on the school's first board of trustees. All that remained was to enroll pupils.[21]

In the midst of settling into his new position and setting up the new school, Howe had his portrait painted by the artist Jane Stuart, the daughter and youngest child of Gilbert Stuart. At the time only twenty-one years old, Stuart had already enjoyed the respect of her now-deceased father and of the Boston community. In the painting, Howe, now thirty years old, looks directly at the viewer with his blue-black eyes. His eyebrows are thick and, like the hair on his head, are jet black. He is dressed in formal business attire appropriate for the time. The portrait reveals why Anna Shaw called Howe "the handsomest man I ever saw." According to Shaw, when Howe rode down Beacon Street on his black horse, all the girls "ran to their windows to look after him."[22] We do not know who commissioned or paid for the painting that now hangs in the entrance of the Howe Building on the campus of the Perkins School for the Blind—probably his father, perhaps Everett, or perhaps Stuart executed the painting on her own.[23]

An Emerging Superintendent

The challenge that Howe faced in securing pupils was threefold. The general public knew little about the new school, those people who did know about it had expressed doubts about the school's ability to teach blind children, and parents of the blind were reluctant to trust their children to a stranger whom, if they knew anything about him, they knew more as a revolutionary than as a teacher. Despite these problems, within six weeks of his return to Boston, Howe had located and admitted his first seven pupils. In December of the same year, an eighth pupil entered the school. Thus, by the end of 1832, eight pupils, whose families had consented to their children's move to the new Boston establishment, had entered the school. Although these pupils gained greater fame because of the novelty of their being a part of the first year of the blind school, they were typical of the population of the school during the first decade of Howe's long tenure as its superintendent.

S. G. Howe by Jane Stuart (1833). Courtesy Perkins School for the Blind.

Following the legislative mandate and his own insistence that the asylum be a school and not a custodial facility, Howe maintained that students who attended the school should be capable of learning. When his first pupil, a fifteen-year-old private-paying boy from Rhode Island, Charles Arnold, showed almost no ability to acquire even basic skills, in December Howe recommended to his parents that the boy return home. What he instituted for his first student became a policy for the institution. If students could not learn, they did not belong at the school. The school would be a place to prepare people for the world, not a place that offered people a mere refuge from the world. For that reason, Howe disliked the custodial association with the label "asylum." Call it an institution of learning or simply a school, but do not think of the facility as a custodial facility, Howe insisted. From the beginning, he believed that the blind should be educated to become fully participating citizens like everyone else. His views had not changed when in 1841 he wrote to a former pupil, A. W. Penniman, now a teacher at the Ohio School for the Blind in Columbus: "I hope you will inculcate upon every blind person the duty of asserting and exercising all the rights of the citizen when they become of age. They should pay their poll tax, vote, go upon juries, be ready to serve as school committee men, and in every possible way mingle up with other citizens, so as to do away with the impressions that they are useless members of society. . . . I trust the time is not far off when blind men may be called to the responsible stations of councilors, judges, spiritual teachers, etc., but we will not anticipate—let us work all together and trust to providence to crown our efforts with success."[24]

Howe believed that unsuccessful learners were likely to have other disabilities in addition to their blindness. He sought in particular to avoid blind students who also had epilepsy or intellectual disability. Apart from the educational difficulties associated with these conditions, "fits" and "idiocy" made integration into the society outside the school more difficult. In his first years as superintendent, Howe had occasionally received negative reactions to his pupils. In 1836, for example, the Unitarian Purchase Street Church led by George Ripley, who in 1841 gained fame as a founder of the Brook Farm community, insisted that Howe give up the pew that he had rented for his pupils' Sunday worship. The parishioners wrote Howe, "The Gentlemen of the Society, or some of them, are afraid of the consequences that may follow to their own families by having the blind children to pass in review before their wives when they are in the family way."[25] It was still believed at the time that a pregnant woman who saw, or especially one who was frightened by, a blind person, might bear a blind child. Howe also received word from James Harris of the New South Society that the congregation would no longer invite "choristers" from the blind school for regular Sunday worship, not because the singers were performing poorly, but because their blindness disturbed members of the church.[26] Since blindness alone frightened some people in the general public, blindness associated with epilepsy and intellectual disability would be an even greater impediment to his students' social integration.[27]

To avoid custodialism, Howe also turned to phrenology to eliminate unsuitable pupils from the blind school. In 1839, for example, he wrote his friend and fellow physician Edward Jarvis about a "half-witted" pupil. "It was easy to perceive" Howe told Jarvis, "at the first glance that so shallow a cranium could not contain the requisite quantum of brain; but I did not like to disappoint his father or to discourage the young man, without being certain by trial of his incapacity."[28]

Howe's second pupil, Thomas Takes, was a trustee beneficiary. Because at age twenty-three Takes was older than the age limit of twenty-one set at the time by the school's state charter, his tuition came from privately donated funds raised by the institution's trustees. Takes spent six years as a pupil and left the school in 1838 to become a piano tuner. He later married a sighted woman. Takes, despite his age on entering the school, fulfilled all of Howe's hopes, seizing the education provided him to become a productive, self-sufficient citizen. Howe also felt Takes's marriage was an appropriate union. Even though he knew that Takes's blindness was the result of disease and not of heredity, Howe believed, nevertheless, that his marriage to a sighted woman would reduce the likelihood that Takes would pass along his blindness to another generation. Like many of his contemporaries, Howe was interested in heredity and retained that interest throughout his life.

Howe's interest in heredity reflected an antebellum, pre-Mendelian perspective. In a long letter to Horace Mann in March 1838, he discussed his views on the heredity of blindness. A perfectionist reformer, Howe claimed that God created man with "a perfect physical organization." But about every tenth person is near-sighted, far-sighted, or otherwise has weak or afflicted eyes. "Now the fact of this departure from the natural state," he wrote, "is not a fortuitous circumstance: if there were but a single case, it must be reducible to a particular cause: and a fortiori, when it prevails in every section of the country & in every generation." This lapse from perfect creation was the "consequence of [a] violation of the natural laws, either by themselves or by their parents: for I hold it to be indisputable that almost every case of congenital blindness is the penalty paid by the sufferer for the fault of the parent or progenitor." But by Howe's view of heredity, the consequences of the hereditary flaw could be prevented. He reminded Mann that much blindness was caused by reading frequently in dim light. School children, he said, were far too frequently subjected to poor classroom lighting. If, for example, they became near-sighted as a result of poor lighting, they could pass along their condition to their children. But Howe held that near-sightedness and its hereditary consequence could be prevented by providing adequate lighting.[29]

Howe's third pupil was Charles Morrill of Wilmington, Massachusetts, who studied at the school for five years and became an accomplished musician. Twenty years old when he entered, Morrill fell in love with another pupil, Sarah Clough, a woman admitted to the school in 1833. When Howe learned of the romance from Clough's relatives, he worked persistently, if unsuccessfully, to suppress their relationship, fearing that, if married, they would likely pass their congenital blindness to their offspring. Frustrated in his attempt to stop their eventual marriage, Howe in the end accepted their union and maintained a long and faithful correspondence with Sarah Clough Morrill, even after Charles Morrill's death in 1865.

The fourth student to enter the school in August was Maria Penniman. The first pupil from Boston and the daughter of a wealthy family, Penniman studied at the school for nine years and returned to her family's home, where she enjoyed a long and comfortable life.[30] Penniman, like other wealthy blind pupils, Howe realized, needed education not to prepare for a life of work but to gain the social graces peculiar to the wealthy. Howe's views of the wealthy were always mixed. They had political influence and paid the private tuition necessary for the survival of the school, but the wealthy were also idle, rigid, and conservative.

The fifth and sixth pupils of that first year were the sisters Abigail and Sophia Carter, whom Howe and Fisher found in Andover, Massachusetts. The sisters became among the most famous of Howe's students as much for stories of their transformation from small-town backwardness to urban sophistication and productivity as for claims of their rescue from "blind ignorance" into enlightenment. Throughout the 1830s, the story of their rescue appeared in newspapers throughout Massachusetts and occasionally in the out-of-state press. Because they were attractive and, at the ages of eight and six years, younger than his other pupils, they often accompanied Howe (always with a female chaperone) on his trips around the region to advocate for the establishment of public facilities for educating the blind. Before Laura Bridgman became world famous, the Carter sisters were the New England Institution's best-known pupils. Their fame and their pleasant dispositions, no doubt, accounted for the later misrepresentation that they were the blind asylum's first pupils.

In 1842, when the sisters were in their late adolescence, they both graduated from the school and returned to their family home in Andover. In a letter to their mother, Howe warned that his expectations made a decade earlier for a community that would willingly employ blind graduates had not been fully realized. Yet he remained optimistic that the sisters, who were bright, attractive, and especially gracious in a womanly way, would find work to support themselves. But in October 1844, Sophia wrote Howe that her efforts to find employment had repeatedly failed. With polite deference, no doubt knowing that Howe expected her to depend on the resources and skills she had learned in the blind school, she asked her former teacher to allow her to return to the institution, "I shall endeavour to do all in my power to make myself as useful as I can. Of course I shall not expect to remain there longer than until the close of the next term." Breaking from what up to that time had been his policy never to allow pupils to enter the school merely for custodial lodging and care, Howe honored her request. Over the years both sisters returned to the institution for short periods, often to teach but sometimes simply for shelter.[31]

Like many other graduates (especially female graduates), the Carter sisters found too few employers in their community willing to hire them. Those who depended on self-employment, using such skills as broom and mattress making, piano tuning, and organ playing, often found that demands for their skills failed to make for steady and dependable livelihoods. To be sure, some graduates of the blind school reported good employment; usually these successes represented in-home enterprises in rural areas. John Herrick, for example, in 1858 wrote Howe that he missed the institution but was doing well with his broom-making business in his small Randolph, Vermont, community.[32]

Even by the early 1840s, however, Howe received several requests from his former pupils for work at the school because they had failed to find employment. One such request came from Jacob Doughty, who wrote Howe from Brunswick, Maine, in May 1840, assuring Howe, "[I] made every effort in my power to get my [broom-making] business under way." But his friends had been discouraging his attempt to set up his enterprise. Doughty feared having to go to the county almshouse. He pleaded, "I earnestly request that I may be so employed otherwise I know not what will become of me."[33] Two years later, James Tucker's uncle wrote Howe: "Mr. James Tucker formerly in the institution wishes me to write to you to see if you will receive him again in the Institution, for he is out of employment and cannot get nothing to do. He will do anything you will please to have him do. You know dear sir what he can do better than I can tell you. He will be useful in doing something or other he says, as he has before. Please write me as soon as your receive this and inform me what you can do for him."[34]

As Howe's prominence increased, he also received correspondence from educated blind people in other parts of the nation who, despite their capabilities, were frustrated in their efforts to find gainful employment. One especially erudite letter came from Richard B. Holland, a young man from Nashville, Tennessee, who wrote Howe in January 1847 to request further education or perhaps a teaching position at the blind school. He explained that he had been blind since the age of seven from an accident and that his family had educated him in Tennessee and then sent him to St. Charles College in Missouri, where he studied Latin, mathematics, logic, and rhetoric. When his father fell on hard times, he had returned home to Nashville, but because he had since had a falling out with his father and stepmother, he was now on his own. His letter ends with a plea that articulates the frustrations of blind people then and now: "Of my proposition: Oh! Think as a philanthropist, such as you are represented. Receive me into your school; instruct me, and you shall, while the memory retains her place in this Person command services of your humble servant."[35]

Year after year over the decades these requests only increased, and their numbers led Howe reluctantly to modify his earlier insistence that the blind school never become more than a school.[36] After the school's move to South Boston in 1839, Howe developed an adjacent workshop where graduates of the school who failed to support themselves in their local communities could find work. He described it in an 1844 letter to a blind New Yorker who was looking for work: "We are enabled to offer work to blind persons who are of good character, & who are disposed to be industrious, frugal, & temperate. Such & none others will be admitted; & they, we think, can maintain themselves & enjoy a humble but honorable independence. . . . The workmen will be paid according first, to their won earnings; 2nd according to the general profits of the establishment."[37] That same year, Howe acknowledged to William Chapin, superintendent of the Ohio School for the Blind, that he had been forced to modify some of his earlier optimism about the blind finding independent employment in New England communities. To be sure, many of his pupils had done well back home, but usually their success depended on the support of family and community friends in the form of start-up capital. But those who worked for wages and those who set up their own businesses were unable to maintain consistent work. Employers, Howe wrote, "often employ a blind man hoping that he may earn his wages, but they soon find that in spite of industry, zeal & perseverance, he is comparatively unprofitable; he needs much aid, he is perhaps in the way of others, and they finally consider him rather a burden than a source of profit." Reluctantly, Howe advised Chapin to develop a workshop for his pupils who had little prospect for independent employment. In doing so, Howe found it necessary to modify his earlier reformist optimism about the employability of blind people.[38]

Eventually, the school opened its own salesroom at 20 and 22 Bromfield Street, just below Howe's Boston office, where it sold goods (brooms and brushes, mattresses, and doormats) and provided services (pillow and mattress rejuvenation) to the citizens of Boston, especially the well-to-do. Several of Boston's leading churches lined their pews with cushions made by the blind workers of the school's workshop, and many of the city's citizens slept on their mattresses. Laura Howe Richards, Howe's daughter, recalled the "stuffy but not unpleasant smell of feathers and hemp about the place."[39] In 1847, Howe could report to an inquirer from Tennessee: "We have something like twenty-five blind persons who work in our shop, & they can earn from four to ten dollars per month, besides their board. Their fare is very plain & their life seemingly hard, but it is a better one than they can get elsewhere, & they generally like it." Howe insisted that the workers not live at the school or be congregated in a particular facility but that, like other city wage workers, they board out in the community. Most employees of the workshop lived in one of various boarding houses in South Boston, and a few lived in Boston.[40] Howe also consistently rejected the claim that the production of the blind—whether for wages, home businesses, or at the institution's workshop—be based on charity. When he received a letter from a man in England suggesting that he sell the autographs of known blind pupils to support their upkeep, he responded:

> It is a maxim with me in the administration of this Institution to avoid every thing which might cause the Blind to be regarded as mere objects of charity. I charge the pupils to receive nothing in the shape of charity. I have no 'charity box' in sight. I allow no articles to be sold at a fictitious value. I assert the right of the Blind to demand a participation in the advantages which our State provides for every child in the Commonwealth, & I maintain that since they cannot be taught in the common schools, there must be expert provision made for their instruction at whatever cost. This policy has been followed by other Institutions, & the result has been that instead of being regarded by the public as mere Asylums, it inspires them with self respect & makes them aim at a higher place in the social scale than they would otherwise seek.[41]

The last of the seven pupils admitted in August 1832 was Benjamin B. Bowen, a thirteen-year-old boy from Marblehead, a coastal town north of Boston, who, like most of the other students, was a state beneficiary. Since the age of five, when his mother had died, he had been living with his father, a fisherman. Though he was close in age to Charles Arnold, Bowen was intellectually gifted and remained a pupil of the school for six years, until 1838. About a decade after leaving the school, he became a traveling lecturer and preacher. Before that in 1840, he published *Daisies and Dew Drops,* a collection of romantic poems and short sentimental narratives reflective of the times. Several of the pieces pertained to blindness, but just as many

were unrelated to the disability. In the preface, Bowen said he was a graduate of the New England School for the Education of the Blind but had not
yet found employment and implied that the book was a way of providing
income. Howe had sent a loom and weaving materials to his Marblehead
home in 1839, but Bowen, it appeared, had been unsatisfied with being a
weaver and with remaining under his father's roof. The pluck that he showed
in publishing the book should have delighted Howe, but Howe remained
silent, probably because he was put off by Bowen's appeal for sympathy from
his readers.

In 1847, Bowen published a second and even more popular book, *A Blind
Man's Offering*. With the fame provided by the book, he began traveling
around the Northeast giving talks. On the lyceum circuit he earned money
from admission tickets and at churches he received freewill offerings, making
as much as thirty dollars a day. Bowen's growing notoriety along with what
Howe regarded as his begging in public became too much for Howe. When
he learned from the Reverend Charles P. Packard of Lancaster, Massachusetts, that Bowen had privately claimed to be an infidel and an atheist, he
responded:

> Mr. Bowen was for many years an inmate of this Institution, and gave us
> a great deal of trouble. He was a perverse and ill behaved youth. . . . I had
> hopes that after he left school, and began to enter seriously upon the business
> of life he would redeem himself, but I have never had any reason to believe
> that those hopes were well grounded. . . . What your friend says about his
> conduct and conversation on board of the Steam Boat [about being an infidel
> and atheist], corresponds with what I have heard from others. I would be
> charitable, and hope that Mr. Bowen has greatly changed, is indeed a new
> man, and different from the one I formerly knew; but unless he has, I should
> [think] that his presence would desecrate any pulpit.[42]

Bowen may have been resourceful, but his lower-class bravado coupled with
what Howe saw as deceitful showmanship to earn a livelihood made Bowen
little more than another sideshow act of the sort Howe despised.

The eighth pupil to enter the New England Institution for the Education
of the Blind in 1832 was Joseph Brown Smith, who joined the other pupils
just a week before Christmas. The others had all entered in August. Quick,
intelligent, though at times rebellious and independent minded, Smith
became another of the school's famous pupils. After graduating from the
blind school, Smith entered Harvard University at age seventeen. John White
Webster, the Harvard professor who would be convicted and hanged in the
November 1849 murder of his Harvard medical school colleague and Howe's
teacher, George Parkman, helped to find benefactors for Smith's initial

tuition and worked with Howe to find Smith additional funding over his four years at the university. In January 1841, Harvard president Josiah Quincy boasted to Howe: "It will gratify you to know and therefore I state that Professor [Benjamin] Peirce stated last night to the Faculty that J. B. Smith, the blind youth, passed the best examination [in mathematics] of anyone in his class. 'This,' he added, 'I say not with reference to his misfortune but *absolutely* that circumstance wholly out of his class.'"[43] In 1844, Smith became the New England Institution's first student to graduate from college and Harvard's first blind alumnus. With a classical education and a gift for music, he left Harvard to become a teacher of music at the Kentucky School for the Blind in Lexington, which he had first visited with Howe in 1841. There he married and had children. He died at the young age of thirty-six.

A native of Portsmouth, New Hampshire, Smith was poor and the first of his kind supported by the state in an arrangement Howe coordinated. Eventually he made similar arrangements with all the other New England states, and even with some states as far away as South Carolina. Although bright and poor like Bowen, Smith never presented his blindness before the public as a means of self-support and remained within the boundaries of Howe's view of propriety. He neither wrote nor talked about his blindness. His independence and his success came from study and hard work. He depended for his livelihood on a respectable occupation that was not associated with his disability, the teaching of music. Smith, in short, was manly in a manner Howe admired. For this reason, despite his sometimes exasperating willfulness, Howe promoted Smith. What a man was, Howe never failed to insist, was not only what he made of himself but also how he presented what he had made.[44]

Although Howe had deplored the public displays of pupils in the French schools for the blind that he had recently visited, he soon saw that the American public longed for information about his blind school and about the pupils he seemed so miraculously to educate. Soon what he had formerly criticized he now employed, though cautiously. He never put his pupils on display simply for their disability, as he had seen the French schools do, but always insisted that they were to show their educational skills—in reading great literature, in solving complex mathematical problems, or in making beautiful music. Beginning in communities throughout eastern Massachusetts, his students' skills became objects of interest at church services and in public demonstrations.[45] Before long, newspapers in the state reported on the large crowds in Beverly, Waltham, Salem, Newburyport, Gloucester, Quincy, Andover, and other towns that came to witness the accomplishments of the blind young people. According to an article in the *Salem Gazette* in February 1833, for example, Howe spoke at the Woodend Lyceum in the shoe-manufacturing town of Lynn, where he presented two little girls (probably the Carter sisters) "who gave astonishing evidences of improvement and quickness of perception in different branches of Reading, Arithmetic, & Geography." The article states, "So novel an exhibition . . . has seldom been witnessed in Lynn." In April 1833, the *Juvenile Reader* published a story about an exhibition at the Salem Lyceum, where blind pupils played musical instruments and performed "exercises in various branches of education." One pupil recited an original poem. The exhibition raised $150. That same evening another performance at Boston's Masonic Temple resulted in "an overflowing house" and receipts of $400, though Howe had received anti-Mason correspondence objecting to his use of the Temple. An exhibition in Augusta, Maine, 8 February 1834 that was reported in the *Eastern Argus* had as its purpose persuading Maine legislators to appropriate funds for indigent blind to attend the blind school in Boston. The article, which reminded readers that Howe was "the romantic and chivalrous crusader in the cause of Greece," described a musical performance by two ten-year-old pupils of the blind school, a boy and a girl. They both wore a green silk band across their eyes, "they were clean and healthy children," and "their faces looked bright, happy, and intelligent." They performed several musical pieces with the boy at the piano and the girl singing. As they did so, the crowd sat "in breathless and silent listening, as if a cherub's notes had locked their senses in a spell of enchantment."[46]

Before long, participating in concerts and exhibits had become a routine part of Howe's pupils' experience at the school. In September 1837, for example, he informed the Reverend Bailey Loring in North Andover that the ticket price for a proposed concert at his church should be twenty-five cents, that the program should run from seven to nine o'clock, and that he should make plans for sufficient lighting and seating. Two months later he negotiated with John Appleton for a concert in Gloucester. Because of the distance from Boston, overnight accommodations would be necessary. Howe expected four hundred tickets to be sold at twenty-five cents each, assuring him of taking in fifty dollars beyond the expenses of the road, board, etc." Appleton had requested that ten students be sent for the concert, but Howe recommended that the audience would receive a better performance if twenty pupils participated. By his fifth year of operating the blind school, Howe had developed a routine for his concerts for the public.[47]

The exhibition of blind pupils also allowed Howe to tap the public for financial donations. Before the end of 1833 he had admitted twenty-nine more students and desperately needed the support to operate the blind school. In January 1833, his friend Horace Mann submitted a memorial to the Massachusetts House of Representatives requesting that the New England Institution show the legislature the progress it had made in educating the blind. Mann hoped the memorial would elicit additional state funding. It soon became apparent to Howe that his father's Pleasant Street residence housing pupils, a matron, three teachers, and him and his two sisters could no longer accommodate the needs of the growing blind school. The school needed a larger home, and for a larger home it needed additional public and private financial support.

For public support, Howe turned to the Massachusetts General Court, which, beginning in the 1830s, supplied part of the funding for the school. The governor named a minority of members to the institution's board of trustees. Although many law makers visited the school, Howe, despite the discomfort he felt about exhibiting his pupils, visited the legislature at least once a year, bringing with him staff and pupils. On Friday 28 February 1840, for example, Howe wrote: "Morning exercises [were] interrupted by preparations for [the] exhibition. In the afternoon [we] repaired to the State House with most of the pupils at 2 ½ o'clock. By 3 o'clock the House was densely filled with representatives, *citoyens & citoyennes*. Commenced at ¼ past by an address & a rapid *expose* of the course of instruction. The classes were then examined in the various branches of study, & answered questions propounded both by the teachers & the auditors. Their answers elicited much applause, but their music seemed to charm the audience. The Committee & the audience seemed satisfied & the *séance* was prolonged to a late hour."[48]

In April 1841, confident that what worked well in Massachusetts would well just as well in another state, Howe planned with a New Haven supporter of the blind to arouse what he saw as the moribund interest of Connecticut lawmakers who, although they had appropriated funds to send students from the state to Howe's blind school, had not taken advantage of the appropriation. To remedy this failure, Howe proposed "a concert and exhibition" of his pupils "to diffuse a knowledge of the advantages which the institution afford to the Blind."[49]

The school's first major private benefactor was Thomas H. Perkins. When he first offered support, Perkins was a sixty-eight-year-old merchant and shipper who had amassed his wealth in trading tea, silk, spices, and opium in China and slaves in the Caribbean and in investing in North American banking and real estate. Like the Howe family, the Perkins family belonged to the Brattle Street Church, and Thomas Perkins had known Samuel Howe since his birth. Howe's grandfather and father, Edward and Joseph Howe, had no doubt done business with Perkins, and Perkins had kept up with Samuel Howe's exploits in Greece and had read about his recent imprisonment in Prussia. Like others of his social rank, Perkins had contributed to local civic institutions: the Boston Athenaeum, the Bunker Hill Monument, and the Massachusetts General Hospital. With the rise of Jacksonian power and consequent diminution of Federalist authority in Boston, wealthy Bostonians like Perkins found it in their interest to support charitable organizations to insure their public influence.[50]

On 26 April 1833 the *Boston Evening Transcript* reported that earlier in the month Perkins, who for several years had suffered from ocular problems, had made a proposition to the directors of the New England Institution. If the directors raised fifty thousand dollars (no small sum for the time) by the end of May, Perkins would donate his large house at 17 Pearl Street, which he valued at thirty thousand dollars. On 21 April 1831, Perkins had spent thirteen thousand dollars to purchase a lot for his new house on the fashionable Temple Place near the Boston Common. Pearl Street, where he had shared his residence with the Boston Athenaeum before it moved to Beacon Street, was becoming more and more commercial as Boston's emerging Irish immigrant slums moved closer and closer. The fund-raising challenge seemed daunting; but because it came with Perkins's imprimatur, upper-class Bostonians gave it their approval and, before long, approached the task of raising funds with unrestrained enthusiasm. With their participation, the effort to raise fifty thousand dollars was seen as a socially sanctioned and, thereby, agreeable project for Boston's moneyed elite of every political persuasion.[51]

Despite its size and social standing, the money-raising enterprise had one unique feature: it was managed in large part by women. Recent histories have described ladies fairs, as they were known in antebellum America, as abolitionist affairs. And though these fairs reached their greatest public recognition through efforts to raise money for the cause of abolishing slavery, woman in Massachusetts learned the skills of community-fair fund-raising at fairs organized to benefit the blind school.[52] The Salem Ladies Fair, for example, took place on 10 April 1833, even before Perkins made his offer. A local newspaper reported:

> Doors will be opened at 10 o'clock, A.M. Some of the most valuable articles will be offered by auction. Price of admission, 25 cents. The Hall will be open the day previous, from 10 to 1, A.M. for the exhibition of the articles—Admission 1 dollar. Items offered for sale included, Dolls of various sorts and doll clothing and doll furniture, Flowers Birds—Humming bird, East India pheasant, swan, etc. (stuffed), Decorated boxes, cases, Decorated lanterns, glass baskets, Necklaces, Glass ship in a case, Napkins, Flags, Hat trees, Panoramic box, Ladies slippers, Men's slippers, Pincushions, Gentlemen's fine linen collars, Infant shoes, Mittens, Cut paper ornaments, Gingham bonnets, Centre table workbox, Fancy basket of bonbons, Two splendid paintings in oils of scenery near Bristol in England, by Miss Sophia Peabody, Blind Miriam, an original tale, written for the occasion, by Miss Savage, Bust of Dr. Spurzheim, Twenty numbered Landscape illustrations of the Waverly Novels.[53]

In January, Elizabeth Peabody, "the godmother of Boston," the loyal friend of William Ellery Channing and Ralph Waldo Emerson, and soon to be a teacher in Bronson Alcott's Temple School, had visited Howe's institution with the older of her two younger sisters, Mary, and with Horace Mann, then a young attorney and legislator whom they had recently met at Rebecca Clarke's 3 Somerset Court boarding house in Boston. Ten years later in 1843 Mary Peabody and Horace Mann would wed. Elizabeth, who had recently moved from Salem to Boston with Mary, got caught up in the excitement of the fair. Sophia, a third sister and the future wife of Nathaniel Hawthorne, was the family artist and her art, Elizabeth hoped, would become a source of much-needed family income. Sophia had studied painting with Thomas Doughty, and she had received the commendation of Washington Allston for a copy she had painted of one of his landscapes. The headaches that had waylaid her for so many years now seemed to be less bothersome. At the Salem Ladies Fair, Sophia's paintings sold for sixty dollars, the highest amount offered for an item at the fair. Elizabeth, who worried more about family resources than did her youngest sister, consoled herself that the loss of income from Sophia's paintings to the blind school would be made up for by the attention the fair provided for her sister's art.[54]

In Boston less than a month later, a second ladies fair proved even more popular for the affluent elite who operated the fair and for the upper and middling classes who attended. The fair, held at Faneuil Hall, soon became the talk of the town. The wife of Harrison Gray Otis, the mayor of Boston, led the festivities. Few Boston matrons and their daughters failed to join the happenings. Even some of their husbands and brothers got involved. The unusual sight of woman engaging in this peculiar form of commerce led local newspapers to comment about the festivities. Around the time the fair ended, an anonymous writer published a fourteen-page pamphlet, "Scenes at the Fair," that lampooned the fair makers. Despite the lampooning the fair's treasurer, Labiah May Smith, reported to Howe that the women had raised an astounding $11,400 for the institution.[55]

The Salem and Boston fairs, along with other fund-raising events of the time, increased public awareness of the blind institution. What had been a strange asylum hardly a year earlier had now become a legitimate educational facility supported by a wide range of eastern Massachusetts elites. Churches, newspapers, and civic and eleemosynary organizations, along with the ordinary people, soon participated in the enthusiasm surrounding the school. Howe could hardly keep up with the requests for his students to perform their newly learned skills.[56] By June 1833, just as residents of Boston and Cambridge were aflutter about Harvard University's awarding of an honorary doctor of laws degree to President Andrew Jackson (whom an outraged

John Quincy Adam called "a barbarian who could not write a sentence of grammar and hardly could spell his own name"), the New England Institution had raised the funds to match the Perkins legacy, and the next month Howe began renovations to the Perkins home at the school's new location on Pearl Street.[57] As he did so, he arranged for the conversion of the barn into a schoolhouse, and the house's large rooms to living space for pupils and staff. For the first time, he had a real school building and real dormitories for his pupils; yet, within a few months, it was clear that the growing prominence of the school continued to generate its principal challenge. As the second year of the school began in the fall of 1833, Howe received requests for admission that exceeded both the space available for housing and educating his pupils and the funds available for hiring new teachers and new caretakers. Because of these limitations, the school admitted fifteen students in 1834 and ten in 1835, together fewer than the twenty-nine who entered in 1833.[58]

A Social Critic

Around this time, Howe began writing on matters not necessarily associated with blindness. Following a pattern that would continue throughout his life, he produced annual reports for the institution and wrote about blindness and Greece and Poland for popular journals, but he also published articles that reflected his diverse interests and the varied causes that aroused those interests. These interests and causes included atheism, slavery, the education of women, and a topic that would fascinate him for the next three decades, phrenology. Howe's writings on all of these topics reflected his confidence, first developed at Brown and Harvard, in human perfection through social reform and improvement.

Two of the most influential articles of his career appeared in the March 1833 edition of the *New England Magazine,* where he had published articles in 1831 and whose editorship he would assume for a short period between the fall of 1834 and the summer of 1835, and the July 1833 edition of the *North American Review.* Although the articles had the same title, "Education of the Blind," they had quite different purposes. The *New England Magazine* article was descriptive and empirical. In it Howe argued what the public was just beginning to believe: the blind can be educated. The confirmation of this remarkable new information, he said, lay in Europe, where blind people were learning to do nearly anything that sighted people could do. Howe concluded the article with a bold claim: "Nothing but prejudice has or will prevent the blind from becoming first-rate teachers of music, of the dead and living languages, of mathematics, and many other sciences. Nothing but prejudice would prevent an educated blind man from finding employment as a counselor at law, or becoming an able and efficient preacher of the gospel." The *North American Review* article presented the historical and philosophical underpinning for blind pedagogy. The *Review* was the leading magazine of New England and, among America's staid intellectuals, one of the nation's leading journals. Publication in the *Review* left little doubt that, at the age of thirty-one, the son of the rope maker Joseph Howe had become a respected member of New England's thinking elite.[59]

In the *Review* article, Howe noted that over the ages people had kept the blind in listless inactivity because they had assumed them to be helpless. Often left to beg or, at best, sent to the almshouse, the blind were likely to degenerate into burdensome "idiocy." Howe claimed that the loss of sight had some inevitable drawbacks, that blind people were, for example, left with a "weak sexual propensity" because sexual attraction was dependent on sight, a sense the blind could not draw on. Nevertheless, their loss of sight was usually made up for by their sense of touch and hearing, both of which, because of the blind person's greater dependence on each, developed precise acuity. Howe expressed confidence that though the European schools had led the way for educating the blind by showing that the blind could learn, these schools—even the best of them—fell short of achieving the potential that American schools were destined to reach. In Europe, he wrote, "the blind man has to struggle against stubborn and cruel prejudices; people are so accustomed to consider the blind as ignorant and degraded dependents that if two organists equally well qualified, should apply for a place in a church, one of them be blind, he would probably lose it." In the United States, however, blind people had neither to confront the prejudices of class differences nor to fall victim to prejudices associated with their disability. What was possible for educated blind people, therefore, was not only an ordinary role in the social order but also a new citizenship, filled with potential and free of bigotry.

In a brief but telling aside, Howe commented on the education of deaf mutes. In Germany, he claimed to have witnessed educators who taught deaf pupils to speak to hearing people and who, in turn, discouraged their pupils from communicating with each other through the use of manual signs. In 1833, when he wrote the two articles, and throughout his life, Howe never questioned his belief that the public communication of vocal language between the nonhearing and the hearing was preferable to the private communication of signs between nonhearers, whose gestures he imagined could hardly be a true language. He noted, "We are sorry that this plan [of vocal articulation] has been abandoned in the Hartford School, which (otherwise) is one of the best in the world." Howe's 1832 observations of deaf Prussian children speaking had nearly as profound an effect on him as had his Berlin imprisonment and would shape a lifelong conviction. Speech and lip reading, Howe concluded, has ushered deaf people into an integrated world where the hearing and the deaf alike could communicate on equal terms. No longer would deaf people be left to communicate only among themselves by the use of privately understood manual signs. As we shall see, his concern for public communication would extend to his insistence that blind people learn to read from raised letters, even after the more efficient but private Braille system became widely available.

A month later, in August 1833, Howe published "Letter on Slavery," in the *New England Magazine*.[60] The magazine printed the article without attribution, but its readers soon learned that Howe was its author. As the title indicated most of the article was a long letter that Howe had written earlier in the summer to an unnamed North Carolina correspondent. The article was important not only for what it revealed about Howe's position on slavery and for what it showed about his views on human nature and human progress But it was important also for what it revealed about Howe's attempt—just as he was enlarging his reputation in Boston—to reconcile the institution of Southern slavery with those views. The North Carolinian had written about New England abolitionists and in particular about the recent development of the immediate abolitionism associated with William Lloyd Garrison and the New England Anti-Slavery Society. He had asked Howe about the number of abolitionists and about what Howe identified as "information about the feeling of New England with regard to the means of removing the evils of slavery."

In his reply, Howe began by affirming his view of American exceptionalism. Unlike Europeans burdened by the economic and social cost of kings and priests, by the necessity of diplomacy and territorial conquest, and the large standing armies and police forces that those foreign civil wars and domestic oppressions require, the United States, "the promised land of republicanism," he said, had, "become [the land of] the most intelligent, the richest, and the happiest people on earth." What the young nation owed to its European ancestors was an example that the tired, corrupt, and oppressive old-world nations could emulate. Sixty years before the founding apostle of American exceptionalism, Frederick Jackson Turner, had launched a view of American moral and political superiority, Howe boldly claimed that the American experiment gave a lie to the European assumption that human beings were fundamentally fallen and must be controlled for their own good by divinely appointed aristocrats. Instead, he argued, what the United States had shown—and in fifty years it would show even more clearly—was the "accelerat[ion of] the great march of mind, to facilitate the progress of the human race, in its course toward the nearest possible attainment of political, moral, and intellectual perfection."

But the experiment, the very hope of the new world and the old, had at its core an evil institution—slavery. Howe was blunt about his feelings about slavery; it was "a system which violates the laws of nature, and the laws of God." And true to his revolutionary reputation, he admitted that "were the slaves of the South now in general insurrection, and in open war with the whites, and *were I forced* to choose one side or the other, I would join the insurgents, and strike with them for the rights of man; and though, father and brother were in opposing ranks, still would I strike for the liberty of the human race."

Just as his revolutionary republicanism reached a crescendo, however, Howe pulled back from the radicalism of the Garrisonians. In place of radicalism came his gradualist sensibilities, and with these sensibilities his commitment to resolve social problems by appealing to individual reason and freedom. Although he acknowledged that "I am called an optimist because I believe that there is force enough in truth, and virtue enough in man, to produce not only the final Abolition of slavery, but many other great changes in the world," he just as quickly denied being, "a representative of *l'extreme gauche*." Immediate abolition, he claimed, would lead to social chaos and, hence, would be as foolish for the slave as it would be for the master. Better to have the planned and rational migration of individual slaves to African colonies, which would insure remuneration to planters for the loss of their property and provide a way for individual slaves to return to the land of their heritage. Such colonization, Howe was quite aware, was a direct challenge to the ideas Garrison put forth in his 1832 book *Thought on African Colonization*.[61]

Besides these matters of economic and social concern, Howe pointed out, is the more important issue of nature. Slavery in the face of republican progressive values must inevitably end. Human progression (and ultimately perfection) unleashed by republican values would do what immediate abolitionism could never do—end slavery by peaceful means. These abolitionists, Howe concluded, were rare in New England, and their absurd doctrine had the respectability of another peculiar sect, "the Mormonites." What should happen, Howe argued, is that South and North alike must continue a rational dialogue and "candidly . . . discuss the question, 'What shall be done with the blacks' "? Reason and nature, Howe stated confidently, would prevail. Joining a tradition held by many Americans—Daniel Webster, John Marshall, Henry Clay, Lyman Beecher and his daughters Catharine and Harriet, Henry David Thoreau (before 1846), Dorothea Dix, and Abraham Lincoln, Howe accepted what he saw as the good sense of colonization.[62] And with this acceptance Howe affirmed the position of the American Colonization

Society founded in 1816. He would ask the same question, "What shall be done with the blacks?" again in war years of 1864 and 1865. By that time, his plan for ending slavery had changed considerably, but, curiously enough, his anticipation for the slaves' integration into American society had become only more sanguine. Though Howe remained an optimist, his optimism over the years would alter as his confidence in individual change gave way to faith (though tentative faith) in structural change. But whether he was arguing for individual reform or structural reform, his views remained grounded in reason provided by education.

During the same month he published "Letter on Slavery," Howe began a correspondence with Almira Phelps and her sister, Emma Willard, on the education of women in postrevolutionary Greece. This correspondence led to the publication in 1834 of a letter in Willard's *American Ladies Magazine*.[63] Earlier that year, young women laboring in the cotton mills of Lowell, Massachusetts, had gone on strike after their wages were reduced by 15 percent. Boston newspapers had carried daily articles about the women's actions. So the issue of women's education was more than an abstract concern to Howe and other social critics. The view Howe expressed in his letter to Willard, the nation's most prominent proponent of women's education, and to her Troy Society for the Promoting Female Education in Greece was progressive for his time. Women, he said had a proper—and by proper Howe meant natural—role to play in society. They were not, as was so often assumed in semi-barbarian society, merely the handmaids of men or mere servants who provided labor and ornamentation. Rather, women played a role in society that was as important as, though different than, the role men played. Women provided "softer and more refined feelings" that balanced the "fiery nature" of men. Yet kept as mere laborers in the service of men or reduced to decoration, women were unable to provide the refinement that nature required of them for the good working of the social order. Under Turkish rule, the Greeks had lost the social balance that women had once provided. Freed from the "Asian" diminishment of women, the newly independent Greek republic could restore what centuries of oppression had kept submerged.

For women to take their natural place in Greek society, Howe argued, they need education. Although he gave no suggestions about how to carry out such education or about what the education should contain, Howe expressed confidence that Greek women, like other European women, were intelligent and resourceful and thereby would respond to efforts for their instruction. Thus, women had a true and prescribed place in God's natural order. As such, like men, women benefit from education when that education prepared them for their natural social roles. In his mother, Howe had seen the embodiment of refined feelings, and in his sisters he daily observed the feminine "soft" balance to the aggressive "hard" force of men. There was no doubt in his mind that women should be educated; the soft side needed instruction for its natural maturation just as much as the hard side needed instruction. Among the girls and women whose education he championed at the Perkins Institution, he never wavered in his confidence. But his progressive views would find their limit when women, in particular, his wife, Julia Ward Howe, moved beyond the boundaries of what his saw as their natural social roles.[64]

Howe's writings give us some insight into what Howe saw as women's natural role in the social fabric. His sentiments were typical of his day. "No lady," he wrote to Abigail and Sophia Carter's mother, "can go before the public as a performer, or a musician, and preserve her fair name, unless she does it under the open and constant protection of her husband, father, mother, or some one in whom the public has perfect confidence. . . . As for their going about with, or appearing in public with young men, who are not their natural guardians and protectors it ought never to be thought of for a moment; for although they may make a few dollars they might too repent it all their lives. The character of young ladies is bright as glass, and like glass too it can never be mended ever if it is cracked, ever so unjustly." Women, Howe held, were constitutionally able to maintain standards of purity and refinement that men could never attain. By appearing in public as a performer or champion of causes, women compromised their own purity and, in a sense, society's purity.[65]

Women, in Howe's view, provided a moral guiding light for men as well as for mankind. In their standard-setting purity women offered comfort, kindness, sympathy, gentleness, and womanly strength. In short, they were the mothers that all human beings (but especially men) needed and wanted. Although Howe would disagree with his fellow Unitarian Lydia Maria Child about the abolition of slavery, his perspective on women was close to hers. Child's 1829 book *The Frugal Housewife* would launch the antebellum view of women as purveyors of domestic economy and society's moral compass.

Howe reflected on these motherly sentiments in a letter he wrote to the Massachusetts novelist, Unitarian, and early feminist Catharine Maria Sedgwick about his requirements for the position of matron of his blind school. Holding the most central position at the school, after his own, the matron had to be a woman of all women. He told Sedgwick he wanted "a kind *motherly* woman to whom the pupils would run with all their little sorrows and joys." She must also be "a thrifty housewife who would oversee and direct all the domestic operations; an intelligent person whose judgment would decide a hundred minute details without definite instructions"; and "a lady like woman whose manners and address would be agreeable to visitors and whose conversation would be instructive to the pupils; a conscientious and religious person who would not be satisfied with keeping the ten commandments but feel the obligation of ten thousand; whose actions would be prayers, whose whole life a sabbath, and whose cheerful resignation would be constant thanksgiving."[66] Howe maintained a long and regular correspondence with the Connecticut poet Lydia Sigourney, who with the wealth provided by her husband and generated by her writings sponsored a blind and indigent pupil, Charles Henry Sandford, at the blind school. Sigourney's dealings with the blind school (and with Howe) were discrete and generous. To Howe, her interest in, and most important, the manner of her concern for poor Charles made her an ideal female.[67]

Howe's thoughts about the purity and the motherly ways of women did not preclude his expressing sexual interest in women. Although he never let down his puritanical Yankee guard, throughout his life, Howe kept an eye out for attractive women. Legend, never confirmed by Howe, claimed that back from Greece in the early 1830s, he struck an unusually handsome figure, as he did back in Boston on his black horse. In February 1834 Elizabeth Peabody, in a gossipy letter to her sister Mary reported that Howe was engaged to Mary Ann Marshall. Given to "coquetting" and one of Peabody's poorest students, Marshall seems to have broken off the engagement before much was made of it.[68] In a 1828 diary entry written while quarantined on the island of Gibraltar on his way back to Greece from the United States, Howe reflects on the dark beauty of Spanish women:

> The women whom I saw (the Spanish) were decidedly fine looking, that is the kind of beauty that pleases me, not regularity of features, not the rose and lily, these women had none of them, but their complexions would be called dark with us. The clear olive skin, black hair, eyebrows, and jetty sparkling eye through which flashed the soul and lit up the whole countenance with spirit and intelligence. It is the soul, the soul, which gives to woman her power of fascination; it is the feeling heart, speaking in the intelligent face; it is the beauteous mirror of the mind that we worship, and not the waxen doll, not the red and white, secumdum artem beauty. . . . I saw some girls at the art-less age of twelve or thirteen playing together, and in every one of them I saw what I had preconceived to be the characteristic appearance of Spanish females. Those I saw were principally of the middle and lower ranks, and there was an appearance of ease and freedom about them which though not amounting to forwardness exactly, yet it is generally a pretty certain sign of a want of modesty. They court not the gaze of the stranger, yet they shrink not from it, and they endure his scrutiny with a sangfroid that we should like to see at home.[69]

How much of a ladies' man Howe became in the years before his marriage in 1843 is hardly known. There are no reports in letters to his friends and associates about romantic interests or sexual affairs. In May 1840 he challenged the attorney and future mayor of Boston John Prescott Bigelow to disavow his claim that Howe had obtained and spent money illegally, not the least of which was for the purpose of having "improper intercourse with a married woman."[70] Howe was clearly distressed by rumors conveyed to him by J. K. Mills and John D. Fisher that Bigelow had spread, but nothing seemed to have come of them. A year later in May 1841, reflecting on human nature and friendship, Howe confided to Horace Mann his feelings for the fair sex. At the age of thirty-nine, he was too old to have a boylike wonder for women, but he was clearly a man who remained sexually unfulfilled. His daughter, Laura Howe Richards, omitted this passage from the letter in the edited volume of her father's writings:

> It is true, I am as sentimental as Jacques, just now, for I have been engaged in a most delightful occupation—reading the ms. letters of a pure warm hearted girl of seventeen to her friend & playmate, who was slowly sinking in a decline. The writer is a daughter of a friend of yours, who is rich, & who lavishes upon her every means of enjoyment. She was away from the city & surrounded with gaiety & life, and yet, she writes day after day to her rich friend very long letters, which are absolutely gushing over with kindliness & love. This was years ago, and the friend is dead, but by chance the letters came under my eye & have given me a most refreshing glance into one of the brightest spots of humanity.
>
> God! With how much of the noblest kind of beauty has profusely endowed the heart of woman. What a well of deep feeling hast thou sunken in her nature, what an inexhaustible spring of love hast thou planted within her soul. But how often is that moral beauty unheeded or blasted, how often does the very depth of her feeling come the deeper woe, & how is the foundation which should pour forth love & affection made to give out bitter waters of depravity & deceit!
>
> As there is nothing in nature so beautiful as the fresh young heart of the guileless girl, so there is nothing so hideous as the passions of a depraved woman.[71]

In Howe's vision of women lay the physical and the ideal. Even in his sexual longings, a woman was never divorced from her purity, her goodheartedness, her "moral beauty." Howe's ideal woman never fully departed from the mother he lost as a young college student. In 1868, when he discovered that two of his employees at the blind school, Sarah McLane and a man identified only as Mr. Hallard, were living together unmarried, he immediately discharged both of them. A woman especially, Howe insisted, must maintain propriety.[72]

In October 1834, he had become the editor of the *New England Magazine.* Shortly before taking over his new position, he described his aspirations for the magazine to Henry Wadsworth Longfellow, a little-known professor of literature at Bowdoin College. "We propose," Howe informed Longfellow, "to change the character of the work to make it partly political, to make it resemble the standard *Monthlies* of London. We intend to make the work an engine for promoting sound republican principles, and exposing in a calm and dignified, but firm & fearless manner the dangerous tendency of the measures & principles of the dominant political party." The "dominant party," was the Jacksonian Democracy, and Howe made clear that his own allegiance was not to that party.[73]

Howe increased his literary efforts as he laid out a curious political theology in two articles published in the December 1834 and January 1835 issues of the *New England Magazine,* both with the provocative title, "Atheism in New England." Goaded by the free-thinking claims made by the Universalist preacher Abner Kneeland in his newspaper, the *Boston Investigator,* Howe argued that although the denial of the existence of God was anyone's right to make, Kneeland's egregious public claims made in print and at his "Temple of Reason" in Boston's Federal Street Theater threaten the very fabric of society. Private atheism was one thing, but public blasphemy was another. Public infidelity, Howe explained, was a social, not just a religious, evil because, in the place of education, infidelity accompanied destructive class warfare that, though often precipitated by the arrogance and illiberality of the rich and powerful, was ultimately destructive of the social order. Class inequality was best dealt with through education and human improvement, and by philanthropic social services for members of society who could not fully provide for themselves. Ignorance and selfishness—for the rich and the poor—were the great common enemies. The social order needed religion to maintain social stability, and it needed religion for the flourishing of education, social elevation, and the common good. Inflamed by irreligious, class warfare (and the leveling principle that it implied) merely led to ignorance, animal passions, and illiberality. Without grounding in the laws provided by Providence, freedom became a license for "blasphemy, ribaldry, and obscenity." Even the sanctity of marriage turned to the "licentious indulgence" of the likes of Fanny Wright and Robert Dale Owen, and the rights of property dissolved into the thievery of the "dividers of property." Had not Owen advertised his *Moral Physiology,* a book about birth control, in Kneeland's *Boston Investigator* and offered copies of the book for sale in Kneeland's newspaper office?

The social fabric, Howe insisted, depended on religion for the harmonious stability of its members, and this religiously based harmony and stability depended on an educated public.[74] Although he never indicated it explicitly, Howe implied that infidelity, class warfare, and moral licentiousness were associated with Jacksonian politics.

Howe linked the blasphemy of Abner Kneeland and the politics of Andrew Jackson and his followers to what he regarded as the pomposity of the evangelical Calvinist Lyman Beecher. (Howe did not make the distinction between the Calvinism of Beecher and the Arminianism of Charles Grandison Finney.) To be sure, Howe, a Unitarian among emerging Unitarians, rejected the claims of what he saw as premodern religious superstitions, the superstitions of Trinitarian Calvinists like Beecher. Beecher, who referred to Unitarianism as the "icy system," at the time was regularly preaching anti-Unitarian, as well as anti-Catholic, sermons at his Congregational Society Meeting at Bowdoin Street on Beacon Hill. But the rejection of those superstitions, Howe insisted, was necessary to open up a true Christianity based on the promise of reason refined by education. Abner Kneeland and Lyman Beecher, as different as their theologies might be, had in common religious claims that lacked reason. Thus reason, and not the sort of irrational class warfare that he witnessed in Europe in 1830, was necessary for religion to thrive in American society. Ordinary Europeans living under ancient prejudices, fixed class divisions, and irrational religious traditions might need revolutionary class conflict, but in the United States without those rigid social fixtures, class warfare was not only unnecessary, it was harmful. Religion in the nation would remain a barrier to class division and conflict as long as it remained rational. For it to remain rational, religion depended on a well-educated populous.

For Howe, the most significant threat to a rational religion was embodied in the Second Great Awakening, personified in Beecher, Jackson, and even Kneeland. A movement lasting from around the end of the 1700s into the 1840s, the awakening led to a rise in individual conversions to evangelical Christian faiths, church membership, and new Protestant denominational sects, along with overt expressions of religious sentiment in churches, in writings, and most important in traveling revival meetings. And it accompanied the politics of Jacksonian class warfare and, paradoxically, Kneelandian atheism. Howe would have none of it. Even in 1829 in Greece, he had regarded with disdain the efforts of American and English missionaries to convert Greeks to evangelical Protestant Christianity. Since he had no doubt about the superiority of a liberal Protestant faith, he had no use for many orthodox Protestant wearers of "black breeches." In his diary of the period he reflected on two missionaries he met while traveling on mules between the colony at

Washingtonia and the Greek village of Vostitza. The missionaries had with them letters from his sisters and father, and he was grateful for their gifts. But of their profession, he had little good to say.

> These men are missionaries: Mr. Anderson, a man apparently of good mind, inquiring disposition and shrewd judgment; [and] Mr. Eli Smith, a methodistical, self-sufficient, narrow-mind, vulgar appearing little body, who have come probably to spy out the land and see whether there be any hope of propagating their dogmas—humbug. Avaunt all licensed and regular priests, God has no need of self-created pioneers in the great march of man toward perfection, nor has man need of the help of such rotten sticks to lean upon— sticks made from the same tree of which he is a branch. I do most purely abominate the idea of having religion made a worldly business. I *think* it is unnecessary that a man in order to fulfill his duty to his kind should be set apart from them and before them, that he should read black letter or wear black breeches, or look black on the foibles of his neighbors. I reverence the Christian religion. I admire its sublime principle. I firmly believe it the best guide to earthly, individual and national happiness, and I think it my duty to my fellow men to use my endeavors to extend it. And [I] do think that without preaching, praying, or acting the black coat, I have done more toward bringing Greeks to it than any licensed retailer of religion. I argue even with the people. I ridicule their idle ceremonies. I dispute with their priests before the people. I accommodate myself to the person and his capacity. I try to throw down one thing before setting up another. As yet I have known but one American missionary do any good, [and] that was Brewer. As for King— the sanctified, hypocritical, selfish and bigoted Jonas King, the deuce knows where he will find a proselyte with all his prayers and fastings. The Greeks are not the old grannies to be humbugged by any such unnatural demeanor. He is mocked and deceived.[75]

Howe's views on "methodistical" preachers and their revivalist theology had changed little in the decade since this encounter. Yet as he continued to observe the effects of Trinitarian revivalism, especially among his blind pupils, he began to notice its detrimental effects not only for the social order but also for the individual's well-being. In October 1839, for example, he expressed concern to the father of one of his pupils, William Dewitt, about the boy's recent religious conversion. William, Howe reported, was well behaved and studious, and though not a bright student, he was diligent in his efforts—a quality that Howe admired. But something unfortunate had happened. After attending a religious revival, the boy, Howe reported, was now in what the revivalists call an "anxious state," which had left William in a frame of mind "induced by gloomy and fearful expectations of human depravity, divine wrath, and the torments of a material hell, with all the appendages of gnashing teeth, and undying worms." The problem, Howe made clear, was that such irrational conversions ensured, "a state of mind which gives degrading views of the human soul, and of the Divine Nature, a state of mind which in my view, is at utter variance with true religion, and which substitutes for it selfish hopes of Heaven as a reward, and selfish fear of hell as a punishment, and which unfits us for doing good for the love of goodness, and serving God for the love of God." For Howe, there was no small irony in this fallen state. Converted Christians in their "anxiety" about their fall from grace were lost to doing exactly what God would have them do—serving God by serving others. But beyond their obvious theological irrationality, these conversions, Howe asserted, were unhealthy and he confided his concern: "It is a state of mind which operates very injuriously upon the physical health, which deprives many of reason, and dooms them to a mad house and which cannot therefore be of God. Now William is of a nervous, sensitive nature. His bodily organization is easily deranged, and much excitement of this kind may injure his mental powers very essentially without at all promoting his temporal or spiritual welfare."[76]

Despite his uneasiness with the social and personal effects of the irrational religious revivalism of the time, Howe remained optimistic that education led to reason, and, in turn, that reason led to a natural theology—one that rejected Calvinism masking as evangelicalism on one hand and atheism masquerading as Jacksonianism on the other. This natural theology arose from God in the teachings of wise men, who in their observations and study of nature understood God not through superstition and special miracles but through reason and observation. This reasoned theology, made available through education, was open to all thinking people, not just a select few. Most especially, Howe maintained, people were not fallen, but rather they had within themselves the capacity to grow, to learn, and to uncover truth. In September 1836 (the same month that Ralph Waldo Emerson published his first book, *Nature*), the first volume that the New England Institution printed in raised letters was the Christian New Testament. Along with other Unitarians of the time, Howe advocated that the Bible be widely distributed—in his case, to blind readers.[77] If ordinary people read the scriptures and discussed their readings in small Bible studies (the kinds of studies that Unitarians first created and called for during the 1830s and 1840s), they would come, Howe believed, to appreciate the rational claims and simply beauty of God's word, for the peace that the biblical claims made for their own lives, as a motivation to do good in the world, and for the stability it provided for just and well organized social arrangements. At the root of this rational Christian faith was Howe's belief in the power of education to develop and sustain what God would have us do through our natural and social selves. Phrenology appealed to Howe because it showed God's laws working in human beings. Man, for Unitarians like Howe who believed in phrenology, was subject to natural, God-made laws, not to metaphysical speculation, and education was the crucial link between human understanding, human perfection, and God's laws.

The printing press of raised-letter books eventually produced a catalogue of many titles for the blind on various topics, as well as the scriptures. Howe received hundreds of letters from around the nation, Canada, and occasionally even from Great Britain requesting books for blind children and adults whose parents and relatives, after hearing about Howe's teaching method, wanted to use it to teach their children and siblings. Usually Howe sent one or more books and often included recommendations about teaching methods and the order in which the student should read them.[78]

CHAPTER FOUR
A Phrenologist and a Superintendent

Howe's confidence in phrenology marked a prominent fissure in his idealism, returning it to the Enlightenment truth, reason, and natural theology that his Romantic idealism had neither entirely abandoned nor entirely absorbed. It was not as if phrenology did not claim its own idealism. To be sure, the followers of the leading phrenologists—Franz Joseph Gall, Johann Spurzheim, and George Combe—were moved by contemporary German and English Romanticism. But the American followers of phrenology grounded their idealism in the materialism provided by the brain. The brain, phrenologists claimed, was divided into discrete regions, each of which was assigned to a certain mental faculty (labeled with terms such as constructiveness, destructiveness, approbation, affection, and veneration). Through the measurement of the regions of the brain in the dead or of the head itself in the living, phrenologists, therefore, had a science of the mind. Thus, mental functions and sentiments became meaningful through cranial measurement. From the phrenological measurement of the regions of the skull taken with calipers, rulers, and other devices, scientists like Howe were able to discover what they believed were the strengths and weaknesses of people's mental abilities and their moral sentiments, along with their behavioral propensities.

Howe's earliest notice of phrenology likely came during his medical training under William Ingalls and John Collins Warren, and he probably heard lectures and discussion about the new science during his studies in Paris in 1830 and his travels to European blinds schools in 1831 and 1832. But the arrival of Johann Gaspar Spurzheim in Boston on 20 August 1832 sealed Howe's enthusiasm for phrenology. For eleven weeks Warren and other Boston medical men escorted the fifty-six-year-old Spurzheim, one of the founders of the brain science, on a course of almost nonstop lectures and demonstrations around eastern Massachusetts. Before medical societies, at public lectures, at educational and public institutions, and before religious societies, Spurzheim told the story of phrenology and showed the way "the anatomy of the brain" revealed the mental, intellectual, and emotional faculties of individuals. Within a week of his arrival, his lectures were attracting the attention of Bostonians of all stripes, and local newspapers were heralding his new science as a medical revolution, or even more so as a revelation in basic human understanding. Spurzheim brought to his lectures a secular gospel compatible with the liberal Christianity that was already prominent among most Boston elites. He presented phrenology as a science based on the physiology of the regions of the brain and held that understanding those regions allowed the scientist to know the workings of the mind. The mind rested in the brain, for the brain was the organ of the mind. The brain, as any anatomist could see, was composed of regions, or distinct parts. Each region of the brain matched a particular human faculty. Specific areas of the brain influenced, even controlled the behaviors, attitudes, sentiments, and personality traits of human beings. By measuring an area of the skull that corresponded to a particular region of the brain, the phrenologist could specify the strength or weakness of the particular faculty, which that region of the brain was responsible for influencing. Finally, Spurzheim told his audiences that the regions of the brain could be modified through the use of those regions. If, for example, a person had allowed a region of the brain to become underdeveloped by inactivity, he could exercise the related faculty, thus causing that region to grow. Brains influenced faculties, but the use of a faculty, Spurzheim insisted, could just as certainly change the brain. With this latter claim, Spurzheim's phrenological materialism became an easy pill for liberal idealists like Howe to swallow. The brain might be the seat of the mind, even the beginning point of the mind, but like all of God's material creations, the material brain was pliant, readily changed by the influences of the immaterial world, and therefore dependent on the material but never fixed by it. In phrenology Howe the doer found a way to reconcile the material and the ideal.[1]

Spurzheim's visit to Boston came to an abrupt end on 10 November 1832 when, despite the care of Boston's most prominent physicians, Spurzheim died from typhus. Before his death and feeling certain of its imminence, he made arrangements to have his American followers procure his brain and body parts for a postmortem examination. At his funeral at the Old South Church on 17 November, arranged by a committee made up of Boston mayor Harrison Gray Otis, Harvard president Josiah Quincy, the navigator Nathaniel Bowditch, and others, were three thousand mourners who heard an extended eulogy from the Harvard professor and German immigrant Charles Follen, along with a specially prepared ode sung in memory of the deceased by Boston's Handel and Hayden Society. So stirred by Spurzheim during his brief time in Boston were the men most closely associated with his visit in the late summer and fall of 1832 that they formed the Boston Phrenological Society within hours of the funeral. The group elected Samuel G. Howe as its recording secretary. Before Spurzheim's remains were finally laid to rest in the recently opened Mount Auburn Cemetery in Cambridge, a team of physicians, including Warren and Howe, removed and preserved most of Spurzheim's vital organs. No one was at all surprised that his brain weighed fifty-seven ounces. Eventually Spurzheim's skull became the most prized article in the society's collection of skulls and plaster casts, which included Spurzheim's own collection of similar specimens. Until 1847 when the Harvard Medical College acquired it, Howe kept the collection at the Perkins Institution.[2]

Spurzheim's visit and untimely death generated a wave of interest in phrenology in Boston. In 1835, for example, the young lawyer Charles Sumner, accompanied by his partner, George Hillard, had a phrenologist read his head. The reader reported that Sumner lacked self-esteem but showed the makings of being a good public speaker. "You must rouse up your self respect—take opportunities which do not try your mettle too much & learn to analyze the talents of others & think it easy to equal others," he advised.[3]

A three-year visit from 1838 through 1841 by Spurzheim's student, the Scottish lawyer George Combe, sustained Howe's commitment to phrenology. Nine months before Combe arrived in the United States, Howe had delivered a lecture, "A Discourse on the Social Relations of Man," before the Boston Phrenological Society. In anticipation of Combe's visit, Howe began his lecture by affirming a fundamental phrenological principle: phrenology "teaches that our immaterial and immortal spirits, though essentially independent of matter, are, in this state of being, entirely subjected to, and dependent upon corporal organization for the manner and extent of their manifestations." From this affirmation, Howe moved quickly to the social implication of his talk. People who have fully functioning and well-developed organs, he explained, whose "original formation . . . is according to the general laws of nature" can exercise free moral agency. But, people whose "original organization is unnatural, or when it becomes diseased, or when the organ sleeps" do not have free agency. Human beings have a natural propensity to be in social relations with other human beings. Although this propensity is natural, it requires education of the intellect to provide a moral foundation for such relations. Social institutions, regulations, and rules best facilitate moral relations if they are built on the authority of phrenological principles. These principles are grounded in an understanding of "propensities, faculties, and sentiments" of human beings. And these principles, Howe reminded his listeners, never fail to account for the equilibrium and harmonious interaction of the "organs of the three cavities of the body, the cranium, the thorax, and the abdomen."

In North American society too much attention, Howe claimed, was given to the cerebral, to the neglect of the other bodily cavities. Stressing what would become his lifelong support for physical activity, Howe noted, "The great errors seem to me to be a neglect of the physical nature of man, the custom of treating boys too early as men, and sending them too early into the world to act for themselves, the existence of too much political excitement, and too extravagant notions of personal and political liberty, the fact that we are too zealous, devout, and untiring worshippers of mammon, and that we mingle passion under the name of zeal with our religious feeling." Howe concluded, "The physical nature of man is sadly neglected and abused in this country, and many of our Institutions tend to increase that neglect and abuse." In urban areas especially, men in their quest for material gain had become puny, sick, and weak because they tended to neglect the balance between the physical, the mental, and the moral. Industry, Howe claimed, was a socially valuable trait; but insatiable greed or (as he labeled it phrenologically) "acquisitiveness" was not. Women also suffered from the neglect of physical well-being and exercise. In their fascination with dressing their hair and corseting their waists and hips, women sacrificed the natural for the unhealthy and artificial.[4]

Howe reported with much satisfaction that his male students especially were benefiting from their daily physical exercise. In his school journal, he noted, "The progress & improvement of the boys in basic gymnastic exercises is very gratifying. They no longer esteem it a drudgery but run out cheerfully from the School at 10 & at 12 o'clock & go through all the exercises with spirit. Most of them get into a perspiration. Their brains and nervous system is recruited & they return to School after 15 minutes recess with renewed zest."[5]

As he emphasized the physical part of the well-balanced human being, Howe used the opportunity to talk about a topic that would concern him throughout his life—masturbation. To the twenty-first-century reader, Howe's near obsession with the issue seems quaint, maybe amusing, and certainly wrongheaded. But in his time, and in keeping with his phrenological assumptions, Howe's concern with "self abuse" made sense. Many others shared his concern. His colleague Samuel B. Woodward, the medical superintendent of the lunatic asylum at Worcester, saw the vice as a certain road to insanity, idiocy, and other horrible conditions. And Sylvester Graham, who made popular the whole-grain cracker that bore his name, also made popular a general social anxiety about "self abuse" through his 1834 *Lectures to Young Men on Chastity.* In 1838 the Boston publishing firm of Otis and Broaders printed a translation of the influential *Treatise on the Diseases*

Produced by Onanism, Masturbation, Self-Pollution, and Other Excesses by the Parisian physician Leopold Deslandes. Like Woodward, Graham, Deslandes, and many others, Howe believed that masturbation left perfectly healthy young men (and he remained concerned only for the effects of masturbation on men) "pale, wan, and feeble," at risk of both consumption and insanity. In ignorant pleasure, he told his audience, these young men were driving themselves into a permanent, irretrievable state of physical weakness and ill health, leaving themselves unable to participate in the demands of life. But more than "disease," gratification of the physical through masturbation was a departure from the natural equilibrium of the mental and the moral parts necessary for healthy living.[6]

Howe concluded his lecture to the Boston Phrenological Society with remarks about education and religion, pointing out, "Our system of education is calculated to bring boys and girls too rapidly forward, to educate them superficially, and to develop too strongly their self-esteem." From Howe's phrenological perspective, the love of "approbation" joined the love of "acquisitiveness" as a significant social barrier to educating young people. Children wanted more things, and they wanted praise—not praise for the learning they were capable of achieving but merely from the teacher. Too often, Howe claimed, a teacher's praise and approval become for the child a form of "cheap reward" for a learning process that was developmental and, thereby, naturally slow.

Howe insisted that phrenology was a compliment, not a threat, to religion. The phrenologist knew that religion was a gift from God, a linkage of the material with the immortal, and that when religion was reduced to the mere faculty of "veneration," the cerebral organ became excited, often overly excited to the detriment of the intellectual. Religion, Howe claimed, was more than intellectual, but it was still intellectual. So veneration was a mental, natural faculty that, like all the faculties, had to be regulated by the intellectual. Without the governing regulation provided by the intellectual, religious veneration often degenerated into the farcical, as when teetotaler Connecticut churchmen, having decided to abandon communion wine, vigorously disputed whether to substitute buttermilk for the wine. Religious revivals too, Howe noted, did little more than arouse people's excitement to drunkenlike states. Apart from the folly and fanaticism of these religious revivals, the events compromised the good health of individuals and of communities. Howe was uncompromising, "Excessive cerebral action, strong and continued nervous excitement is always injurious; nature knows no exception to her laws; and it is absurd to suppose the Holy Spirit arrests their operation in these particular cases." Finally, like masturbation, the religious excitement generated by religious revivals, to Howe, was associated with serious health problems, in this instance with dyspepsia and insanity. Thus, religious zealots in their excitement tended to have perpetual digestive problems, and they were prone to madness.[7]

Even before he had met Combe, Howe had publicly pledged himself to the new science of phrenology. Combe delivered his first lecture on 28 September 1838 shortly after his arrival in Boston. On Monday, 8 October, the day Horace Mann and the Dorchester Democrat Nahum Capen first met Combe, they escorted him to the Perkins Institution on Pearl Street, where Howe toured the visitors through the facility. Of special interest to Combe was Laura Bridgman, the blind and deaf girl who after a year at the blind school had already become a regional marvel and was on her way to becoming a national and international sensation. At the end of the day, the excited Mann wrote in his journal that Combe's book, *The Constitution of Man,* "will work the same change in metaphysical science that Bacon wrought in natural." On 10 October at Boston's Masonic Temple, Combe began a new series of sixteen two-hour lectures on phrenological themes. Howe and Mann had read his *Outline of Phrenology* and were attracted to his ideas. Even Ralph Waldo Emerson, who read Combe's *Constitution of Man,* called the phrenologist's writing "the best sermon I've read for some time."[8] In the absence of Spurzheim, Combe had become the world's leading exponent of the science. Not surprisingly, his visit to the United States was a great occasion for Howe, so much so that in anticipation of it, he had prepared a raised-letter edition of *The Constitution of Man* for his adolescent and adult blind pupils to read. Twenty-four blind pupils attended the 10 October lecture, having learned about Combe's ideas from the special edition Howe had provided them.[9]

Howe maintained a close friendship with Combe during Combe's long visit to the United States between 1838 and 1841 and during Howe's visits to Europe in 1843 and 1844, and again in 1850. Apart from those times, they exchanged frequent and regular correspondence. Throughout the 1840s, Howe lectured on phrenological topics before audiences of the Boston Lyceum. One of his most popular titles, "Phrenology of the Senses," on more than one occasion followed the lyceum lecture given by Emerson.[10] In 1857, Howe prepared a revised raised-letter edition of *The Constitution of Man* for his own pupils and for general blind American readers. When Combe was not available for phrenological consultations, Howe could turn to Mann, whose commitment to phrenology paralleled Howe's. Mann had accompanied Combe for nearly two months in March and April 1840 during his travels to Philadelphia and in the Western Reserve. Often during times of particular stress, Howe and Mann would remind each other to "conserve energy" and not to over exert the brain. Their correspondence was often filled with phrenological language and expressions that had meaning only to the phrenologically initiated. In February 1842, for example, Howe on a trip to New Orleans, wrote Mann about his recent visit with the physician Edward Jarvis, who at the time was living in Louisville, Kentucky. Howe's private comments about Jarvis reflect the language of phrenology.

> You have I suppose received letters from Jarvis respecting the L[unatic] Hospital. You know him & can judge for yourself, but my opinion can do no harm. I know few persons who *on the whole* would do better than he, although he has disturbing forces. His caliber is not very large. He has benevolence, modified by acquisitiveness. He has good intellect & great industry, qualified by self esteem which hides from him his deficiencies. Naturally combative he has subdued his irritability by conscientiousness & approbativeness and is very conciliatory & pleasant in his deportment. He has been the life & soul of the common schools of Louisville a[nd] all acknowledge his services in other matters of public good, but he is nevertheless unpopular. They call him *mean.* I do not know why.[11]

In 1849, Howe arranged with John Collins Warren to transfer the Boston Phrenological Society's large collection of skulls and other phrenological artifacts, including most prominently the skull of Spurzheim, from the Perkins Institution where it had resided for over a decade to the Harvard Medical School. At the time, the society had not had a meeting for five years because interest in phrenology had begun to wane in the late 1840s. And Howe, believing the collection would best be preserved at the medical school, readily relinquished it.[12]

Superintending the Blind School

Although his writings associated him with several local, and even some national, issues in the 1830s, Howe's principal responsibility remained the blind school. Between 1832 and 1839, the school admitted 119 students, whose successful education increased the fame of the school and its superintendent. Besides being a place of interest to local visitors, the blind school had become an attraction for American and foreign tourists visiting Boston. It was a common practice at the time for ordinary people to visit public establishments—prisons, jails, poorhouses, schools, and asylums. In late April 1834, for example, Abram V. Courney, a twenty-eight-year-old blind student from Albany, New York, escorted the Tennessee politician and recently defeated member of the U.S. House of Representatives David S. (Davy) Crockett from his lodging at the Tremont House to the blind school. Crockett, who two years later would die at the Battle of the Alamo, spent the afternoon meeting with Howe and observing students in their classes and at work. The British author Harriet Martineau visited the school in 1836, during a winter she spent in Boston before resuming her visit to the Midwest and Great Lakes regions in the spring and summer. In 1838, back in Great Britain, she described the blind school as a "melancholy place," an identification that distressed Howe but nevertheless led to a two-decade friendship and correspondence between the two. After Martineau, the penologist and "child saver" Enoch C. Wines visited the school and in 1838 wrote about his observations.[13] In the early autumn of 1840 Charles Sumner escorted the Austrian dancer Fanny Elssler to the school for a tour led by Howe.

Despite the array of visitors, life went on at the school. In late February 1837, Howe wrote several letters to the parents of his pupil Martha Granger, a private-paying student, eighteen years old, from Rochester, New York, who had been at the school only since the previous October. On 25 February Howe informed Mrs. Granger that on the previous Thursday Martha had become seriously ill and he had bled her. When her condition did not improve, Howe called in two doctors, John Homans and John Fisher, to consult. Homans diagnosed the sickness as "hysteria arising from derangement of the menstruation," but a later diagnosis was "brain fever." Howe assured the mother, "My sister, to whom she is very much attached is with her & will continue so; she has every possible attention, she is not left for [an] instant alone, & be assured, all that human means, all that medical skill & kind careful attention can do, shall be done for Martha: she is much beloved by all here, & I am sure as much will be done for her as though she was at home." A few days later, Howe wrote to Mr. Granger that Martha was stable but no better. On 7 March Howe informed the family of their daughter's death. His words reflect the genuine pain that he felt over her death. She was not the first pupil to die at the school, but she was the first who had died so unexpectedly and so suddenly.

> Now after my [previous] letter was written she began to grow feeble; but so gradual & easy was the change that she seemed like one sleeping; and as there was no pain, no movement, no consciousness it could hardly be said at what precise time her spirit took its flight. As she had been so many days insensible, and as she sank away rather like going into a profound sleep than into death it is probable that our supposition was correct & that water had collected upon the brain. She had all the aid that human skill could give her; she had the sincere prayers & assiduous attention of many who loved her much; but all availed nothing for it pleased her Maker & God to summon her pure spirit to that bright world where the weary find rest. . . . Every respect will be paid to her remains, the minister of the church she attended will officiate; & she shall be laid in the family tomb where sleeps my mother.[14]

In December 1838, the Mount Washington House, a hotel in South Boston located at the corner of H Street and Broadway, became available. A five-storied luxurious lodging, the hotel had caused its backers to incur enormous construction costs. The Panic of 1837 beginning in May produced bank and business failures, a commercial slowdown, and high unemployment across the country. By the last months of 1838, it was apparent that the hotel had failed to attract the vacationers to South Boston that its owners had projected. Howe and the blind school's trustees persuaded Thomas H. Perkins to allow the school to exchange his Pearl Street residence for the hotel, at a sizable loss to the hotel investors. On 29 May 1839 the school moved to the newly built hotel.

Howe was delighted. The facility was spacious, even plush. Perched on a high hill, the facility included about an acre of grounds. Maud Howe, his youngest daughter, remembered: "The Institution was a large brick building, with a classic façade and big white Doric columns. It stood on an elevated plateau above Broadway. Its windows looked out over Boston Harbor. . . . The rooms were large and well proportioned with extra high ceilings. The corridors were paved with squares of gray and white marble. An imposing staircase rose, circling round and round a deep central well, to the giddy height of five tall stories. . . . There was a polished mahogany handrail."[15] About a month before the move, Howe described the hotel to his former pupil A. W. Penniman, now a teacher at the Ohio School for the Blind.

> The House itself is a most beautiful building erected four years ago, at an expense of 110,000$. It is 120 feet front and ninety feet deep in the two wings which run back leaving a court of 45 feet square in the rear. It is five stories high; through each story runs a noble entry way lighted by windows at each end of the House, and by a circular opening in the centre which opening found a sort of circular gallery through each of the five floors and terminates in a glass cupola on the top. The basement of the first floor is laid in white marble, and from each end winds up a broad circular flight of steps. On the basement is a suite of rooms 80 feet long, by twenty wide for work shops. Here also are the boy's washing and bathing rooms[,] dining—the girls['] dining room, and the kitchen. On the second floor or parlor floor there is a room fifty feet by forty feet for the girls' school room, on the other wing, one smaller for the boys, but having across the alley these large rooms united or separated by folding doors for music. Leading from the boys['] school room is an entry which opens to a room 60 feet long, by twenty wide, destined for a bowling alley and gymnasium.
>
> Over the girls' school room is a magnificent Hall sixty feet long, by forty wide, and 20 feet high which we shall use as an exhibition room.
>
> The rest of the House is in keeping with these parts that I have described; there are about 200 apartments in all, and we here shall be able to have every accommodation that is desirable.[16]

Perkins Institution (ca. 1850). Courtesy Perkins School for the Blind.

The hotel was located in what at the time was sparsely populated South Boston, an oddly shaped peninsula emerging from Dorchester Neck and separated from Boston by the South Boston Bay. In 1840 the entire population of South Boston was only 6,176. Located away from the hustle and bustle of Boston, the new facility was near the Boston Harbor, where students could bathe in the salty ocean waters, a convenience that Howe highly valued. In the new facility, students had clearly separated dormitory rooms and educational spaces. The staff too had separate living quarters, and in his apartment, Howe could now house and display his growing library of books and phrenological artifacts.[17]

A typical day at the New England School for the Blind began at 5:00 A.M. when the domestic staff woke to begin the day. At 5:30 a trumpet sounded to

wake the male students, who shortly thereafter assembled in the gymnasium
for Howe's daily inspection of their cleanliness and good health. A matron
carried out a similar process for the female students. At 5:40, which in the
1850s Howe extended to 6:00, devotional services were heard in the pupils'
classrooms on every day but the Sabbath. The services consisted of a reading
or a sermon, usually delivered by Howe, followed by a hymn and the recitation by all attendees of the Lord's Prayer. After prayers, pupils returned to
their rooms to make up their beds, which had been allowed to air out. At
7:00 students ate a plain but wholesome breakfast of milk and wafers. Bread
and butter with gingerbread were occasionally added to the menu. After
breakfast, male students did physical exercises, and the female students did
housework and took walks. Then all students took cold baths. Throughout
his life, Howe believed in the salubrious effects of cold-water bathing and
insisted that cold baths would arouse the mental powers of his students. From
time to time parents objected to the baths, especially in cold weather, but
Howe was unmoved. The students ate a full lunch at one o'clock and a lighter
supper around six. As Howe noted, the meals were "simple but healthful and
abundant." Students were encouraged to eat as much as they wished. Meat,
usually pork or chicken but occasional beef or lamb, was served four times
a week; and fresh fish, salted fish, and baked beans were each served once
a week. Pudding was served almost every day. Never fond of sweets, Howe
discouraged the serving of cakes and candies but allowed for seasonal fruits.[18]

In the evening at 7:45 students assembled in their schoolrooms, where a
local daily newspaper was read to them. In June 1839, shortly after the school
moved to South Boston, some pupils formed the Lyceum Society. At first
only six pupils participated in the society's activities, but soon its membership increased to eighteen. Most weekly meetings consisted of a question for
debate, such as, Does the end ever justify the means? Is it right to remove the
Indians west of the Mississippi? Of the lyceum, Howe noted, "At each meeting the zeal & interest increased; each maintained his side of the question
with tenacity & manifested eagerness to collect information which would aid
him." Staff members sometimes read to the students about current issues. On
Sunday evening, 13 June 1846, for example, the students heard William Ellery
Channing's letters on the annexation of Texas.[19] In 1840 Howe also initiated weekly evening poetry readings. The female students and staff seemed
especially eager for these events. "Their fondness for poetry," he wrote, "is
very remarkable & they will sit by the hour together listening with the greatest eagerness to any tolerable reader of tolerable poetry. It is not merely the
meter & rhyme that interest them but they seize upon the ideas, & brilliant
poetic image is sure to call forth vivid feeling which expressed upon their
countenances."[20]

At the new facility in South Boston, Howe, whom both the students and staff always referred to as "the Doctor," also began hosting social gatherings of male and female students, which usually took place in his apartment at the institution. He justified the gatherings by claiming that students "have much need generally of opportunities for improving their deportment in society." Sometimes the students left the school to attend concerts or plays in Boston or Salem. Howe encouraged these outings, as much for the students' edification as for what he believed was the need of ordinary citizens of eastern Massachusetts to become comfortable in the presence of blind people. When well-known musicians and actors, such as Jenny Lind, Charlotte Cushman, and Edwin Booth, gave performances in Boston, Howe rarely failed to persuade the hosting theaters to provide tickets for his students.[21] On Saturday and Sunday evenings, students often attended concerts of Boston's Handel and Hayden Society, and from time to time, they went to the Tremont Temple to hear the Philharmonic Society perform. Howe always insisted that only a few students go to each concert—never more than a half dozen—lest the blind pupils call undue attention to themselves. Howe told a Canadian colleague that schools for the blind should be founded only in cities, never in small towns, because cities provide venues for good music.[22] His emphasis on the importance of music to the blind is recorded in a comment by the reformer Enoch Wines, who, in a visit to the blind school on 14 August 1834, noted that the school's organ and thirteen pianos "never appear to be still." For Wines, the emphasis on musical education was a matter of "political economy, to encourage a taste of music in the blind, and to afford them every possible facility for the cultivation of such musical talent as they may possess." With music, blind people could most advantageously compete with the sighted.[23]

On 6 July 1839, as he did on a few occasions, Howe spoke to the male pupils about masturbation, the topic, as mentioned earlier, that would concern him throughout his years at the school. He recorded his remarks in the third person: "A long and very serious address was made by the Director to all the assembled boys upon the wickedness and mischief of masturbation. The disgusting character & pernicious consequences were set forth & substantiated by extracts from various authors. . . . [All the boys] were very much interested, & those who were suspected of being guilty of it were agitated & two came to the office afterward, acknowledged the fact & promised abstinence. It is a long time since there has been occasion to speak to an individual on this painful & dreadful subject, & never before have I deemed it necessary to address the whole, but having detected two or three, & being suspicious of others I thought it best to [bring] up the whole subject. . . . I have always found the best way to be a free & full explanation and the causes & consequences; an address to the self esteem & self respect of the masturbator."[24]

The small children went to bed at eight o'clock and the older students went at nine. Beside their beds, the students recited the Lord's Prayer and usually sang a hymn. All lights were out in the facility by ten thirty, and the institution's furnace shut down for the evening.[25]

The first of several hour-long classes began at eight in the morning with boys and girls in separate classes, grouped by their age. The typical curriculum included reading, spelling, grammar, mathematics, geography, music, and work skills. Each class ended with a fifteen-minute recess. For about the first fifteen years of the school's existence (and on occasion in later years), Howe taught natural philosophy, history, grammar, and physiology to all of the older boys. Male students, whom Howe destined for college enrollment, also studied Latin and Greek from four o'clock to five under his tutelage. During the 1839–40 academic year, for example, three young men studied Latin and Greek with Howe.

Howe described his own teaching style and methods in an 1839 letter to William Chapin, superintendent of the Ohio Institution for the Blind: "My way is to read over several books on the subject of my lectures, & then taking a *heading* from my text book, I talk to my class for an hour." On Mondays and Thursdays he lectured on natural philosophy, on Tuesdays and Fridays on history, and on Mondays and Saturdays on grammar. He made extensive use of tactile maps and globes. To supplement his natural philosophy lessons he used models of animals and plants that the blind students could touch. He reminded Chapin that these models did not need to look good; rather, for the blind, how they feel must be instructive.[26]

Students who did not pursue college preparatory subjects, and that was the majority of students, spent the hours between two and five in the afternoon in manual-skills education. Those younger than twelve years tended to learn work skills, and those who were twelve and older were likely either to perfect those skills, especially musical and academic skills, or to spend the afternoon in the manufacture of objects—especially brooms, mats, chair cane, needle work, cushions and mattresses—for the school's sales room on Bromfield Street. Students were assigned to work-skills classes in keeping with conventional male and female roles, with boys weaving, picking hair for cushions, or making mattresses and brushes, and girls sewing, braiding, doing fancy needle work, or preforming domestic tasks.

Even before the school's move to South Boston in May of 1839, Howe boasted about the school's advanced teaching equipment. Tactile maps of the world graced several classrooms. On them, Howe's blind pupils learned geography through their sense of touch. Around 1838, Howe ordered a globe with a thirteen-foot circumference made especially for the blind school that, like the maps he used, gave pupils tactile information about the world. The globe cost a princely four hundred dollars. After visiting the school, Wines observed: "It is undoubtedly the most perfect article of the kind in the world, and no one who visits Boston should leave the place without seeing it, that is, if his curiosity leads him to extend his observations beyond the cotton goods, fish barrels, and granite rocks."[27] Besides the maps and the impressive globe, Howe continued to acquire embossed, wooden, and stuffed animals and plants for his students to handle. They might not be able to see the world of living creatures, but, Howe insisted, they could come to appreciate the diversity of creation by touching preserved artifacts.[28]

Howe believed strongly in the benefits of physical education. During the long days of summer, the students frequently went out for picnics or took walks to the sea or across the wooden drawbridge into Boston, and the boys went fishing and swam in the ocean *au naturel*. Around 1846 Howe instituted ocean bathing for the girls, but in their case *habillées*. On 4 September 1846, ten boys and a steward sailed to Lovell Island, where they fished all day and ate their catch. Howe reported: "No accident occurred or any thing to mar the happiness of the party except the sea sickness of 2 or 3 of them which luckily was not very severe or of long duration. Oliver in particular seemed highly delighted; he caught several fishes some of them quite large."[29]

In winter when bad weather and short days limited his students' outings, Howe had the students perform calisthenics. He opened a bowling alley at the school that proved especially popular among both the students and the staff. Blind pupils learned to bowl by aiming the ball at the voices of sighted staff members.[30]

On Sunday, students attended church services in a denomination of their parents' choice or, if they were older students, of their own choice. By the 1840s, Howe was directing his pupils not congregate in a few churches but to try out the many churches around South Boston and in Boston. Although the students were required to attend church regularly, Howe discouraged church membership, especially for his younger students. By 1850 it had become his policy to allow none of his students to join a church, even the one they attended regularly. Because the school lacked the staff to escort students to so many different churches, Howe asked churches to provide companions for his blind students. Throughout his superintendency, Howe prided himself on keeping the school a nonsectarian institution. "We inculcate no Sectarian principles. We do not teach or even consider religion as a thing apart from the duties & occupation of every day; but that which should animate the conduct & the feelings upon all occasions and at all times. Every pupil is required to attend some place of public worship (selected by his parents) twice every Sabbath," he wrote in 1839. When in 1850 Ambrose Wellington, a teacher at the school crossed the sectarian line to proselytize among his pupils, Howe quickly put a stop to the action. "I inculcate," he wrote to Wellington, "only those general religious & moral principles, which are recognized by all sects, & by good sense of all religions. I must require my assistants to do the same."[31] In 1842 he refused to allow the baptism by total immersion of his fourteen-year-old pupil Cynthia Ford who, he believed, was too young for such a decision.[32]

During the same decade with the establishment of the Know Nothing Party, Boston elites showed their widespread prejudice against Boston's Irish Catholics. Even Howe's good friend Henry Wadsworth Longfellow insisted to his publisher, James Fields, that in screening for household servants, "No Irishman need apply."[33] Howe, however, maintained a close relationship with the Catholic churches of South Boston. His Catholic pupils always attended mass, and he hired Catholic staff even in positions that were more than custodial. When in 1853 his friend the reformer Dorothea Dix, who was corresponding with Laura Bridgman, revealed her nativism by insisting that Howe employ "none but an American" (that is, not an Irish Catholic) as a new companion for Laura, Howe replied that he would not have Dix "circumscribe the limits of my choice by any national prejudice or proscription."[34] As late as 1870, he responded to the inquiry of an elected official: "In the Institution which I have the pleasure to administer there is entire religious equality, and although the catholic priest is not permitted to perform his rites within the walls, neither is the protestant clergyman. The pupils are sent every Sabbath to church and to Sabbath School of their own choice, and there hear whatever priest or clergyman chooses to teach them."[35]

Howe believed that the Christian scriptures, readily available for people to read and study, were the best means for combating the ignorance, sectarianism, and religious fanaticism embodied in, what he believed was, a Trinitarian orthodoxy of emotionalism and irrationality. What was true for the ordinary citizen must also be true for the blind. Like other Unitarians in the 1830s and 1840s who worked through the American Bible Society to make the printed scriptures available for lay readers, Howe worked for a decade to have first the New Testament, then the Psalms, and shortly before his marriage in April 1843, the entire Bible printed in a six-volume raised-letter edition for blind readers. So committed was he to the project that he even spoke before the evangelical Park Street Church, which awarded him two hundred dollars toward the printing of the Bible.[36] He spent much time during the 1840s distributing raised-letter Bibles to blind readers throughout the English-speaking world. He did so under the unflinching assumption that by reading and studying the scriptures privately and in small Bible study groups, people would come to the sublime truths of God's word. Rather than producing anxiety and worry over one's own salvation, the Christian scriptures, he believed, opened a course for living and created a way to fulfill what God would have one do. For Howe, Christian truths were always more a means to action than they were a set of orthodox beliefs to think about, debate, and fret over.[37]

Whereas Howe printed the scriptures without worry over his own or anyone else's salvation, he was not so insouciant about the art of printing itself. Having worked in 1832 and 1833 with twine and rope fibers to construct letters that he glued to paper, Howe had by the end of the decade begun to produce several raised-letter books for blind readers. The testaments of the Bible in raised-letter editions were Howe's first effort at printing, but soon he was involved in producing other raised-letter books. These included John Bunyan's *Pilgrim's Progress,* Shakespeare's *Hamlet* and *Julius Caesar,* and Milton's *Paradise Lost;* and textbooks such as his own *Diagrams, Illustrating a Compendium of Natural Philosophy for the Use of the Blind* (1836), *The Reader; or, Extracts in Prose and Verse, from English and American Authors* (1839), and *An Atlas of the Principal Islands of the Globe, for the Use of the Blind* (1838). At the 3 May 1837 monthly meeting of the board of trustees, Horace Mann made a motion that a copy of the *Atlas* and the New Testament be printed at the institution and "[be] sent to each of the Governors of the U. States, one to the Library of Congress, one to each of the colleges in Mass., & one to each of the Institutions for educating the Blind in Europe." By doing so, Mann argued, the blind school would be showing the world what the blind could accomplish, as well as showing the good works produced by the school's press.[38]

In later years, Howe published histories, anthologies, and novels for the blind. Much of his correspondence between 1838 and his death in 1876 involved the printing and distribution of reading material to the blind. Throughout Howe's professional life, the Perkins Institution was one of the few sources of such material in the nation. As his correspondence reveals, Howe became involved in several controversies, which may seem esoteric to the twenty-first-century reader, about printing type. Today we would refer to these as font or raised-letter font. Although Braille type had been developed for the blind, Howe continued to champion the raised-letter Boston Line Type as the best type available for blind readers. Through trial and error, he concluded that this type was the easiest and most reliable for blind readers to discern as they read with their fingers.[39]

School records reveal that, along with the daily routines, Howe attended to the inevitable problems of running an institution. One evening in January 1840, two girls and two washerwomen were nearly suffocated after a chimney had blown down, causing a malfunction of the flues entering their bedrooms. Just in time Howe dragged the girls and the women out into the cold but fresh winter air. He wrote: "Soon they began to breathe freely, then to rave most violently, to cry out & gibber and weep like excited maniacs. After a few hours they became rational then calm & no bad symptoms remained but headache & debility."[40]

Other problems were recurrent, among them, an overworked staff. Teachers and other staff members worked long hours, but they rarely complained about the work. Most employees considered the work to be pleasant, and Howe usually had far more applicants for positions than he could hire. But from time to time he received complaints. In February 1848, for example, Mary C. Paddock, a faithful and long-term teacher, wrote: "Now I would ask, how much is expected a person can do consistently with good *health* & good *spirits* besides teaching six hours in school, walking with the children for exercise, & reading one & a half hours in the evening, & feeding & hearing the children about here till nine in the evening?" When the matron, Margaret McDonald, asked her to add waiting on the girls' tables during dinner to her duties, Paddock had reached her breaking point.[41]

Supplying pupils with sufficient clothes was another reoccurring and unending source of trouble. Throughout his tenure at the blind school, Howe cajoled parents, family members, guardians, and sometimes town selectmen to obtain clothing for them. By the 1829 Massachusetts legislative charter of the blind institution, neither the school nor the state was responsible for acquiring or paying for the clothing students wore.

Another reoccurring problem was disciplining students who misbehaved and broke school rules. Howe deplored corporal punishment, which he allowed to be used only on rare occasions. In one instance, in April 1840, Howe called together the older boys of the school after receiving a report that Mr. Nelson, a teacher, had struck a student named O'Brien. As Howe reported the matter, the students "were under very great excitement, and being invited to express their opinions they gave [what] was very strong expressions of feeling. They considered that the use of physical force was an insult & degradation to them." The boys reminded Howe that he had inculcated the advantages of moral suasion over corporal punishment. "It was clear that their esprit de corps had been strongly excited, and that they considered the whole class of the blind had been outraged," Howe added. He affirmed to the boys that physical force should be rarely used and that he would never use such force. But when the boys insisted that Mr. Nelson be censured, Howe defended the teacher, saying that although he had not acted in the best manner, he had acted "under a sense of duty." But Howe ended the journal entry: "It is hoped that the result of the conference will be to convince the pupils that a due regard is felt for their rights."[42]

On another occasion, Howe witnessed a teacher threaten a student with a leather strap. When he confronted her, the teacher claimed that she a done less than what she had seen other teachers do. Shortly thereafter Howe discovered that another teacher had employed a leather belt to discipline students. He dismissed that teacher and warned the one who had threatened her pupil with a strap.[43]

Most students who violated rules were deprived of amusements, such as an ocean swim in the summer.[44] For extremely offensive behavior they were likely to be "excommunicated" or shunned by the Perkins community. In June 1839, for example, Howe reprimanded Edward Carter for telling lies and announced that for a week no student or staff member would speak with Carter. But, he added, "If he shall show a proper feeling of repentance & sorrow, & promise better conduct for the future the affair [is] to be passed over & all pupils forbidden to make any reference to it or even to upbraid the offender."[45] Howe dealt with, Robert Cunningham, a habitual "self abuser," by informing his guardian in New York: "My plan is to give him the cold shower bath every time I discover his fault. If this does not cure him, I shall set a person to attend him constantly, and thus shame him before the school."[46]

Making arrangements for students during the school's two three-week vacations, in spring and fall, was often vexing. The expectation was that the students would return home for these weeks to be with family and friends. But during economic hard times or because of sometimes ill-defined family issues, some families pleaded with Howe not to send their child or sibling home for vacations. In other instances, once their child was home, the family might be reluctant to return him or her to the institution. Over the years, Howe chastised parents for making their children tardy for a new academic term. To prepare for vacations, Howe had to organize their transportation by rail, boat, or stage coach. Traveling in antebellum America was a challenge even for the sighted; for blind people it was harder. Drivers, vessel captains, and station masters were frequently reluctant to help blind people, and fellow travelers were sometimes frightened by them. Despite the problems, Howe insisted that institutional vacations continue because of the benefits of the time off for pupils and staff and to encourage the integration of the students back with their families and into their communities. So committed was he to time off that Howe would occasionally send blind pupils without families or guardians to a local (or even the state) almshouse before he would allow them to remain at the school during the three weeks of vacation. For Howe, the goal of educating the blind was always their reintegration into ordinary American communities. Despite the problems they created, vacations were important for that goal. But Howe also insisted that his pupils maintain a sense of home, believing, "every human being ought to have the home feeling; & to get it strongly & deeply only during the years of childhood & youth." For these reasons, he never failed to shut down Perkins Institution twice a year.[47]

Howe faced an especially difficult problem in the admission and retention of his pupils. Admitting pupils to the blind school meant making decisions about who was appropriate for the school and who was not. These decisions led to questions about the purpose of the school. From the beginning, Howe had insisted that the New England School for the Blind be a school and not a custodial facility. Students who enrolled at the institution should be children whose ages were similar to the ages of children in typical schools throughout Massachusetts. These students would arrive at the blind school, receive a curriculum of instruction in ordinary academic subjects, learn a trade, and graduate from the school. A few (always male students) would go on to higher education, but most would return to their home communities as educated young people to assume the normal roles that their sighted peers typically assumed. Howe expected that the school would receive all students who could learn and repeatedly insisted that the ability to learn would be the only criteria in retaining students. Those who were not able to learn would be dismissed. All other students—no matter their sex, class, or religion—would receive an education (but only an education) at the school.

He was adamant that both sexes receive academic education and vocational training. Most activities, including performances before the public, involved boys and girls. The ages of his pupils, however, proved to be another matter. As the school became better known to the general public, many families, along with local physicians and clergy, made recommendations to Howe to admit students who were older than traditional school-aged children. Especially in the 1830s and 1840s, first-time admission requests came for children in their teens, and even from adults in their twenties. From the beginning, Howe allowed older children and adults to enter the school, but he did so reluctantly and never without complaining about what he perceived to be the bad influences of the worldly older pupils on the immature younger ones. Soon after he moved the school to South Boston, he wrote in his journal: "Report of bad language used by Margaret Harris, recently admitted. The evil effects of admitting pupils of adult age are made manifest in almost every case in which we deviate from the rule of not admitting any over 16 years old. . . . The evils are not confined to evil or vulgar habits, low or improper language, or any tangible faults, but the whole bearing &

demeanor & conversation of ignorant & prejudicial adults is very injurious to the morals & manners of children. It is to be hoped that in future we may be rigid in adhering to the rule respecting the age of beneficiaries."[48]

Howe proudly acknowledged that blind pupils of all religious faiths received an education at the Perkins Institution. That meant low-church Methodists and Baptists received an education along with mainline Congregationalists and Unitarians, and even Catholics, though they were a minority. And in keeping with Howe's belief that the economic class of a blind child's family should never be a barrier to the child's education, the poor were admitted along with the well-to-do. Poor students received tuition either from appropriations of the Massachusetts General Court or from public funds from one of the several state legislatures that contracted with the school to educate their blind children. Other poor students became trustee beneficiaries, having their tuition paid from private funds raised and managed by the school's board of trustees. Through the 1830s, the annual cost of tuition and board was $160.[49]

Howe's perspectives on age, sex, class, and religion were liberal for his time. But his outlook on race was more complicated. As noted earlier, in his August 1833 article on slavery in the *New England Magazine,* he made his abhorrence to slavery just as clear as he had made his preference for African colonization. Around the same time, an unnamed black woman presented her four-year-old daughter for admission while the school was still in Joseph Howe's house on Peasant Street. Howe refused the admission on the grounds that the child was too young for the school, but told the woman to return with the child when she was older. In reaction to reports of Howe's decision, Horace Mann informed Elizabeth Peabody that he had written Howe to express his distress over his friend's refusal to admit the black child to his school. Howe, Mann reported to Peabody, feared that a black pupil among his student body would offend his wealthy Boston supporters. At the time, the school had existed for only one year, and little attention was paid to the matter. Yet because the rumors persisted, the board of trustees at its 3 October 1833 meeting felt it necessary to affirm (probably at Mann's initiation), "It [is] the duty of the Institution to receive colored pupils." The rumors, however, were never entirely mitigated by the board's decision, and at the New England Anti-Slavery Society Convention the following May, the Reverend John M. S. Perry of Mendon, Massachusetts, one of the society's secretaries, denounced the refusal of the blind institution to admit a "colored boy" from Uxbridge. Most damnable of all, Perry claimed that Howe had justified the exclusion by saying, "We may have some pupils from the South, and if we admit this blind colored boy into our Institution, it may make it unpopular there." After Perry concluded his remarks, William Lloyd Garrison introduced a letter that Benjamin Davenport had sent to Effingham L. Capron, his Massachusetts legislator and the society's vice president, the previous January. Davenport's letter confirmed what Garrison called Perry's "melancholy and disgraceful" disclosure. According to Davenport's letter, Howe and John Fisher were willing to exclude black children to placate Southern sensibilities. Although Davenport had no way of knowing it, the school did admit its first white Southern student, Harriet Garnage of New Orleans, the following July. No sooner were the convention's proceedings concluded than the matter of the blind school's excluding black applicants received scorn first in Boston's and then from the nation's abolitionist press.[50]

In July 1835, less than two years after the publication of her controversial book, *An Appeal in Favor of That Class of Americans Called Africans,* Lydia Maria Child, an active and outspoken leader of the Anti-Slavery Society and a participant in its 1834 convention, wrote Howe to recount the revelations made public by Perry's claims and confirmed by Davenport's letter. Shortly thereafter, Howe responded to Child's letter. As he would show at other times, Howe was never more provoked than on those occasions when he felt falsely accused, and he felt so accused on this occasion. To Child, who at the time was receiving significant criticism for her antislavery writings, he acknowledged that he felt bound to consider the survival of the institution when he considered the admission of applicants to the blind school. Yet, as Howe saw it, his "candid admission" as stated at the convention was "a garbled one sided and uncharitable statement as some people delight in hearing & judging by." In his own defense he insisted "I always stated that I considered it to be the imperative duty of the Trustees to admit colored pupils as soon as possible." One problem, he implied, was space. First in the cramped quarters of his father's house and then in the only somewhat larger quarters of the Perkins mansion, there simply was not room for additional pupils, "colored" or otherwise. Yet, despite this space limitation, Howe expressed confidence that by the fall of 1835 the school will be ready to admit a black student. The letter ends: "No one even supposed you admitted the possibility of anybody else doing any good but in your way." Seventeen years later Howe happened on a copy of his letter to Child and confessed to Charles Sumner, "I blushed when I read what I had written." As he would often do in his life, Howe expressed regret for his outburst of anger, and as he usually (though not always) did, he followed his expression of regret, in an 1853 letter to Child, with an offer of apology for his "want of courtesy" in 1835.[51]

The first black pupil admitted to the school for the blind was Sullivan Anthony, the same "colored boy" from Uxbridge whose admission Howe had refused two years earlier. He entered in May 1836 as a trustees' beneficiary and remained at the school for four years. By 1853 Howe could report, with some satisfaction, that the school had admitted "six other colored persons." In 1839 he also approved the admission of two Chinese girls referred to him by the American Board of Foreign Missions, acknowledging the benefit of an education to both girls. Typical of Americans of his time, Howe saw in their education a means for civilizing nonwhite people whose betterment depended on their acculturation to, what he believed to be, white New England Protestant values of prudence, modesty, restraint, and thrift.

In August 1839 Howe reported to Capron on Anthony's progress over the past three years. The legislator, whose 1834 letter from Benjamin Davenport had so inflamed the Garrisonians in 1834, had sponsored the boy's admission to the blind school. Howe assured Capron that he caused Anthony "to be treated in every way like the rest of our pupils." He attended the same classes, ate at the same table, and received the same treatment as other students. Yet, Howe claimed, the boy remained immoral and crude. Principal among his bad habits was masturbation. But also he was "vulgar and filthy in his conversation, dirty in his person, and lazy in his habits." Despite efforts to correct what Howe regarded as his crude and immoral behavior, Howe said, "he has so little moral sense that no effectual appeal can be made to it." To be sure, Howe is quick to acknowledge, Anthony "deserves more pity than censure for all these things." His natural organization, that is, his intellect, "is so narrow that he has made almost no progress, and if he continues here I shall treat him as I have some white boys who are imbecile—take him entirely from school and keep him at work." Howe begged Capron to use his influence during the October vacation to exact a change in Anthony's habits, which he attributed to his low early associations. Not all of the other nonwhite students who became pupils at the blind school experienced the same outcome as Anthony did. Like other students, some succeeded and some had problems adjusting to life at the institution. And like their white counterparts, their success depended in no small part on what Howe regarded as the quality of their natural organization and their associations.[52]

Laura Bridgman

This linking of the natural organization, which in Howe's thinking manifested itself in material phrenological faculties, and human association, which kept Howe grounded in the liberal New England idealism of his time, saw its clearest appearance in Howe's most famous pupil, the blind and deaf girl Laura Bridgman.[53] Within a few years after she arrived at the blind school, Laura became known personally to the thousands of people who flocked to the school to visit and view her, and by millions of Americans and Europeans who read about her journey from a world of dark and silent ignorance to one

Laura Bridgman (ca. 1860). Courtesy Perkins School for the Blind.

of enlightened and communicative knowledge, from primitive isolation to
civilized interaction.[54]

On 4 October 1837, Laura Bridgman entered the Institution for the Blind,
at the time still located in the mansion on Pearl Street in Boston. Daniel
and Harmony Bridgman, who had traveled from Hanover, New Hampshire,
with their seven-year-old daughter, were reluctant to leave her with the
school's superintendent, a man they had met only a few months earlier. The
preceding spring, James Barrett, a student at Dartmouth College who was
helping the town with local tax assessments, had visited the Bridgman family
on tax matters and observed their daughter, whom he found "sprightly and
joyous of spirit," despite having been left blind and deaf at the age of eighteen months from a bout of scarlet fever. Barrett reported what he had seen
at the Bridgman household to R. D. Mussey, a local physician and member

of the college's medical department. Mussey knew about Howe's work for the blind, and on one occasion in 1833 in Salem had shared a lyceum platform with him. In May, Mussey observed Laura for himself, and later that month wrote to Howe about her. Howe quickly wrote back, eagerly affirming Laura's need for education and speculating about the appropriate way to educate her: "May she not be placed in some situation where the channels to her intellect will be widened, her mental powers developed & her life be made happier to herself & more useful to others? . . . It strikes me also that she could be taught more advantageously by the method used in the instruction of the Blind than of the Mutes inasmuch as a considerable part of the apparatus of instruction is adapted to the sense of touch, which she possesses, it seems, in a high degree of perfection." Laura's case, Howe told Mussey, will be "useful to science by throwing light upon some point of intellectual philosophy." Citing reports and his own observation of Julia Brace, a blind and deaf woman who had languished at the American Asylum for the Deaf at Hartford, he also told Mussey that he was certain that there had never been a successful attempt to teach a blind mute "any artificial language of signs, much less any system of tangible letters." But true to his phrenological assumptions, he added, "I am confident that a child whose nervous system is well developed & whose brain in the perspective region is of usual size & in good condition, much might be done." The only obstacle to her education was her parents. Expenses for Laura, Howe wrote, would not be a problem, and she would be kindly treated and "every effort would be made to improve her mind." Indeed, because of the financial hard times brought on by the Panic of 1837, the family might be relieved to be freed of her care. But, he asked, are the parents intelligent enough to see the advantage of parting with their child for the sake of her education at the institution? Not knowing the answer to his question, or even having observed Laura, Howe assured Mussey with his abiding reformist optimism and perfectionism "It appears to me, she might be taught to converse & read. . . . At any rate, the attempt is worth making & the labor & expense should not be an obstacle; for a human soul thus clogged & trammeled calls upon us as strongly for aid as a living man buried under ruins."[55]

In late July 1837 Howe traveled to Hanover with three of his friends, the poet and recently appointed Harvard professor Henry Wadsworth Longfellow and two attorneys, George S. Hillard and Rufus Choate, as well as Samuel Eliot, a Harvard student. While his traveling companions participated in the Dartmouth College commencement ceremonies, where Hillard gave the commencement address, Howe visited the Bridgman home, about seven miles from the college, with Mussey. There he observed Laura as she showed her interest in the strange visitors by darting about in delighted curiosity.

Years later when Howe recalled his first encounter with Laura, he remembered her vitality, her interest, and her sweet disposition. He immediately saw in her a well-functioning brain that contained an active but undeveloped mind ready to be liberated from the sensory deficits that had limited her learning. Her alertness showed that her mind was intact. Despite her disabilities, she was no "idiot," and Howe had little doubt that she could learn.[56]

Within six weeks the Bridgmans were convinced, however reluctantly, that Laura would benefit from enrollment in the Boston blind school. Less than three weeks after her education began, Howe wrote two of his former blind pupils, still in their teens, about his new student. He told one: "She is as happy as a bird & apparently as intelligent as many children of her age with all the senses. . . . I hope to be able to teach her many things, though access to her intellect is very difficult." Despite the challenge, Howe remained optimistic, explaining to the other former pupil; "The immortal spirit within her, although in darkness & stillness like that of a tomb, is full of life & vigor, is animated by innate power & triumphantly refutes the doctrine that the soul is but a blank sheet upon which education & experience write everything."[57] To these young women, his former pupils, he reaffirmed a most adult position that he had articulated before but never so succinctly. The mind, or the soul as he called it, was not an empty surface passively awaiting external data mediated by the senses to create its essence, the claim British empiricists, such as John Locke, and French sensualists, such as Etienne Bonnot de Condillac, had made in previous generations. As a good phrenologist, Howe knew that the mind held in the brain was, despite the brain's physicality, full of life and vigor and was therefore immortal. It had within it its own essence. It was therefore more than what was merely imprinted on it. It was the immortal God that was in each mortal. Laura Bridgman's disability, then, was not so much the blockage of sensory data to her brain as it was the sensual blockage of her brain's immortal force from revealing itself.

In November and December 1837, while local newspapers were filled with the news of the mob killing of the antislavery editor Elijah Lovejoy in Alton, Illinois, Howe sent two letters to the Bridgman family to report progress in Laura's education. "She was rather dull for two days after [you] left here & cried two or three times but after that she became very lively & I do not think that she repines at all for home now," he said in November. By December, a little more than two months after Laura entered Perkins Institution, Howe wrote a long letter detailing what he regarded as the remarkable changes in her behavior: "We have succeeded in making her understand several words in our raised print & I am very sanguine in the hope that she will learn to read & perhaps to express her wants in writing." By the end of March 1838 he reported that under the tutelage of her teacher, Lydia Drew, Laura had learned all her letters and could easily give and receive information through the use of finger spelling, which involved forming the shapes of ordinary letters to produce words on the hands of the communicants. He noted that she responded to commands and remained obedient. Finally, he raised a new issue with the family. Although she had been at the school only six months, her fame had spread throughout Boston, causing "hundreds of people" hoping to view her to come to the school. He assured the Bridgmans that even on days of public exhibition he avoided having Laura too much on display. Often, he declared, Laura remained "in her chamber" or went with a teacher on a walk during these exhibitions.[58]

Contrary to what Howe told the Bridgmans, the public could not be kept away from the new phenomenon. Local and regional newspapers and journals published stories about the transformation of the little blind and deaf girl. Eventually the stories spread to national and international publications. From likely and unlikely sources, people wrote to Howe about Laura. In Laura's first five years at the school, Howe received letters inquiring about her from the poet Lydia Sigourney, from the leading Calvinist cleric of the time, Lyman Beecher, and from the industrialist Amos Adams Lawrence. Lawrence was touched by the occasional letters Laura sent him and by the visits he made to her.[59]

As the years went by, the interest in Laura only increased. After the school's trustees published Howe's *Ninth Annual Report* in 1841, information about her penetrated the nation as newspaper and periodicals printed excerpts of the report. Not wishing to display her too overtly to an admiring public, but well aware of its desire to see her, in late summer 1841 Howe commissioned Sophia Peabody—the fiancé of Nathaniel Hawthorne, who at the time was having second thoughts about his involvement with the Brook Farm commune—to make a bust of Laura. Throughout September, Peabody made regular trips to the institution to work on the bust. After she completed a clay portrait bust, Howe asked her to make several plaster casts for his upcoming journey into the nation's West and South, which would keep Howe away from Boston between November 1841 and March 1842. Before leaving Boston, he wrote to people that he planned to meet, informing them that he was bringing with him the busts of Laura Bridgman. Having known the three Peabody sisters for nearly a decade, Howe was only mildly annoyed when Elizabeth, who was always concerned about the family's pecuniary needs, wrote him to suggest that additional casts of Sophia's sculpture of Laura might well be sold for ten dollars at the institution.[60] In July 1842, when Elizabeth learned of the impending resignation of Laura's principal teacher, Mary Swift, she

Bust of Laura Bridgman by Sophia Peabody (1841).
Courtesy Perkins School for the Blind.

applied for the position, but Howe hired Sarah Wight instead.[61] (In March 1841, Howe had turned down an application for a teaching position at the blind school from Henry David Thoreau.)[62]

The journey—the longest in distance and time that Howe ever made through the nation—had as its purpose the development of schools and services for the blind in the states that Howe planned to visit. He calculated that, with Laura's fame at a national peak, he could boost his efforts with inexpensive plaster busts of the blind and deaf girl that he could exhibit and on occasion leave with admiring benefactors. His friend Francis Lieber, a German expatriate on the faculty of the University of South Carolina, who was visiting Boston during the summer of 1841, had a similar thought. Before he arrived in the United States in 1827, Lieber had been under duress and was eventually jailed by Prussian authorities for his liberal views, which had found their way into songs that threatened Prussian authorities. In Boston, he edited the *Encyclopedia Americana* before taking the position in South Carolina. If you cannot take Laura with you, Lieber told Howe, bring instead a replica of her, and you will quickly win states to your cause. Lieber spent the summer observing Laura and discussing with Howe the issues of her education and what her education revealed about language.[63]

Travels South and West

The trip would include a stop in Washington. As early as December 1836, first in a letter from his representative in Washington, Abbott Lawrence, and then from Senators Henry Clay and Daniel Webster, Howe had received requests to visit the nation's capital so that elected officials could "see the pupils under your care." "We doubt not," Lawrence had written, "that many gentlemen here will be happy to witness their proficiency and to become better acquainted with the course of instruction pursued in the asylum under your superintendence."[64] The journey south began in late November 1841. Howe took with him Abigail and Sophia Carter, a female teacher as their chaperone, and his prized pupil Joseph Brown Smith. For twenty-five years, Anthony Bowden, who was later the institution's steward, served as Howe's tour advance man and business agent in a time when American mode of travel was all too often haphazard and unpredictable. Bowden planned the tour that would take Howe and his party as far south as South Carolina and Georgia, back up to Washington, D.C., west into Kentucky, south to New Orleans, and back to Boston by sea.[65] Howe set out with confidence in his ability to sway elected officials to the cause of education for the blind. Earlier that summer he had said in a letter to Otis Sutton, a Louisville, Kentucky, businessman: "And let me say that there is no such powerful appeal to be made, as can be made by the appearance and appeal of blind children. With such children as I could select, I would agree to carry the hearts of your Legislature by storm and get a bill through both branches before the members could have time to wipe the tears away from their eyes." A few months later he boasted to Francis Lieber, who was now back in South Carolina, "I have exhibited our pupils before the Legislatures of 7 states, and not one . . . hesitated to do all I asked for the Blind."[66]

Progressing slowly because of bad weather, Howe traveled first to Washington and then to Richmond, where in a letter to Charles Sumner he expressed his disdain for what he saw as a land corrupted by the institution of slavery. "No one has his prescribed duties," he wrote. "The master scolds and drives, the slave dawdles and shirks; and if anything *must* be done, it takes one white longer to hunt up two Negroes and force them to do it than it would take one uncorrupted Saxon to finish it alone." Shortly before Christmas, Howe arrived in Georgia where, as he had in Virginia and South Carolina, he addressed the state legislature on services for the blind and exhibited the reading and writing skills of the Carter sisters and the mathematical abilities of Joseph Smith. From Georgia he sent more thoughts about slavery, this time employing unrestrained sarcasm in two letters to Horace Mann. On 23 December he wrote: "The physical condition of the slaves is unquestionably better in the Carolinas and in Georgia than that of the free blacks or the poor whites of the South, and perhaps better than that of the free blacks of the North." But why? The answer to the slaves' superior physical condition is "physical education." He continued:

> The only clean, well organized and thoroughly administered institutions which I have seen in the South are the Slave Depositories, if I may so call them. That in Charleston is a large, airy building, with ample court-yard and well ventilated rooms. Every part is kept scrupulously clean; everything is well adapted to its purpose; every officer is active and energetic. Its tread-mill and its whipping post are the *ne plus ultra* of their kind. Into this place are brought for safe keeping and for board the gangs of slaves which are to be sold in the market. To it also a master may send his slaves to be boarded merely, or to be confined and whipped, or punished by solitary confinement. . . . The gangs for sale and the mere boarders are not punished however, nor even confined, except at night. On the contrary, they are incited to walk about in the courtyards. They are well fed, they lodge in large, airy, clean rooms, and are daily promenaded in clean clothes to take the air, even out into the country.

Three days later Howe admitted to Mann that, although he never failed to acknowledge his antislavery sentiments, he also tried to reassure his Southern hosts "that [slavery] was a matter in which the North ought not to interfere."[67]

After Georgia, Howe and his companions returned to Washington, where they remained through the first week of the New Year. Howe had hoped to persuade Congress to do for his blind school what Henry Clay had persuaded it to do for the American Asylum for the Deaf in Hartford. In 1820 Congress had given the school twenty-three thousand acres of the Alabama territory. Proceeds from the sale of the land (stolen from Native Americans) provided the core of an endowment that the deaf school enjoys to this day. But Howe was not to have his way with Congress. With John Tyler in the White House and Jacksonians still strong in both houses of Congress, lawmakers had no interest in this kind of public works project.[68]

From Washington, Howe sent his now exhausted Carter pupils back to Boston with their caretaker, and he and Joseph Smith traveled through Virginia to Kentucky, where he planned to address the state legislature. The journey through Virginia on the National Road, the nation's first federally funded road, was rough, and he was sick by the time he reached Wheeling. Most likely he was suffering again from the recurring ill effects of the malaria he had contracted in Greece in 1829 and that had laid him low in England in 1832. While recuperating in Wheeling, he sent a request to William Chapin of the Ohio School for the Blind (and later of the Pennsylvania School for the Blind) to allow several of Chapin's students to meet Howe in Cincinnati to accompany him to Frankfort. With these students, along with his own pupil,

Joseph Smith, Howe was able to make a presentation before the Kentucky legislators. He felt matters went so well that he boasted to Sumner, "There is no doubt about its success in the Senate, for all Frankfort is so interested in the blind that I am afraid some mammas will put their children's eyes out." But he was put out that Chapin had come along too to capture some of the glory for himself.[69]

In Frankfort, Howe reconnected with a Brown University classmate, George D. Prentice, who helped him advocate for a blind school in the state. Prentice, the author of a biography of Henry Clay who was heavily involved in Kentucky Whig politics, put Joseph Smith's exceptional mathematical abilities on display to impress the legislators. He gave Smith an especially difficult problem, which he promptly solved. In 1844, after graduating from Harvard, Smith returned to the state to take a teaching position at what became the Kentucky School for the Blind.[70] The trip to the Blue Grass State was especially effective. As Horace Mann commented to in a letter to George Combe, "Dr. Howe gave an exhibition to the Kentuckians, and carried them away as by enchantment."[71]

Howe and Smith continued from Kentucky downriver to New Orleans. From Vicksburg, Mississippi, Howe wrote Mann that his visit to Kentucky had gone well and that it appeared that state officials would likely ask one of his former pupils, A. W. Penniman, to serve as the first director of the proposed blind school. Of the "west," he wrote: "It appears like a great hollow gourd—a squash! I do not mean the country itself, for its resources are vast, inexhaustible, but the social, mercantile, political structures. There is inflation, grandiloquence, gasconading beyond anything I had conceived. They brag, and swagger, and lie with all the self-complacency and all the assurance in the world."[72] Unlike New Englanders, Howe concluded, the westerners could hardly control their passions. Their bravado might be droll, but lacking the restraint provided by reason, it was never manly.

Except that Howe charmed elected officials in Baton Rouge and visited several of the state's charitable institutions, little is known of his travels on behalf of the blind after he arrived in Louisiana. In New Orleans, however, he observed an event that affected him profoundly and would, after the publication of a letter about it, move him (despite his resistance to being so moved) to an overt antislavery position. In the city in which the expression "selling a slave down river" fulfilled its quintessential meaning, Howe witnessed a slave beating and wrote to Sumner about what he had seen. The event had occurred in a New Orleans slave prison that Howe happened to be visiting in his tour of Louisiana institutions. Several months later, Sumner received a request from the abolitionist Maria Weston Chapman to submit a short article for the 1843 *Liberty Bell,* a publication that her antislavery society used to raise funds for their Massachusetts Anti-Slavery Fair and to extend the message of abolitionism. Sumner replied that he had nothing to contribute but that he had recently received a letter from his friend Howe describing the public whipping of a female slave he had witnessed in Louisiana. The letter, Sumner informed Chapman, might be just the testimony against slavery that she was looking for. With Howe's permission, Sumner gave the letter to Chapman, who included it in the next edition of the *Liberty Bell.* Appearing with articles by such well-established opponents of slavery as Henry I. Bowditch, George S. Burleigh, Harriet Martineau, and Theodore Parker, the radical abolitionists William Lloyd Garrison, Wendell Phillips, and his earlier antagonist, Lydia Maria Child, Howe's description of the slave beating in New Orleans, entitled "Scenes at a Slave Prison," became a highlight of the 1843 publication and quite suddenly linked Howe with abolitionists with whom he had previously avoided any association. His description, written originally for Sumner's eyes only, shows slavery in its brutality and irrationality. "In the negroes' department I saw much which made me blush that I was a white man," Howe confessed.

> Entering a large paved courtyard, around which ran galleries filled with slaves of all ages, sexes and colors, I heard the snap of a whip, every stroke of which sounded like the sharp crack of a small pistol. I turned my head and beheld a sight which absolutely chilled me to the marrow of my bone. There lay a black girl, flat upon her face on a board, her two thumbs tied and fastened to one end, her feet tied and drawn tightly to the other end, while a strap passed over the small of her back, and fastened around the board, confined her closely to it. . . . Below the strap she was entirely naked; by her side, and six feet off, stood a huge negro with a long whip, which he applied with dreadful power and wonderful precision. Every stroke brought away a strip of scarf skin and made the blood spring to the surface. The poor creature writhed and shrieked, and in a voice which showed alike her fear of death and her dreadful agony, screamed to her master, who stood at her head. "Oh! spare my life—don't cut my soul out!" But still fell the horrid lash, still strip after strip was broken from the skin, gash after gash was cut in her flesh, until it became a vivid and bloody mess of raw and quivering muscle.[73]

By the last week in March 1842, after nearly four months in the South and West, Howe returned home to South Boston. In his absence, the twenty-nine-year-old English novelist Charles Dickens, who had claimed that the two most important objects that he wanted to visit during his 1842 tour of the United States were Niagara Falls and Laura Bridgman, had had the second wish fulfilled on 29 January. In addition to Laura, Dickens met Oliver Caswell, another blind and deaf pupil at the school, who was from Rhode Island. In Howe's absence, accompanying Dickens on his visit to the school were Whig Boston mayor Jonathan Chapman and Charles Sumner. Although he observed all the blind pupils in their class work and daily school activities, Dickens was especially taken with Laura Bridgman. When his *American Notes* appeared after his return to England in late 1842, an already famous Laura Bridgman became even more famous. One newspaper claimed, without much exaggeration, that because of Dickens's report of his visit to the Perkins Institution, no other female, besides Queen Victoria, was at the time better known than Laura Bridgman. Of course, the fame of the pupil extended to her teacher.[74]

Howe finally met Dickens in June in New York City. In Kentucky, around the time that Dickens toured the Perkins Institution and while the frenzy associated with his visit had fully captured Boston, Howe added a marginal note to a letter to Sumner that reads: "If you have [a] chance, give my love to Dickens—no respect but my love—for I do love him because he loves humanity." Laura Richards omitted the remark from her edition of her father's letters.[75] In *American Notes* Dickens reproduced large parts of Howe's 1841 annual report, in which he described his successful education of Laura. He also praised the "civilized" society of Boston, while panning New York, Washington City, and nearly every other locale in the nation as "uncouth." Soon after the publication of Dickens's book, Howe began to receive letters from some of Europe's most influential intellectuals. The renown would serve him well when, in the spring of 1843, Howe left for his honeymoon tour of European charitable institutions.

While Dickens ensured the Perkins superintendent's worldwide fame, Howe's article "On Universal Language," first delivered as an address at the annual meeting of the American Institute of Instruction in New Bedford, Massachusetts, on 17 August 1842, provided Howe the intellectual legitimacy he always longed for. The hour-long speech was one among five presented at the meeting and later printed in a volume of their proceedings. The other speakers were Horace Mann, Gideon F. Thayer, George B. Emerson, and Henry Barnard. Howe's delivery showed the confidence he had developed during his recent trip to the South and the West.[76]

Howe began his talk with a blunt assertion. Language is an innate disposition, an impulse, as he put it, to "exteriorise" the self. Neither an inspiration nor an invention, he said, language is a gift from God and of God, whose purpose is the improvement and perfection of human beings. For teachers to understand this purpose and guide it in ways intended by God, they need the insights of phrenology, which explains "that intimate and wonderful relation between the immaterial spirit and the material body, which makes the activity and power of the mind dependent upon the quality and condition of the physical organization, which modifies every mental manifestation, and

makes the outer man correspond with the inner." With phrenological understanding, language becomes a natural expression of emotions and passions
of the mind; yet, these moments of expression gain meaning only through
"the medium of signs." Signs come in two basic forms. The superior way is
through vocal sounds, aided by bodily gestures; the inferior way is by gestures
alone. Ancient civilizations and primitive peoples relied on gestures; more
highly civilized people depend on vocalization. Added to these auditory signs
are ideographic signs captured in drawings and written signs. All of these
signs, Howe claimed, in anticipation of Noam Chomsky's assertion more
than a century later, "are derived from the principles of universal grammar."
Yet, despite their universality, signs are also progressive, developmental, even
(though he did not use the word) evolutionary. People in civilized, advanced
cultures give priority to vocal language. Language dependent on gestures is
quite possible, and the exchange of signs made by deaf people verifies their
utility. But, Howe stressed, just as God put human beings on a course toward
progress and advancement, so too did God make vocal signs the highest,
most advanced form of signs. Thus, vocal language is the most superior form
of language because with vocalization language has reached its final outcome—the outcome God established for human beings. In short, to speak
vocally was for human beings to "exteriorise" themselves most perfectly.

Referring to his own boyhood education as "imprisonment," Howe
insisted that children learn language by experiencing it in the day-to-
day activities in which they naturally participate. Howe opposed what he
regarded as the unnatural teaching activities of many school masters, who
imposed unfamiliar language on children more as an exercise in rote memorization than as the natural rhythm of growth. Language develops, Howe
argued, as it unfolds in the daily circumstances that children encounter.
Better to give children new encounters that require new language than to
impose new words divorced from their use and meaning. For this reason,
children had best learn formal grammar late in their schooling, just before
they are ready to leave school. Forcing grammar on young children is merely
to ensure that they will regard language as "a knell of sorrow."

The fame provided by Laura Bridgman, a tour of the nation on behalf
of public education for the blind, and the publication of a major lecture on
language, all in his tenth year as director of the blind school, had made 1842
an active year for Howe. Yet the year included a final important event that
would forever shape the man. In the June on the same trip to New York
to meet Dickens, he began to fall in love with Julia Ward. His close circle
of friends—Horace Mann, Henry Wadsworth Longfellow, Charles Sumner,
Cornelius C. Felton, George S. Hillard, and the dying Henry Cleveland—
could not have been happier.

CHAPTER FIVE
Private Lives, Public Causes

In 1842 Samuel Howe's closest friend was Horace Mann. The two men had known each other since they were both students at Brown University, where Mann had been the studious older tutor, and Howe (at least for the first few years) the ill-behaved undergraduate. After medical school and his years in Greece, Howe had renewed his acquaintance with Mann through their common interest in the blind school. Mann had been a legislative sponsor of the school's charter in 1829 and one of its first trustees. By the early 1840s they had extended their friendship through their mutual support for the humane treatment of insane people, and for public school and prison reform. Working together for improvement, Howe, the physician organizer, and Mann, the attorney legislator and since 1837 the secretary of the Massachusetts State Board of Education, made an effective team for social reform. Howe acknowledged to Mann, "I owe you much, very much—your influence & your example have gone very far towards forming what few & humble aspirations for true usefulness & real nobility I may have, & I'll strive not to disappoint you & disgrace myself by 'butterflying' it before I have wings."[1]

Besides Mann, Howe's oldest acquaintance and dearest friend was the young lawyer Charles Sumner. Born, along with a twin sister, Matilda, in 1811, Sumner was a child of an ordinary, hard-working but not particularly prosperous Boston family. In 1826, his father, for whom he was named, was appointed sheriff of Suffolk County, the county in which Boston resides, allowing him the wherewithal to send Charles to Harvard University. Studious like Mann, Sumner was nevertheless not as outgoing as Howe's older friend, and he was more given to self-doubt and worry. Howe and Sumner remembered first meeting when each man was drawn to the Broad Street riot on 11 and 12 June 1837. On that warm late spring day that followed by a month the start of the economic Panic of 1837, Protestant volunteer firefighters

Horace Mann (ca. 1850). Library of Congress.

coming from a fire in Roxbury confronted a march of Irish Catholic funeral mourners in the heart of the city. Before the day was over, fifteen thousand Bostonians had taken part in the riot, forcing Mayor Samuel A. Eliot to call for the state militia to halt the mayhem. Besides Howe and Sumner, Robert Winthrop, Abbott Lawrence, Josiah Quincy Jr., and Sumner's father were among the group of citizens who attempted to stop the riot before the state militia arrived. Howe and Sumner deplored the growing hostility that native Protestant Bostonians were developing for Irish Catholics, whose numbers were increasing rapidly because of their immigration into the city. Howe and Sumner, along with their friend Horace Mann, would come to view the Broad Street riot as a foreshadowing of the vice, corruption, and irrational passion that threatened the social and moral stability of Boston society.[2]

Later that year, Sumner went to Europe, where for nearly three years he studied law and toured the continent, learning languages, meeting literary and political figures, and establishing himself among Europeans as an exceptionally well-read and urbane American. On his return to the United States in 1840, he renewed his friendship with Howe, with his appointment to the board of trustees of the Perkins Institution and their mutual association with the Five of Clubs.[3] In June 1841 Sumner described Howe to Francis Lieber, the German expatriate and their mutual friend: "He is the soul of disinterestedness. He has purged his soul from all consideration of self, so far as [a] mortal may do this; and his sympathies embrace all creatures. To this highest feature of goodness add intelligence and experience of no common order—all elevated and refined by a chivalrous sense of honor, and a mind without fear. . . . Both [of us] have been wanderers and both are bachelors, so we are together a good deal; we drive fast and hard, and talk—looking at the blossoms in the fields, or those fairer in the streets."[4]

The Five of Clubs was actually made up of six members. Probably the founding member was the gregarious and shrewd professor of classical litera-

Charles Sumner (ca. 1860). Library of Congress.

ture and later president of Harvard University Cornelius ("Corny") Conway
Felton. Felton had known the second member, Henry Wadsworth Longfellow, when he taught at Bowdoin College and was influential in bringing
him to Harvard in 1835 as a professor of modern languages. In the group
Longfellow was affectionately called "Longo," as much for his name as for his
stature. Among his friends, he was by far the shortest. The third member was
Henry Russell Cleveland, whose marriage to a wealthy woman allowed him
the time to indulge his interests in classical and modern literature. When
Howe met him, Cleveland was editing the works of the Roman historian
Sallust and writing a biography of the seventeenth-century English navigator
Henry Hudson. Cleveland, who was suffering from tuberculosis, had, like
many other ailing young men and women of the period, tried environmental
cures. Before his death in Havana in 1843, Cleveland gave up his place in
the Five of Clubs to Howe. The final two members of the club were George
Stillman Hillard and Charles Sumner, attorneys who were eventually law
partners. Hillard, who was married to Howe's distant relative Susan Howe,
was one of the first Americans to see the literary merit of Nathaniel Hawthorne, whose opposition to Garrisonian abolitionism he shared. Sumner, in
contrast, would grow in his opposition to slavery. Both men were the favorite
students of Joseph Story, a Harvard professor and Supreme Court justice. As
partners, Hillard proved the better practicing lawyer, though Sumner understood the law better.[5]

What brought these men together were their common literary interests
and their need for male companionship. All had traveled internationally,
and except for Cleveland, all had spent time in Europe. They spoke multiple
European languages, and they read and corresponded with European intellectuals and literary figures. That Howe spoke only French and Greek put
him at a disadvantage to Longfellow, Felton, and Sumner, each of whom
spoke several more languages. Despite this limitation, Felton made Howe
one of the dozen or so men who annually quizzed Harvard students in their
perfection of written and spoken Greek. In this capacity Howe came to
love the classical literature he had failed to take seriously before his years in
Greece. The Five of Clubs liked food, especially oysters and beefsteaks, and
long talks into the early hours of the morning, often with a bottle or two of
wine, even though some of the members, including Howe, supported the
Temperance Movement. Under Mayor Eliot in 1838, Boston had passed the
so-called Fifteen-Gallon Law to restrict the sale of intoxicating liquors to fifteen gallons or larger amounts that the poor were unlikely to afford. But they
were not poor, and wine, after all, remained a connection to the European
ways that they so revered. The men also talked about women. Cleveland,
Felton, and Hillard—the married club members—were ever interested in

marrying off the unmarried Sumner and Howe, as well as Longfellow, who was a widower.[6]

Sometime in June 1842 it became evident to these friends that Samuel Howe was falling in love with Julia Ward, a twenty-three-year-old New York woman who had spent part of the past two years in Dorchester with an unrelated family of Wards. Mary Ward, who was Julia's closest companion among the Dorchester Wards and was engaged to Julia's brother Henry, had introduced Julia to Margaret Fuller and Ralph Waldo Emerson.[7] According to Julia Ward Howe's memory nearly a half century later, she had first met Samuel Howe a year earlier on a visit with her two sisters, Mary Ward, Henry Longfellow, and Charles Sumner to the Perkins Institution in South Boston. They had gone to the school to see the ten-year-old Laura Bridgman and to meet the man who had gained fame as her teacher, only to find Howe absent. After observing Bridgman and Lucy Reed, another blind and deaf young woman, who "had been accustomed to cover her head and face with a cotton bag of her own manufacture," the party of visitors was about to leave for Boston when Howe appeared on his black horse. Julia remembered that the doctor "made upon us an impression of unusual force and reserve."[8] The force of the impression was so great that Julia began to call him "Chev," the nickname his friends had given him after he received the Chevalier of the Greek Legion of Honor.

Julia Ward came from a wealthy New York family. Her father, Samuel Ward, a partner in the banking firm of Prime and Ward (later Prime, Ward, and King), had made a fortune in banking and real estate. When she was five years old, her mother, Julia Cutler Ward, died in childbirth, leaving her and her three brothers and two sisters in the care of her father, her uncle and aunt, John and Eliza Cutler Francis, and servants. Julia was the oldest daughter. Influenced by her father's and her older brother Sam's interests in languages, Julia at an early age developed fluency in French, German, and Italian. Like many other well-to-do young women of the time, she sang and played the piano and became an accomplished artist.[9] But unlike her peers, Julia had little use for the domestic arts. She disliked cooking and she had no skills in sewing and needle work. Although the absence of these domestic skills concerned her father, no one else in the family seemed to mind.[10]

Her oldest brother, Sam, had studied at George Bancroft and Joseph Cogswell's prominent Round Hill School in Northampton, Massachusetts, which employed German pedagogical methods. Though he excelled in mathematics, modern languages, and drawing, Bancroft predicted to Sam's father that he would not likely excel in business. After a stint at Columbia College, Sam avoided the obligation of associating himself with his father's banking firm by traveling to Europe in October 1832. What was planned

Julia Ward Howe (1846). Collection of the author.

to be a one-year stay in Paris ended up being a four-year sojourn, the last three of which were in Heidelberg, where he strengthened his knowledge of French and mastered German. During his last year in Heidelberg he met Longfellow through the poet William Cullen Bryant, who was spending the winter in the German city.[11] Two years after he returned to the United States, he married Emily Astor, the daughter of the richest man in the nation, John Jacob Astor. When his father died in November 1839, Sam succeeded him at Prime, Ward, and King. Two years later Emily Ward died giving birth to a son, who also died.

The other members of the Five of Clubs met Sam Ward through Longfellow. On a visit to the recently widowed Sam at the Wards' summer home at the corner of Bellevue Avenue and the old Beach Road in Newport, Rhode Island, Longfellow had met Sam's younger sister Julia.

Five of Clubs members frequently went to New York to visit Sam Ward, who returned the visits by often traveling to Boston. Howe's letters to Ward during this time were joyful, playful, and filled with puns and word plays, and in one instance, thanks for a pot of oysters.[12] On 24 August 1842, for example, he wrote Sam about the recent Harvard University Commencement, mentioning his fellow club member, Cornelius Felton.

> Things have gone off well at Cambridge. The old generation of pupils passed away with self complacence, & the new one, in equal numbers takes its place full of hope. But the most interesting freshman who entered (the world) on Commencement day was a little girl. I am told she passed a very good examination, & the Professor of Greek has taken her under his especial protection. His wife was rather pained by this new accession to their family but Feltonius laughed more heartily than ever, wiped the moisture from his glasses repeatedly & declared it was very funny. He will name her Sappho Deutega, and she will be to him the sweetest creature in all the world. What a beautiful provision it is, is it not, that in every nook & corner of the earth, from the equator to the poles, in every hovel as well as every palace there is the very sweetest little creature in the world—there is a pearl above all price—there is a pledge of affection, which would not be bartered away for the wealth of India! This God scatters broad-cast over his creation and among all his creatures. But stop, I forget who I am writing to and what I am writing about & if I do not stop you will [stop] reading.

So, although Samuel Howe and Julia Ward first met in the summer of 1841, the two certainly knew of each other even earlier through Samuel's contacts with Sam Ward.[13]

The following summer Samuel and Julia met again in Boston and New York. On 27 June 1842, Sumner wrote Lieber in South Carolina that he suspected Howe would marry, adding, as Howe's close friend, "What will become of me?" Some of the Five of Clubs, especially Howe, hoped that Sumner would take a liking to Julia's sister Louisa. But nothing beyond small talk with one of the other "Three Graces of Bond Street" (so named by Cornelius Felton) came of the hope. Almost three weeks later and two weeks after Mann had delivered Boston's traditional Four of July oration, Felton wrote Sam Ward a long letter detailing the growing romance between Howe and "Diva Julia," a nickname that referred to Julia Ward's singing at house parties and before other groups of friends—a pleasure that she sometimes protested but "endured" happily until old age. That same summer in New York, an unnamed diarist recalled seeing the couple: "Walked down Broadway with all the fashion and met the pretty blue-stocking, Miss Julia Ward, with her admirer, Dr. Howe. . . . She had on a blue satin cloak and a white muslin dress. . . . They say she dreams in Italian and quotes French verses. She sang very prettily at a party last evening, and accompanied herself on piano. I noticed how white her hands were."[14]

A year earlier, Howe had written Mann about his view of a "true woman." At the time, he had been reading the letters of a woman who had died at a young age. "The writer is a daughter of a friend of yours," he wrote Mann, "who is rich, & who lavishes upon her every means of enjoyment. She was away from the city & surrounded with gaiety & life, and yet, she writes day after day to her rich friend very long letters, which are "absolutely gushing over with kindliness & love." Reading her letters had caused Howe to become what he described as "sentimental." In that state he wrote: "God! With how much of the noblest kind of beauty has profusely endowed the heart of woman. What a well of deep feeling hast thou sunken in her nature, what an inexhaustible spring of love hast thou planted within her soul. But how often is that moral beauty unheeded or blasted, how often does the very depth of her feeling come the deeper woe, & how is the foundation which should pour forth love & affection made to give out bitter waters of depravity & deceit!" But he ended his description with a caveat, "As there is nothing in nature so beautiful as the fresh young heart of the guileless girl, so there is nothing so hideous as the passions of a depraved woman."[15]

A month later when Felton wrote to Sam Ward about Howe, he said nothing about the budding relationship with Julia Ward. Instead, Felton informed Sam that Howe was ill and distraught—ill with fever and distraught over the death of "one of his [blind] boys," a nine-year-old named Orrin Moore, who had been at the school only ten months. At the time, Howe had just delivered his lecture "On Universal Language" at the American Institute on Instruction, and he was about to introduce the Boston Whig community to Dorothea Dix's prison findings in a series of letters published in the *Boston Daily Advertiser.*[16]

A few weeks later (and with Howe presumably in better spirits), Howe caught Julia Ward in a parlor game of blind man's bluff to great delight of the fraternity of club members, who now assumed that the marriage of the two seemed inevitable. In November, Sumner claimed as much to Julia's brother Sam. Sometime that winter Julia wrote her sisters Louisa and Annie that she, Mary Ward, and George Hillard had taken a sleigh ride to South Boston, where Howe took them to visit with Laura Bridgman. This was Julia's second encounter with Laura. But on this occasion she did not see Lucy Reed, who had returned to her Vermont farm family. Howe had had little success teaching her to communicate. No doubt, Howe believed, "the old lady" to whose house Lucy was to return and who was "coarse & makes a pipe (not a cigar!)" would "think nothing but indulging her animal appetites."[17]

Howe had asked Julia to wear her snake bracelet so Laura could feel the shape of a snake. But Laura, who said, "I do not want a snake," seemed more interested in Julia than the bracelet. "I gave her my hand." Julia reported. "She felt of it and said, 'Where does she come from? Whose friend is she? The Dr.'s. Do[es] he go to see her? Very often indeed,' replied Hillard with a quizzical laugh." At a party that evening Sumner joined the group, and Julia told Louisa and Annie, "Sumner got Mary and me under a curtain, held it down, called us his dear wives, and said it was the commencement of his domestic bliss."[18]

The engagement became final on 21 February 1843 and plans were prepared for a European honeymoon. "I am no longer in love with you Julia," Sam wrote a short time later, dropping his usual reserve. "It is something more than love, & yet, adoration is not its name. It seems that I have no longer any *me,* what formerly was *me* is taken away, & you hold its place. I do not think of myself, of my own identity but yours seems to have monopolized mine. You will not understand me, perhaps I do not understand myself, I only know I shall not be restored to myself until I am restored to you."[19] Around the same time, Howe wrote Sumner, "I want to see you—embrace you. I am too too happy. I do not deserve such love from such a woman. . . . May I have but the power to make her happy & I ask no more of God in this world. I cannot wait here. I must run about or I shall be crazy with joy. I must tell my dear sister." He ended with another of his persistent efforts to get Sumner to marry too: "Good bye, and if you would be blessed, go & win a woman like Diva! Go Sumner go this very evening & begin to love. You have only to do it & be beloved in return."[20] In March Longfellow told Sam Ward: "Everybody seems delighted with Julia's engagement. She is wise as well as witty. Howe is a grand fellow, and deserves his good fortune. This everybody feels and acknowledges."[21]

Families in both Boston and New York threw parties for Samuel and Julia to celebrate their engagement. When the Harvard professor and literary historian George Ticknor for example, honored the couple with a gathering at his house on 10 February, most of the Boston elite who attended did so just as much to show their respect for the New York Wards as for Samuel Howe. Just as there were parties given by acquaintances, so too there were invitations for Julia to visit with Samuel's relatives. In late January, she confessed to Louisa and Annie that she had met Samuel's father and disliked him.[22] In another letter to her sisters, she complained that despite having a sore throat and a headache, she had put on a ball dress to attend a party at the home of her future brother-in-law, Joseph N. Howe Jr. But she had stayed for only forty minutes for what turned out to be merely a light supper. She described one of Samuel's sisters as "very quiet and dignified and gentle in her manner." Her first encounter with the Howe family, subdued and brief, was no doubt quite a contrast to the vivacious life of the Bond Street Wards.[23]

On 18 April 1843, Felton, Sumner, Longfellow (back in December from his third trip to Europe), and Howe left for the New York ceremony. On Sunday, 23 April, in the evening, Samuel Howe and Julia Ward were married in the home of Julia's uncle John Ward at 8 Bond Street. Julia's maternal uncle the Reverend Dr. Benjamin C. Cutler officiated. Julia's dress was "white embroidered muslin, exquisitely fine . . . worn over a satin slip." Samuel was attired in bright blue broadcloth with gold buttons and white velvet brocaded on a satin wedding waistcoat. (In later years, Howe's children used their father's wedding attire when they played "dress up.") Charles Eliot Norton, the future editor, literary critic, and Harvard professor, remembered attending the wedding as a boy of fifteen. Charles Sumner, he recalled, had been the groom's best man and the victim of a practical joke at the wedding reception when Julia slipped several silver spoons into Sumner's his coat pocket and then in jest claimed he had pilfered them.[24]

Less than two weeks later, on May 1, the Reverend James Freeman Clarke married Samuel's best friend, Horace Mann, to Mary Peabody. The couple had first met at Clarke's mother Boston boarding house at 3 Somerset Court. The wedding day had begun with such torrential rains that Sophia Hawthorne could not traverse the muddy roads from Concord into Boston for her sister's wedding. Other family members, however, including her sister Elizabeth Peabody and her parents, Nathaniel and Eliza Peabody, were present for the ceremony at Elizabeth's West Street bookshop in Boston. After losing his first wife, Charlotte Messer (the daughter of Brown University president Asa Messer), to tuberculosis in 1832, Mann had taken many years finally to propose to Mary Peabody. It seemed to have taken George Combe's admonition "to rise above fate & admit the idea of another partner of your affections" to push Mann to marry again. It had also taken Mary Peabody's comforting patience to win over the often dependent widower. According to Howe, however, in a letter written many years later to his friend in Greece, George Finlay, Mann "was rather enticed into [marriage] than chose marriage." Soon after, the two newly married couples sailed on the new British steam liner the *Britannia* for its maiden voyage to Liverpool. By the time that the two newly married couples departed, the rain had stopped and the sun shone brightly. The only problem occurred five days after their departure, when Howe seriously injured his leg and was reduced to walking with crutches.[25]

Between the engagement and the honeymoon trip, Howe had received two unexpected and unsettling requests from Julia's brother Sam and her uncle John. Just a few days after the announcement of their engagement, Ward assured his younger sister that he approved of Howe and of their forthcoming marriage. To Howe, too, he blessed the joining together of the two. But three weeks later, in a friendly but firm letter Ward insisted that the couple travel to Europe not from New York by a sailing ship but on the *Britannia,* a new steamer of the Cunard White Star line. Ward said he was concerned with the safety of the voyage. The steamship, he was certain, would be the safest means of crossing the Atlantic. Howe showed no objection, especially since Ward offered to lend him money to pay some of the travel expenses. Less than two weeks before the wedding, Ward again wrote Howe a letter. This one was long and referred to a letter Howe had sent to Julia that had upset her. Although Ward did not reveal the content of Howe's letter, he was concerned enough about it that he mildly chastised Howe for its contents. Around the time of this letter, Howe received an "ante-nuptial" agreement that Sam Ward and his uncle John Ward had had their attorney draw up for Howe's and Julia's signatures. Feeling uneasy about it, Howe consulted Sumner, who advised some modifications. On the day of his wedding with little other choice short of calling off the ceremony, Howe and Julia Ward signed the document, the crux of which guaranteed that Julia's assets, all of which she had inherited from her father, would remain in a trust fund controlled by Sam Ward and John Ward. The proceeds from the fund would be distributed to Julia biannually. Neither Samuel Howe nor Julia Ward would have any control over the fund, and neither, it appeared, was pleased with the document.[26]

Samuel Howe's previously friendly and open relationship with Sam Ward would never be the same. It was hardly surprising that such contrasting personalities, as relatives, would remain friends. Ward lived between periods of excessive wealth and abject poverty. He dressed lavishly and wore diamond studs and a sapphire ring, he dined with friends and clients at the most expensive restaurants, and he drank the finest wines. He was a Democrat who loved the South and white Southerners, and he despised abolitionists of all stripes. During the Civil War, he was accused (falsely) of being a Copperhead and in later years he peddled influence as a well-rewarded lobbyist. Like Ward, Howe lived a life of excitement and change, but, unlike his brother-in-law's, his life was guided by thrift and his purse was never heavy. Howe's appearance was always clean, but his manliness was never showy. He remained modest in his diet and was a temperance man, even though he occasionally drank wine. As a Free Soiler and later a Republican, Howe had no use for slavery and the social system that maintained the peculiar institution. In short, the brothers-in-law were exceedingly different men.

A third, unexpected matter was Julia's announcement that she would refer to herself as Mrs. Julia Ward Howe, not Mrs. Samuel G. Howe. In Boston on the day of her departure for Europe, she wrote her aunt Eliza Cutler Francis about her decision. She might now be joined to her husband as a Howe, she said, but she would never abandon her own name to become a mere appendage of her husband. Samuel Howe was likely surprised, but there is no evidence that he objected to her decision.[27]

Surviving letters from Julia suggest a turbulent courtship, an early sign of future tensions in the marriage. Samuel and Julia loved each other and were deeply attracted to each other. But their personalities did not complement each other. Samuel was serious, sometimes even stiff, while Julia loved to joke, to be ironic, and to tease. Samuel had been surrounded by women—his mother, his sisters, and women of the blind school—who assumed the traditional role of homemaker and caregiver. Julia had grown up in a household of men, who, with the exception of her father, appreciated her love of languages, drawing, poetry, and music. And these men—brothers and uncles—expected (or at least did not object) to Julia's public performance of her talents.

On 1 May 1843, Howe and Julia, accompanied by her sister Annie, and Horace and Mary Mann, sailed from Boston for Halifax on the way to Liverpool. The fourteen-day voyage with nineteen thousand letters, "fifty bushels of newspapers," seventy-three "well-mannered and congenial inhabitants," and a crew of ninety-four men on board was uneventful.[28] The travelers found little but pleasant things to say about the ship and its crew, despite the problem Samuel had negotiating the decks of the ship with his injured leg, and some nausea Julia experienced at the beginning of the voyage. The camaraderie of the ship's guests, the favorable strong winds, and the generally pleasant weather, it seemed, made up for the pain and inconvenience caused by the bad leg, the occasional choppy sea, and the persistently cold temperature. They arrived in Liverpool on 14 May and spent two days in the port city. There they attended a Unitarian worship service led by Harriet Martineau's brother James, who, according to Mann preached on the topic "the nature and inspiration of sculptures."[29] James Martineau knew of Howe from his sister's earlier visit to the Perkins Institution. From Liverpool, the party journeyed on to London, where they took an apartment at 31 Upper Baker Street, across the street from Regency Park. They intended to meet the city's noted reformers. But first they would observe the final Parliamentary debate on an education bill.

Howe and Mann had planned to use their trip to Europe to visit charitable and educational institutions and schools, but Howe's injured leg limited his mobility and his reoccurring malaria caused many days of fever and sickness. They did visit a few of the city's charitable institutions, however, despite Howe's difficulty walking through them. On 23 May, with a police escort, they toured a covered market where "sacks and bundles of old clothes" were being sold, and later that day they visited London's "Jews corner."[30] But unlike Mann, who kept up a nearly nonstop review of charitable sites, Howe spent several of his days at his apartment. Since he could not easily go out, visitors arrived to pay their respects to him. Lord Morpeth invited him to dinner and escorted Julia Howe, Annie Ward, and Mary Mann through Westminster Abby and the House of Lords. Samuel and Julia went with Lord Morpeth and the Duke of Richmond to the newly opened Pentonville Prison. Samuel found it quite an improvement over Westminster Bridewell, the prison he had visited with Charles Dickens, "where the treadmill was in full operation." The visit recalled to Julia Dickens's comment to her husband, "I cannot blame a woman for killing her own child, if she sees he will become such a man as one of these."[31]

Another visitor to the Howes was Thomas Carlyle, who could talk of nothing but Laura Bridgman.[32] Julia, sometimes with Samuel and sometimes not, attended parties given by British and American families in London.[33] In his diary Edward Everett, who was serving at the time as U.S. minister to Great Britain, wrote: "Mr. [Sidney] Smith *badinant* told Mrs. Howe she must take an English master, that there were some twenty false pronunciations she must cure. He had had me in hand, and I greatly profited from it. He instanced in her case a wrong pronunciation of the word 'Lords' which he said she called 'Luords.' "[34] At the same party, Smith introduced Howe, who was held in high esteem there for his work with Laura Bridgman, with the salutation, "Gentlemen, Prometheus!"[35] "If you saw what people here think of my husband," Julia confided to her aunt Eliza Ward Francis, "you would think him more than good enough for me. Every body comes to see him and to talk about Laura Bridgeman [*sic*]. . . . Tell the dear Dr. [Uncle Francis] that London has rung with my husband's praises."[36]

Mary Mann, who was newly pregnant, stopped attending parties as frequently as Julia and did not accompany her husband on a visit to Windsor Castle. She wrote her friend Rawlins Pickman in Salem: "Dr Howe, who is not well, has gone to bed. His ladies have gone out to dine." She added later in the letter, "Dr. Howe and I have been doing our best to enact the Saint, for he, poor man, is lame & fastened to a sofa, ever since he has been in England."[37] On 2 June Samuel wrote Charles Sumner that after a month of dealing with his bad leg, a sprained neck, and fever, he was at last able to walk on crutches to take breakfast with the Duke and Duchess of Sutherland.[38] By 8 June, Howe was able to join the others on a trip to Edinburgh, with a tour of York Cathedral and Newcastle on the way. They met their mutual friend George Combe in Edinburgh. Although Howe had been too lame and too sick to accept some of the many invitations he received, he did meet with William Wordsworth, who, he wrote sardonically to Sumner, had most of his money in American investments.[39] Having missed so many institutions and with many people still to meet, Howe at the end of June decided to stay longer in Great Britain while the Manns departed for the continent.

For the next month, Samuel Howe, who was feeling better, made up for time lost. From late June to late July, the Howes and Annie Ward visited prisons, schools, hospitals, and poorhouses in Ireland, Wales, and England. In Ireland, they dined with the Anglo-Irish novelist and children's writer Maria Edgeworth, and at Hanwell, Samuel met John Conolly, a prominent insane asylum superintendent who soon became interested in the education of "idiots" and whose interest would influence Howe's efforts in 1845 on their behalf. Shortly before they left for the continent, they had tea with Harriet Martineau and then paid a visit to the grave of the poet Robert Burns, where, Julia reported, "I had nothing to give him but my silent tears."[40]

In the journal she kept during her honeymoon, Julia left entries and poems that show she had mixed feelings about her marriage. At times she reassured herself, describing the new people and new European scenes she was experiencing. But at other times she expressed uncertainty about her new role as the spouse of a famous philanthropist. In a journal poem entitled "The Present Is Dead," she said, "Methinks the soul is ebbing from the clay" and concluded with the ominous lines

> I am content to live, content to die,
> For life and death to me are little worth;
> I cannot know, through all eternity
> A grief more deep than those I know on earth.[41]

At the end of July, Samuel, Julia, and Annie moved on to the continent, where they learned that Samuel's imprisonment in 1831 had led Prussian authorities to prohibit his entrance into the country. Disappointed and not a little perturbed, the three set off for Frankfurt, where, unexpectedly, Samuel ran into the Manns. The families joined together again and toured Heidelberg. By month's end the Howes were at Baden Baden, where Samuel enjoyed the baths. For the next three months, the travelers toured sights and institutions in Switzerland, Austria, and northern Italy. A letter John Fisher wrote Samuel on 15 October acknowledged the news Samuel must have told him earlier, that Julia was pregnant. Fisher advised Howe to settle in Rome for the winter and the birth and for Julia not to "remain indoors for weeks before the anticipated event arrives" but to get out and enjoy the warm days of the Roman autumn. "Such unreasonable, unnecessary, and unphilosophical practice," he said, "is injurious in all respects—injurious to parent and to offspring." By early November the Manns had returned to Boston, while the Howes, following Fisher's advice, settled into a pleasant apartment on the Pincian Hill.[42]

Julia Ward Howe was indeed pregnant, and her husband could not have been happier. In November, back from Paris, where he had had his teeth filled, he sent Sumner a letter that he marked "Confidential." "I am back again & happy with my dear Julia," he wrote. "How do you think the sweet one was occupied during the days of my absence? Going to the opera, playing & singing, writing poetry? In none of them so much as (you cannot guess) in working upon a *baby frock!* God bless her & hers! She is a true woman!"[43] By January 1844 he continued to effuse his joy. He assured Sumner that Julia "grows everyday stronger, heartier, as well as courageous & cheerful." They walked for an hour on the Pincian, and Julia "[drove] three or four hours about the beautiful environs of Rome."[44]

In letter after letter to Sumner from Rome, Howe teased, cajoled, and pleaded with his friend to get married. In one letter he said: "I tell you how delightful it is to be married, then would I discourse to you of the tenderness the deep strong tenderness of a high woman—of a woman like my Julia—till you should gird up your loins & your resolution & go & do as I have done." In that same letter, he expressed his attachment to his friend in the Romantic language of the era: "Would you were here just now, your straps unbuttoned, your waistband also, your feet in my red slippers, a glass of orvietto in your hand, your sweet smile on your lips, just as you used to sit in my easy chair of a Saturday night."[45]

In Rome that season, the Howes found a community of British and American tourists that included George Combe and his wife, who had traveled

from Edinburgh to Rome, provided frequent companionship. Samuel and
George toured the sculptures in the Vatican's museum, making phrenological
observations as they moved among the art work. And the two wives took carriage rides through the city. Also visiting the Howes that winter and spring
were the writer Sidney Brooks and the Italian Marquis Auconiti, along with
their wives. The Howes also met Thomas Crawford, an American artist who
was in Rome studying and producing sculpture.[46] Charles Sumner had first
met Crawford while touring Italy in 1839 and was so taken by the artist
that he had written to his Boston friends, urging them to buy Crawford's
works or at least to write about them. In the spring of 1843, Sumner arranged
for the Boston Athenaeum to purchase (at the lavish price of twenty-five
hundred dollars) and display of Crawford's Neoclassical piece *Orpheus*. In
December 1843 Julia's sister Louisa joined her sisters and new brother-in-law,
and that winter they met the thirty-four-year-old Unitarian minister from
Boston Theodore Parker, who had settled in Rome for the winter with his
wife, Lydia. Although Samuel knew about Parker, and Julia hardly knew him
at all, on 27 March 1844 Parker baptized the new baby, Julia Romana Howe.
Before the ceremony, Julia's sisters had expressed concern that an iconoclas-
tic, "free church" Unitarian like Parker would perform the rite of baptism.
But Parker assured Julia's sisters that he would baptize the child in the name
of the Father, the Son, and the Holy Spirit. Named for her mother and the
city of her birth, Julia Romana, the delight of her parents, also became the
delight of the American Roman community.[47]

Samuel and the sisters had remained with Julia throughout her labor,
which had lasted eight hours. Samuel wrote Sumner exuberantly not only
about the event but also about his views of true womanhood.

My letter of the 12th announced to you the happy delivery of my dear Julia
from the perils of her condition, & the birth of a healthy & beautiful daughter. This event has made our cup to run over with gladness. It has fused our
souls more completely into one, & it has given me still further knowledge of
the depth & strength of woman's nature. While Julia seems to love me more
than ever, there has sprung upon her heart an intense & yearning love for her
child. There have been hours when it seemed doubtful whether she could be
its nurse, & those were hours of bitter heart—burnishing sorrow followed by
delicious joy at her successful efforts. Her strong nature develops itself with
greater intensity in this new relation than in any other, & there is even well-
ing up from the depth of her heart a gush of affection which is most touching
to behold. She said after she had been a mother for only twenty four hours
that should the child die, or she die herself, she had already tasted enough of
the sweets of a mother's love to repay her for all her inconveniences and all
her pain.

How beautiful, how wonderful is nature. Only a year ago, Julia was a New York belle—apparently an artificial, possibly by some thought a beautiful one. Now she is a wife who lives only for her husband & a mother who would melt her very beauty, were it needed, to give a drop more of nourishment to her child.

To see her watching with eager anxious eyes every movement of her off-spring, to witness her entire self-forgetfulness & the total absorption of her nature in this new object of love is to have a fresh revelation of the strength & beauty of woman's character & new proof of her superiority over us in what most ennobles humanity—love for others.[48]

The time in Rome with friends and family, with new sights and a new culture, with the birth of Julia Romana, and with a time away from Boston's harsh winter was a good occasion for the newlyweds—at least from Samuel's perspective. At the end of March, with a routine in place for the baby and with the assurance of Annie's and Louisa's help for Julia, Samuel left for a month's stay in Greece. It had been fourteen years since he had been to the country, and he was both delighted and heartbroken to see the changes that had occurred and the things that had not changed since his departure in 1830. After landing in Corinth, where a reception awaited him, he traveled on horseback to Megaris and Eleusis, where he saw the site of the Washing-tonian colony. Some of the residents recognized him, and pulling him from his horse, they took him and his traveling companions to a house for a meal in his honor. An American newspaper recounted the event: "Cushions were strewn for them to sit upon, a table was set before them, and they were forced to eat and drink, and then began the long series of questions and answers about the events that transpired during the fifteen years of their separation." Soon nearly the entire community was in the house, and others were outside looking in the windows. A few days later, Howe traveled to Athens, where the local newspaper reported his visit to the city as an "indescribable delight."[49]

In May, soon after Howe returned to Rome, and the family moved to a new residence in Paris, where the late spring and early summer would be cooler than in Rome. Thomas Crawford, who was now actively courting Louisa Ward, followed them to Paris. In Paris too were Charles Sumner's brother George and Francis Lieber, who was in Europe for the season. George, who had the sense of humor that his brother Charles often lacked, informed Howe that Julia had written him that she had burned all of her books by Madame de Stael. He added jokingly, "I have had a copy of *Corinne* and *L'Allemagne* bound in Asbestos cloth. In that state, I seek now the first favorable opportunity to send them to Lady Howe."[50] As the friends social-ize, gossiped, and saw the sights of Paris, Crawford continued to pursue the only slightly reluctant Louisa. Her brother Sam, who had the previous

September married his second wife, Medora Grymes from New Orleans, and her uncle John, however, were worried. With Crawford, they feared that Louisa might marry a poor artist, one who had hardly established himself and had no known reputation for stability. The Wards saw in Samuel Howe the only family member to keep control over Louisa. Letters between Howe and the Wards soon began to travel across the Atlantic. And Howe, with some amusement, found himself in the role of arbiter. At first he regarded Crawford as "a strange, unpolished jewel," but he eventually came to like and admire Crawford. As he told Sumner: "I like Crawford better the more I see him. . . . He seems to be doing pretty well . . . certainly has very great talent, more than any other American sculptor whose work I have seen. . . . He has exquisite taste, fertile imagination, & a correct eye."[51] In Parisian cafés Howe plotted with Lieber and George Sumner to persuade Crawford to delay the marriage plans until he and Louisa had returned to the United States. Though they were convinced that Crawford would make a good partner for Louisa, despite the possibility that he might remain a poor artist, Howe and the others advised Crawford to placate the Wards by making himself known to them. That way he would then be more likely to win the Wards' and Louisa's confidence and affection.[52]

With matters still unresolved about Louisa Ward and Thomas Crawford, the party of travelers moved from Paris to London in mid-July. There, shortly before they left from Liverpool on 17 August, Julia and Samuel visited with the Nightingale family at Embley. Julia remembered their daughter Florence, who, at twenty-four, was a year older than she, as "then a young girl, dreaming of Protestant nunneries and great benevolent enterprises."[53] When Florence asked Samuel if she might become a nurse to serve the poor, he responded that though it would be a public position, the work would be appropriate for an unmarried but proper and upright young woman like herself. A decade later, during the Crimean War, Nightingale would acquire the world fame that she has held to the present. The Howes would maintain years of correspondence and visits with the woman who launched the nursing profession.[54]

Sometimes around the first of September, the Howes and the Ward sisters returned to New York, where Annie, Louisa, and Julia remained with baby Julia Romana, while Samuel traveled on to Boston. On 4 September Cornelius Felton happened upon Samuel and later commented to Sumner how thin he looked. It had been a happy honeymoon, Howe informed Felton, and there had been the birth of his first child. But Samuel Howe had been injured and sick for much of the sixteen months he had been away from Boston.[55]

Public Causes, Public Controversies

On 28 March 1841 when Dorothea Dix began visiting the East Cambridge jail to teach a Unitarian Sunday school class for women, she was nearly forty years old and unmarried. Influenced by William Ellery Channing, minister of the Federal Street Society and founder of American Unitarianism, she had become part of a movement of Unitarians and Trinitarians who brought Sabbath school education to children who did not attend school and to adults in unusual circumstances.[56] Dix was appalled by what she found in the jail on that Sunday afternoon. Among the women congregated in the facility were law breakers but also women whose principal offense was their "insanity" or their "idiocy." Massachusetts, she knew, had a public facility for insane people at Worcester that had received its first patients in January 1833 and that was publicly funded through efforts begun in 1829 by Horace Mann. Also, in December 1839 the city of Boston had opened the Boston Lunatic Hospital in South Boston, a facility for insane paupers not far from the Perkins Institution. Why then, Dix wondered, were there "lunatics" in this and, presumably, other local jails and in local poorhouses in the Commonwealth and at the state prison at Charlestown? Later visits only increased her questions. What she soon discovered was that the 1830 legislation creating the hospital at Worcester did not provide for pauper lunatics who were already in local jails and almshouses.[57]

Howe's interest in the plight of the state's insane citizens had begun even before he met Dix. In June 1842 he had written John G. Palfrey, who at the time was editor of the *North American Review* and had recently been elected to the Massachusetts House of Representatives as a Whig, urging him to publish Edward Jarvis's article on the insanity and insane asylums in Massachusetts. Howe wrote: "I am just now deeply interested in the Subject of provision for those of our lunatics who are unprovided for, & desirous of bringing the subject before the public in some way. Would an article, *in extensor,* on the subject of insanity, from Doct. Jarvis or myself be acceptable to you? If so I know no better way of bringing the subject before the public." He added in a footnote to his letter, "Dr. [Samuel] Woodward of Worcester writes that he is sometimes obliged to turn away 30 patients a week for want of room."[58]

It is unclear when Howe first met Dix—perhaps in church, perhaps after she had written him in July 1842 about a blind boy in Maine who she felt could benefit from instruction at the blind school. Certainly by August 1842 he knew her. That month an article in the *Boston Courier,* using information Dix provided, exposed conditions in the East Cambridge jail. In the ensuing criticism that the exposé elicited, Howe backed up Dix's findings with the publication of two letters in the *Boston Daily Advertiser* in September.[59] On September 8, Howe wrote: "The article in the *Courier* tells not half the horrors of that demonic den. . . . [In the East Cambridge jail], "twenty unfortunate creatures, unsuspected of any crime, incarcerated with the felon and the homicide, were cramped up within narrow cells, breathing a fetid air, and festering in their own filth! . . . The condition of the unfortunate insane in the Cambridge jail was, at that time disgraceful in the highest degrees to a Christian Community." Howe appealed to an enlightened community to find proper accommodations for the insane people in jails, though at this point he did not suggest where that place might be. A week later Anson Hooker, the jail's physician, responded to Howe's charges by claiming that the jail segregated the insane from the felon and that the facilities were cleaner than Howe had charged. On September 27, Howe responded to Hooker by asserting that several witnesses had confirmed the poor condition of insane people in the Cambridge jail. He refused to back away from any of his earlier charges.

Besides the East Cambridge jail, Howe, at Dix's suggestion, inspected jails in Beverly and Danvers. "God grant there may not be many such!" he wrote after the inspections. He assured Dix that he was willing to visit additional jails, adding, "Several years ago, I visited the Alms house in Cohasset & saw some idiots in shocking conditions. Did you see them [?]" Howe suggested that Dix and he coordinate their inspections of jails and almshouses.[60]

In January 1843, during the only term Howe served in the Massachusetts House of Representatives, he introduced to the legislature Dix's memorial on the conditions of the "insane and idiotic" in Massachusetts jails and poorhouses. While giving credit to Dix for her humanitarian work on behalf of these vulnerable citizens, Howe used his influence with Horace Mann, Charles Sumner, and Robert C. Waterson, a Unitarian minister, to provide legitimacy for Dix's findings. The ultimate goal of the memorial was to enact legislation that would prohibit the placement of "insane and idiotic" people in the state's prisons. To affect this goal, the General Court appropriated public funds to enlarge the hospital at Worcester. In the same month that he introduced the memorial, Howe published a review of Edward Jarvis's "What Shall We Do with the Insane?" in the *North American Review.* Before its publication, Howe told the editor, John Palfrey: "I have some misgivings about your inclination to publish some statements that I may feel obliged to make, such as that there are *at least* six insane persons within twenty miles of Boston who are kept *chained* up like wild beasts, & that two of these are *women!*" But he urged Palfrey to stand with him: "Disgraceful as these facts may be deemed to the community they must be made public, for it is only by so doing that they can be effectively cured." The memorial and the article in the *North American Review* ensured that the issue of treatment for the mentally ill, and especially the indigent mentally ill, was before the public.[61]

Over the remainder of the decade and into the next, as Dix traveled the nation advocating for the humane treatment for "insane" people, she and Howe continued their correspondence. The topics were usually about reform—the prison discipline controversy, blind reform, instruction for "idiots," or heredity and insanity. In 1853 Dix persuaded the U.S. Congress to authorize the sale of western lands for the support of hospitals for "insane" citizens only to have the authorizing bill vetoed by President Franklin Pierce. After 1853, their correspondence waned, though it did not stop. In an 1861 letter to Massachusetts governor John Andrew, Howe referred to Dix, soon to be appointed superintendent of the Union Army's nurses corps, as a "one woman power."[62] This label summed up what recent historians have noted about Dix. She worked best by herself, campaigning for causes that required legislative reform while, by necessity, leaving to men the day-to-day political maneuvering that the legislation she advocated for required.

In 1842, Howe and Dix held the same beliefs about the proper place of women in the public arena and about the abolition of slavery. They both disliked abolitionists, especially of the antipolitical, Garrisonian stripe. Tied to their anti-abolitionism were their views about women (and especially married women) in public. Both saw a place for women in social change, but that place had to be as a proper moral force. Women might call attention to moral flaws in society and even advocate for a morally decent new direction, but they must never actively engage in the male-dominated process of political-legislative change. Women might be moral arbiters, but women were never to be the primary arbiters of social and political change. Howe's views about abolition would change in the late 1840s and into the 1850s, but his views about women's proper place in the social fabric would not. This perspective would have implications for Julia Ward Howe, who over the years became an increasingly public and political person.

Howe's perspective on women in the public arena departed from that of most of the Garrisonian abolitionists. Certainly, among the Garrisonians were several married women, such as Lydia Maria Child, Lucy Stone, and Angelina Grimke, who would assume roles of moral suasion, but they would do so with the knowledge that they enjoyed full equality in the home and in the public arena. These women found in their marriages a foundation of marital and public equality that was reinforced by the radicalism of the community of abolitionists. In short, for these abolitionists, male and female alike, the abolition of slavery was intimately linked with the full equality of women inside the home and outside of it. Samuel Howe could never identify with the Garrisonian brand of abolition, nor could he relate either to their claims for the liberation of women in the home or to their calls for the active entry of women into the public sphere.[63]

Once Dix opened a new place for Howe's involvement in social reform, Horace Mann opened up new opportunities for that reform to become controversial. Two months after Horace and Mary Mann arrived back in Boston from their honeymoon in Europe, Horace Mann, in his capacity as superintendent of the Massachusetts State Board of Education, published his *Seventh Annual Report,* an important paper that proved controversial. Having visited and observed many schools and charitable institutions in Europe, Mann was struck by what he had seen in Scotland and Prussia. Especially in Prussia, he had observed that ordinary people regarded teaching as an honored profession. Teachers were respected by their communities and by society at large for their knowledge and their teaching competence. As Mann observed, teachers in Prussia, and only to a somewhat lesser extent in Scotland, knew the subject matter they were teaching, but, more important, they knew how to teach what they knew. Both national school systems reinforced a position Mann had for several years argued before the Massachusetts State Board of Education—that the state's teachers should be better educated to be competent teachers. Mann argued that there were scientific principles and methods that teachers could acquire to make the learning process more effective for students. He noted that good European teachers did not rely on rote memorization and recitation as much as Massachusetts teachers traditionally did. They used a variety of teaching activities, they made classroom work enjoyable and challenging, and they were co-learners with their students in the educational process. Furthermore, good teachers rarely used corporal punishment because they rarely needed to employ such punishment to elicit good learning from their pupils.

Although he had toured Europe primarily to observe regular schools, Mann was interested also in educational practices in schools for the deaf. What he had seen in Europe had reinforced and expanded the perspective he had held before he left Boston. That perspective was based in large part on what Howe had told him about his tour of Prussian schools for the deaf in 1832. Unlike French schools for the deaf, which used manual language, Prussian institutions had explored and were employing lip reading and oral communication with what Mann thought was great success. In these Prussian schools, teachers instructed young pupils to understand receptive communication by viewing the lips and mouth movements of the person speaking. Because of their success with this method, Prussian educators had come to emphasize oral communication, which involved vocalization as well as lip reading. By feeling ordinary speakers' voice boxes and by observing the movement of their mouths, deaf pupils learned to speak orally. Both lip reading and vocalization required much practice, and students never developed perfect communication—either receptive or expressive. Nevertheless, Mann was now more convinced than ever that oral communication for the deaf, about which Howe was so enthusiastic, would prevail because it allowed for the integration of deaf people into the mainstream of ordinary, day-to-day spoken language. Like Howe, Mann was an integrationist, and like Howe, he would have little use for what today we call identity politics.[64]

After Howe returned to Boston in September 1844, he was soon caught up in matters that had awaited his attention at the Perkins Institution, in Mann's school reforms, and what would soon become controversies about deaf education and prison reform. He was happy to learn that one of the graduates of the blind school, John Sturtevant, had enrolled as a freshman at Dartmouth College. The college had covered the costs of tuition, and Boston friends had raised a subscription to cover his board and laundry. Sturtevant would fulfill Howe's highest expectations when he became superintendent of the school for the blind in Tennessee, later leading that institution through the trying years of the Civil War. Like Joseph Smith at Harvard before him, Sturtevant represented Howe's highest aspiration for his most capable pupils.[65]

On 23 November, Howe wrote Daniel Bridgman, Laura's father, that he was about to begin Laura's religious instructions. "I shall teach her the existence & the attributes of God, her dependence upon Him, & her obligation to love Him & obey His commandments," Howe assured Laura's father. "In order to avoid all sectarian bias, & all narrow views, I shall teach her only the general doctrines of Christianity as revealed in the New Testament." Following his liberal Christian perspective, he concluded, "To me it seems best not to teach her any special creed, but to make her love & reverence Jesus Christ, & to live in that charity to all mankind, & in the practice of those virtues which he taught by his precepts & by his example."[66] Three years earlier Howe had written to Lyman Beecher, the leading American proponent of Calvinism, in response to a letter from Beecher about Laura's religious education of Laura: "I should feel obliged to you if your leisure permits for your own views upon the case, and especially upon a question which gives me much anxiety, viz. whether to attempt to indoctrinate her in what may be called the dogmatical part of morality and religion, or to lead her by example into the practice of their inculcations. Should I inculcate moral and religious actions as *duties* or should I not?"[67] Despite the deference Howe showed to Beecher, there is every reason to believe that Howe's anti-Calvinistic perspective in 1841 was well formulated and solid.

During the time Howe was preparing to begin Laura's religious instruction, he exchanged several letters with Francis Lieber in which the two men discussed Howe's aspirations for Laura and explored the link between language and Laura's acquisition of faith with language. Howe soon discovered, however, that while he was in Europe, orthodox Trinitarians had, probably with the knowledge of her teacher Mary Swift, exposed Laura to the very thing that Howe had tried to avoid having her encounter—sectarian indoctrination.[68] What had been accomplished could not be undone. Now holding to orthodox Trinitarian notions about God, Laura could no longer become a "pure" experiment in the natural unfolding of religious sentiment that Howe so longed to demonstrate. Howe also learned, probably to his relief, that Mary Swift would leave the school early in January to marry Edwin Lamson. At the same time, ironically, word appeared in the press that Howe was instructing Laura in nonorthodox, presumably Unitarian, religious instruction. Soon orthodox clergy were attacking Howe as a Pelagian heretic for trying to manipulate Laura's religious commitment in the direction of Unitarianism. Such charges were moot; Laura had already accepted the very doctrines of which these evangelicals feared she was being deprived.

Mary Swift's replacement was Sarah Wight. Unlike Swift, Wight was a Unitarian and therefore held religious views more in line with Howe's. Laura was curious about God, about Jesus, about death, and about heaven. Wight's liberal Christian, naturalistic faith did not jibe with the evangelical theology Laura had acquired in 1844. In the appendix to the school's *Eighteenth Annual Report,* Howe explains that Laura's expressions of pietistic faith are not like his own faith and that because of the influence of other people on Laura during his absence, she acquired the orthodox sectarian notions now implanted in her mind.[69]

Besides dealing with these matters, Howe was advocating for a national library for the blind, for services for "insane and idiotic" children, and for the establishment of a new blind school in North Carolina (whose local proponents had asked Howe to recommend the name of a person who might direct the new school as long as that person was not "an agitator on the subject of slavery"). He corresponded with fellow superintendents of schools for the blind about the national library. But when he went to Washington two years later, at the end of April 1846, to lobby Congress to fund the library, his effort failed. In November 1844 Howe began to exchange a series of letters with Samuel Woodward, the medical superintendent of the Worchester Lunatic Asylum, about the proper way to educate and treat children with "insanity and idiocy." Woodward was well known in Massachusetts and beyond the state as a progressive champion of moral treatment for the insane. When John Conolly, whom Howe had met the previous year in England published an article about French schools for "idiots," Howe and Woodward's interests in the education of "idiots" only increased.[70]

Francis Lieber, back from Europe in the summer of 1845, finally met Laura

Bridgman, about whom he had had such curiosity. For Lieber, as for Howe, the most intriguing thing about the blind and deaf girl was her acquisition of language. How could someone who could neither see nor hear have a "sense" of language? What did language mean to someone who could communicate only with her fingers and from the palm of her hand? How could blind and deaf people construct "pictures" of language in their minds? Language was obviously dependent on a sense for people to communicate, but was language not an essential reality independent of particular senses? Soon, Howe was more interested in Lieber's questions than in Laura's religious instruction. Besides, by demonstrating the essentiality of language, perhaps the essentiality of religion also might be implied. While Lieber met and communicated with Laura on this and other occasions, he planned to publish a paper with Howe on the acquisition and meaning of language. In the papers of the Perkins School are handwritten manuscript pages on language in Howe's hand that Howe never published. But despite Lieber's requests, Howe never completed a formal paper on Laura's acquisition of language as Lieber would do for the Smithsonian Institution in 1851. As Howe told Mann, who had also encouraged him to write a book about the education of Laura Bridgman, he had little spare time to write, only an hour and a half between prayer time and breakfast. Furthermore, Howe complained: "I can't keep my hand off of John Calvin, & if I could, I would not. Why should I; is not my mission belligerent; did not God intend my destructiveness for something, & though my gun be but a pop, shall I not pop with all my might? Is not Calvinism the greatest obstacle to all kind of human progress, the enemy of God, the libeler of his noblest son, our great elder brother? What though it be a giant, & I not even a dwarf & unpossessed even of a sling, shall I not smite my baby smite though my tiny knuckles are broken upon the monster's iron head?"[71] Nevertheless, his interest in language initiated by Lieber diverted his attention away from religious instruction of the blind and deaf girl.[72]

In October 1845, Howe joined Mann in his efforts to change public education in Massachusetts. Mann's 1844 *Seventh Annual Report* had called for new ways of teaching and new ways of educating teachers in so-called normal schools. Such a school had opened in Lexington in 1839, but Mann's report called for more schools to educate teachers. The report also called for the use of oralism in deaf education, arguing that Massachusetts officials should establish a school of oral instruction rather than send the state's pupils to the Hartford school, where signing was the method of instruction. About a month after his return to Boston, Howe had advised Mann to ignore an article in the *North American Review* that was critical of oralism. About a month later, however, Howe's advice had begun to change. With the onset of criticism from the Boston School Masters, along with criticism from orthodox clergy, Howe argued that Mann must stay firm in his claims for oralism and for public school reforms. Of the latter he privately wrote his colleague William Chapin at the Ohio School for the Blind:

> The one thing needful in this country at this time is a proper system of *training* teachers; for the only hope of preserving the purity of our institutions rests upon our common schools, & our common schools never will be what they ought to be until they are placed under teachers *who have themselves been taught to teach.*
>
> By the present arrangement the teachers learn their business by practicing upon our children, who suffer several years from their ignorance & errors, & when the teacher has learned something of his business he leaves it for something more profitable, & is succeeded by another ignoramus who causes suffering & loss of opportunity to another generation of children. It has often occurred to me to compare the new teachers in a common school to the barber's apprentice, who learns to shave upon the chins of his master's less favoured customers, & our common schools are the less favoured customers. After the apprentice has drawn blood enough & made blunders enough in them he is promoted to [the] private school or academy.[73]

Howe worked with Mann in the effort to establish normal schools in Massachusetts. His election to the Boston School Committee in December 1844 gave him an opportunity, he believed, to advocate for Mann's reforms. In May the board had appointed him to the Grammar School Committee, which was charged with examining Boston's public grammar schools. But before he could begin this work, the Massachusetts General Court passed legislation, guided by John G. Palfrey, chair of the House of Representatives' Committee on Education, to provide part of what Mann and Howe had recommended—teacher training in state-sponsored normal schools.[74]

With several schools proposed, Mann began making decisions about where to locate the new normal schools, while Howe went about examining Boston's elementary schools. Although Mann had won the fight over teacher training, Howe and he, along with Charles Sumner, were now engaged in a contentious struggle with the Association of Boston School Masters, who had strongly disagreed with Mann's *Seventh Annual Report,* specifically with its claims about the poor quality of education many of the schools' teachers were offering.

Like other idealists of the period, Howe rejected the Lockean notion that the mind is a tabula rasa on which sensory material is written, seeing in it the rationale for rote memorization and routinized learning. He believed that the mind had within it a divine essence, independent of the senses, and so the role of the teacher was to help the student "recognize and cultivate his internal principles."[75] Although Howe never read Kant, Kantian idealism influenced his views on education. What he knew about Kant he had learned principally from Mann (who had learned most of what he knew from Elizabeth Peabody) and to a lesser degree from Julia Ward Howe (who became one the nation's most thorough readers of Kant). Another new friend, well read in Kant and other German idealists, was Theodore Parker, with whom Howe had struck up a friendship in Rome. Back at his West Roxbury congregation, Parker preached a sermon entitled "Public Instruction," which supported Mann's vision for public education. Later, Parker transformed the sermon into a lyceum lecture entitled "Education," which he delivered on at least nine occasions between 1844 and 1845.[76]

On 6 May 1845 the Grammar School Committee got under way with three members—the Reverend Rollin H. Neale, a Baptist minister, Theophilus Parson, a teacher of classics and later a professor of law at Harvard University, and Howe. Since they were all committed to reform, they decided to break with tradition and shift the annual investigation of the schools from oral examinations to written tests. Throughout the summer the three men worked assiduously, administering tests to thousands of children in the city's nineteen grammar schools. They also asked the school masters to answer surveys. Neale also administered written tests in Roxbury, Hartford, and New York, the results of which were to be used for comparison with the Boston test results. On 7 August the Grammar School Committee read its report to the full committee. It took three hours. The report expressed nearly complete condemnation of Boston's grammar school education. Although the subcommittee noted that there were good teachers among the schools, too many of the pupils had become accomplished only at memorization and not in thinking. High percentages of pupils tested poorly in grammar and geography. As Mann informed Howe two weeks after the report appeared, "On the whole it is a more terrible Report than any human imagination could conceive. If the masters give me another chance, I think I can so reply as to make it redound to the glory of God."[77]

The report recommended hiring a superintendent for the entire Boston school system, and it called for a single headmaster for each of the nineteen grammar schools. The report concluded with recommendations, consistent with what Howe had been calling for several years, that the schools put less emphasis on memorization and recitation, and less emphasis on the employment of corporal punishment. Within days of the report's public offering, newspapers in the city either praised or condemned it. For some Boston citizens, the report was a long overdue exposé of poor educational conditions in Boston's public grammar schools. For others the report was an exaggerated depiction of a school system with limited resources but with dedicated teachers. In the end, Howe and some of the other reformers removed themselves from the Grammar School Committee and most of the school masters survived the calls for reform. Nevertheless, some modifications were made in the school curriculum and teaching methods, and the use of the corporal punishment became less and less common. Howe and the other committee members may have exaggerated the poor quality of Boston grammar school education, but fewer school boys would learn the way Howe had learned—by rote and the rod.[78]

In late winter 1845 Howe published four letters in the *Boston Daily Advertiser* about "insane and idiotic" children. The letters combined what Howe had learned from Conolly's report on his visits to French schools that attempted to educate "idiots" and Woodward's report that touched on what Woodward called "congenitally insane children." Of "idiots," Howe claimed there were probably five or six hundred in the Commonwealth, while there were likely a hundred "insane" children. He mentioned that Conolly's report had referred to the successful education of "idiotic" children at the Bicêtre. "Driveling idiots" had never been considered candidates for education; yet, the French had shown that even "idiots" are amenable to instruction. Such education, Howe noted, improved both the physical and mental abilities of the "idiot." While never claiming a cure, Howe insisted that education is appropriate to develop the lot of even the lowest-functioning human beings. Besides "idiots," Massachusetts had children who were "insane" from birth. Although autism would be a century away from Leo Kanner's creation of the label, Woodward's and Howe's descriptions of the children suggest the condition. "Insanity" had almost always been associated with adults; Howe in the *Advertiser,* however, argued that children too can have a particular form of mental illness. These children tend to be unfocused and easily distracted. They are often out of control, and except at sleep, are in constant undifferentiated motion. They rarely speak, but they often make repetitive noises and screams. Although he was vague about the cure of such a mental condition, he advocated for the treatment and education of children who exhibited these behaviors. Even if only one in ten improved as the result of intervention, the intervention would be worth the effort.[79]

By the spring of 1845 Julia was pregnant again, and Howe, busy with the day-to-day operation of the blind school and his efforts to advocate for new services for "insane and idiotic" children, as well as controversies associated with public school education and the education of the deaf, found another cause to take up his interest and time: prison reform. Reformers throughout much of the nation had debated the issue of prison reorganization since the emergence in the early part of the nineteenth century of two models of reform—the Auburn and Pennsylvania systems, each named for the location of a prison. The prison in Auburn, New York, which opened in 1816, housed prisoners in congregate accommodations during the day. Prisoners remained in silent confinement and slept in solitary cells, but they were allowed to interact, though in silence, during daytime manual labor and at meals. The other model was embodied in the Eastern State Penitentiary, which opened in 1829 at Cherry Hill just outside of Philadelphia. The facility had its origins with local Quakers. There prisoners were kept in identical private cells apart from all other prisoners. Prisoners worked in their own cells, and for about an hour a day penitentiary authorities allowed them to go outdoors, but in locations where they maintained their isolation. Silence was the prison policy; food was brought to each prisoner in silence, and waste was removed in silence. By 1843, a controversy had begun to brew over which type of prison, Auburn or Pennsylvania, was the preferred model. In Massachusetts, the controversy erupted in the Boston Prison Discipline Society, whose members split their support between the two systems. Howe, following the ideas of his friends Sumner and Mann, believed that the Auburn Prison, overcrowded and out-of-control, had given up on reform and degenerated into brutality. The "silent system" had failed. The prisoners were more in control of the facility than were the authorities, newly incarcerated felons merely perfected their criminal skills, and immoral behavior ran undisciplined when not observed or cruelly disciplined when discovered.

Howe's relationship with the Prison Discipline Society remained tenuous because, although he had been a member since the late 1830s, as early as 1840 he had begun to question the society's preference for the Auburn system. In March of that year he responded to a request for information about the American penal systems from a Prussian social scientist, Nicholaus H. Julius, by sending him a package of material produced by the Boston Prison Discipline Society. Although he sent the material, Howe was critical of what he identified as its lack of impartiality in favoring the "social system." For Howe, the social, or Auburn, system overlooked "some important principles of human nature": "the consciousness which the criminal feels that the moral sense of the community in which he lives approves of the crime for which he is committed and the appearance that he has the *sympathy* of nine tenths of those about him."[80]

Howe's doubts about the society's loyalty had their origins in at least three sources. First, and most important, Sumner and Mann preferred the Pennsylvania system. Second, Howe believe that the rigidity and sloth of the secretary of the society, the Reverend Louis Dwight, an orthodox minister and graduate of Yale, kept the society from ever considering any of the potential merits of the Pennsylvania system. The Auburn system reflected the efforts of orthodox, evangelical Protestants, while the Pennsylvania system was the work of progressive Quakers. Third, Howe had visited the Eastern

State Penitentiary (as had Mann, accompanied by George Combe, in March 1840), and he had been most impressed by what he had seen. He was also impressed that most European travelers to the United States, including Francis Lieber, Alexis de Tocqueville, and Frédéric Auguste Demetz, had praised the Pennsylvania system of penitentiary management. Howe expressed his doubts in a letter to Julius. "I think [Dwight]," he wrote, "entirely overlooks some important principles of human nature which militates against the Social system of improvement. Indeed the very attempt to reform *in masses* is necessarily attended by a very great evil."[81] Howe remained so frustrated with Dwight that he plotted with Lieber to take over the orthodox minister's position.[82]

Howe's first foray into the politics of prison discipline occurred before his marriage in early 1843, while he was a member of the legislature. When the society made its usual request to the General Court for funds to publish its annual report, Howe, under the influence of Sumner and Mann, questioned the predictable praise that the society gave to the Auburn Prison and then used his influence to block the annual appropriation for the report's printing and distribution. After his return to the United States in September 1844, Howe renewed his interest in the society, especially since his visits to European prisons had convinced him that American systems were superior. Around this time, he also arranged for the publication and wide distribution of Dix's *Remarks on Prisons and Prison Discipline in the United States* as a pamphlet. In this and other writings, Dix, a strong proponent of the Pennsylvania system, claimed that the annual reports of the Boston Prison Discipline Society contained errors and inaccuracies. He also kept up an ongoing correspondence about prison reform with Dix. In June 1845 he wrote: "We are involved in quite a war here in consequence of the question raised at the Annual Meeting of the Prison Dis. Soc. about the infallibility & omniscience of Lewis [*sic*] Dwight, & now that his great supporter champion Mr. Samuel Eliot has returned we are in danger of being pulverized. . . . "I did not know that there was so much illiberality & ill temper among philanthropic & intelligent individuals as I have seen manifested within a few days, & I really begin to fear that somehow or other I must have grown illiberal & ill tempered myself in order to have provoked such an exhibition of it." In July 1847 Howe urged Dix to publish her latest findings about the nation's prisons that she has visited, confident that her report would justify the Pennsylvania system.[83]

In May 1845 Dwight charged Eastern State Penitentiary officials with fraud in what he claimed were misrepresentations in their annual report. Howe and Sumner disputed the charge. After what could only be described as strong discussions bordering on name calling by both sides, the society appointed a committee with Howe as its chair to determine whether Dwight's claims were fair and appropriate. Although Sumner and Mann were appointed to the committee, most members, including Samuel A. Eliot, a former mayor of Boston and in 1850–51 a congressman and strong defender of the Fugitive Slave Law, Walter Channing, a physician, and George T. Bigelow, a Brahmin attorney, were loyal to Dwight, who also appointed himself to the committee.

The conclusion of the majority was that Dwight's claims about the cost, flaws, and prisoner recidivism of the Pennsylvania system were accurate. To his frustration and after various committee machinations, Howe was obligated to issue a minority report with Sumner and Mann. The report, with Howe as its author, appeared in early summer 1846 as a one-hundred-page booklet entitled *An Essay on Separate and Congregate Systems of Prison Discipline.* The ever-faithful benefactor Amos Adams Lawrence subsidized the publication.[84] The report, reflecting the strong perspective of Howe, Sumner, and Mann, was remarkably respectful. Howe argued that the Pennsylvania model as reflected in the Eastern State Penitentiary was not a perfect system. Its public costs were, at least in the short run, higher than those incurred by the congregate, or Auburn, system. Yet, according to data on costs and outcomes he provided, Howe was persuaded that the solitary confinement provided in the Pennsylvania system made that system the better of the two. He referred to the Auburn prison as a "school of vice." Rather than rehabilitating convicts, the system merely reinforced their immorality, while the prison received labor from them at little cost to the state. Young, first-time offenders were especially vulnerable. Usually sentenced to only a few years in prison for minor offenses, these convicts soon learned from veteran offenders how to be better law breakers. Furthermore, Howe argued, contrary to the claims in Dwight's report, solitary or separate system at the Eastern State Penitentiary did not cause undue numbers of prisoners to go insane. Although unable to associate with other prisoners, prisoners at Eastern could speak with prison officials, with clergy, and with honorable visitors like Howe. Thus, they model their behavior not on that of other convicts but on upstanding citizens who point them in new law-abiding directions. Howe said that during his visits to Cherry Hill that the prisoners seemed well behaved and content and well occupied with work, reading, and gardening. Most important, they were not learning how to be hardened criminals. Instead, they were being treated like individuals, rather than as a criminal class. As such, they are far more likely than the Auburn convicts to leave prison to become law-abiding citizens. For Howe, then, the Philadelphia solitary system of incarceration allowed for the improvement, if not the perfectibility of wrongdoers.[85]

In an address to the Prison Discipline Society in June 1847, Howe gave a more personal reason for his support for the separate system.

Sir, shall I be pardoned if, for the first time in my life, I speak publicly of my personal experience of the effects of prison discipline; shall I be free from the charge of egoism, if I say that I know, what no other member of this society knows, the actual workings, in my own case, not only of the separate but the solitary system? But, sir, no matter what may be said, or thought, I think I see my duty in it, and I will speak.

I have been a prisoner, sir; I have known what a weary length of time is a day passed in a gloomy cell, without occupation, without books, without hope; what an eternity is a month, dragged out in a lonely cell, where, though it was not dark, I could see no sun, nor moon, nor stars.

Among the first portion of my imprisonment, in the Prussian prison at Berlin, for the offence of aiding the Poles in their struggle for liberty, I was kept *au secret,* as it is called—that is, no one was allowed to see me except the turnkey who brought my food; I could not know my offence, I could not tell when I was to be tried, I could not tell what was to be my fate, I could not receive a letter or newspaper, or know what was going on in the world. I bore up under this depressing and purposely agonising [*sic*] treatment, as well as one who had youth, strength, and an ordinary share of courage could; but it was evident that my health could not endure long in my narrow cell, and my entreaty to be allowed exercise was complied with. I was led out into a court yard of the prison, and I can assure you sir, that, though the fresh air was most delicious, and the bright sun was most welcome, I never cared to go there again. On either side were convicts in their cells, and they came to the gratings, and the men began to talk ribaldry, the women to becken [*sic*] to me, and because I shrunch [*sic*] away, they blasphemed and cursed me, until I was glad to find refuge in my cell; and I thanked God for its silence and its solitude. It seemed to me a paradise, in which I could live contented, when contrasted with the hell it would have been, if such wretches as I had seen, had been inmates with me.[86]

Howe's experience in the Prussian prison would have an additional implication in 1859 when he feared trial and incarceration in a Virginia prison after the events at Harper's Ferry.

After publishing the four articles about "idiocy" in the *Boston Daily Advertiser,* Howe maintained his interest in the subject even as some Bostonians found the idea of educating "idiots" to be little more than nonsense. In February 1847 he received a letter from George Sumner describing his observations after a visit to the "idiot" school led by the French alienist Félix Voison and its principal teacher, Édouard Séguin. Although Howe had doubts about what he called "French charlatanism," he trusted Sumner and therefore was impressed by the description of the school's philosophy and educational techniques. Later in the year he read Séguin's important work *Traitment moral, hygiene et education des idiots.* He was most impressed with Séguin's techniques and the results that he was obtaining, but, as a phrenologist, he could not abide the author's sensualist perspective grounded in the writings of Condillac.

The previous April, Howe had himself appointed chair of a state commission "to inquire into the condition of Idiots of the Commonwealth, to ascertain their numbers, and whether any thing can be done in their behalf." During his service on the commission, Howe and his fellow commissioners observed "five hundred and seventy-four human beings who were condemned to hopeless idiocy" in sixty-three towns and villages. In almost all of the cases that the commission members located, the "idiots" were "left to their own brutishness." Impressed by the commission's findings, supported by the reports that were coming from France about the successes there educating "idiots," the Massachusetts General Court passed legislation in May 1847 to appropriate public funds for an experimental school for "idiots." In October 1847 Howe admitted his first "idiotic" pupils to the school for the blind. In February 1848, Howe summed up the commission's finding and his own experience of five months of educating "idiots" with his *Report Made to the Legislature of Massachusetts upon Idiocy* and later that summer published "Causes and Prevention of Idiocy" in Theodore Parker's *Massachusetts Quarterly Review.* Edward Jarvis was so taken by the report that he wrote a detailed review for the April 1849 issue of the *American Journal of the Medical Sciences,* thus ensuring that Howe's report would receive large national and international notice.[87]

In his *Report,* Howe reminded the legislators that their charge to the commission was to ascertain the number of "idiots" in Massachusetts and, from that number, to determine what could be done for their improvement. A count of the number of "idiots," Howe pointed out, is dependent on a precise and careful definition of idiocy. Linked to that is an understanding of the causes of idiocy, which is also associated with the improvement of the lot of "idiots."

To ascertain the numbers, the commissioners had sent out a written circular to all the town clerks in the state and then followed up these circulars with personal observations of "idiots" in private homes and public almshouses. Of the 574 "idiots" they examined, the commissioners concluded that 420 were true "idiots." Extrapolating from general population data, the commissioners concluded that there were between 1,200 and 1,500 school-aged "idiots" in the Commonwealth, of which between one-third and one-half were paupers. For Howe, idiocy was fundamentally a physical matter "found in the condition of the bodily organization." In some, idiocy manifest itself in the "size and shape of the head"; in other persons, it affected the nervous system, the temperament, or the development of the chest and abdomen. At the same time, idiocy was related to the "sins of the fathers." These sins in Howe's pre-Mendelian world, had consequences for future generations of "idiots." If Massachusetts wants truly to do something about the number of "idiots" in the future, Howe maintained in the report, it will enlighten ordinary citizens about the violations of God's natural laws that caused idiocy. These include alcohol drinking, tobacco smoking, masturbation, and working without adequate rest, all of which could cause idiocy in the next generation.

Howe was dissatisfied by the traditional and even the legal definitions of idiocy. Fundamental to idiocy as a physical condition, he believed, was a lack of intellectual or mental capacity. Nevertheless, this lack of intelligence might take on different manifestations; some "idiots" have extraordinary intellectual capacities in particular areas, while they are utterly deficient in many other areas. The definition that Howe found most appropriate was the one supplied by the French alienist Jean Etienne Dominique Esquirol. This definition identifies idiocy not as a disease but as a condition in which the intellect is so little developed that an "idiot" is one who fails to respond to instruction commensurate with the instruction that he and other people would normally receive at their age. In this context, "idiots" might be differentiated by the degree of their lack of intellectual development. The most limited form of idiocy is the "absolute idiot," that is, "the unfortunate creature who has hearing, but seems not to hear; sight, but seems not to see; who never learns to talk; who cannot put on his own clothes, or feed himself with a spoon, or learn to do the simplest thing." Next on the developmental continuum is the "imbecile." He "cannot take care of himself at all, but can do pretty well under the direction of others." Next is the "simpleton," "who thinks he is a man, and who hangs on the skirts of society, the victim of some and the butt of others, until at last he comes upon the public for support, and usually degenerates into idiocy as he advances in age." Added to these degrees of idiocy is the uniquely separate "moral idiot" or "moral imbecile," who has little or no moral intelligence. These people are immoral because they lack a moral faculty; they do not know how to be moral.

Howe insisted that despite their inevitable disability, "idiots" have a "place in the human family": "We maintain that they have a germ of the human faculties and sentiments, which in most cases may be developed. Indeed, the number of persons left by any society in a state of idiocy is one test of the degree of advancement of that society in true and Christian civilization." Although Howe believed Séguin's assumptions about the will as an independent faculty were flawed, he acknowledged that Séguin had shown that idiots can learn. Howe concluded that it is therefore important that the Commonwealth of Massachusetts do for "idiotic children" what it has done for deaf and blind children. Education cannot remove their disabilities, but it can open up ways for "idiots" to learn and from their learning, to become at least partially independent. But, Howe claimed, because so many of the state's "idiots" are either in almshouses or in the homes of poor families, the best place to educate them is in an institution.

Howe wrote "Causes and Prevention of Idiocy" in the *Massachusetts Quarterly Review* not for legislators but for an educated public audience. He was therefore more speculative and more opinionated than he had been in his report. Writing in the context of the European revolutions of 1848, Howe linked idiocy with the oppression of the laboring class. "The seed of our thought is this great truth," he wrote, "that the mental and moral condition of men is made by nature to be mainly dependent upon the structure and condition of their bodily organization." Whether human beings labored as slaves in the cotton and sugar fields of the South or in the factories of England or in domestic services in New England, he explained, they were deprived of the rest, fresh air, and mental stimulation all people need. The quest for riches among a few had led to burdens for the many. This violation of physiological laws set forth by God had consequences not only in the moment but also for future generations. Idiocy—both physical and moral—was principally the result of hereditary conditions caused by the misery of the laboring classes. Thus idiocy was not inevitable, he argued. It was not the result of some necessary human failure. Rather, idiocy had become part of human social relationships, especially because of the harsh working conditions of the laboring classes. Thus, grinding work in poor conditions for long hours led to idiocy, if not in the first generation, then in the next. Four-fifths of Massachusetts "idiots" were born to families whose working conditions were harsh and whose labor was exploited for the benefit of a few. "There can be no manner of doubt," Howe claimed, "that those social institutions which require that great classes of men shall spend their whole time and their whole energies in bodily labor are radically wrong. We have seen that, when pushed to their extreme, such institutions ·cause a great degeneracy of the race, and great frequency of moral and mental idiocy." Every human being is born with "nervous fluid." We waken in the morning after a good rest with this creative energy and use it in creative, productive tasks to learn and to create a better world. Some of the energy is mental and some is physical. Kept in balance, the mental and physical parts of the "nervous fluid" ensure that human beings will do and be what God created them to do and to be. Cheated from flourishing or thrown out of balance, the creative energy begins to tear down the organs of the body and eventually leads to flaws in the next generation. The laboring classes, he said, were especially vulnerable to idiocy because in their grinding labor they were deprived of the "nervous fluid" that should be directed to mental energy. After working from sunup to sundown, they are interested in little more than sleep. It was no wonder that so much idiocy, Howe claimed, was concentrated in the exploited laboring classes. "Surely, the millennium will never come on earth; surely, mankind will never display a hundredth part of its vigor, its goodness, its capacity for almost indefinite improvement, until the laboring class, which composes such an immense majority, is redeemed from the degrading thralldom under which it actually lies."

Toward Antislavery

Until 1846 Howe resisted involvement in the antislavery movement. He had little use for Garrisonian abolitionist, and in 1834, he had dismissed their claims that he prohibited the admission of black students to the Perkins Institution as the accusations of extremists more interested in raising allegations than in knowing the truth. He had made explicit in his 1833 article "Letter on Slavery" that he abhorred slavery but preferred African colonization to the integration of former slaves of African descent into the dominant white American social order. His trip south from the fall of 1841 to the spring of 1842 had given him his first opportunity to see the South of white masters and black slaves. When Garrisonians published his article about the New Orleans slave whipping in 1843, he became associated with the ultra-abolitionists but still he would not identify himself with abolitionist sentiments and suppositions.

Howe's shift to a more explicit antislavery position grew out of his friendship and association with Mann, Sumner, and even Longfellow, who had published *Poems on Slavery* in 1842 after first reading the poems to the members of the Five of Clubs. In 1846 Mann, Sumner, and Longfellow were no more explicitly antislavery than Howe was, and all were becoming less aligned with dominant Whig politicians of the period. After their work on the Boston Public School Committee and their minority report on the Boston Prison Discipline Committee, Howe, Mann, and Sumner began a process of departing from the Whig Party. Although the party, which was controlled by dominant Boston elites, was only a decade old, by 1846, in the face of several issues, but especially slavery, it was beginning to unravel.

This unraveling had its origins in several occurrences beginning in the mid-1840s, but none was more prominent than the annexation of Texas into the federal union. Even before the election of James K. Polk on 4 December 1844, his one-term predecessor in the White House, John Tyler, had his eyes on Texas. Mexico had outlawed slavery, but slavery was a crucial part of the agricultural economy of the Republic of Texas. By joining the Union, Texas would throw off the delicate balance established by the 1820 Missouri Compromise. Polk had made it clear that he favored territorial expansion, and Texas was crucial to that expansion.

Ten days after Polk's inauguration, Wendell Phillips delivered a fiery speech in Concord, Massachusetts, condemning slavery and denouncing Texas annexation. Listening to the speech that day, among others, was Henry David Thoreau, who later wrote an anonymous article for William Lloyd Garrison's *Liberator,* favorably reviewing Phillips's speech.[88] On 15 June 1845 Polk ordered General Zachary Taylor to cross the Sabine River into Texas to protect Texas interests, and within a week the Congress of Texas voted to accept the annexation of the republic into the United States. In reaction Charles Sumner gave one of the most important speeches of his career, later published under the title *The True Grandeur of Nations,* in which he argued that peace, rather than armed aggression, characterizes the truly great nation. On the same day of Sumner's speech, 4 July 1845, Thoreau moved to his cabin on Walden Pond. Visiting Boston at the time, Lieber in his diary called Sumner's speech, "one of the worst reasoned speeches I have ever heard." Within a few years, Lieber would have equally harsh comments to make about Sumner's (and Howe's) antislavery activities. Howe wrote Sumner to praise the speech, and Theodore Parker gave a sermon in full agreement with its content. But fellow Five of Clubs member Cornelius Felton agreed with Lieber and urged Sumner not to dwell on the topic of peace, for "peace men are weak."[89]

Throughout the summer and fall, antislavery, anti-annexation forces held meetings in Boston, Salem, and Concord. On 22 September 1845 John Palfrey, who had recently freed slaves that he had inherited from his father's estate and transported them at his own expense from New Orleans to Boston, met with antislavery citizens in Concord about the Texas annexation. In October Howe also met with a group in Cambridge who opposed Texas statehood. Despite the protests, in December Texas became the twenty-eighth state to join the Union. With the declaration of statehood new fighting broke out between Mexico and the United States. On 23 July 1846 Thoreau refused to pay his poll tax as a protest against the war and spent a night in jail before his neighbor paid the tax for him.

In February 1847 General Taylor's forces defeated the army of Mexican general Santa Anna at the Battle of Buena Vista in Monterrey. Eventually, U.S. troops occupied Mexico City and the war ended on 2 February 1848 when Mexico and the United States signed the Treaty of Guadalupe Hidalgo, ceding to the United States not only the Texas territory but also what is today California, Arizona, New Mexico, Nevada, and Utah. Slavery now had the potential to expand into a vast new area. The discovery of gold at Sutter's Mill in California a month earlier would put the expansion to its first crucial test.

All of Boston was caught up in the politics and daily happenings of the Mexican War. Even at the Perkins Institution the conflict drew interest and debate. On 6 February 1847, for example, the students of the blind school gave a concert at the Massachusetts State House with about six hundred legislators and private citizens in attendance. Among those present was the governor of New Hampshire, who was visiting as a guest of the Massachusetts governor. Everything associated with the concert went off as planned until the two governors began talking with Laura Bridgman. Through her translator, she badgered the officials with questions about the war with Mexico, leaving them amused but astonished to learn how deeply the war had penetrated all parts of the New England society.[90]

Almost two years later, in November 1848, Howe responded with annoyance to a Massachusetts legislator who had objected to one of Howe's blind teacher's voting in the recent general election. He was certain that Howe was merely pressuring blind men, like the teacher, to vote the antiwar, Free Soil ticket. Howe assured him, "We endeavor, by all means in our power, to inspire the Blind with a proper degree of self respect; we educate them for the world, for citizens of a free country, & when their education is finished, we bid them go out into the world, & take their place among men." He added, "I might have sent more than a half a dozen [blind] persons to the Polls from this house every one of whom, probably would have voted the Free soil ticket."[91]

If Texas annexation and war were crucial parts of moving Howe toward a firm antislavery position, two other matters also shaped his willingness to change in the direction of a more explicit antislavery stance. Not long after John Quincy Adams joined Congress in 1831, he began introducing petitions sent to him by abolitionists asking Congress to end the slave trade in the District of Columbia. The District of Columbia had become a major location for the large slave trade coming out of Maryland and Virginia. Slaves in these states were frequently sold to cotton states in the Deep South, and Northern abolitionists were strongly opposed to the nation's capital city being used for such slave trading. Adams did not entirely agree with the abolitionists, especially the Garrisonians, because he was concerned about preserving the Union. Nevertheless, he was certain that the right of citizens to petition their government was a fundamental Constitutional principle. For years he submitted petitions sent to him, even when he did not agree with them, to the ever-growing frustration and eventual fury of his Southern colleagues in Congress, who were incensed that frequent petitions were being placed before Congress and that the federal postal service was being used to transmit them. Finally, in 1836 Congress passed the so-called gag rule, which prohibited the introduction of antislavery petitions and was later used in an attempt to limit the postal service's delivery of such petitions by allowing the administration to permit postmasters to hold or destroy them. In 1842 the House of Representatives voted to censure Adams for his repeated attempts to introduce antislavery petitions. Even though the gag rule was rescinded in 1844, the efforts to censure the former president outraged New Englanders like Howe.[92]

Howe and his friends were further outraged by the growing attempts by Southerners to capture slaves who had made their way to Boston. Some of these fugitive slaves had been in the city for many years; others were recent escapees who had been in Boston for only a short time. The resentment Northerners like Howe felt over Southern intrusion into the affairs of the North would only increase after the passage of the 1850 Fugitive Slave Law.

Boston had a small but thriving black community. By 1850 there were about two thousand black residents of the city. Although their numbers had grown over the past two decades, the influx of many European immigrants (primarily the Irish) had actually reduced the percentage of black Bostonians from 3.1 percent of the general population in 1830 to 1.5 in 1850. Much of the black community resided in the city's Sixth Ward near the northern edge of Beacon Hill and in the North End. The social life of the community centered in predominately black churches, such as Twelve Baptist Church, led by the activist pastor Leonard Grimes, and the Boston African Methodist Episcopal Church. The growing presence of the Irish in the 1840s and especially in the 1850s meant greater competition for jobs that had been traditionally occupied by blacks.[93]

Against this background, Howe's turn toward antislavery began quite rapidly. On 1 September 1846 Howe attended the twenty-fifth anniversary of his graduation class at Brown University, along with fifteen other members of the class of 1821. It was a time of reacquaintance and jolly story telling. In September 1846, Henry Ingersoll Bowditch, son of the famous navigator, invited several men, including Howe, to his home at 8 Otis Place to form what he and the other men in attendance began to call the Vigilance Committee to protect runaway slaves from the Southern slave catchers in Boston who were intent on returning them to the South. A particular incident had triggered the meeting. A slave named Joseph or Joe had stowed himself secretly on the ship *Ottoman,* bound from New Orleans to Boston. After the ship was well out to sea, crew members found the slave hidden below deck, nearly starved and exhausted from the July heat. Unable to transfer Joseph to a ship headed back to New Orleans, the *Ottoman* proceeded to Boston, where the stowaway was put in prison to be shipped back south. He managed to escape and made his way to South Boston, where he was recaptured and eventually sent back to New Orleans. In the process Boston antislavery sympathizers and abolitionists learned about the plight of the slave but remained helpless to stop the slave's return. Newspapers around the city carried the story of the slave's plight.

Twenty-two men attended the meeting in reaction to this abduction and the many other abductions of slaves occurring in the city. Howe, along with John Andrew, an attorney who would later to elected governor of Massachusetts, Richard Hildreth, editor of the antislavery *Boston Atlas,* and Elizur Wright, editor of the *Massachusetts Abolitionist,* were at Bowditch's parlor that Sunday afternoon and were appointed to a committee to make arrangements for a larger meeting at Faneuil Hall. The next day Sumner and Howe met with Adams. Congress was out of session, and the men asked him to preside at the meeting that was planned for 24 September. To their relief, the sometimes cantankerous former president agreed, with the stipulation that his sore throat be better by the time of the meeting.[94] The committee also asked John G. Palfrey to speak at the meeting. Placards posted around Boston announcing the meeting, and a gallery was reserved for women who were accompanied by men. Howe was to introduce Adams and present a "statement of the case," and Sumner and George B. Emerson were to collect subscriptions for the activities of the committee.

When the Faneuil Hall meeting opened on that hot September day, the rhetoric was like the temperature. The hall was so packed that many people were turned away. Howe, as chairman of the Committee of Arrangements, called the meeting to order and made some preliminary remarks that successfully warmed up the audience. He was hardly a great orator in the tradition of Daniel Webster and Wendell Phillips, but Thomas Wentworth Higginson, an antislavery Unitarian minister from Worcester, remembered that each of Howe's sentences was like "a sword thrust." Howe began by recounting the plight of the fugitive slave Joseph and then moved to condemn the misfortune of the poor slave by appealing to the fair play of the audience. Over and over Howe asked rhetorical questions and used rhetorical pronouncements to advocate for human beings like Joseph whom Boston authorities treated like brutes. Help for Joseph was too late; he was on his way back to New Orleans. But the "action which this meeting proposes," Howe announced, should ensure that no escaped slave will ever again be sent back to the land of his enslavement. Boston, the foremost city of American liberty, can no longer stand by and do nothing while fellow human beings who desire only liberty are returned to the lash of slavery. Throughout his remarks the crowd shouted in agreement, and the applause at the end of his talk could hardly be stopped.[95]

After the meeting, a permanent committee of forty men was organized that included Andrew, Hildreth, Sumner, Henry Bowditch, Francis Jackson,

Samuel May, William I. Bowditch, William Channing, Henry B. Stanton, Wendell Phillips, and George Dodge was set up to maintain the anti-slave-catching momentum established at the meeting. Adams's presence added legitimacy to the gathering, but clearly the workings of the group were in the hands of a younger generation of men. Howe stayed involved with the group through the summer of 1847. Several times the men met in his second-floor office at 20 Bromfield Street. Walking up the steep and narrow steps, the agitators found a large, sunny, open room with "an oil-cloth carpet, a large desk, three Windsor chairs, and an open Franklin stove." Centrally located just a few blocks from the State House, Howe's Bromfield Street office became the meeting place for all sorts of plotting during the decade of antislavery campaigning.[96]

During that fall of 1846, as his involvement with antislavery politics increased, Howe agreed to stand for election to Congress as a "Conscience Whig" against the "Cotton Whig" Robert C. Winthrop. Howe agreed to run only because he knew that his election was nearly impossible. He had little interest in taking up politics in Washington City. Like another candidate for a seat in the U.S. House of Representatives, Abraham Lincoln, who candidacy in Illinois's Seventh Congressional District was successful, Howe did little campaigning. Edward Everett, Howe's one-time champion, described about the circumstances leading up to the election in a letter to his brother.

> Our home (state) politics are at this moment in rather an "abnormal" state. A paper was set up or rather adopted by Charles Adams last spring, the "Boston Whig," the object of which appeared to be to place the Whig party under abolition influences without destroying its identity. The leaders in this movement besides himself were Charles Sumner, Dr. S. G. Howe, & Dr. Palfrey. It was thought it would result in an attempt to disturb the usual preparatory organization of the Whig party, but this did not take place. The nominations of the Old Whig candidates for state officers & Congress were made with great enthusiasm & unanimously, & this although much pains has been taken to render Col. Winthrop unpopular for voting for the bill furnishing the means for carrying on the Mexican War. A few days ago, a long letter addressed to Col. Winthrop was published by C. Sumner with his name in the Boston Whig, at the same time an advertisement for an "Independent Rally" appeared in all the Boston papers & last evening the aforesaid rally took place. . . . It is doubtful whether this proceeding will cost Winthrop a vote. It may impair his majority, but is more likely to stimulate his friends & the Whig party generally to extraordinary efforts.

When the final election results were tallied, Howe came in third, with 5,975 votes cast for Winthrop, 1,674 votes for the Loco Foco candidate, and 1,340 votes for Howe. Having never expected to win the House seat, Howe ended his run. He would never again stand for an elective public office. What happened in the fall of 1846, however, set Howe in an antislavery direction that he would follow for the next twenty years. His greatest disappointment from the election was to learn that George Hillard, his fellow Five of Clubs member, had voted for Winthrop.[97]

Family Matters

By July 1846 Samuel Howe was exhausted. Since his return to Boston from Europe, he had successfully advocated for a blind school now scheduled to open in Raleigh, North Carolina, but he had been unsuccessful in persuading Congress to fund a national library for the blind. He had written a major report on prison reform and edited the reports of others. Between the fall of 1844 and the summer of 1846 orthodox theologians had criticized him for the form of religious instruction he planned to give Laura Bridgman. Others had criticized him for his views on deaf education and prison and public school reform.

In March and again in September of 1847, Howe received the most public, though not the most potent, criticism of his religious instruction of Laura Bridgman from the orthodox Boston minister A. W. McClure. In his journal the *Christian Observatory,* McClure, who had previously used his magazine to denounce the reforms of Horace Mann, claimed that Howe was suffering from Pelagian heresies. Contrary to Howe's Pelagian assumptions, McClure asserted, human beings are not by nature innocent and holy. In Howe's own reports over the years of Laura's behavior, there were numerous examples of her sinful nature. Laura needed orthodox religious instruction, McClure claimed, because she was like every other human being: fallen and in need of Christ's atonement. The controversy over Laura Bridgman's religious instruction was linked, at least indirectly, with Howe and Mann's controversies with the Boston School Masters, many of whom held orthodox perspectives.[98]

Although he never made a definitive response to McClure's criticism, Howe summed up his views on the substance of Laura's faith and her soul in a letter to Julia Ward written before their marriage. Julia had commented in an earlier letter about Laura's religious sense, and the comment elicited a strong and moving response from Howe.

> Yes! There is in her a soul, there is in all our souls a revelation deeper than that made eighteen hundred years ago—revelation without which Christ might have been crucified over again every day since that day on Calvary, and we have been no better. Thank God for that portion of his spirit that he has implanted in every one of us, and for the right culture of which, and not for what we *think and believe* we are accountable. Laura never heard of God, never heard of Jesus, never made a prayer; yet she is a Christian, yet

she praises her creator daily, yet she shows forth his goodness and love, and renders him more an acceptable homage than thousands who daily bend the knee, and hug themselves with the belief that they alone are the *elite* who are to keep God company in the upper world. . . .

[W]e ask them [religious sects] for bread, and they give us stones and serpents; we ask them for soul's religion and they give us stern dogma; we ask for aid and encouragement to the feeble yet God-like aspirations which we thinks are within us, and they tell us we shall be surely damned unless we believe we are utterly unworthy to be saved. We think we have found a path to heaven, and they shout and say we shall certainly bring up in hell unless we travel on their turnpike, and pay toll at their gate. I am sick and tired of them all and mean to go to heaven in my own way and to take Laura with me in spite of their howlings. I know the way as well as they do. I know God as well as they do. I see him in every sight, I hear him in every sound, I feel him in every sensation. The world is full of him, but were everything and every being except for myself and one insect swept out of existence, I should see in myself and in that insect proof stronger than Holy Writ of the power, goodness, and love of my God, and the insect's God.[99]

On 25 August 1845, the Howes celebrated the birth of Florence Marion Howe. The new daughter was born at the Perkins Institution and named for the not-yet-famous Florence Nightingale and her mother's relatives. Julia's pregnancy had been difficult, especially since she became pregnant less than three months after giving birth to Julia Romana. In January 1846, she told her aunt Eliza Ward Francis. "I still live the same subdued, buried kind of life which I used to live when you were with me, but with some ameliorations." Her voice, she said, was silent, and her poetry was "chained down by an icy band of indifference." She lamented, "I begin at last to believe that I am no poet and never was one, save in my own imagination." "But then," she added, "this winter, I have had good servants, excellent health, fine weather and two nice horses, who make the journey to and from town very easy, so that I have not patronized the omnibus once since you left me." She had spent the past three weeks in Boston, where she had communed with her friends Jeanie Belknap and Mary Ward, and was enjoying learning to sing Giovanni Battista Pergolesi's *Stabat Mater* "in very good style." She concluded: "[Samuel] is very kind and good, and his health has greatly improved. I am quite happy nowadays. My children are a great delight to me."[100]

A month later, Julia confided to her sister Louisa her sense of what it would take to make her marriage work.

May God teach him to love me and help me to make him happy. For our children's sake and for our own, we must strive to come nearer together and not live such a life of separation. We must cultivate every sympathy which we have in common and try mutually to acquire those which we have not. He must learn to understand those things which have entirely formed my character. I have to come to him, have left my poetry, my music, my religion, have walked with him in his cold world of actualities. There I have learned much, but there I can do nothing. He must come to me, must have ears for my music, must have a soul for my faith. My nature is to sing, to pray, to feel. His is to fight, to teach, to reason. But love and patience may bring us much nearer together than we are.

Julia concluded her letter by telling Louisa that Chev had purchased the Packard farm house in South Boston and intended to refurbish it. With an expanding family and Julia's uneasiness about making her home at the institution, Samuel had purchased property that the family would eventually name "Green Peace." "There at last," she wrote, "I shall not hear the noise of the children [of the Institution] & can sit all day under my own trees & think of you."[101]

By the time the family arrived in Brattleboro, Vermont, for the cold spirit waters in July 1846, Julia, with two small children, was just as exhausted as her husband. Although Samuel had to spend time proofreading corrections Sumner sent him on his prison discipline report, he told Sumner: "I am perfectly in love with the cold water cure, that is with cold water itself in any form. A fortnight since I could not wash my body in cold water without taking cold. Now I leap from bed into cold spring water, I flounce about in a cold bath at noon, I am showered & douched several times & sit with my feet in cold water before going to bed. It will give me a new lease of life & health."[102] Julia indulged in reading, drawing, and talking with other spa vacationers. Three weeks into the vacation, she wrote Louisa that she had drawn a sketch of her daughter Julia Romana *au naturel,* adding, "Chev has almost died over this sketch of mine."[103] To Annie she reported her delight that Samuel had chosen to print her poem "The Roman Beggar Boy" in a raised-letter collection of poems for the blind.[104]

After Samuel and Julia returned from Europe in September 1844, Thomas Crawford continued to court Louisa Ward, and the Howes continued to act as mediators for the couple and the New York Wards. At one point, Crawford found Louisa "so cold" that Sumner had to be brought in to assure him. But the two lovers finally married in November. For Julia and Samuel, the issue of the ante-nuptial continued to strain the relationship between them and the Wards. Although Sumner advised Samuel not to contest the agreement he had signed on the day of his marriage but instead to draw on the semi-annual interest of the legacy and to keep those funds separate from his own, Howe was annoyed by his in-laws' control over what he saw as property that was more his wife's than her brother's and uncle's concern. He had had to request funds from Julia's inheritance to pay for the extended stay in Rome and Paris and to go toward the payment for the new property in South Boston. Letters traveled between Boston and New York and even to Julia's brother Francis in New Orleans about the legacy. In the end, Sam and John Ward relaxed the ante-nuptial agreement to allow Julia and Samuel easier access to the interest her legacy provided.[105]

In February 1846, another one of the "Three Graces of Bond Street" was considering marriage, Annie Ward, who was being wooed by Adolphe Mailliard, a relative of Napoleon now living in the United States. As he had with Louisa, Howe wrote Sam Ward about his assessment of the proposed marriage. He began his letter with an affectionate, "Dear Wardie." Annie was twenty-one, but to Howe she was still young in body and spirit. Nonetheless, she was clearly in love, he told Sam, and he and Julia were delighted that Sam and Uncle John had approved of the marriage. He wrote: "You stand now in a better position, if he turns out to be the right man, why all will go well. If you are obliged, from any course to protest, you will stand a better chance of being listened to, than if you had always been in the opposition." He then explicated his views of marriage: "Marriage may effect a favorable change in her whole system, *but then maternity may make a total wreck of it.* . . . But she will not hear any thing of this. She looks down from the ethereal height of transcendentalism upon all physiological considerations with contempt. She listens only to the voice of feeling, as though God did not make the body & prescribe the laws of its constitution, as well as those of the soul."[106] Rarely had Howe articulated with such bluntness the priority of the physiological-phrenological over the transcendental as he did in this letter.

Yet within two years, complicating the matter of the trust fund and the purchase of Green Peace was the September 1847 collapse of Sam Ward's banking house, Prime, Ward, and King. The bank's failure was precipitated by Ward's excessive speculation in commodities. At the same time, it became evident to Julia that her trust fund was insolvent because of her brother's risky, failed investments. For Sam Ward, the bank failure meant not only the loss of his family's fortune and trust but the end of his marriage. Medora Grymes Ward had no intention of keeping herself and her two sons under the same roof with her now bankrupted husband, and she soon moved with her sons back to be with her mother in New Orleans. Adding to the tragedy for the Ward family was the news of the death from yellow fever of their brother Francis Marion Ward in New Orleans.[107]

Despite the financial stress associated with its purchase, Green Peace was a home, though for Samuel it never held the affection that it did for Julia. At

Green Peace, she could have a garden and flowers, and her children would have a place to play apart from the constant crowd of pupils and visitors at the Perkins Institution. To Louisa she wrote:

> I confess my spirits have risen wonderfully since I left the Institution. My little corner is so green and pretty, so quiet and hidden from all. I have not those dreadful stairs to go up and down. All the rooms are so near together. I need not lose sight of the children at any time. The new parlor is built on the left of the old one. . . . It is adorned with a beautiful paper and with the furniture of my best parlor at the other place. The old parlor is covered with shelves stained brown with a narrow hanging of blue trimmed with fringe. It contains almost all our books, and with the blue carpet from your room, table, secretary, etc., it makes a snug library. The old wooden mantel piece is covered also with a little curtain of the merino trimmed with fringe. . . . I have my (your) little work basket table in the library and sit there to sew Dudie's [Julia Romana's] flannel petticoat, etc. . . . There is a nice oil clothe on the floor. The old window seats have Turkey red cushions, the old mantel piece has a red hanging. My own little bookcase that stood in your room has undergone a great change. I have lined the inside throughout with crimson silk (an old curtain dyed)[,] covered the shelves with morocco paper of the same color, taken out one of them to make room and arranged in it my alabaster things & Crawford's mother and child, and made it a beautiful little cabinet. This is in the dining room.[108]

At Green Peace too, Julia could entertain friends and hold the parties that she dearly loved. The original house was two hundred years old at the time the Howes occupied it. The ceilings were low, and heavy posts stood at each room's corners. Small windows let in light and in summer, air into the rooms. Cupboards were squeezed into an uneven staircase wall. The living room was large, and there was a conservatory on the house's south side. Down a long hallway rested Lord Byron's helmet that Howe had purchased in Greece. In the living room was a large fireplace. A Gobelin carpet with a medallion of Napoleon and Maria Louise in its center that the Howes acquired from Annie after her marriage to Adolphe Mailliard covered the floor. The Howe daughters remembered fondly dancing on the carpet as their mother played the piano. A tall sixteenth-century cabinet stood near the fireplace, and other European pieces that the Howes had acquired on their honeymoon filled the room. Near the house were a greenhouse and a bowling alley, and on each side of the house lay an oval lawn, with a laburnum tree on one lawn, and three hawthorn trees on the other. Directly in front of the house were two large Balm of Gilead trees, and the entire property was surrounded by a yellow fence. Samuel found pleasure in working with his English gardener, Mr. Arrow, to tend the fruit trees and garden on the property's six acres. He was especially fond of his pear and peach trees, but cherry and apple trees also graced the property.[109]

In May 1846, anticipating her move to Green Peace, Julia wrote Chev, "I am strong, my darlings are well, and besides, it is summer not winter, that I have to look forward to. I must say also that the thought of going to our own house is a very pleasant one to me. How snug & quiet we shall be there."[110] To Julia, Samuel was a man of action, a man who lived in the moment, with little appreciation for the spiritual and artistic longings that made Julia who she was. In another letter five months later, she wrote candidly about her feelings: "I would have no secrets, if I have not told everything & shown you everything, it is not because I have not the disposition, but because you have made me feel that, in spite of all your kindness, you could not take much interest in my spiritual experience, such as it has been. . . . It has seemed to me therefore both wiser and kinder to sink all these things, and to live only in the present and future, which are all that I possess in common with you. These three years of married life have wiped out, as with a sponge, all living memory of the past. I have gone with you into a new world, and am become in many things, a new creature, and I think a better & happier one." But being a new creature, as she put it, had come with a price. "I firmly resolved when I married you to admit no thought, to cultivate no taste in which you could not sympathize. You *must know* that my heart has been very loyal. It was long before I learned that you neither desired nor appreciated this renunciation on my part. This last year has destroyed more illusions than either it's [*sic*] predecessors." To gain Samuel's love she must lose herself. "Still, I assure you I am nearer the attainment of peace of mind than I have been. I will not expect too much from you. I will enjoy all the moments of sunshine which we can enjoy together. I will treasure up every word, every look of your's [*sic*] that is kind and genial, to comfort me in those long, cold, wintry days when I feel that you do not love me" Just as she expressed her fears and longing, she backed away. "Excuse all this, dear husband. I am sure you cannot know how highly I prize you, how far above other men I place you. When you are affectionate to me, I am too proud, too happy. Je serais toujours belle et joyeuse, si tu m'aimerais toujours."[111]

Julia so loved to entertain that Samuel once quipped that if Julia "were on a desert island with no other inhabitants but one old nigger, [she] would give a party."[112] After Longfellow's marriage to the wealthy Fanny Appleton, the Longfellows were frequent guests. As their families grew, well into the late 1850s, the Howes and the Longfellows would take the "Hourlies"—the horse-drawn omnibuses that traversed the seven miles between South Boston and Cambridge—for frequent visits between the two families. Charles Sumner was also a frequent visitor, and his sister and brother, Julia and George, and his mother were occasional visitors. Florence Howe Hall remembered visits from other Boston friends, including George L. Stearns, Edwin P. Whipple and his wife, and James T. Fields and his wife. She also recalled a visit from the English poet Arthur Hugh Clough, Florence Nightingale's unsuccessful suitor. Other foreign visitors the Howes entertained at Green Peace were the Hungarian patriot Lajos Kossuth, the Swedish traveler Frederika Bremner, and the American Arctic explorer Elisha Kent Kane.[113] In the summer of 1857—in the heat of the afternoon—John Brown visited the Howes at Green Peace, and during the war Julia provided a wedding reception at Green Peace for Edwin Booth and his new wife, Mary Devlin. At the reception was Edwin's brother, John Wilkes Booth.[114]

At one of the gatherings of the Five of Clubs, Julia boasted: "I gave them a neat little dinner, soup, salmon, sweetbreads, roast lamb and pigeon, with green peas, potatoes *au maitre d'hotel,* spinach and salad. Then came a delicious pudding and blanc-mange, then strawberries, pineapple, and ice-cream, then coffee, etc. We had a pleasant time upon the whole." During the Christmas season of 1845, Julia wrote to Annie about having a party for her daughters, the sons of her brother and sister-in-law, the Wales, and a few other children. She acknowledged anxiety about the party but confessed that everything turned out nicely. That evening she and Samuel attended a party at the Ticknors'; just a few years later the Howes' antislavery position would preclude their receiving further invitations from the Ticknors. She confessed to Annie that she really did not want accept the Ticknor's invitation, but, she said, "Chev insists upon my going out."[115]

Julia sometimes entertained women friends of her own, among them the writer Margaret Fuller, whom she had met before she married Samuel. Especially close to Julia Howe in the late 1840s were Jane Belknap, her old friend Mary Ward, and Sarah Hale. In 1847 she told Louisa: "I had last week a little meeting of the *mutual correction* club. . . . This society is organized as follows: Julia Howe, grand universal philosopher; Jane Belknap, charitable censor; Mary Ward, moderator; Sarah Hale, optimist. I had them all to dinner and we were jolly, I do assure you."[116]

The Howe children remembered fondly the evenings when the family and their guests put on plays. When the family performed Thackeray's *The Rose and the Ring,* Laura Howe Richards remembered, Julia took the role of Countess Guffanuff, Samuel played Kutasoff Hedzoff, the future Massachusetts governor John Andrew played Prince Bulbo, Florence played Angelica, and Julia Romana was Betsinda. These plays were a frequent family activity until the children were grown and had left the home.[117]

Balancing the happiness of the first decade of the Howes' marriage were losses and moments of stress in the final years of the decade. In late May

1846, Samuel's sister Maria became seriously ill with puerperal fever. Maria had worked with her sister Jennette at the blind school before she married Thomas B. Wales, a banker who had served for several years as treasurer of the Perkins Institution. Julia and Samuel were both deeply affected by Maria's death on 2 June at the age of thirty-five. Death from puerperal fever, which Oliver Wendell Holmes Sr. in 1843 had first associated with lack of cleanliness in child delivery, was a common source of death for women of child-bearing age. Julia's own mother had died in childbirth in 1824, and her brother Samuel's first wife, Emily Astor Ward, had also died in child birth. Less than two years later, in March 1848, Thomas Wales married Maria's sister Jennette, and brought her to live at the Tremont House on the corner of Tremont and Beacon Streets, where she took over the upbringing of her sister's children. Jennette had been with Samuel since the opening of the blind school in 1832. As Mrs. Thomas B. Wales, Jennette become an active member of the Boston Female Orphan Society and the Needle-Woman's Friend Society, whose salesroom was on Washington Street.[118]

Julia's fears about childbirth were not merely the result of the death of her mother and her sisters-in-law but derived from the births of four of her own children between 1844 and 1850: Julia Romana in March 1844, Florence in August 1845, Henry Marion in 1848, and Laura Elizabeth in 1850. For parts of four of her seven years of her marriage, Julia Howe was pregnant, and with each pregnancy, death was always a real possibility. Apart from the threat of death, birthing and the raising of children was an unending chore for a woman who, as a rule, preferred the company of adults. To her sister she commented on the labors, if also the joys, of raising baby Florence.

> Flossy, as Julia calls her, is as healthy a child as one can see. She creeps on the floor all day, and can pull herself up by a chair, and stands for a long time though she is just nine months old. She has three teeth and is getting a fourth, but with little trouble. She is backward about her teeth, but I am glad of it. She will suffer less for it. She is still my little bed fellow and floods my bed every night. I shall begin to feed her in the course of the summer, and shall not probably nurse her beyond fifteen months, as she is very strong and I am somewhat weakened by the long nursing.

Samuel often seemed more interested in his various causes than in matters that concerned Julia. Usually Julia, who was moved by his speeches and writings, expressed pride in his work, but he failed to provide the emotional support that she expected from her spouse. The sentiments in her letters to her sisters fluctuated between frustration with Samuel and pleasure in her married life. Sometimes she even claimed that she would have preferred never to have married Samuel; other times she expressed great affection and admiration for her husband. These fluctuations summed up Julia's feelings in the seven years after her marriage and in the years before they traveled to Europe in 1850.[119]

Julia's vehement denial in a letter to her sister Louisa in June 1848 that she would ever behave like the Boston sculptor Sarah Fisher Clampitt Ames reveals the limits of her rebellion. Julia had known Sarah Clampitt, who was two years older than she, before Sarah's marriage to Joseph Alexander Ames, a portrait painter. Much of Boston society knew that the marriage was open and free. Sarah was at the time living apart from Joseph but was fully engaged in Boston social life without him—at least in those homes that would have her. Julia wrote: "Now for a word about Clampit, or Ames, as you call her. Dear sister, for God's sake do not suppose that her morale is mine, or that I ever could talk & feel as she does. Her state of rebellion and discontent is almost wicked, and it has shocked me excessively to find that she is very indiscreet and unguarded in her expression of it." These remarks led her to comment on marriage as she saw it five years after her own. "Marriage is not an affair simply of happiness. It does not promise us a boundless gratification of any taste or feeling. It is a contract into which people, for the most part, enter voluntarily, knowing that it has certain advantages and certain disadvantages. It is a relation in which we assume grave obligations to other people, & it is quite as important that we should make them happy as that we should be happy ourselves." She then compared the relationship she had with Chev to the relationship Sarah Clampitt Ames had to her husband.

> I never could assume toward my husband the position that Clampit does. If we do not suit each other, it is quite likely to be my fault as his. I am grateful to him for many kindnesses, for much that embellishes and elevates my life, and he has certain rights & privileges, a certain supremacy and dignity, as a husband, which I wish him ever to retain, as much for my own sake as for his. If I could be free tomorrow, it would be difficult for me to find as kind a guardian, as pure and noble a man. The children too, what a point of union do they make! Could I ever leave them? Could I ever take them from him? Could I ever wish them fatherless? No, dear Wevie, I do not think as Clampit does. My nature is a more contented, perhaps a gentler one. I cannot pretend to say that I am perfectly happy or that there are not vast and painful longings of my soul which, in this life, will never be satisfied, but I am to live forever, and I shall be more likely to attain happiness hereafter by cultivating in this life, a spirit of humility, of gratitude, and the loves of *uses,* upon which my Swedenborg so insists.[120]

During the second half of the 1840s, when Julia was worn out by and concerned about her frequent pregnancies, she was worried too about Samuel's recurring sickness. Although no one identified it as the return of malaria, its symptoms suggest that his "Greek fevers" were still with him. In October 1845 Julia told her sister Annie that Samuel was deathly sick. Nothing could stop his fever, headaches, nausea, diarrhea, and "blue devils." Julia and a maid and a manservant had all tried to ease his pains, but none could do more than merely watch over him. When Dr. Fisher saw him, Samuel looked near death, or as Julia described him, "[he] has been sick as a dog," she reported, "and still remains as weak as a rat."[121]

CHAPTER SIX
For Free Soil and Free Men

A few days before Christmas 1846, Amos Adams Lawrence, accompanied by a British cousin, Arthur Lawrence, visited Laura Bridgman at the Perkins Institution. American and European guests like the Lawrences made frequent requests to view the remarkable blind and deaf girl, to see her read and do needle work, and to observe her communicating through finger spelling. The wealthy merchant and manufacturer had supported the school over the years and had recently contributed to the publication of Howe's minority report of the Prison Discipline Society. All of his funds were given privately with the caveat that he would receive no public recognition. His support continued even though he was, at the time, a committed Cotton Whig with little use for Howe's growing turn toward antislavery politics.[1]

During the same month, Howe's friend Horace Mann and his family moved to the hamlet of West Newton. Also in December, John G. Palfrey won a run-off election as a Whig candidate to the U.S. House of Representatives and became the primary Massachusetts voice to oppose slavery in Congress. Before the winter was out Henry Wadsworth Longfellow had published his long epic poem *Evangeline: A Tale of Acadie.* The members of the Five of Clubs had heard the poem for months and had, with Longfellow's blessings, edited it. When it was published Howe wrote to Longfellow, "A book! A book that pleases, instructs & improves people, what a gift it is to the world!" Howe also received tributes, for his Prison Discipline Society minority report. Charles Sumner called it a work of genius, and Mann, who despite grumbling to Sumner about Howe's terrible punctuation, lauded the work for its lofty sentiments. From South Carolina, Francis Lieber thanked Howe for the copy of the report he had sent him. He suggested that Howe distribute it throughout Europe and America, and he assured Howe that Louis Dwight's "villainy" was best ignored for the foolishness that it was.[2]

Through the spring and summer of 1847, the Boston Vigilance Committee continued to meet in Howe's Boston office on Bromfield Street. In May Howe attended a six-hour meeting at the home of Theodore Parker. The meeting concerned fugitive slaves and marked the beginning point in a deepening friendship that Howe had with one of the most brilliant and controversial ministers in Boston. Howe came to admire Parker, who had baptized Julia Romana in Rome in 1844 and who, in January 1846, had been installed as its minister by Boston's Twenty-Eighth Congregational Society. Parker's congregation met in Boston's Melodeon Theater and later in the Music Hall, a grand facility that had the seats for the largest Sunday morning audience in Boston. An eclectic group of parishioners attended the society's meetings: Longfellow, William Lloyd Garrison, Elizabeth Peabody, Louisa May Alcott, Moncure Conway, and, on occasion, the Howes. They were just as likely to be in attendance as were artisans, laborers, and small shop owners. People were known to read their favorite newspaper during parts of the service they found boring, but never during Parker's sermons—brilliant, controversial, provocative, but never boring. More than anything else, Bostonians came to the Music Hall on Sunday mornings to hear Parker deliver blunt denouncements, often naming particular people who had not lived up to his heroic expectations. Parker, for example, was merciless to Judge Edward G. Loring after the Anthony Burns affair in 1854, and he repeatedly denounced the various Curtis family attorneys who served the interests of Boston's Cotton Whigs. When the English poet Arthur Hugh Clough visited Boston in 1852, spending two weeks in November with the Howes, he attended services at the Music Hall to hear one of Parker's sermons. After dining with Parker at Green Peace, Clough commented to his fiancée, "Theodore Parker has been preaching some very infidelical sermons proclaiming himself in Miracles and all that—by which the genteel Boston mind is a good deal disturbed, poor thing." Clough was also left uneasy by Parker's, and the Howes', antislavery rhetoric and readings. And he was shocked to learn that Parker and the Howes had participated in the Underground Railroad.[3]

Parker's theological and political positions had made Parker even more radical than Ralph Waldo Emerson, his Concord contemporary—so radical that most Unitarian ministers refused to exchange their pulpits with him. Influenced by German higher Biblical criticism and the writings of Immanuel Kant, Parker rejected the truth of miracles and denied the authority of Hebrew and Christian scripture and the divinity of Jesus. In May 1841 in South Boston he preached what became his most famous sermon, later reprinted for wide distribution under the title *A Discourse on the Permanent and Transient in Christianity.* In the sermon, Parker argued that the Hebrew and Christian scriptures do not in themselves hold truth, that human beings experience God intuitively rather than through Biblical revelation because

God is "immanent in matter and man." In the process Parker alienated Boston's orthodox Christian community and offended most of his fellow Unitarians. Howe had concerns about Parker's theology. He agreed with Sumner that Emersonian transcendentalism was "the great mystagogue."[4] If Emerson's transcendental theology was so insubstantial, would Parker's be any less so? While Emerson would surround his theology with ironic aphorisms, Parker spoke his theology in a straightforward manner. There was little doubt about the radical bent of what he believed, or did not believe. In June 1847 he wrote to the fathers of two of his pupils who wanted to attend Parker's Sunday meeting. Before he allowed his pupils to be exposed to a minister that he would not let his own children hear on Sunday morning, he felt he must consult with their fathers.[5]

During the same month, Howe received word from the executors of the estate of William Oliver, a wealthy Bostonian, that the Perkins Institution had received a forty-thousand-dollar legacy. Always strapped for money, Howe was delighted to receive this large, undesignated bequest. It would ensure that the school would remain on a good financial footing even if the legislature should fail to provide necessary funding. And it also made possible the expansion of the Perkins Institution's workshop facilities for school graduates who could not find regular community employment. Over the years Howe had become increasingly less optimistic about his graduated pupils' becoming fully integrated into the everyday life of their local communities after leaving the institution because of the lack of opportunities for viable employment. In 1852, he responded to a blind man who had expressed frustration over his inability to find steady work: "Every year's experience shows one how hard how very hard is the lot of those blind persons who are obliged to labor for a livelihood; and it shows me too that it is becoming even harder. Every year mechanical inventions are diminishing the number and reducing the profits of simple handicraft. . . . It is becoming very difficult for blind men to support themselves by manual labor even with the indirect assistance given them at our work shop. There are there many most worthy intelligent and industrious men who labor hard, fare poorly, and economise in every way, and yet who can hardly pay for their board and clothing."[6] Howe increasingly saw that with the growth of New England wage-worker industrialization, the kinds of handicraft work that his blind graduates could perform was becoming more and more superfluous. Although he had never wanted a workshop tied to the institution and had resisted its creation, the institutional workshop was becoming a more and more important source of employment for some of his graduated students.

In a thoughtful mood made possible by the Oliver bequest, Howe responded to an inquiry about Laura Bridgman from Henry Scott, a professor of moral philosophy at King's College in Scotland about help. Scott had inquired about Laura Bridgman, and the inquiry allowed Howe to give his private thoughts on the topic of help.

> In the present rude state of civilization men are so continually & sorely pressed by the calls of individual or family conservatism & are obliged to accustom themselves to live unmoved by the want & suffering around them that they seem utterly selfish; but let a case like that of Laura Bridgman occur & straightway good men from all parts of the world hasten to see if they can suggest anything for her aid, or at least to express their sympathy for her, just as the neighbors all run to see if they can help to dig out a man who may have been buried alive by the caving in of a mine or a well.
>
> Not long ago a horse ran away furiously with a wagon in which was a little child. A crowd followed, & among the rest was an old woman who, with tears in her eyes & [a] quivering voice, enquired of a gentleman the child's fate. "I don't know my good woman," said he. "God preserve the poor little fellow; but why do you run bareheaded after him; *is he your child?*" "Oh, No," said she, "he is not my child, *but he is somebody's child!*"
>
> There was more eloquence in that poor sentence than in an oration of Demosthenes! The woman demonstrated Gods love by magnifying the love He had implanted in her, more clearly than Paley could do in a whole volume.[7]

Always the optimistic liberal reformer, Howe in his letter to Scott showed that at the core of his vision of philanthropy was the linkage of family and friends beyond immediate kin to the wider community. A child was, for Howe, always someone's and everyone's own child in the sense that the community had responsibility for each of its children. And for Howe, as civilization moved toward greater concern for the well-being of all of its members, the closer that civilization moved to perfection. And there were signs of that movement. The revolutions in Europe in the spring of 1848, despite their mixed outcomes, only reinforced Howe's optimism. He was equally optimistic about the Massachusetts General Court's decision to pass legislation in March 1848 to establish the nation's first municipal library to be open free to the public for its edification and learning.

In his pre-Mendelian curiosity about heredity, Howe was also ever the optimist. As his interest in "idiocy" grew and as he developed education for this group, he became increasingly taken by what he suspected was a link between lineage and the development of disabilities. In December 1847 he sent surveys to various authorities asking for their perceptions about the link between heredity and deafness, blindness, "idiocy," and "insanity." The surveys reveal his growing interest in understanding heredity and its place in the onset of these conditions. From the information that he received, Howe concluded that heredity reflected acts and conditions that led to flaws in God's natural order. Thus, an intemperate woman or man could produce children who were disabled. Overwork, lack of clean air, or abject poverty might also cause one of these disabling conditions. As Howe understood heredity, it was a human-environmental relationship that could be changed for the better, and therefore many of the conditions that contributed to disability could be overcome by changes in a person's circumstances. The intemperate parent could learn the value of remaining sober. Or, to insure the good health of their progeny, people could improve their working conditions, for example, by working fewer hours and enjoying greater leisure. As the environment improved so too could the heredity of one's offspring improve.[8]

On 19 November 1847, Samuel and Julia Howe accepted the invitation of James Freeman Clarke and Theodore Parker to join what the two Unitarian ministers had decided to call the "Conversational Club." A week earlier, Clarke and Parker had called in John Andrew to discuss the formation of a club that might rejuvenate discussion of the things of the mind and of the spirit. The three men agreed that with the recent disbandment of the Hedge Club and the demise of the Brook Farm experiment, Boston's liberal thinkers lacked a forum for perceptive discussion. At the time, Julia was four months pregnant with her third child and was delighted at the prospect of being in the regular company of men and women interested in philosophical and theological matters. Samuel, who was equally delighted, told Clarke, "Secluded as I am from the world all day by my calling, I feel the need of living, talking books to commune with of an evening." During the first week of December the group met for the first time at Parker's home. Joining the Howes were the spouses of Clarke and Parker, along with Andrew, Henry I. Bowditch and his wife, Eliot Cabot, J. W. Browne and his wife, E. H. Chapin and his wife, Edward Jarvis, Samuel Downer Jr., George W. Bond., Susan Burley, Hannah Stevenson, and Henry N. Rogers. The club met biweekly and explored such topics as "Woman," "Evil: Is Human Sinfulness a Positive or Merely a Negative Matter, and What Explanation Can Be Given of the Existence of Evil?" "What Shall We Do to Elevate the Laboring Classes?" and "The Recent French Revolution and the Prospect of a Permanent Government in France." Although the club failed to meet after April 1848, it solidified the Howes' relationships with Clarke and Parker, creating connections that were especially important to Julia's intellectual growth and to her friendships and Samuel's.[9]

When Henry Marion Howe was born in April 1848, Howe expressed his delight in a letter to his sister-in-law Louisa Ward Crawford, now back in Rome with her husband, Thomas.

I suppose you know that [Julia] had a very pleasant accouchement, absolutely an *enjoyable* affair which began with a laugh at ¼ before eight o'clock, soon grew into a growl, & terminated with one short yell on the part of the mother and a continuous scream on the part of *the boy* who came into the world in less than twenty minutes after he began to knock for admission. As in the case of Flossy, no soul was in the room or house even when Henry Marion came except his Paternus.

The thing happened thus: Julia was out walking until seven o'clock & came in & sat entertaining Sumner in the Parlour. I came in at 20 minutes before eight & Sumner said Julia has just gone up stairs. Presently I heard the Old Bird singing from the top of the stairs in her sweet voice—Chevie—Chev-ie. I went up & she said sweetly, "Somebody is coming." So I went down & dispatched the man servant for the Doctor, sent Sumner for the midwife, & the girl for some chloroform. The girl carried off the Cook for protection, the children's nurse was out, & before a soul of them could get back, I was holding *my son* in my arms & performing for him & his mother the various duties of surgeon, nurse & midwife. I had got through with the most important operations & was about to proceed to the ablations when the nurse, doctor, apothecary & all came trooping in, but all too late. . . .

Julia is very well. She rode out at the end of three weeks & has been out every day since. On Sunday she walked with me about the Commons.

She begins to receive her friends & to be as gay & brilliant as ever. Today we have the Club to dinner, Felton, Longo, & Sumner. If Hillard is with you tell him we shall drink his health *first,* second that of Pio Novo. On Friday we are to give a "Reform Banquet." My friend Horace Mann has just been elected to Congress & we are to have a gathering of "Reformers."

Finally, Howe assured Louisa that Julia rode out in her carriage three weeks after the birth and had ridden every day since, and on Sunday had walked with Howe about the Boston Common. He concluded, "She begins to receive her friends & to be as gay & brilliant as ever."[10]

Two weeks after Henry's birth, Julia described to her sister Louisa her joy in having a son, and especially a son who had become so easy to care for. He never cried, she told Louisa, and nursed on a regular schedule, requiring only one feeding at night. "He is a perfect prince of a baby." But she worried that his placid temperament might be the result of the melancholy that had possessed her during her pregnancy.[11] Nearly a year later, Francis Lieber, who had not yet learned the name of Howe's son, teased him, "Have you baptized him Sumner Longfellow Parker Wilmot Howe? In 1849, Lieber in South Carolina could still tease his Massachusetts friend about the Wilmot Proviso.[12] But those days would soon end.

As Howe informed Louisa, his close friend Horace Mann had been elected on 3 April 1848 to the Eighth District seat in the U.S. House of Representatives, replacing the recently deceased John Quincy Adams. Only a month before the election, Mann had written to Howe, "I always feel 'sort of lonely' when I do not hear from you for several days. I can get along passably without oxygen, but there is a certain moral *supporter of life,* that I must have, or languish."[13] The two men had been friends for more than twenty years, and now Mann would be off to Washington. Howe dreaded the departure of his oldest friend, but he continued to remind the somewhat reluctant Mann that his duty was in the capital city where he could do good things for Massachusetts and most of all for the antislavery cause. After Mann arrived in Washington, Howe prodded him to become involved in antislavery legislation. But Mann demurred, not yet feeling he had properly established himself in the ways of the House of Representatives. Two weeks after his election, however, an event occurred that would eventually transform Mann into an overt antislavery man.

On the night of Saturday, 15 April 1848 the schooner *Pearl,* filled with seventy-seven slaves—men, women, and children—sailed down the Potomac River toward the Chesapeake Bay. The plan of its captain, Daniel Drayton, was to sail through the Chesapeake Bay to New Jersey and to freedom for the slaves. But owners of the slaves got wind of the escape and sent out the steamer *Salem,* which, on 17 April, with a crew of thirty white volunteers, overtook the *Pearl.* Drayton and his two white accomplices, Edward Sayres, the owner of the schooner, and Chester English, were arrested and on 18 April were paraded through Washington City on their way to jail. The slaves were removed to holding facilities. Crowds of Washington citizens, angry at the prisoners' actions, soon formed a mob that stormed the jail. For several days they made it difficult for supporters of the arrested prisoners to get safely into the jail. When the antislavery congressman Joshua R. Giddings of Ohio tried to visit the ship's crew, the mob nearly killed him. Its fury was not limited to the jail. On the night of the arrest, the proslavery crowd threw rocks and broke windows of the offices of the city's only abolitionist newspaper, the *National Era.*[14]

The mob's anger was a reflection of a growing antagonism in the South to Northern opposition to slavery in the District of Columbia. As noted earlier, Northern abolitionists and antislavery proponents had begun to petition Congress to end slave trading in the district. With the increased need for slaves in the cotton-growing states of the Deep South, and with the diminished need for slaves in tobacco-growing Virginia and Maryland, the District of Columbia had become a major location for slave trading from the upper South to the Deep South. The great fear of slaves like those who tried to escape on the *Pearl* was being sold "down South" and thus being separated from family members. Slavery sales in the district were most often of that sort where families were torn apart, never to see each other again. Between 1790 and 1860, about one million slaves were transferred from the upper South to the Deep South.[15] Northern abolitionists and slavery opponents had petitioned to end slavery in Washington, arguing that because much of the United States was free of slavery, the nation's capital too should be free of the institution. Many of the petitions John Quincy Adams had spent years introducing in the House of Representatives were to stop the slave trade in the District of Columbia.

After the capture of the *Pearl,* committees to raise a defense for Drayton and his crew began to organize in several Northern cities. In Boston on 25 April 1848 a committee of fifteen men, including Samuel Howe, held a public meeting at Faneuil Hall to denounce the arrest of the crew and to raise money for its defense. Most of the men, such as Samuel May, Samuel Sewell, and Elizur Wright, were traditional abolitionists. After meeting with the committee, Howe concluded that the membership was more interested in the purity of their cause than in the practicality of defending the accused slave stealers and that many of them, committed more to principle than to practice, were *"impracticable, mulish."*[16] The committee's members had trouble deciding on the best person to give legal representation to the *Pearl* crew. Howe suggested Horace Mann.

There were at least two advantages to having Mann lead the defense of the *Pearl*'s crew members. Having just been elected to Congress, he was in the capital city, and therefore, unlike several of the other names mentioned for the task, accessible to the defendants. More important, Mann was well known to the Boston Committee and fairly well known to abolitionists in Philadelphia, the other major source of funds. The principal disadvantage was that Mann was viewed principally as an educational reformer, and his antislavery credentials were untested. That he opposed the extension of slavery no one doubted, but how strongly and how faithfully he would pursue the antislavery positions was unknown. And after he had arrived in Washington, he had done little to reveal his position. Despite letters from Howe and the other members of the committee, Mann was at first reluctant to take the case. He had hardly had time to adjust to his new position, and now he was being asked to defend slave abductors in a city that had nearly killed Giddings when he visited the defendants. Furthermore, as a state legislator and then chair of the Massachusetts State Board of Education, Mann had not tried a case in more than a decade.

During the first week of May a letter signed by Howe and eleven other men appeared in the *Boston Evening Transcript* opposing slavery in the District of Columbia and denouncing the imprisonment of the crew of the

Pearl. About the same time, Howe and Julia took a trip south. While Julia stayed in Bordentown with her sister Annie and her family, Howe proceeded to Washington to persuade Mann to take the case. Howe wrote Sumner: "[Mann] takes hold with great zeal & enthusiasm, though he uses his subtle wisdom in all his movements." As he had on other occasions, Mann took on the case more out of duty than for any other reason.[17]

The trial began in July. Howe informed Mann that the Boston Committee had received offers of help with the trial from both Salmon Chase of Ohio and New York's William Henry Seward. Although they trusted Mann's judgment, most members felt that only Chase's help was worth having. The initial trial lasted for two weeks, and then the case lingered until May 1849. In the end, Drayton pleaded guilty to seventy-four charges of illegal transport of slaves, and Sayres too eventually pleaded guilty to a reduced charge. No one among the Boston Committee was pleased with the outcome, but neither was anyone particularly surprised by it.[18]

Back in Boston through the summer and fall of 1848, Howe dealt with the ongoing needs of the blind school. For several years, neighbors had been complaining about his blind boys bathing in the sea. The boys might not be able to see their own nudity, but their South Boston neighbors certainly could. After the attorney John M. Williams told him that nude bathing in the ocean was considered indecent and for that reason was illegal, Howe decided to be more prudent in the daily bathing the boys enjoyed but, otherwise, he ignored the law.[19]

Howe did not attend the first national convention of the Free Soil Party held in Buffalo beginning 9 August 1848. Around twenty thousand delegates, Democrats, Whigs, and Liberty Party members from eighteen states, took part in the event, determined to found a new, viable party. The new party nominated former president Martin Van Buren for president and Charles Francis Adams of Boston for vice president. Although Howe did not attend the Buffalo convention, he attended a state Free Soil meeting on 22 August, where he was elected one of several vice presidents of the meeting. At that same meeting, Charles Sumner gave a provocative speech in which he linked the interests of the Southern "lords of the lash" to the interests of the Northern "lords of the loom." The election of the Louisiana slave owner Zachary Taylor, Sumner insisted, had been supported not only by the cotton South but also by business interests in the North, some even from Massachusetts. On 16 September Abraham Lincoln would be in Massachusetts, speaking at rallies first in Dorchester and a few days later at Tremont Temple in Boston for the Whig candidate, Taylor. Lincoln remained loyal to the Whig Party, but Howe, like many other New Englanders, could not abide the Louisiana slave owner as his candidate.[20]

In August Howe wrote Mann about his delight that Mann had spoken out so strongly against slavery. The next month he consoled Longfellow on the death of his seven-month-old daughter, Frances.

> It is said no man can taste the bitterness of death twice, but surely the parent who loses a child feels a sharper pang than any his own death bed will bring. So it seems to me, at least, for I have just gone through in apprehension what you have suffered in reality. I believed, for some time, that my dear Flossy would certainly die, and as I held her writhing form in my arms & tired in vain to soothe her pains, I saw the hour rapidly coming when she would be a corpse, so it seemed to me that all the hours & days after that would be so blank & cheerless that nothing could enliven them. It seemed to me the most desirable thing would be to be buried with her & next to that to live alone, separated from every one & to cherish her memory. . . .
>
> The rescue of my dear child from death does not fill me, as I supposed it would do, with joy. It makes me apprehensive. It makes me tremble for the future. It makes me think of others who are bereaved. It makes me desire to lessen every mourner's grief. Would, my friend, I could do something for you besides assure you of my sympathy![21]

In July, Christophoros Plato Castanis, one of the Greek orphan boys whom Howe had brought with him to the United States in 1828, presented a lyceum talk in Boston. The event was billed as "Greece, the First Garden of Liberty Struggling to Shake Off the Yoke of Turkish Tyranny." With Howe's support, Castanis had received an education at the Mount Pleasant Classical Institution in Amherst, Massachusetts. Beginning in the late 1840s, he began touring the nation dressed in Greek warrior attire. He had with him "the identical sword of Lord Byron," and he recounted his own experience of surviving the massacre of Scio. The four books he had written were offered for sale at the lecture. Although Howe had so vehemently objected to blind people using the speaker's platform to make a living, he did not object, it seems, to Castanis taking to the lecture circuit.[22]

In November, Howe was invited by Brown University to give the annual Phi Beta Kappa lecture at the university. For the prankster during his undergraduate days, the invitation must have come as a surprise but also as an affirmation of his renown as a teacher of the blind.

At the new school for "idiots," his lead teacher, James Richards, and the school's matron, Margaret McDonald, were not getting along. Richards was a bright young man and a skilled teacher; yet, before long Howe backed McDonald, and Richards eventually left to teach at the Pennsylvania School for the Feeble-Minded. By February 1849, Howe was once again feeling the effects of malaria. Mann was so worried about him that he wrote to his wife, "I have never contemplated the idea of Howe's dying before I should."[23] So that month Samuel and Julia journeyed to Northampton for the water cure, leaving Julia Romana and Flossy with the Hillards and taking baby Henry with them. Howe had a lifelong faith in the salubrious effects of hydrotherapy, even in the middle of a Massachusetts winter. A few years earlier, on taking the water cure at Saratoga Springs, New York, he had written, "You would be materially benefited I know, by the use of the waters, which would *astonish your bowels.*"[24]

In May Howe wrote Mann in Washington about the noon-day hanging of the convicted murderer Washington Goode. Goode was a black man. There was little question that his conviction had been just. But Howe expressed outrage that in the year 1849 the state of Massachusetts would still turn to capital punishment to deal with a crime, even a horrible crime like murder. Despite his indignation, Howe was relieved that three years later, in 1852, the Massachusetts General Court passed legislation that stipulated that the crimes of rape, arson, and treason would no longer be considered capital offenses but might now be punishable by life in state prison.[25]

By June, Boston was in the grip of a cholera epidemic. More than seven hundred people in the city, including several students and a teaching assistant at the Perkins Institution, eventually died from the disease. Because poor Irish immigrants in crowded neighborhoods were most likely to suffer from the disease, most of Boston's upper class associated cholera with what they believed was the dissipation of the Irish. Cholera sicknesses became so frequent that Julia encouraged friends to stay at Green Peace, where, she said, cholera had not struck.[26]

In the midst of sickness, Howe was called to municipal court to translate for two Greek immigrants who had been accused of horse thievery. The *Salem Gazette* reported that as Howe interpreted for one of the defendants who had addressed the court before his sentencing, "the tears began to roll from the interpreter's eyes, and the translation melted the court, bar officers, juries, and bystanders into simultaneous tears." The Greek thieves were given the lightest possible sentence. Howe's translation, and his tears, had had a good effect.[27]

Despite the cholera outbreak, Howe participated in a meeting at Tremont Temple in October of Boston citizens opposed to the use of navy flogging. With the other meeting participants, Howe, echoing his sentiments on the subject of capital punishment, argued that in a civilized society like the United States, there was no need for flogging. It was brutal and unnecessary and merely showed the mean-spiritedness of the flogger. Better methods were available to discipline sailors.

At the end of February 1850, Julia gave birth to her fourth child and third daughter, Laura Elizabeth, named for Laura Bridgman, now a young woman.

Like Henry's birth, it was an easy one. Julia had enjoyed tea with Theodore Parker that afternoon when she felt contractions. A nurse and Samuel were called to her bedside around nine that evening. Samuel left the room to complete a letter to Mann, saying he would return to the birthing room when he heard Julia cry out. Samuel's expectation made Julia determined not to cry out, and she did not. About ten thirty Laura was born, Samuel arrived to tie off the cord, "and everything was just right," Julia told her sister. But with four young children, even with servants, Julia's role as mother had truly become trying—everything indeed was not just right.[28]

New England and the nation suffered shattering political controversies in 1850. The Mexican War of 1846–48 had left the United States with large new territories open to the expansion of slavery. The Missouri Compromise of 1820 had already begun to unravel as a result of the war. Now with such huge western lands open for settlement, the earlier compromise seemed hardly adequate for the new realities. In December 1848 the discovery of gold in northern California had reached the eastern presses, exacerbating sectional tensions. Within a few months men were heading west to search for gold in California. Among the tens of thousands of Americans who set off for California hoping to strike it rich was Julia's brother Sam. This quick shift in population meant that the "forty-niners" were soon petitioning Congress for statehood for California. Suddenly, the question of slavery and its extension into the new territory taken from Mexico had immediate political and economic consequences. Would California enter the Union as a slave or a free state? How would its status be resolved? The Wilmot Proviso that had passed only in the House of Representatives in 1846 had indicated that the new territory acquired from Mexico would be free of slavery. But the proviso was not law. Still unresolved were two related issues: the slave trade in the District of Columbia and the enforcement of the 1793 Fugitive Slave Law's mandate for the return of fugitive slaves to their owners.

Through the spring and summer, Congress debated the issue of slavery in the new territories. On 1 March 1850 Howe wrote Sumner: "There is a dull & blameworthy indifference here to the wicked & dangerous work going on in Washington." Yet Howe assured Sumner that the indifference was merely a prelude to "some terrible quicknesses to the hearts & consciences of the people by some gross and palpable outrage" like "civil war in Kansas or servile war in the South."[29] A week later, on 7 March, Daniel Webster delivered a three-hour speech before the Senate that called for passage of Henry Clay's compromise bill on the slave issue, including a provision for the return of fugitive slaves to their owners. Most of the Whig elites of eastern Massachusetts—George Ticknor, Jared Sparks, Samuel A. Eliot, Benjamin R. Curtis, Nathan Hale, editor of the Whig's *Daily Advertiser,* and Edward

Everett—were pleased with the compromise and pleased with Webster. Even Howe's brother Joseph would add his name to the city's Webster Association, an organization that rallied behind the senator. The debate and the maneuvering of the legislation continued until September, when Congress passed several pieces of legislation that became known as the Compromise of 1850. The compromise had four provisions: balancing Texas, which had been admitted as a slave-holding state, California would enter the Union as the thirty-first state and as a free state; the citizens of the New Mexico and Utah territories would, at a future date, vote whether to join the Union as slave-holding or free states; the residents of the District of Columbia would be allowed to continue to own slaves, though the District was prohibited from further engagement in the slave trade; and by the provisions of the Fugitive Slave Law of 1850, all American citizens in the North and South were obligated to assist in the capture and return of runaway slaves to their owners in the South. The law most egregiously provided a captured fugitive slave with no trial by jury, only a hearing before a judge. No longer could fugitive slaves find refuge in the North; now Canada and Europe were the only safe destinations for runaway slaves. For many of the black population of Boston who were fugitives, the law became an immediate source of grave concern. Beginning that spring, individuals and families of black Bostonians left for Canada. In the process the city lost some of its most capable and militant antislavery citizens.[30] With an active Underground Railroad in the North, the provision that required Northern citizens to participate in the capture of fugitive slaves was especially galling to antislavery proponents. In Boston, beginning in the spring and reaching a crescendo in the fall of 1850, anger from abolitionists and antislavery forces directed their most acute wrath at the Fugitive Slave Law and at one of its leading sponsors, Daniel Webster.

Only one day after the Webster's speech, Mann wrote to his wife that Webster's life was a "vile catastrophe." While Boston was preoccupied with another Webster—the John White Webster, on trial for the gruesome murder of his Harvard Medical College colleague George Parkman—Daniel Webster quickly became a pariah among Boston antislavery citizens as they talked among themselves about the speech. On 21 March, Howe invited antislavery and abolitionist forces in the city to assemble at Faneuil Hall for a meeting to discuss "the recent speech of Mr. Webster." Although the meeting proved more an opportunity to denounce the compromise than to develop measures to protect fugitive slaves, it brought together antislavery men and women like Howe who were becoming doubtful of the Whig Party's ability to stand against the expansion of slavery. Traditional abolitionists such as Wendell Phillips were also at the meeting, thus merging, if tenuously, the two groups opposed to slavery. On 4 May the denunciation of Webster's speech reached a new level when Mann published a detailed criticism in the *Boston Daily Evening Transcript*. While friends like Howe were delighted by the letter, Mann soon found that the Boston Whig establishment was so displeased that they were ready to purge him from the party. Even his old friend from law school Edward G. Loring published a series of articles in the Whig *Daily Advertiser* that praised the new law and, in effect, denounced Mann's position. In November 1850 Mann ran not as a Whig but as a Free Soil candidate, winning the election by only forty-one votes.[31]

While the Compromise of 1850 was a uniting force among groups opposed to slavery, it was divisive elsewhere, including among Howe's circle of friends, where it led to the breakup of the Five of Clubs. Howe and Sumner were, in their actions and words, clearly opposed to Webster. And Longfellow, more out of his loyalty to his two friends than for any other reason, agreed quietly with that opposition. But Hillard and Felton supported Webster. For Hillard, Sumner's law partner, the professional break was gradual but decisive. Hillard had shared Sumner's antislavery views since the early days of their law partnership, but the attacks on Webster were more than he could bear. Furthermore, Hillard could not abide what he saw as Sumner's increasing interest in social change based on abolitionism and reformism. Although they would remain friends, the close relationship that had marked earlier years was gone. For Felton, a strong-willed man but with an equally strong sense of humor, the friendships lingered for a while, despite the differences. But when he published a letter in the *Advertiser* critical of Mann's attack on Webster, Mann asked Sumner to respond to Felton's criticism. As the exchange of printed letters using stronger and stronger words continued, relationships frayed. The Five of Clubs was never the same after Felton became one of the eight hundred signatories (including Oliver Wendell Holmes) to a letter supporting Webster's 7 March speech. Felton saw in Sumner's words arrogance and rigidity, and he could tolerate neither. Two years later, in a letter that he marked "burn up this letter, when read," Felton wrote Howe about his relationship with Sumner.

> I think you are mistaken, by a natural partiality for [Sumner], in judging of the temper of his political course, and in the view you take of his quarrel with me. *I did not break from him, but he broke from me*. . . . When he spoke of Felton as "drawn into the abyss of infamy" "so that it were better for that man that he had never been born" (I quote from memory, but you will find it even more strongly expressed in the printed speech in Faneuil Hall) and when he stigmatized Webster as a Traitor and worse than a murderer, he employed language wholly unfit to be used by a gentleman, of gentlemen: language that if sincere, makes any intercourse with those to whom it is applied disgraceful; and if not sincere, is inconsistent, of course, with honesty of purpose in

him who used it. Now, when I went to Washington, I passed a few days in Baltimore, on my way.[32]

Felton's assumptions may have been too harsh, for Sumner had written Howe at the beginning of the storm, "[I] hadn't the heart for the controversy with my ancient friend."[33] Sumner had supported Felton in 1844 and 1845 during the days of his wife, Mary's, illness and eventual death. Interestingly, Howe would remain cordial with each of the members of the Five of Clubs, but a break had occurred. Never again would the men enjoy times together in mutual friendship and admiration, reading and talking about literature and art. Slavery had destroyed yet another institution.[34]

Replacing the Five of Clubs for Howe—if not in intimacy at least in intensity—was the Bird Club. Organized after the passage of the Fugitive Slave Law by the East Walpole paper manufacturer Francis ("Frank") Bird, the club was made up principally of non-Garrisonian antislavery men in Boston. Howe had met Bird in the early 1850s because of their mutual interest in the *Boston Daily Commonwealth.* Among the club members, besides Bird and Howe, were John Andrew, Charles Sumner, George L. Stearns, Franklin Sanborn, James W. Stone, Edward Keyes, John G. Palfrey, William S. Robinson, Henry L. Pierce, Charles W. Slack, and Elizur Wright.[35] The club met on Saturday afternoons at 2:15, at first at Young's Hotel and later at the Parker House for dinner and talk about current political issues. The dinner cost one dollar, without wine, and a bit more with it. Usually between thirty and forty men attended. The club prided itself on having no president, no officers, and no rules, "nothing to hold it together but similar political and social affinities, and a common need and love of good fellowship." Virtually all of the members were aligned with the Free Soil Movement, most having come out of the Whig Party, but some had been aligned with antislavery Democrats, while others had identified themselves with the anti-immigrant Know Nothing Party. What they had in common, Howe claimed, was being "straight & impractical republicans."[36] As such the club was a place where Boston men of similar minds could hear about and discuss the latest happening in the antislavery movement.[37] The club also proved beneficial to Howe personally. Besides its camaraderie, the club provided Howe a friend in Frank Bird. Several decades younger than Howe, Bird became a close confidante, especially after the deaths of several of Howe's contemporaries.

In June 1850 Samuel and Julia left Boston for Europe, taking with them their two younger children, Harry and newborn Laura, along with Margaret McDonald (whom the children always referred to as Dee Dee), the matron of the idiot school, as nurse and housekeeper. The older children, Julia Romana and Florence would remain in Concord with the Edward Jarvis family. Samuel planned to return in early October for the fall term of the

Perkins Institution, but Julia would go on to Rome to be with Louisa and Annie. Julia Romana and Flossy would join their father on his return. The older daughters had never been separated for so long from their parents, but they knew the Jarvis family and, more especially, were friends with the older Jarvis children. The decision to travel to Europe, less than six years after their honeymoon trip, was somewhat impulsive. Julia wanted to be with her sisters. Louisa was in Rome and pregnant, and Annie had decided to visit there. Samuel, whose health continued to be poor, longed to be away from the responsibilities of the blind and idiot schools and to enjoy the mineral waters he expected to get in England and on the continent. Besides, there would be George Combe to spend time with. For the younger Howe children, Henry and Laura, there would be their much-loved Dee Dee, whom Laura remembered dressed in summer in pure white dimity. She had a "store-closet all full of glass jars, and the jars were full of cinnamon and nutmeg and cloves and raisins, and all manner of good things."[38]

The trip was more important for Julia, however, than for Samuel. Four babies in six years had taken its toll. Even with servants to tend to children, Julia's life had become dull and predictable. In May, she encapsulated her fatigue and indifference in a four-line ditty written to her sister Louisa.

> *Oh! that the sofa were my dwelling-place,*
> *With one big nigger for my minister!*
> *That I might all forget the Baby race,*
> *And, nursing no one, wallop only her!*[39]

The trip across the Atlantic went smoothly. The babies did well, especially Harry, who was just beginning to walk and, as Julia wrote her sisters, became the spoiled mascot of the ship's captain. Julia also reported finding interesting people on board, including the American actress Charlotte Cushman, who was heading to England after one of her acting engagements in the United States. Julia assured her sisters that she and Cushman had "become quite good friends."[40] Samuel reported to Sumner that Julia had been seasick for a few days but that he had been free of seasickness because of his careful diet. He described among the passengers Miss Hayes, who "takes brandy at lunch, whiskey punch before bed time, & . . . smokes *cigars,* not cigarettes, but real bona fide Havana cigars." A week later, at Great Malvern in Worcestershire, where he took the water cure, Samuel wrote Sumner to ask him to remind Jarvis to send frequent news about his children, about Laura Bridgman, and about happenings at the institution.[41]

While in London in July Samuel learned of the death of Zachary Taylor from cholera and the elevation of Millard Fillmore to the presidency. Not long thereafter the new president invited Daniel Webster to be his secretary of state. That same month Webster resigned from the Senate to accept Fillmore's offer, and in his place Robert C. Winthrop, the man who had defeated Howe in the congressional elections of 1846, was appointed to the Senate. Although no one at the time could have foreseen the outcome of these changes, it would eventually have important consequences for Howe and especially for Sumner. In April 1851, after three months of balloting, the Massachusetts General Court elected Sumner to replace Winthrop in the U.S. Senate. During the time, Sumner had carried the Massachusetts Senate and had consistently received the highest number of votes in the House, but not a majority. The decision had taken so long because a coalition of Free Soilers and Democrats had difficulty, despite the skillful and persistent maneuvering of Henry Wilson, coming to an agreement on Sumner. Howe, who had his doubts about the coalition, was nevertheless elated by his good friend's election. Whigs like Robert Winthrop, however, complained, "But I should find my stomach revolting from Sumner."[42] Now, three of Howe's closest friends—Mann, Sumner, and Palfrey—would be elected officials in Washington.

In August 1850 the Howes moved from London to Paris where Samuel renewed his friendship with Charles Sumner's brother George, who would shortly learn of the death of their youngest brother, Horace. Horace Sumner, along with Margaret Fuller, her husband, the Marchese Ossoli, their infant son, and several other passengers drowned on 18 July after the sinking of their ship in a storm off the coast of Fire Island, New York. Charles had gone to the sight of the wreckage in the vain hope of finding Horace, as had James Freeman Clarke in search of his cousin Margaret Fuller. Henry Thoreau and Ellery Channing had also gone to Fire Island hoping to find Fuller's manuscript on the history of the Roman Republic. Referring to his brother Horace as an "invalid," Charles Sumner wrote Howe about his visit to the site of the vessel's destruction and of the sadness of the loss of his brother. He also commented that he had read Mann's "notes on Webster" concerning the Compromise of 1850 and had found them to be well written, but as he put it, "too personal."[43]

While he was in Paris, Howe visited the schools for "idiots" at the Bicêtre and the Salpeterière. At the Bicêtre, he concluded that M. Vallée's much-commended success in educating "idiots" was actually the result of his pupils' being primarily epileptic rather than "idiotic." Howe credited Vallée with much talent and many skills, but he did not recognize that the school was for "idiots." At the Salpeterière, Howe observed a small school for "idiotic girls." "I found," he reported, "only a girl who was not particularly skilled in the art of instruction trying to teach some other girls to read & little else." He left

Paris not at all convinced that the reports about Parisian success in educating "idiotic" students were accurate.[44]

By the middle of August Julia and the children moved on to Italy to be with the Crawfords and Annie, all of whom had earlier in the month stayed with the Howes in Paris. Samuel gossiped in a letter to Sumner that both Crawford and George Sumner had acquired a belly, and that George had complained about not getting enough credit for his letter about the idiot schools at Paris.[45] Samuel remained at Boppard in the Rhineland taking another water cure. For much of the time he was in Paris, he had not been feeling well. To Sumner he confided, "Parting from Julia & my children & being left alone in the world (as it seemed) so affected me as to bring on a *crise des nerfs* & to prostrate me." But his mood was improving, and he assured Sumner, "I am now pulling up fast & have improved very much in strength, weight & vigour. I can eat my weight in any thing edible, climb the steepest crags, & warm up a wet sheet in very few minutes."[46] From Boppard he returned to Paris, and then moved on to London, where he met with George Combe. In the middle of October he sailed for Boston.

A School for "Idiots"

When he returned home to his two daughters and the blind school, Howe also came back to the newly opened school for "idiots." Howe's interest in the education of "idiots," which had begun in the mid-1840s in his exchange of letters with Samuel Woodward, was followed by the publication of Howe's letters in the *Boston Daily Advertiser* in 1845. Those letters had generated public curiosity, ridicule, and hope. On 22 January 1846 Rep. Horatio Byington of Stockbridge persuaded the Massachusetts House of Representatives to appoint a committee to inquire into the condition of the state's "idiots" and whether anything could be done to improve their circumstances. Having known of Howe's interest in the education of "idiots," in February, Byington wrote a long letter asking him for information about the needs of "idiots" that might be used by the legislative committee to gain state appropriations, perhaps for a school. On 12 March 1846 Howe responded in writing to Byington's request, and the committee included the response in its first report issued on 25 March. Howe was clear that the education of "idiots" was possible, and, furthermore, it was a duty of the state to educate its "idiotic children." He asked, "It is a saying with us that every child in the State has a right to be taught at the public expense, & shall we overlook or neglect those who are helpless children all their lives long?" For too long, Howe argued, "idiots" have merely been sent to almshouses where they have wasted away at public expense, when it is clear that they could learn and become productive members of society. Their gifts might be meager, but they have gifts. It was the duty of the state to educate these children so that they might become industrious and active citizens.[47]

On 11 April 1846, the Massachusetts General Court appointed a second committee to inquire into the conditions and needs of "idiots" in the state. On this occasion, the legislature named Howe as one of the three members of its new committee. Over the remainder of the year, Howe and Byington continued to discuss strategies to pass legislation and to secure appropriations for a school for "idiots." Each man knew that getting money from lawmakers would not be a simple task, especially about a cause that seemed to some legislators to be as quixotic as did the education of "idiots." The letter Howe received the following February from George Sumner in Paris about the school for "idiots" at the Bicêtre confirmed and expanded on John Conolly's reports on the success of educating "idiots." (Recall, however, that when Howe visited the French schools in Paris in August 1850, he was not impressed with the education he found there.) On 15 March the committee issued its second report, which included Sumner's letter. Howe was the author of that report.

On 8 May 1848, just as Howe was persuading Mann to defend the crew of the *Pearl,* Massachusetts governor G. A. Briggs signed legislation that established a three-year experimental school for "idiotic" children. The legislation did not assign the responsibility for operating the experimental school, but in August Howe agreed to begin a class of "idiotic children" at the Perkins Institution. Governor Briggs, who had no other options to house the new school, agreed to Howe's offer, and on 1 October 1848 the first pupil entered the school. By November, three men, including Mann, had agreed to serve on the board of trustees of the new idiot school. People around the nation began to notice what was happening in Massachusetts. In February 1849, for example, the *Southern Literary Messenger* published "Education of Idiots"; and in June the same journal published "Idiocy in Massachusetts" by Matilda F. Dana. In January 1851 the *Christian Examiner* published "Dr. Howe's Report on Idiocy" by George B. Emerson.[48]

In the eighteen months of the experimental school's existence, Howe demonstrated to legislators and to the curious public that his "idiotic" students could learn. On 4 April 1850, before the Howes left for Europe, the Massachusetts General Court approved the incorporation of a permanent school for "idiots" to be located at the Perkins Institution. Soon after Hervey B. Wilbur, a physician who had begun a private school for "idiots" in Barre, Massachusetts, wrote Howe about taking disabled pupils whom Wilbur could not accommodate. Because of the public discussion about educating "idiots," people who knew about them were becoming interested in having these children served. In June 1850, for example, John Greenleaf Whittier wrote an article in the *National Era,* in which he said, "All the pupils have more or less advanced. Their health and habits have improved, and there is no reason to doubt that the experiment . . . will be found to have been quite as successful as its most sanguine projectors could have anticipated."[49] With information about the Massachusetts idiot school in the press, the states of Connecticut, New York, Pennsylvania, and Illinois in the early 1850s began to debate the opening of a similar public educational facility in their states.

As he had for his blind pupils, Howe had insisted that only pupils who could learn would receive education at the idiot school. When one of his first pupils, Warren Crane Masten, did not show signs of learning, Howe sent him back to the almshouse at Walpole from which he had come. This policy continued into 1867 when he dismissed Cornelius McCanley, whose father was an acquaintance of Howe's friend Longfellow. "He would be comfort-ably housed, clothed and fed and be free from abuse at either" Deer Island for local paupers or Tewksbury for state paupers, Howe assured Longfellow. At the same time, he was interested early on about the possibility of boarding out some of his "idiotic students" to the homes of people in South Boston. In November 1850 he wrote his lead teacher, James B. Richards, about the idea. As Howe saw the matter, capable residents could learn at the institution but live near the school with an ordinary family during the day. Before he tried the experiment, he informed Richards and the parents of some of his pupils, he would invite the pupils to spend two weeks in his own home, where he would observe the daily interactions between the pupils and his family.[50] Growth in the population of South Boston during the 1840s made Howe's plan more feasible. Between 1840 and 1850, the population of South Boston rose from 6,176 to 13,309, more than a 100 percent increase in residents. This rise in population meant that there were more boarding houses available for his pupils.[51]

At the idiot school, the first classes of pupils learned elementary reading and writing. Always a champion of physical education and convinced that a weak mind was linked to a weak body, Howe also had his pupils engage in outdoor and indoor gymnastic activities. During other parts of the day, students participated in what today we would call arts and crafts, and Howe insisted also that his pupils learn a trade for a time after they left the school. Although he knew that not all his pupils were capable of holding full-time employment, he was concerned that students be prepared to return home to be as little a burden to their family and community as possible. In December 1850, after his return from Europe, he reported, "The experimental School for Idiots has been thus far very satisfactory. In eight out of ten cases, the improvement is very marked and decisive. Their filthy habits are corrected; they can control their evacuations; they observe the laws of decency; they can feed themselves, dress themselves, and do many things which they could not do before. They are gradually acquiring the use of speech, and some can read and count. The most we can expect to do is to correct all vicious and uncleanly habits, to make them observant of decency, to strengthen the body and give activity and dexterity to the limbs; and to train them to simple manual labour."[52]

After receiving a five-thousand-dollar appropriation from the state legislature in April 1850, Howe moved the idiot school out of the Perkins Institution to a home nearby. But as requests for admission to the school increased, the new and temporary facility proved to be inadequate. For a time in 1854 the school took over Green Peace and the Howe family moved back to the blind institution.[53] But with Julia pregnant again, it was the worst of all locations for the family. In 1856, after a visit to the idiot school, the legislature appropriated another twenty-five thousand dollars for a permanent home for the school on the condition that the school's trustees raise another five thousand dollars. Know-Nothing governor Henry Gardiner vetoed the bill, but the outcry was so great that the governor rescinded his veto. Especially surprising was the support of Caleb Cushing, the Whig-turned-Democrat and champion of proslavery politics. Cushing, representing Newburyport (William Lloyd Garrison's hometown) in the General Court, rose to the defense of additional funding for Howe's idiot school, much to Howe's surprise and gratitude.[54] Eventually the money was raised and the trustees purchased land for the idiot Massachusetts School for Idiotic and Feeble-Minded Youth between L and M Streets in South Boston. By October 1856 a new building was completed and at last the school had its first permanent home, into which all pupils had fully moved by January 1857. The pupils of the new facility, like their blind counterparts, enjoyed bathing in the sea water in summer months. Although it was clearly now separated from the Perkins Institution, the idiot school was within an easy walking distance of the blind facility. When he was in town, Howe made a daily visit to the idiot school.[55] When he was away from South Boston for extended periods, Edward Jarvis would come from Concord to superintend the school.

In November 1857, Howe delivered an address at the ceremonial laying of the cornerstone for the new institution for "feeble minded" children at Media, Pennsylvania. Dorothea Dix, who had been involved in the founding of the school, had been expected to attend, but because of illness, she was unable to be a part of the event. Joseph Parrish, superintendent of the new school, was there, as were Hervey B. Wilbur, superintendent of the newly opened New York State Asylum for Idiots at Syracuse, and George Brown, who had taken over Wilbur's private school at Barre, Massachusetts. There was a spirit of hope and perfectionistic zeal in the air. If society willingly cared for its lowliest members, Howe told the audience, then surely human beings were reaching a point of high civilization. Massachusetts, New York, and now Pennsylvania had founded schools for the weak minded, and Connecticut and Illinois were contemplating similar institutions.[56] Progress and liberality were marching forward.

> Upon what ground, then, shall we put the appeal in [idiots'] favor? Clearly, upon the broad grounds of humanity—upon the fact that they are human and helpless—we, human and strong.
>
> Your community is civilized enough to hear and admit this claim. There has been some organized effort among you for years in behalf of this unfortunate class, and the building which is to be reared upon the foundations you this day lay will be one of the results of those efforts.
>
> The material structure, however, will be small account compared with the principles upon which your institution shall be conducted. . . .
>
> We must recollect that public charitable institutions, as they are called, are in many respects social evils, and only to be tolerated as long as they remedy or lessen greater evils.
>
> While we recognize the facts that idiocy constitutes one of the present phenomenal conditions of our race—that of every million children born a certain number are idiots—that this will doubtless continue for some generations—we must still bear in mind that this phenomenal condition is not inherent and essential, and not necessarily permanent.[57]

Opposing Slavery and Other Reforms

In a letter Samuel sent Julia in Rome after his return to Boston, he told her about a fellow passenger, a lawyer from New York in the stateroom opposite him who had become ill and soon appeared to be in "a dying state." He had no friends or acquaintances on board, so Samuel attended him. "I was with him, and nursed him, and cheered him all I could, and read the bible to him, and so raised his spirits and his hopes of reaching his family, that he rallied and was better during three days, then he began to sink." When the man died, and Samuel argued that his body must be delivered to his family in New York. But his argument was to no avail; the man's body was sent down into the sea. The man was about Samuel's age. He was married, and like Samuel, had four children. "He left home hardly more ill than I had been," Samuel wrote. Life is short and tenuous, he confided to Julia.

Samuel's letter also contained the news that on his visit to Julia's uncle John Ward in New York, Samuel had found him pale and thin but "in good spirits and very kind and genial." The next day when he went to Concord to pick up their older daughters from the Jarvis household, Flossy had come running out of the house shouting, "Papa, Papa." Samuel wrote: "She was in my arms in a moment, and soon Julia was there also, and my heart took its feast of affection, and I wept for joy as freely as ever I have wept for sorrow. . . . I have been with them four days, and yet they hang round me all the time. They kiss me every moment and seem willing to give up any play to come and love me." He reported to Julia how the girls had grown and matured in their absence. He planned to spend the winter at Green Peace with his daughters.[58]

Julia remained in Rome until after the birth of her sister Louisa's child, Mary Crawford. While she remained in the ancient city, Julia developed a close friendship with Horace Binney Wallace, an American would-be poet and follower of the French philosopher Saint Simon. Unlike Samuel, Wallace understood Julia's passion for the life of an artist, her desire for expression, and her need for public recognition and affirmation. At a time when women's proper place was considered to be the home, and certainly not the marketplace, the legislative hall, or the lecture circuit, Wallace saw Julia for who she was and for who she hoped to become. There is no evidence of a physical relationship, but they became close. Julia returned to Boston with the younger children in early September 1851. When she learned in January 1853 that Wallace had committed suicide the previous December, she dressed in black. Samuel and Julia had been apart for nearly a year; not long after her return Julia was in mourning for a man her husband hardly knew.[59]

Howe had only just arrived back in Boston when he heard about the potential capture of two fugitive slaves, William and Ellen Craft. On 25 October 1850, he brought the news to Theodore Parker that slave hunters had obtained warrants for the Crafts' arrest and return to Georgia. The Boston Vigilance Committee had just formed, and the cause of the Crafts seemed a perfect test of the committee's resolve to frustrate the new Fugitive Slave Law. Soon handbills describing the slave hunters were distributed around Boston. Mobs of citizens began to harass them. At his home, Parker married the fugitive couple and kept them in hiding. He also gave firearms to William. By the first week in November, the Crafts were sailing for England and freedom. The Vigilance Committee was proud of its work. It had successfully rescued two human beings from the clutches of slavery, and it had done so with no bloodshed.[60]

On 15 February 1852, the Vigilance Committee became involved in the case of a runaway slave named Shadrach Minkins. Minkins had escaped from Virginia in 1850 and was working as a waiter in a Boston restaurant. On the day of the committee's first meeting, federal marshals had arrested Minkins and placed him in custody. But shortly thereafter, primarily black members of the committee rescued Minkins from his cell and put him on a train to Montreal. As a test of the new Fugitive Slave Law, the rescue of Shadrach Minkins proved an embarrassment to the Fillmore administration as well as an embarrassment to Daniel Webster. With the escapes of the Crafts and of Minkins, federal and state authorities took greater care and stronger measures to carry out the Fugitive Slave Law.

Two months later, on 9 April, the Vigilance Committee was called together at Tremont Temple to protest another fugitive slave abduction. The runaway slave was Thomas Sims. Sims had escaped in February by stowing away on a ship leaving Savannah on route to Boston. Slave hunters representing Sims's Georgia owner had Boston officials arrest the slave. At the Vigilance Committee meeting tempers were high. According to Thomas Wentworth Higginson's memory of the event, Howe was ready for revolution. Plans were prepared for a rescue, but officials made sure that they did not have a repeat of the escape of Shadrach Minkins. On 12 April two hundred Boston police and volunteers escorted Sims to a waiting ship that took him back to Georgia.[61] On his return to Georgia, Sims was publicly whipped as a warning to other slaves.[62] The Minkins and Sims fugitive slave episodes took place as the Massachusetts General Court was deciding the senatorial seat that in April would go to Charles Sumner. Both events, no doubt, affected the outcome, because the coalition of Free Soil members and Democrats in the House finally arrived at a decision that put Sumner in the U.S. Senate.

During 1851, Howe became the editor of the Free Soil newspaper the *Boston Daily Commonwealth.* From the beginning of its publication, the paper, like its predecessor, the *Republican,* was in financial trouble.[63] Over the three years of its life, it nearly folded at least twice. But one of the paper's first tasks was the public support of Sumner's candidacy for the Senate, which during the winter and spring was before the Massachusetts General Court. To find material for the paper, Howe turned to his friends; Mann, Palfrey, Parker, and Sumner supplied articles. After her return to Boston, Julia also contributed articles to the paper. She told Annie that she enjoyed her "various squibs and spays," as well as the praise that Holmes was giving her articles in his lyceum lectures.[64] Eventually Samuel dealt with the political matters of the paper, and Julia with social and literary matters. But when Samuel was sick, Julia took over responsibility for editing the entire paper. And from time to time, Samuel even contributed articles about the arts. He wrote, for example, about an unnamed black singer who some critics claimed had a voice more powerful and original than the voice of Jenny Lind, who at the time was performing in Boston. A comment Howe made to Sumner about the singer reveals an attitude about race that was typical even of slavery opponents of the time. "My theory," he said, "is that however much of melody the blacks may have, & they have much[,] they have not the *fibre* & the nerve ever to generate magnetism enough to electrify a large audience. It is not merely Lind's music, it is partly her animal magnetism that charms."[65] Free Soil in its orientation, the paper became an important, though short-lived, journal for antislavery forces in Boston who remained within the framework of political action. Unlike the Garrisonians, the readers of the *Boston Daily Commonwealth* tended to be Free Soil New Englanders who saw politics as a way of resisting slavery, and especially of protecting the fugitive slave.

Howe also used the newspaper to advocate for the Hungarian patriots and statesmen Lajos Kossuth and Ferenc Pulszky, whose independence movement had been crushed by the Austrian Empire. Kossuth began touring the United States in late 1851 and continued through 1852, hoping to receive financial support for his revolutionary efforts. Pulszky spent time in 1853 as a visitor of the Howes. Although Howe and others in the nation were sympathetic to the aspirations of the Hungarians, the Monroe Doctrine inhibited U.S. support for their cause. Nevertheless, Kossuth and his talkative wife became friends of the Howes. The Kossuths and Pulszky spent many evenings at Green Peace, sometimes chatting in English but usually conversing in French with the Howes and with many of their friends. On one occasion, the guests included Theodore Parker, James Lowell, George Sumner (recently back from Paris), Henry and Fannie Longfellow, Richard Henry and Sarah Dana, and Catharine Sedgwick. After dinner, the Howes brought in Laura Bridgman, and the conversation moved from her education to the exploits of Kossuth in Hungary. Howe was struck by Kossuth's aversion to killing animals merely for sport, while Howe's young daughter Florence was taken by Kossuth's top hat with its unusual black feather, an extravagance unimaginable in proper Boston.[66]

Charles Sumner delivered his inaugural speech before the U.S. Senate on 9 December 1851. It was a resolution welcoming Kossuth to the nation. But Sumner went beyond the resolution to comment on the United States' noninterference in the conflicts among European nations. The speech echoed his 4 July 1845 speech condemning the Mexican War. As a gesture of respect and friendship, Sumner sent Howe a copy of the speech. On 28 December Howe responded with a lengthy letter in which he expressed some of his strongest criticism to one of his closest and dearest friends. Howe had praised Sumner for his 1845 address, but six years later his perspective had changed, principally because of the revolutionary activities of 1848 and 1849. To Howe, Sumner's call for peaceful noninterference was a call for an end to a battle for freedom that had begun with the American and Greek Revolutions and continued with the revolutions of 1848 and 1849. Although Howe hated war, his view of human progress did not preclude the use of armed force. Thus, Howe reminded Sumner, peace is a noble achievement among human beings. But human beings are not driven by principles alone; they are also driven by feelings and instincts. Over the course of history, tyrants have used calls for peace, in the name of law and order, to suppress people and to keep them in bondage. Although all civilized men strive for peace, peace should never become the tool of oppression. People have the power and can use force when they have no other recourse to secure their freedom, especially in the face of tyranny and despotism. "Why tell the Despots," Howe asked, "that under *no circumstances* will we ever resort to the kind of interference which *alone* they fear, or care much for?"[67]

Eighteen months later Howe wrote another letter to Sumner, this time to encourage him to show leadership in the Free Soil movement. He admonished his friend, "Now you, and you alone among [politicians], are able to be the exponent and defender of the principles and the *morals* of the Free-soil party—of the free Democracy. Depend upon it, that [the] party is sound at the core, and it will answer from the heart and from the *conscience* to an appeal from you, in a way that will astonish those who imagine that they are not only the leaders but the owners of the party. . . . [Most of] our party would say amen to any declaration like this—let our basis of representation be respect for man, *as man,* and not as villager, townsman or city man; let other things be considered duly, but let no consideration of expediency, so thought of how the coming election may be affected, no regard for temporary effect, induce us to violate a plain rule of right." Howe concluded, "All men are *equal* as well as free, and let us not ask what advantages or what disadvantages of wealth or position a man may have; as poverty shall not disfranchise him, so wealth shall not."[68]

Although increasingly more of his time was spent on antislavery affairs, Howe remained involved in other reforms. In November 1853, for example, he wrote Foster Hooper, chairman of the board of trustees of the state lunatic asylum at Worcester. As a board member, Howe had received comments about the poor conditions at the institution. Like other facilities of its kind, the Worcester hospital was overcrowded. More and more community poorhouses and families were requesting that the asylum take local residents. Howe, who inspected the hospital during the day and at night, saw that with greater numbers of inmates, the Worcester facility had less staff time to focus on the treatment of patients and thus had more pressure to become custodial. Howe's letter to Hooper was strong. Each of its short paragraphs began, "I protest." Howe protested that patients were in the courtyard of the institution. Some were on benches or even the bare ground, simply lying about idly. They were involved in no activities; they had nothing to do, no distractions, and certainly no treatment. Howe protested that male patients were sometimes in the women's wards. With his concern for heredity, he worried about the consequences of the intermixing of the sexes. Howe protested that the facility had poor drainage and poor ventilation. The odors at the hospital were strong, and the inadequate sewage and ventilation systems aggravated an already bad situation. Howe protested the lack of employment and recreational opportunities for the patients. From his perspective, the best place for Worcester patients was back in the community. If patients were going to have a chance to re-acclimate to communities, they would need to acquire social and occupational skills that they had best be taught at the hospital as a part of their plan of treatment. Howe was committed to recovery as the primary purpose of the hospital. What he saw, what he feared in 1853 was custodialism.[69]

Howe also became involved with a proposed state reformatory school for wayward girls. In 1850, after his return from Europe, state representative William Appleton asked Howe for his opinion about such a school. Massachusetts already had the House of Reformatory for boys in South Boston not far from the Perkins Institution, so Appleton and other elites sought a facility for girls. At the time, Howe was a director of the board of the boys' reformatory. On Christmas Day 1850 Howe wrote Appleton a long letter in which he explicated his opposition to a state reformatory for girls. But the letter remained unpublished, and the state made no effort to establish the facility. Three years later, however, a group of commissioners were again considering the development of a girls' reformatory school. This time Howe wrote the commissioners about his opposition and published his letter along with his 1850 letter to Appleton.[70] Because Howe had been a director of the boys' reformatory, his letter carried weight. To Horace Mann in 1851, he summarized his original position: "My ground is that we should not build a great Central House of Reformation and gather the girls there, because the principle ought to be that of separation and diffusion, not of congregation of vicious persons, because the girls will be exposed to public gaze, and get the character of bad girls, and learn to think themselves such."[71]

Howe's position followed from his 1844–45 views about the two forms of prison, congregate and separate. For Howe, who always rejected custodialism, congregating girls into one large and centralized facility was the worst possible policy. Although there were, no doubt, some "vicious" girls whose constitutions placed them beyond the hope of reform, the vast majority of fallen girls were amenable to reform, if reform was provided. Institutions often looked good on the outside with their massive and imposing architecture and their well-kept grounds, but on the inside these large institutions were usually the breeding ground for wrongdoing, Howe insisted. The character of wayward girls could go to the good or to the bad. Most girls were in the large category that Howe identified as open to good environmental influences. Their moral identity was formed not at birth but in the daily exchanges they had with other people in their various social encounters. Girls who grew up among law-abiding, upright people would most likely become decent women; girls who grew among lawbreakers would most likely become fallen women. Large congregate institutions only made the prospect of the latter more likely.

The simplest and most cost effective way that the Commonwealth of Massachusetts could provide reform for its wayward girls, Howe believed, was through a system of what today we call foster care. Under such a system, girls would be placed in the homes of ordinary, upright families who would instruct them in proper morals and social graces. Rather than being incarcerated in a central institution, the girls would be widely distributed throughout the state. To ensure that the system worked well, the state would appoint a superintendent and a matron to place the girls among Massachusetts families. Workers under the supervision of the superintendent would periodically visit the girls in their foster homes to inquire about their behavior and moral rectitude and insure their well-being and safety. To prevent the girls from being used as household servants, Howe insisted that the families be paid a stipend of fifty to one hundred dollars a year for the training and supervising they would be doing. Anticipating labeling theorists by a hundred years, Howe argued that the girls would leave their foster families to become ordinary members of society. Yet if they were to leave from an institutional reformatory, they would be forever marked by their association with the institution. Although some citizens might object to the cost of the annual stipend for the families who take in the girls, Howe claimed that the stipends and the pay for the inspecting workers would be far less than the costs of building and maintaining a large facility like a public reformatory. Besides, large institutions, especially those that congregated socially devalued people, always became mere training grounds for deviance and greater devaluation. As he had argued and would continue to argue, Howe stood for decentralized and dispersed social services.

In late December 1853, Ticknor, Reed, and Fields published forty-six of Julia's poems in a collection entitled *Passion Flowers*. Within weeks of its publication, Samuel, who apparently knew nothing about the poems before their publication, sent letters to his friends asking what they thought of the poems. Sumner responded that he considered the collection "a work of genius" and declared, "The genius is rare." Samuel's old acquaintance Nathaniel Willis, who acknowledged that he had read only a few of the poems, published in reviews and in newspapers, assured Samuel that Julia's poems were of the highest quality. At first none of Samuel's friends seemed to see (or at least to reveal to him) that several of the poems suggest a woman struggling with domestic discord. And from what Samuel wrote to his friends, there is little indication that Samuel was initially disturbed by the poems. John Greenleaf Whittier's January 1854 review in the *National Era* seemed to have assured him that the anonymously published poems, whose authorship was known to virtually everyone in Boston, was a respected and respectable collection. Besides, with a third edition of the poems coming out in March 1854, Julia was destined to make nearly two hundred dollars from the sales of the book, and Samuel was never one to despise income.

It is hard to know whether Samuel ever learned of the question that Nathaniel Hawthorne, who praised the poems highly, posed about the collection, "What does her husband think of it?"[72] Yet by the spring and again pregnant, with her fifth child, Julia reported to her sister Annie, "[Chev] has been in a very dangerous state, I think very near insanity," adding in another letter, "Chev is as cold and indifferent to me as a man can well be. I sometimes suspect him of having relations with another woman."[73] It is quite likely that Samuel finally read the collection of poems or heard unsettling rumors about them and became resentful and angry. Around this time Julia told her sisters that Samuel had talked about divorce. Almost no letters between the couple during the early and mid-1850s have survived. We know from Julia's letters to her sisters that in these years Julia found little love and comfort in the marriage.[74]

Free Soil and the Massachusetts Emigrant Aid Company

During those difficult mid-1850s, Florence and Julia Romana attended the Stevenson School in Boston. Five days a week they rode the omnibus from South Boston into the city and back again. Their classmates regarded them as odd because their parents were identified with the Free Soil Party. Florence remembered their being called "Little Free-dirters" to the roaring laughter of the children.[75] In January 1852, Howe reported to Sumner in Washington that the Free Soil Party was defunct, "or at least sleeping." But he expressed gratitude that Ralph Waldo Emerson, in a lecture Howe had attended the night before, had "sent several hot shots right into the ribs of hunkerism."[76] Soon the Free Soil movement would take on a new urgency.

At the beginning of 1854, the U.S. Congress began to discuss the fate of the Kansas and Nebraska territory. Following the debate about the territory won from Mexico, the issue about the latter territories had to do principally with slavery. Would slavery become part of the social and economic fabric of the new territories? And as potential new states, would the fate of the territories affect the balance of power between slave-holding and free states in the U.S. Congress?

The fate of Kansas and Nebraska had its implications in the territories and before the Congress, but the question of how Kansas and Nebraska would enter the Union also had profound implications in New England. Traditional Whig elites like Abbott Lawrence, Amos Adams Lawrence, and John Murray Forbes—men who had supported Webster in 1850—had begun to see that, with a Congress favoring the interests of the cotton South, the manufacturing interests of the North would soon suffer. What had been loyalty to Webster and compromise with the South began in 1854 to give way to antislavery sentiment among elites like the Lawrences and Forbes. As these and other wealthy manufacturers and merchants shifted their perspectives, they also began to put their money into supporting antislavery causes. Although never Garrisonian abolitionists, New Englanders like the Lawrences and Forbes, along with other Whigs like Howe's friend the wealthy industrialist and merchant George L. Stearns, were willing to add their names and especially their money to the cause of keeping Kansas and Nebraska free of slavery. Their antislavery perspective in 1854 had more to do with their concern for the protection of free labor, which, as they had recently come to see it, was threatened by the South's system of chattel slavery.[77]

In February 1854, using funds supplied by Amos Adams Lawrence, Howe joined other Free Soilers to form the Massachusetts Emigrant Aid Company. The purpose of the company was to encourage New Englanders to emigrate to Kansas. The territory bordered Missouri, where slavery flourished and where slave interests were determined to keep Kansas open to slavery. Howe and other Free Soilers were just as determined to keep the state free of slavery. By offering support for New Englanders to emigrate to the Kansas territory, where they awaited inexpensive farm land—far better than the land available in rocky New England—the Boston Free Soilers tried to shift the Kansas population balance in favor of antislavery interests. On 16 February, the Free Soil convention aroused the interests and passions of increasingly more Bostonians for the antislavery cause.[78]

No cause turned more New Englanders to antislavery than two occurrences during the third week of May. On 22 May the U.S. Congress, over the objections of Sumner and most of the delegation from New England, passed the Kansas–Nebraska Act, which had been shepherded through the Congress principally by Illinois senator and Democrat Stephen Douglas, and on May 30 President Franklin Pierce signed the legislation. Two days later after the passage of the act, a twenty-three-year-old fugitive slave named Anthony Burns was arrested in Boston. The arrest led to a riot on Friday, 26 May and to a meeting that filled Faneuil Hall that evening.

Early in the afternoon before the Faneuil Hall meeting, the Vigilance Committee, about two hundred men, met at the Tremont Temple. Because of the questionable legality of the committee and the meeting under the Fugitive Slave Law, attendance was carefully monitored by the committee's leadership. Howe proposed a plan of rescue that required a group of fifty or so men to proceed immediately to the Court House to demand that Burns be turned over to the group. If the marshal refused to release Burns, the group would use force to retrieve him. Although some members of the committee supported Howe's plan, the majority rejected it, preferring instead to await the judge's decision on the matter. The meeting ended with a commitment of the members to "wait and see" how the process developed and to prepare for a meeting the next evening.[79]

The headlines in the *Boston Herald* on the day after the Faneuil Hall meeting were "Immense Meeting in Faneuil Hall" and "Tremendous Excitement." Among the speakers were Wendell Phillips, Francis Bird, Theodore Parker, and Samuel G. Howe. Faneuil Hall was packed with men in the auditorium and many women in the galleries. Trains and wagons had brought several hundred people from Worcester and Concord to join the throng. Officers were elected to the Vigilance Committee with Howe, one of the several vice presidents. By the time Howe reached the podium the crowd had worked itself into cheers of "Fight!" and "Down with the Tyrants!" When it was his turn to speak, Howe reminded the audience that the seal of the Commonwealth of Virginia, the state to which Burns might be forced to return, reads, "Resistance to tyrants is obedience to God." He then quoted the seventeenth-century political theorist Algernon Sidney, "That which is not just is not law, and that which is not law is not to be obeyed." The South had resolved not to keep faith with freedom; therefore, the North in the name of freedom and the living God must never keep faith with slavery. Howe proposed a resolution that the assembled audience approved with loud cheers: Every man should be a free man, and the freedom of each man represents God's will. By implication, Howe claimed, to deny freedom to a fugitive slave from Virginia was to deny God's will for that and any other man.[80]

Despite the best efforts of the attorney Richard Henry Dana and the protests of Boston's black and white antislavery forces, Suffolk County Judge Edward Greely Loring on June 2 ruled that Burns be remanded to his master for return to Virginia, and under the riotous circumstances ordered the U.S. marshal to send him immediately south. Angry and disappointed, Howe wrote Theodore Parker a short note on the evening of the decision: "I must go or choke in this disgraced & degraded community. I am sick at heart, & sick in body. But one thing I want done. Draw up a brief, terse strong address to E. G. Loring stating that the community has lost confidence in him, that we cannot trust our orphans to the charge of such a man. Put it round at once for signatures. If done *now*, it will receive the signatures of a great majority of the people."[81]

Two weeks later when Howe wrote to Mann, who had recently become president of Antioch College in Ohio, about the Burns affair, he was just as angry but, with the turn toward more and more antislavery sentiment, he was also a bit more optimistic. Howe knew that "Ned" Loring had been a law school classmate of Mann's at the Litchfield Connecticut Law School and later the two men had been close friends in Boston, where they both practiced the law. That friendship ended in 1850 when they took different public positions on the Fugitive Slave Law. Mann had been surprised and affronted by Loring's articles in the Whig *Daily Advertiser* expressing unequivocal support for the 1850 law. Howe wrote:

> As it is, poor Burns has been the cause of a great revolution. You have no idea of the change of feeling here. Think of Sam'l A. Eliot, the hard, plucky and "sort of honest" Eliot, coming out for repeal of Nebraska or disunion!
>
> Things are working well. God will get the upper hand of the Devil, even in Boston, soon. As for Loring—old Ned Loring, whom you loved, and who, for a while you *boosted* up on your shoulders into a moral atmosphere, he has sunk down, and will die in the darkness of despotic surroundings. I wrote him, and talked with him before the decision; I have had a letter from him since, but it is a hard and heartless one. I have liked him much; and am loth [*sic*] to lose the last of my association in that circle; but I must. If he is white, I am blacker than hell; if he is right, I am terribly wrong.[82]

On 4 July 1854, responding to the Kansas–Nebraska Act and the Anthony Burns affair, William Lloyd Garrison burned a copy of the U.S. Constitution, declaring the document "a covenant with death and an agreement with hell."[83] On the same day, Henry David Thoreau delivered his speech "Slavery in Massachusetts" to a Framingham audience. A week later Howe's newspaper, the *Boston Daily Commonwealth,* reported that the first group of settlers sponsored by the Massachusetts Emigrant Aid Company would move to the Kansas territory.

On 14 July Howe began a correspondence with William M. Langhorne of Lynchburg, Virginia. Langhorne had written Howe on 29 June and again on 3 July. In the first letter he said he had contacted his local state representative to gain permission to educate blind slaves to read, write, and play musical instruments. Many of his friends considered Langhorne's idea to be "an idle and visionary scheme," but he was determined to give blind slaves some useful occupation. "I believe," he said, "there is scarcely an owner of such a servant that would not gladly clothe and board him for twelve months and permit him to remain a term of years provided they were satisfied he would be well taken care of and returned a tolerably good mechanic and performer on one or more musical instrument." Langhorne ended the letter with the claim, "Negroes have fine taste for music and I will esteem any information that will further my object a special favour."[84]

The irony of the arrival of this letter shortly after the Burns affairs must have struck Howe. Burns, whose sight was perfect, was sent back to slavery in Virginia, while blind slaves in Lynchburg had a champion who wished to teach them the skills that slaves like Burns were otherwise prohibited from learning. Laws in Virginia made it illegal to teach a black person to read and write, and the assumption of the day was that slaves of African descent were naturally musical. To teach a slave to read and write was simply illegal, and why should a black slave receive instruction in music? In his first response to Langhorne, Howe began by saying that he had no way of knowing whether Langhorne's scheme for educating blind slaves would succeed. He said he had only limited knowledge about the capacity of black people to learn and acknowledged his doubts: blacks may not have great abilities to learn. Nevertheless, he added, "like all of God's children however they have capacities capable of improvement. He forbids us to bury even the one poor talent in a napkin; & He will reward you for any honest & earnest effort in behalf of the unfortunate even if it should not be crowned with earthly success."[85]

Two years later, in September 1856, Howe again wrote Langhorne about his scheme for educating blind slaves. He was blunt but kind.

> You ask me whether in my opinion "you would not take from northern fanaticism a potent weapon by a vigorous & systematic plan of moral & religious instruction of our (your) negroes." I answer that any plan for the moral elevation of the blacks must have a higher motive than that of human favor or disfavor. Never mind what fanatics in the North who would give to slaves their freedom may say; never mind what fanatics in the South who would deny them freedom may say; but go on, in God's name, & give to the negroes moral & religious instruction.
>
> But, in order that they may obey the Scripture command, & be able to give a reason for the faith that is in them, —enlighten their understandings; improve all their faculties; teach them to reason; to understand all the laws of God whether revealed in his book of nature or in the Bible; to know their rights & their duties, & the rights & duties of others. Do not bury their good talent in a napkin, but improve & multiply it. Do to them as you do to your own children; develop all the moral and all the mental faculties which God has implanted in them (& to smother which is quenching the spirit) train them up to the practice of all the virtues, including self respect & a determination to wrong no man & let no man wrong them; do all this and the blessing of Heaven will rest upon you. If thus enlightened—thus trained—the negroes, on arriving at man's estate—choose to work for the whites without

wages; choose to be considered as chattels; to be bought & sold as cattle are— to be deprived of all those rights which you value so highly—why, then, they may do so, at their own dreadful peril & cost, for it would be selling what they ought to maintain to the last gasp of their lives.

Until you have done all this you should not conclude, as you seem to do that they do not want to be free; anymore than you would take a white child of eight or ten years old & assert that because he said he preferred to be always a child & depend upon you, he therefore renounced the glorious privilege of coming to manhood calling no man master, & bowing down to God alone.

Remember you keep your slaves in mental childhood; you do not help them develop to the uttermost the mental faculties which God gave—as he gives every thing to be used & improved.

Howe added a closing sentence in which he admitted to Langhorne, "Look at this matter, my dear Sir, from the stand point of high humanity—of reason—of Christianity[,] not the *letter* but the spirit of Christianity, & I think some scales will fall from your eyes—they have mine, for I did not always think as I do now about it.[86]

The Question of Kansas

In late June 1854 William Ellsworth, a blind pupil, started a fire that could easily have burned down the Perkins Institution. Howe and several attendants caught the fire before it got out of hand. By the first of August Howe had sent William back to his father. More than any other hazard, Howe feared fire at the institution. With a facility filled with blind students, students who set fires could not be tolerated. That autumn, with Julia pregnant again with her fourth daughter, Maud, the four Howe children came down with the measles. Even with help from servants, the stress on Julia was great. Samuel helped bathe the children to lower their fevers and help them rest. In September the Howes printed the last edition of their newspaper, the *Boston Daily Commonwealth*. Subscriptions and advertisements were simply not large enough to sustain the Free Soil paper.

On 28 July 1854 the first group of immigrants sponsored by the Massachusetts Emigrant Aid Company arrived in the Kansas territory and soon thereafter founded the city of Lawrence, named for Amos Adams Lawrence, whose Cotton Whig proclivities had never been as strong as his father's and were now behind him. The Kansas–Nebraska Act had brought Lawrence into the antislavery movement. His sentiments were now firmly established, and his largess was helping to make Kansas immigration possible. Howe turned to Lawrence, who had been a generous supporter of the Perkins Institution, to provide financial assistance to the free-soil immigrants.

Back in Boston in October Howe organized a series of lectures by speakers who had different perspectives on various topics associated with slavery. Howe invited William Lloyd Garrison to speak, but Garrison refused to participate in what he saw as a series that would include speakers who considered the possibility that slavery was appropriate. A letter Howe wrote to Theodore Parker saying he had tried to include all known perspectives in the series suggests that Parker had criticized Howe for not including more Garrisonians.[87] Howe also extended an invitation and an offer of a one-hundred-dollar speaker's fee to Pierce Butler, the slave-owning senator from South Carolina.[88] Eventually Wendell Phillips, Ralph Waldo Emerson, Moncure Conway, Edwin P. Whipple, and Frederick Douglass agreed to deliver speeches, as did the proslavery spokesmen General Sam Houston and Senator Robert Toombs of Georgia. To his host's surprise, Toombs insisted on meeting Theodore Parker at his home.[89] When he lectured on 10 February 1855, Douglass dined with the Howes at Perkins Institution, where the family had once again settled as it awaited renovations to Green Peace.

On 12 March 1855, at Julia Romana's eleven birthday party, Samuel, Julia, Flossy, and Laura preformed "The Three Bears," to the roaring laughter and applause of Julia Romana's friends. In the role of "Papa Bear," Chev was loud and gruff, and he made all of the children both laugh and feel a little afraid, especially when he roared at dark-haired Flossy, playing Goldilocks. In the midst of Kansas happenings, ordinary family life for the Howes went on.

Settlement in Kansas continued, and in August 1855, the first Kansas convention of Free Soilers gathered at Lawrence and attendees called for the election of delegates to a free-state constitutional convention. A few days later, on 16 August, Wilson Shannon replaced Andrew Reeder as the territorial governor of Kansas, and on 5 September free-state representatives met at Big Springs to form the Kansas Free State Party. On 23 October in Topeka, Free Soilers drafted the "Topeka Constitution," which, among other things, prohibited slavery in the Kansas Territory, and they elected Charles Robinson as their territorial governor. With competing territorial governors and the mixed interests of proslavery and antislavery forces in Kansas, the moment was ripe for conflict. Into this brewing factional divide came abolitionist John Brown and his sons to Osawatomie in late October.

By November Kansas had begun to bleed. Proslavery supporters of Franklin Coleman killed Charles Dow, a Free Soiler, initiating two weeks of fighting that became known as the "Wakarusa War." Proslavery forces near Lawrence also killed Thomas W. Barber, and Free Soil Kansans added an exclusionary clause to the Topeka Constitution that prohibited "negroes and mulattoes" from entering Kansas. (In Kansas as in much of the free states, antislavery did not necessarily translate into antiracism.) The following 10 May 1856 Governor Charles Robinson was arrested in Lexington, Missouri, and held until 10 September, when he was released on bail.

Nine days later, on 19 May, Charles Sumner delivered his speech "The Crime against Kansas" before the Senate. For two days he held the Senate floor, where he labeled the actions taking place in Kansas by the proslavery forces "the rape of a virgin territory, compelling it to the hateful embrace of slavery." He called Andrew P. Butler, the senior senator from South Carolina, Don Quixote clinching "the harlot, Slavery" and said Stephen Douglas was Butler's Sancho Panza. On 21 May proslavery forces ransacked Lawrence, Kansas, marking the beginning of what became known as "Bleeding Kansas." The next day, back in Washington, South Carolina congressman Preston Brooks, Senator Butler's nephew, beat Sumner with the metal head of a cane while the senator was sitting at his desk in the Senate Chamber. A big man, Sumner was unable extract himself from his seat as Brooks continued to beat him, leaving him unconscious and badly wounded. In the midst of the events and as a result of them, at Pottawatomie, John Brown and his sons and associates attacked and killed proslavery men who had been harassing antislavery families in Franklin County. Brown had been driven to carry out the act of murder after reading about the caning of Sumner.[90]

Howe send a message of sympathy to Sumner, noting that the assault had brought men in Boston together in their common outrage. Men like Felton and even Hillard were protesting the assault, though Howe felt that Hillard's protest was too timid.[91] Not long after the events of May, Howe and others called for a meeting at Faneuil Hall to protest the caning of Sumner and to raise money for "Bleeding Kansas." Five thousand people attended the meeting, where the former Hunker and now Know Nothing governor Henry J. Gardner, who, despite having long coveted Sumner's Senate seat, spoke about the need to "rise above party feelings and party bias" to support Sumner "in his hour of trouble."[92]

Sumner would be away from the Senate for more than three years, traveling to spas and seeking out doctors in the United States and Europe in an effort to find a successful treatment for the pain and headaches that resulted from his injuries. During those years Howe and Sumner exchanged letters in which Howe (along with fellow Massachusetts senator Henry Wilson) advised Sumner to rest and not to return to the Senate too soon. Sumner seems to have taken Howe's advice.

In June Howe was appointed a director of the New England Emigrant Aid Company, successor to the Massachusetts Emigrant Aid Company. John Carter Brown, the Rhode Island investor, was chosen president and Amos

Adams Lawrence, treasurer. Around this time Howe wrote Longfellow to report on the sad state of Sumner's health and to encourage him to speak out about Kansas. As the days went on, the news from Kansas seemed only to get bleaker. On 4 July U.S. Army troops under Colonel Edwin V. Sumner dispersed the free-state Topeka legislature. So incensed were residents of Concord about matters in Kansas that on that same 4 July they petitioned the Massachusetts governor to declare unlawful the imprisonment of Massachusetts emigrants in Kansas. Finally, on that Independence Day, Howe left for a trip to the Kansas territory. His plan was to go first to an antislavery convention in Buffalo, then to Chicago and St. Louis, through Iowa and Nebraska, and then down to Kansas.

Although he never arrived in Kansas because of the dangers of travel, Howe developed opinions about what the Kansas immigrants needed. And foremost among their needs were arms. Surrounded by Missouri ruffians who were determined to make Kansas a proslavery state, the New England settlers in the territory were hardly able to protect themselves, their families, and their possessions without arms. As he left Tabor, Iowa, to return to Boston, Howe assured Kansas families that he would work even harder to arm them.[93]

By the time Howe returned to South Boston, New England was abuzz with support for "Bleeding Kansas." On 10 September, in Cambridge, Emerson delivered an address entitled "On the Affairs in Kansas," in which he called for Kansas relief. Throughout the fall Howe raised money for Kansas arms and Kansas relief. The money from Stearns and other donors would go for guns. But some donors stipulated that their contribution not be used for arms. Gifts of money came from all sorts of people. In November 1856, for example, the committee received three hundred dollars from Lady Byron, the widow of Lord Byron. Howe and his associate P. T. Jackson spent much of the winter requesting funds, which they converted into supplies and arms for the Kansas settlers. A few days before Christmas of 1856, Howe wrote to Amos Adams Lawrence, one of the principal funders of the arms and supplies to Kansas. Lawrence had called for generosity of spirit toward the slave powers. Howe was no opponent of magnanimous actions, but he cautioned Lawrence against the failure to carry out the duty of free men to ensure that the bondage of slavery end. "Duty bids us act as we should do if sons of our mothers or children of our loins were among the four million bondsmen." He added with a growing certainty, " 'Let us hold out the olive branch'—to men, yes! To wrong & oppression, no! The olive branch has been held out, & they would denounce it dove and all, as they have been disposed to, if now we waver & hesitate." Justice and humanity required that Massachusetts, Howe cautioned Lawrence, stay firm in its principles, that it not play "fast and loose" with that which was the right.[94]

Sometime in early January 1857, John Brown, back east from Kansas, checked into a Boston hotel. For more than seven months, he had eluded proslavery Kansas forces intent on avenging the Pottawatomie killings. Shortly thereafter Brown met with three of his Boston supporters, Parker, Stearns, and Howe. Joining this group would be Franklin Benjamin Sanborn, a school teacher from Concord, and Thomas Wentworth Higginson. At a later date, John Brown's old associate, the wealthy New York abolitionist and former Liberty Party candidate Gerrit Smith, would join his Massachusetts supporters. Less than two years later this group would come to be known as the Secret Six.

Also that January during an evening reception at Parker's home, Brown met Garrison.[95] Brown had preceded his visit with letters to the Massachusetts men asking them for aid in his quest to keep Kansas free of slavery.[96] Not long after Brown met with his Boston supporters, the Massachusetts Kansas Aid Committee's executive committee authorized rifles for Brown to transport to Kansas and for five hundred dollars. In a letter to Amos Adams Lawrence, Howe made it clear that he supported the Massachusetts public funding of arms, which would, he had no doubt, be a more efficient way of arming Kansas immigrants than the more tedious way of collecting private funds.[97] To this end he arranged to have Brown address a state legislative committee for guns and money for Kansas. Nothing came of the appeal to the legislature. Nevertheless, Brown needed arms and his Boston supporters were ready to supply what they could in arms and money from the private funds they were actively collecting.

While Brown was in Boston drumming up support for Free Soil Kansas, the U.S. Supreme Court handed down a decision that shook the antislavery world. The Court announced the *Dred Scott v. Sandford* decision on 6 March 1857, a mere two days after the presidential inauguration of James Buchanan, a doughfaced Democrat from Pennsylvania. In its decision, delivered by Chief Justice Roger B. Taney, the Court ruled that slaves did not have protection as citizens under the Constitution, that Congress had no authority to prohibit slavery in the territories, that slaves were not allowed to sue in court, and that as private property, slaves could not be taken away from their owners without due process. Less than a week later, John Brown addressed a large crowd in Concord in which he recounted the antislavery struggles in Kansas and denounced the recent Supreme Court decision.

In the midst of his fund-raising for Kansas, Howe continued to carry out his responsibilities with the blind and idiot schools. Around the same time, too, Julia's play *Leonora* opened in New York at the Wallack Theater. Francis Lieber, who had come from South Carolina to explore a faculty appointment at Columbia University, saw the play and remarked in his diary, "Some scenes

[were] excellent."[98] On 3 April 1857 Howe invited the famous British actress
Fanny Kemble, who was performing in Boston, to visit the blind school. Five
days later, she obliged Howe by giving a reading there.[99] Later that summer,
for a second time, William Ellsworth nearly burned down the institution.
Before expelling the boy, Howe wrote to his guardian, the Reverend Charles
R. Fisher, Willie's guardian, about the fire.

> On Thursday last, the house was set on fire, & we very narrowly escaped
> a serious conflagration. Had the discovery been delayed five minutes, the
> building would have been destroyed. . . . Suspicion fell upon Willie, & after
> twisting & turning, & lying, & showing great cunning & adroitness he
> owned that he purposely set the building on fire. The plan was deliberately
> laid; combustibles were gathered, & measures taken which he supposed
> would secure the destruction of the building. . . . Moreover, he confessed that
> he once set a barn on fire with the purpose of destroying the cattle of a man
> who had offended him, & that he once set a shed on fire.[100]

Howe spent much of his time in the spring and summer of 1857 raising
funds for Kansas. In late April the Massachusetts Kansas Aid Committee
authorized an additional five hundred dollars for Kansas aid and funds for
the purchase of two hundred Sharpe rifles. In Springfield, Brown took pos-
session of the funds and the rifles, much of which had come Stearns, Lawrence, and Forbes.

In late May Howe set out on his second trip to the Kansas territory.
Julia, along with her daughter Laura, accompanied him as far as Louisville
but turned back when Laura became sick. Julia was also worried about her
play.[101] Samuel went on without them but was accompanied by Senator
Henry Wilson and the Free Soil Unitarian minister John Pierpont. Howe
and his companions arrived in Kansas on 27 May, and that evening all three
men spoke at the Unitarian church in Lawrence. Howe stayed in Kansas for
about two weeks, traveling around the territory to assess the condition under
which free-soil Kansans were living. On the way home he visited Mann at
Antioch College. Soon after leaving Mann he wrote him a letter about what
he had seen in Kansas and admitted that he had "half a mind to pull up and
go to Kansas."[102]

In October, Kansas free-state forces scored a victory in the election for
the territorial legislature. Vacationing at Newport, Rhode Island, Howe
was overjoyed by the election returns. Throughout the fall of 1857 and into
the winter of 1858 Howe continued to correspond with Kansas authorities.
Among his correspondents was Captain John Brown.

John Brown

On 22 February 1858 John Brown met with Gerrit Smith and Franklin Sanborn at Smith's home in Peterboro, New York. Smith's support for Frederick Douglass had resulted in the alienation of Douglass from most of the Massachusetts abolitionists led by William Lloyd Garrison, for Smith, like Douglass, advocated for political involvement in the elimination of slavery. Smith had known Brown since 1848, when he granted him 244 acres of land at a dollar an acre at North Elba, New York. Smith had established the North Elba community primarily for the settlement of blacks. Sanborn was a young teacher from Concord, who in 1862 would express an amorous interest in Emerson's daughter Edith (which Emerson would put a stop to). Like Smith, he was a radical antislavery man. What Brown had to tell these men on that cold but bright February day was that he had plans to lead an uprising of slaves. He was evasive about the time and place for his plot but explicit that his plan involved a slave insurrection. Less than two weeks later, Howe, Sanborn, Stearns, Higginson, and Parker met with John Brown in his hotel in Boston. Brown repeated the plan he had described to Smith and Sanborn in Peterboro. The men agreed to advise Brown and raise money for his efforts.

Around this time, James Freeman Clarke, an antislavery man and the minister of the Church of the Disciples, where Howe often attended services, recalled meeting Howe on a Boston street. "Ossawattomie Brown," Howe greeted Clarke, "is in my office. He has a plan in view, and if you would like to help him, he will tell you something about it." At Howe's invitation, the two men proceeded to Howe's Bromfield Street office, where they found John Brown alone. Soon Brown was describing his work of carrying away slaves from Missouri to freedom in Kansas. Clarke remembered his saying that "he intended doing the same thing, on a larger scale elsewhere," but about where and how, Brown had said, "I keep to myself."[103]

Around the end of 1857 Brown had had a falling out with a British soldier of fortune, Hugh Forbes. Brown had hired Forbes to train his men for future combat. Money was at the root of the differences; Brown had not paid him. Forbes had sent "abusive" letters to Sanborn, Sumner and others.[104] On 1 May 1858, Howe and Sanborn also received letters from Forbes saying that he had revealed Brown's plan to New York senator William Seward. Rumors about Forbes's complaints began to circulate around Congress. Henry Wilson wrote Howe that he "better talk with some few of our friends who contributed money to aid old Brown." He warned that money used for purposes other than those directed to Kansas might adversely affect the men who had contributed to Brown's cause. Howe had come to respect the working-class senator, whose native intelligence made up for his lack of formal higher edu-

John Brown (ca. 1850). Library of Congress.

cation and social upbringing. Soon five of the Secret Six agreed to postpone
sending money to Brown, with only Higginson disagreeing with the delay.
Stearns sent a letter to Brown warning him that the arms sent to him were to
be used only for the defense of Kansas and for no other purposes.[105]

On May 24, five of the six (with Smith present and Higginson absent) met
Brown at Smith's room at the Boston's Revere House. They discussed Forbes's
actions. The men agreed to give Brown money but sent him back to Kansas
and thus delayed the invasion plans. On June 2 Brown met with the Secret
Six, this time including Higginson. With more money, Brown returned to
Kansas.[106] Although Brown still did not say when or where, or even how
he planned to develop slave insurrection, the Secret Six had no doubt that
insurrection was Brown's intent.

On 3 February 1859, Samuel and Julia sailed to Cuba with Theodore
Parker and his wife. Parker was ill with tuberculosis, and like many other
people with the disease in the nineteenth century, he sought a warmer climate in the futile hope that such an environment would effect a cure. During

the previous month, Parker's lungs had hemorrhaged, and doctors told him that he would likely not recover from the consumption that he had suffered for several years. In New York, shortly before sailing to Cuba, Howe wrote to John Murray Forbes to introduce John Brown. Howe urged Forbes to support free-soil Kansas by providing funds for Brown. With Brown's financial needs cared for, the Howes sailed for Cuba, where they spent February and March. Samuel and Richard Henry Dana, who also happened to be in Cuba, toured the Cuban military hospital and the Presidio, the notorious Havana prison.[107] On the way home Samuel and Julia spent two weeks near Columbia, South Carolina, with the Wade Hampton family, whom they had met in Cuba. Wade Hampton was the scion of a wealthy planter, whose family had owned hundreds of slaves over several generations. His wife, Sally Baxter Hampton, was a native of New York and, like Parker, suffered from tuberculosis. (She would die from the condition in 1862.) From the letters Sally wrote to her mother, it appeared that the Howes and the Hamptons got along exceptionally well. Back in South Carolina Howe even prescribed a poultice for Sally, the "effect [of which] was miraculous." It was the only time in Samuel's life that he would spend so much time with white Southerners in the South. As he reported to Parker, "We journeyed together, & disputed together about slavery, & [Hampton] was rather taken with the novelty of a northern man talking rank abolitionism."[108] By mid-April the Howes were back in South Boston, while the Parkers later in the spring sailed from Santa Cruz to Europe, where, in Florence, Theodore Parker would die a year later.

In March 1860 Ticknor and Fields published Julia's book *A Trip to Cuba*. It had first appeared in 1859 as a series of articles in the *Atlantic Monthly*. Written in the travelogue style popular at the time, the book records Julia's impressions of her sojourn through Nassau and of her longer stay in Cuba during the previous winter. The condescending images and language Julia used and her assumption that blacks needed the white culture to elevate them from brute to human being are typical of upper-middle-class Yankees in the nineteenth-century. She wrote, for example: "The negroes [in Nassau], as they came nearer, suggested only Christy's Minstrels . . . and we strained our eyes to see the wonderful ape, Jocko. . . . But you must allow us one heretical whisper—very small and low. The negro of the North is an ideal negro; it is the negro refined by white culture, elevated by white blood, instructed even by white iniquity. . . . The negro among negroes, is a course, grinning, flat-footed, thick-skulled creature, ugly as Caliban, lazy as the laziest of brutes, chiefly ambitious to be of no use to any in the world. . . . View him as you will, his stock in trade is small; he has but the tangible instincts of all creatures—love of life, of ease, and of offspring. For all else he must go to school to the white race, and his discipline must be long and laborious." This passage ends with her suggesting that enforcing labor on blacks to work was not a bad thing.[109]

Samuel's reaction to Julia's articles and book was much less vitriolic than was the reaction of William Lloyd Garrison. Samuel expressed his take on Julia's work in a letter to Parker in Florence: "Have you read Julia's Cuba? Some things in it make me sad, e.g. the question whether viewing the actual condition of the negro enforced labor is not best!—as if anything would justify the perpetuation of such wrong by the stronger race."[110] To Garrison, the claim that blacks are fit only for hard labor was demeaning. Blacks, Garrison chided Julia, are neither naturally lazy nor brutish.

By March 1859 Brown, who at the time was holed up in Springdale, Iowa, wrote Howe, who was in Cuba, a letter that was vague but nevertheless suggested his continuing plan for a slave uprising. Always in need of money, Brown said: "To effect a good seasons [sic] work we ought to begin early, & all that I know of to hinder our doing so is the want of a trifling sum for an outfit. The entire success of our experiments ought (I think) to convince every *capitalist*." Through the spring and summer of 1859 the Secret Six continued to raise money, which they designated for Kansas, knowing also that it was destined for other purposes as well.[111] In early May, Brown arrived in Concord as Sanborn's guest and soon thereafter visited with Emerson and Thoreau. On 9 May he moved to the Beach Street Hotel in Boston, where Howe found him tired but ready to meet Boston friends. To that end, Howe invited several Boston antislavery supporters, including James Russell Lowell, John Murray Forbes, and Francis G. Shaw, to his Bromfield Street office to "to see the 'original head' for which the Governor of Missouri has offered 3000$, but which the owner, old fighting Brown of Kansas, holds at a higher figure." "Brown, as you know" he added, "is a practical, not a talking abolitionist, but he will be glad to tell you in his rough way something about his mode [of] abolitionizing." By the time that Brown left Boston on 30 May, he had collected over three thousand dollars.

"Abolitionizing" was in the air. Men and women, who had once seen antislavery activity as too radical, now made up a chorus of opposition to slavery. George Sumner, for example, now home from France, gave over a hundred antislavery lectures between January and June 1859. At the annual Fourth of July ceremonies in Boston, Sumner delivered a most scathing address in which he denounced the *Dred Scott* case and its leading proponent, Justice Roger Taney.[112]

On 2 August 1859, Howe's oldest friend, Horace Mann, died in Yellow Springs, Ohio. Learning of the death two days later, Howe wrote the dying Theodore Parker about Mann's death and, Howe insisted, the need for a monument to Mann's memory.[113] Howe was perturbed that state lawmakers had proposed a statue for Daniel Webster to grace the State House grounds. If the Commonwealth could honor a compromising Cotton Whig like Webster, who, Howe commented to Palfrey, had "debauch[ed] the moral sense of the people," how much more did Mann deserve the recognition of a memorial statue on the grounds of the State House? Howe would spend the next several years raising enthusiasm and funds for a statue of Mann that would one day, along with Webster's statue, occupy a prominent place on the State House grounds.[114]

On Sunday, 16 October 1859, the worlds of both the slaveholder and the antislavery forces turned upside down. At Harper's Ferry, Virginia, John Brown and his band of twenty-one followers—five black and sixteen white— took over the town's federal arsenal. Since July, the invaders had rented Kennedy Farm, a Maryland farm near Harper's Ferry, which had served as the group's base camp. There they made preparations for the raid. It was John Brown's plan and the group's intention to use weapons seized from the arsenal to arm slaves. These armed slaves along with their free black brothers, Brown believed, would foment insurrection that would spread south, eventually forming a vast slave insurrection.

It was a daring but fatally flawed plan. Within thirty-six hours of the seizure of the arsenal, President James Buchanan, whom Howe called "the childless old man of the White House," sent federal troops under the command of Captain Robert E. Lee, who, along with Lieutenant J. E. B. Stuart, quickly put down the uprising. Most of Brown's men, including two of his own sons, were killed. Brown himself was wounded. As he had made clear to his Secret Six backers, though not in specific details, Brown had hoped to launch a general revolt of slaves throughout the South, but his plan would be left stillborn after the arrival of Lee's overwhelming numbers. By Tuesday and for the remainder of the week, Boston newspapers, like their counterparts throughout the nation, were filled with reports about the Harper's Ferry uprising. On 20 October and again four days later, Howe asked Lawrence to help raise funds for Brown's defense and for the support of Brown's wife.[115]

CHAPTER SEVEN
War, Freedmen, and Crete

On 25 October 1859, nine days after the raid on Harper's Ferry, the state of Virginia indicted John Brown on the charges of treason and murder. On the same day, the *New York Herald* began a series of articles reporting information obtained from letters seized at the Kennedy Farm. These letters left little doubt that John Brown had planned a slave insurrection and that he had support—at least tacit support—for his plan from influential Northerners. The headline of one edition of the *Herald* read, "The Exposure of the Nigger Worshipping Insurrectionists." The names Franklin B. Sanborn, George L. Stearns, and Samuel G. Howe appeared in the articles along with the names Frederick Douglass and Gerrit Smith, and Senators William Seward, Henry Wilson, and Charles Sumner, and within days of the *Herald*'s publication, Howe's name was in leading newspapers across the nation.

In reaction to the press reports, Stearns's wife, Mary, remembered that Howe on a visit to the Stearnses' home had a "dread that threatened to overwhelm his reason." Howe feared arrest and was visibly shaken. Ralph Waldo Emerson too was alarmed. He wrote to his brother William that "bushels of letters" were likely to implicate his friends in Brown's raid.[1] Only the next day did Howe get a reassuring opinion from John A. Andrew, who told Stearns and Howe that they were not guilty of treason.[2] From that point on, Howe resumed his work with other Boston antislavery men to find money for Brown's defense and for the care of Brown's family.

On 2 November a circular signed by Howe, Emerson, Samuel Sewell, and Thomas Wentworth Higginson appeared throughout Boston, calling for financial support for Brown's defense. Two days later Brown wrote Higginson that it would serve no good purpose for his wife to come to his jail. At the time Mary Ann Day Brown was in Boston on her way to meet with her husband. She was nearly destitute. Besides searching for support for Brown's defense, Sewell, Higginson, and Howe also appealed to wealthy donors like Amos Adams Lawrence and John Murray Forbes for funds to aid Mary Brown and the remaining members of her family in North Elba.[3]

With his name now closely associated with Brown's raid, on 14 November Howe sent a letter defending himself to the *Boston Daily Advertiser.* The letter appeared two days later in the *Advertiser,* and a day after that in the *New York Herald.* "Rumor has mingled my name with the events of Harper's Ferry." Howe's letter began. These rumors, Howe insisted, were based on the writings of Hugh Forbes, a disgruntled and therefore unreliable source. Although the letter left no doubt that Howe knew and admired Brown, whom he referred to as "the heroic man," Howe insisted that the Harper's Ferry raid was "unforeseen and unexpected by me." "Nor," he continued, "does all my previous knowledge of John Brown enable me to reconcile it with his characteristic prudence, and his reluctance to shed blood or excite servile insurrection." Brown's action, he added disingenuously, "is still to me a mystery and a marvel."[4] In reaction to the Forbes's letters, the *New York Herald* ran an article on 17 November under the headline, "Who Is Dr. S. G. Howe?" The article charged that Howe was a ringleader in both the Shadrach Minkins and the Anthony Burns fugitive slave affairs and that as editor of the *Boston Daily Commonwealth,* he used imprudent language and made unjustified claims against the South and against the lawful institution of slavery. The article also implied that Howe used his position as superintendent of a blind school as a benign covering for what were sinister and socially threatening actions. In short, he might appear to be a philanthropist, but in reality he is a dangerous agitator.[5]

Other reactions to Howe's involvement in the Harper's Ferry raid were more covert. Having developed close ties to Southern elites, Dorothea Dix, for example, privately confided her repulsion that her friend and champion could have been involved in the insurrection.[6] His brother-in-law Sam Ward, too, was horrified that his sister's husband was involved in Brown's treasonous activities.

At about the time that he sent his letter to the *Advertiser,* Howe and Stearns took a train to Montreal, while Frederick Douglass went to Canada and from there sailed to England. All three men had good reason to fear that Virginia governor Henry A. Wise would bring charges against them. He was the same Henry Wise who, while serving in Congress, had tried so vehemently to censure John Quincy Adams when he persistently attempted to introduce antislavery petitions. Later Congress had threatened to try Wise for murder because he had served as a second in a duel that had killed a congressman from Maine.[7] Other Virginians were just as angry as Governor Wise;

one offered a fifty–dollar reward for the "head of that traitor William H. Seward."[8] And according to Lieutenant Robert Gould Shaw, who in March 1862 in Charlestown, Virginia, found in the papers of Brown's prosecutor, Andrew Hunter, a letter from a detective who had been sent to Montreal to arrest Howe but had been unsuccessful.[9]

Howe rationalized that this was the time to go to Canada. For years advocates for blind schools in Canada had invited him to lecture and to speak to Canadian authorities and show them the skills of his blind pupils, and he had just recently received another invitation. Furthermore, John Andrew had changed his earlier opinion about Howe's culpability. Now he warned Stearns and Howe that they might be liable, especially if Governor Wise were to call for their testimony, or even their arrest. Franklin Sanborn, a third member of the Secret Six, had left for Canada back in October. Gerrit Smith, feeling guilty about the deaths at Harper's Ferry and under pressure for a possible Virginia indictment, suffered a nervous breakdown, and his family had him admitted to the New York State Insane Asylum at Utica. With Theodore Parker dying in Florence, the only Secret Six member who stayed firmly in support of Brown was Wentworth Higginson.[10] In a letter to Howe written, but not sent, while Howe was on his way to Canada, Higginson rebuked him for his letter denying knowledge of Brown's plans.[11] Nevertheless, while in Canada, Howe participated in two public events, one on 30 November and another on 3 December, to raise money for Brown's family.[12]

On 2 December in Charlestown, Virginia, John Brown, convicted of all charges against him, went to the gallows. For several weeks before the execution, indignation and outrage had mingled with sadness and despair as pockets of antislavery citizenry throughout the North anticipated Brown's hanging. Back on 30 October in Concord and again on 1 November at Boston's Tremont Temple, Henry David Thoreau gave his address, "Plea for Captain John Brown." Thoreau, whose family had long-held (and long-practiced) abolitionist sympathies, had nothing but praise for Brown. Out of Brown's Puritan heritage, Thoreau said, Brown had been led by a righteous God. Rather than being insane or crazed as some reports claimed, Brown, Thoreau argued, was completely sane. "No man in America has ever stood up so persistently and effectively for the dignity of human nature."[13] Like Thoreau, Ralph Waldo Emerson lent his voice to the cause of John Brown. At an 18 November meeting in Boston to raise money for Brown's family, Emerson referred to Brown as the "hero of Harper's Ferry." He claimed that Brown was an idealist who nevertheless put his ideals into action. Emerson drew his loudest applause that evening when, in a putdown of the Garrisonians, he claimed that Brown "did not believe in moral suasion; he believed in putting the thing through."[14]

Three days after Brown's execution U.S. Senator John Mason of Virginia, the author of the 1850 Fugitive Slave Law, called for a committee of investigation to inquire into matters surrounding the Harper's Ferry raid. The forthcoming investigation left Howe, who was back in Boston from his trip to Canada, again concerned for his own safety. In a letter to Charles Sumner, who had recently returned to the Senate, Howe said he feared that the hot-tempered Wise could have him arrested as he traveled through Virginia should the Senate summon him to Washington. No doubt remembering his imprisonment in Prussia in 1832, Howe contemplated returning to Canada rather than risk facing charges in Virginia. On 14 December the Senate formed its investigation committee with Senator Mason as chairman and Mississippi senator Jefferson F. Davis as its chief inquisitor.[15]

In the midst of these matters, Samuel G. Howe Jr. was born on Christmas Day, a Sunday. Delighted with the birth of his second son, the youngest of six children, and namesake, Howe wrote to Sumner, assuring him that the birth had gone smoothly. He also thanked his friend for giving foreign stamps to his son Harry as a Christmas gift. By the end of the month, Howe was back in Canada, this time with pupils to give demonstrations before Canadian officials. Although still concerned about moving through Virginia, he had decided against avoiding the investigation committee's summons that was issued on 11 January 1860. Even though *Vanity Fair* would lampoon his second trip to Canada for the "treatment of the blind," Howe had been assured by Sumner and the other Massachusetts senator, Henry Wilson, that he could travel safely through Virginia to Washington for his testimony before the committee. Receiving the summons on 23 January, Howe left at the end of the week for Washington. But before departing he received additional assurance from Sumner, who had learned that the committee would "regard such witnesses for the time as under the protection of the Senate." Howe, Sumner insisted, should have no fears of arrest by Virginia authorities.[16]

On 3 February Howe appeared before the Mason Committee, and a few days later Stearns also answered the committee's inquiries. Questioning from the chairman and from Davis were, under the circumstances, remarkably civil. After his testimony Stearns wrote Howe, "The Com[mittee members] were civil and did not press me at all. I answered freely and they took all I said in good faith."[17] In his own testimony, Howe acknowledged that the Massachusetts Kansas Aid Committee had made two hundred Sharp's rifles available to John Brown. But he insisted that, as an earlier and now disclosed letter from Stearns had made clear, the Massachusetts committee had stipulated that the arms were to be used only for the defense of Kansas. Although he answered all questions that were put to him, Howe's memory was frequently incomplete. Within a few days, his testimony was published, in whole or in part, in newspapers around the nation. After visiting with Sumner and Wilson, Howe left Washington to return to South Boston. It soon became clear to Stearns, Howe, and others that the Senate commit- tee was hoping that their testimony would implicate elected officials of the Republican Party, such as Senators Wilson, Sumner, and Seward.

In March and April Howe was back in Canada for a third trip on behalf of that nation's blind schools. From Montreal, he wrote Sumner on the fate of the Union, "We shall have blood." In Boston, Howe's notoriety had inspired letters and requests for autographs, such as the following from Lewis S. Thomas: "Permit me, although a stranger, to address you at this time, to ask if you will be so kind as to give me your autograph? And, if it will not be too presuming, I would ask if you have one to spare of John Brown, the Martyr of the Cause of Freedom?"[18]

With matters associated with the Harper's Ferry affair less prominent in the press, Howe spent much of the spring and summer soliciting sup- port and funds for a memorial statue for Horace Mann. In mid-May Howe learned that his friend Theodore Parker had died in Rome. In a 1 June letter to Sumner, he mourned Parker's death: "You too have been sad & have wept, as men weep inwardly, at the tidings from Florence. We who knew Parker intimately knew how much there was of tender, womanlike affection about him." He also talked about the slow pace of obtaining support for the Mann statue, explaining that Mary Mann had approved a statuette of Mann but that her sister Sophia Hawthorne, who had recently returned with Nathaniel and her family from England, had insisted on changes, which that the artist dutifully made.[19] It would not be until the next year that the final commis- sion for the statue would be given to the American artist Emma Stebbins, then living in Rome.

On 29 August 1860 Massachusetts Republicans met in Worcester, where Sumner gave a rousing speech in which he condemned the machinations of proslavery elected officials, such as John Bell, John C. Breckinridge, and Stephen Douglas. With Bird Club backing, the convention nominated John A. Andrew for governor. In October Boston held a daylong celebration for the visiting Prince of Wales, the future King Edward VII. At the end of the month Irish Americans in the city held a mass rally in support of Stephen Douglas, the Democratic candidate for president. About the same time, Julia received a strong letter from her brother Sam Ward, a long-time Democrat and active supporter of Stephen Douglas, who in his newest incarnation was known as the "king of the lobby" in Washington. He wrote: "The North is playing with fire and a powder magazine, and I expect to see the day when an abolitionist will be obnoxious as were members of the Hartford Convention half a century ago." He was sure that the antislavery activities of Julia and her husband were acts of "fanaticism."[20] Despite the Irish Americans' efforts on behalf of Douglas and Julia's brother Sam's warnings, on 2 November 1860, a day of chilly rain in eastern Massachusetts, Abraham Lincoln, on the Republican ticket, carried Massachusetts by winning a plurality in a four-way contest, and John A. Andrew was elected its new governor. As the likelihood of Southern secession increased, Howe wrote Sumner that rather than preserving the Union it would be in the best interests of the nation to let the secessionists go their own way. Yet after the South Carolina convention on 13 December approved articles of succession, Howe was less sure about letting the secessionists have their way. He wrote Sumner, "The South Carolinians will have the conflict!" A month later, his views of Union preservation had evolved to the point that he was critical of what he called William Seward's "fetish" of Union preservation. If there was to be fighting, let it be for the end of slavery, not merely for the preservation of a slave-ridden Union.[21]

Throughout the winter tensions grew in Boston. On 20 January Howe was part of a group that protected Wendell Phillips as he walked from the Music Hall to his home. Phillips had given a fiery speech, "On Disunion," in which he argued that the Northern states were best freed from union with the slave-owning powers, and that preservation of the Union was possible only with the elimination of slavery. The speech that ended with the pronouncement, "All Hail, then, Disunion!" had created a near riot. "His path," Howe wrote Sumner, "was beset & his way obstructed by a mob of well dressed, but evidently coarse & uncultivated men, who howled & yelled & pressed in upon the body guard which surrounded him." Howe, whose antislavery position had only a few years earlier been far less radical than Phillips's, had now taken on the radicalism of abolitionists like Phillips. By the end of the month, he wrote his friend Frank Bird of his opposition to the upcoming Convention of Compromise, which that he called a "Convention for saving Slavery in the Union." On 13 April 1861, the day after the Confederates in Charleston harbor fired on Fort Sumter (whose very walls Howe and most other New Englanders knew were built from New Hampshire granite), Howe wrote his friend and the newly elected governor Andrew of his hope "that war shall not cease until emancipation is secure." As Adam Goodheart has written, "But now the loss of this two-acre island—lowering of one flag and the raising of another over a useless piece of federal real estate—was suddenly a national calamity."[22] Quickly from all over the North, people who had been unsure of war only a few weeks earlier were convinced that war was absolutely necessary. Howe, now nearly sixty years old, was caught up in the patriotic fervor and offered to do his part for the upcoming war effort. The only duty that he would refuse, he told Andrew, was the work of a spy.

At the Perkins Institution, the growing national conflict began to have an effect. From the beginning of its operations, the school had taken private-paying students from the South. But now the parents and relatives of these students began to have misgivings about allowing their children to remain at the school. J. O. Harris, for example, in New Orleans wrote Howe to insist that his son, Joseph, return home. After the intervention of a relative from Vermont, Harris changed his mind and allowed Joseph to remain in South Boston. Other Southerners, however, withdrew their children. Another concern in the growing conflict was the money that Southern schools for the blind owed to the Perkins Institution for printing. In August 1862, for example, Howe wrote the following to Major General Benjamin F. Butler, the military governor of New Orleans, about money owed by the Louisiana School for the Blind: "If there be any funds within your reach which may be properly appropriated to payment of this account, I know you will be prompt to do justice in the promises."[23]

On 2 May 1861 General Winfield Scott, commanding general of the Union Army, and governor Andrew asked Howe to prepare a survey of the sanitary conditions of Massachusetts troops, which were in Washington protecting the city from an anticipated Confederate invasion. Within five days Howe was in the nation's capital where he complained to Andrew about the poor quality of the troop commanders and about the lack of medical care of the state's troops. "There is more need of a *health officer* than of chaplain, but the U.S. knows no such officer," Howe lamented. "Soap! Soap! Soap—I cry but none heed," he added, "I wish some provision could be made for having washer-women. They are more needed than nurses."[24]

By August, Howe had become more confident than ever that the abstract idea of Union preservation might seem like a necessary rationale for war, but it was not a sufficient one. There was low morale among the troops. To raise the morale of the troops, and the general public, emancipation should be added to the rationale of Union preservation. Howe warned Andrew, "We need something or somebody to magnetize our people with some new word or blow, or else there will be terrible demoralization in less than a month. Popular enthusiasm can never be kept up about any abstraction & the cry for Union is now less than an abstraction, it is a *sham* & the public instinct recognizes it as such. Who shall raise the cry *openly* for *Emancipation!* . . . The north—the people—the world would cry bravo! & new vigor would be breathed into all hearts."[25]

To follow up on his call for emancipation, Howe arranged a meeting of antislavery Bostonians at his office on Bromfield Street on 5 September 1861. On 16 December a second meeting took place attended by William Lloyd Garrison, Wendell Phillips, Franklin Sanborn, George L. Stearns, William

Henry Channing, James Freeman Clarke, Edmund Quincy, and Frank Bird. The meetings led to the formation of the Boston Emancipation League, to which Howe was elected a vice president. Howe, Stearns, and Edward Atkinson formed the league's executive committee. The league published broadsides, newspaper articles, and pamphlets and organized speeches and discussion groups to arouse public enthusiasm for emancipation. The league criticized what it saw as the Lincoln administration's slow response to eliminate slavery. One of its broadsides reads, "The object of this League is to urge upon the People and the Government *Emancipation of the Slaves,* as a matter of justice, and as a military necessity; it being the shortest, cheapest, and least bloody path to permanent peace, and the only method of maintaining the integrity of the nation."[26] As he had done with the free-soil Kansas campaign, Howe turned to Amos Adams Lawrence for financial support for the Emancipation League. On the evening of 16 December at a mass meeting in support of immediate emancipation, Howe introduced the evening's principal speaker, the former governor of the state and one of the founders of the Republican Party, George S. Boutwell. At long last, Howe believed, influential Boston politicians, businessmen, and reformers were beginning to draw together in support of emancipation.[27]

As concerned as he was with emancipation, Howe remained alert to the sanitary conditions of the Massachusetts troops. In response to Governor Andrew's request, Howe wrote a report, which was published in July by the U.S. Sanitary Commission, on whose board he served as a civilian member. Howe began the report, titled, *A Letter on the Sanitary Condition of the Troops in the Neighborhood of Boston,* by insisting that just as the soldier owes his allegiance, even his life, to his country, his country owes the soldier proper living conditions to maintain his strength and "vital force" as a soldier. In previous conflicts from the Mexican War to the more recent Crimean War, Howe noted, more soldiers lost their lives to disease and ill health than to enemy forces. "Government ought to take as much care of the soldier's health as it does for its personal estate, its implements of war, or its horses, but," he argued, "it does not." Good officers who care about the fighting ability of the troops they command will not only be good drill masters but they will also be good sanitarians.

"Most of all we want men of abundant vital force," Howe said, "who can resist destructive agencies of all kinds." He identified the overcrowding of troops in their quarters as the greatest obstacle to good health, pointing out that especially when they sleep, men need fresh air and adequate, dry space. Crowding men into barracks or canvas tents nearly ensures that the "vital force" necessary to each man will be compromised. Howe also pointed out the health hazard of odors from waste, adding that troops also need clean conditions in latrines, sinks, and privies. He made recommendations for dealing with human waste, as well as cooking waste, and concluded the report with suggestions about diet and food preparation. "Men of army age," he wrote, "require daily at least 28 ounces of nutritious food," adding that troops be given a variety of wholesome food and not the bland food that is too often associated with army life. The best way to ensure that food, specifically meat, is nutritious is to broil it. If broiling is not possible, the next best way to prepare the food is by roasting or baking. Frying should be avoided because it "changes the oil into empyreumatic state and hardens the fibre."[28]

In January 1862 Howe wrote Sumner in Washington to secure the appointment of John V. Degrasse as a physician to the fugitive slaves who were accumulating in and around the nation's capital. Howe described Degrasse, a graduate of the medical school of Bowdoin College who had been admitted to the Massachusetts Medical Society in 1854, as "a fine, handsome, bright mulatto, of good education & good address." Although Howe's request was not acted on, Degrasse eventually received an appointment as assistant surgeon of the U.S. Army Medical Corp, where he served as one of eight African American physicians in the Union Army.[29]

In February 1862 Howe published another article, this one addressed to "loyal women" who had asked him about acquiring clothing and hospital supplies for the Union troops. The ostensible purpose of the article was for Howe to advise the women to avoid providing such supplies to Union soldiers because the provision of clothing and supplies was the responsibility of the government, not of civilians. Howe's primary purpose, however, was to argue a case that was even more central to his concerns in the early days of 1862: the emancipation of slaves and the destruction of slavery.

According to Howe, the Northern fighting man had little more than pay to motivate him to fight. The Southern soldier had the protection of his country to provide "passion." But what zeal, Howe asked, did the Northern soldier have? "No! our men in the field do not lack food, or clothing, or money, but they do lack noble watchwords and inspiriting ideas, such as are worth fighting and dying for." The idea of preserving the Union, he claimed, was too abstract, and also it lacked nobility. The Union soldier needed something to fight for that was more concrete and more ennobling. "Intensify the morale of our army by higher purposes, by noble motives, and you will see how much stronger is a virtuous than a vicious cause, when men are made to feel that it is so: and how much more hardy and plucky is a Northern than a Southern man." For Howe, the most concrete and noble cause that could inspire the ardor of the Northern soldier was the emancipation of all slaves and the final destruction of slavery. This letter was the first major opportunity Howe had for advocating in print a position that he had held from the beginning of the war.[30]

Howe used a printed pamphlet to express openly his views on the necessity of emancipation, but he communicated privately his perspective on what he judged to be the blundering of the Union Army's commanding general, George B. McClellan. Of the general, Howe wrote to Francis Bird, in March 1862: "The fact long ago suspected by the instinct of the people begins to get through the scull [*sic*] of the 'Powers that be.' An egregious thunder of McClellan which made a botch & failure of the late *proposed forward march* has convinced the Pres. that he is utterly incompetent to the task of handling a great army. There is a great fight going on over him, & I do not doubt that though his fall may be delayed, it will come soon. I have long thought he was a humbug (an unintentional one) & I think the more he stirs now to defend himself the more plainly will he show his incompetency."[31]

Howe also called for the arming of free blacks and freedmen. As early as January 1862 he complained to Sumner, "It would seem to be the purpose of those in power to prevent the black man from vindicating his own cause and showing his capacity for self guidance by denying him all opportunity of doing any thing for himself." Howe's anger only increased as he wrote, "The policy of the Administration towards the fugitives within our lines is unjust & cruel. Lincoln is a greater slave-holder than the King of Dahomey." The most productive work for free blacks and for freedmen was in the armed services.[32]

Freedmen's Inquiry Commission

In its February 1862 edition, the *Atlantic Monthly* magazine published Julia Ward Howe's poem "The Battle Hymn of the Republic." She had written it in the early morning hours at Washington's Willard Hotel back in November. She had gone to the capital city with Samuel, who was meeting with the U.S. Sanitary Commission. Accompanying the Howes on their trip south were Governor Andrew and his wife and the James Freeman Clarke, the Unitarian minister of the Church of the Disciples. Julia's observations of Union troops moving through Washington had inspired her to write the poem. The *Atlantic Monthly*, founded in 1857, had a wide readership, so it was not surprising that soon soldiers were singing her words to the popular tune of "John Brown's Body." Within weeks of its publication, Julia would begin public recitations of her poem that she would continue for eager public consumption for the remainder of her long life.

Later in the month, Samuel's old friend Cornelius Felton died, and the Howes attended his funeral at the Harvard University chapel. Within three years, three of his closest and oldest friends—Mann, Parker, and Felton—had died. Also, later that month a grand organ was installed at the Perkins Institution. It was one of the most majestic organs in the nation, and it made Howe proud that he had generated from faithful contributors the six thousand dollars necessary to make the organ a reality.

Howe went to Washington several more times in 1861 and 1862 for his work with the Sanitary Commission. His health was not good during these years; he complained frequently of headaches and fever from reoccurring malaria. But he felt obliged to do his part on the commission. The commission, which had been created by Secretary of War Simon Cameron in June 1861, had two principal functions: inspect military hospitals and give advice to Cameron about the establishment of additional hospitals and health-related facilities. During a trip to Washington in December 1861, Howe took time one Sunday while the commission was not meeting to ride horseback into Virginia, the very state he feared entering after the Harper's Ferry affair just two years earlier. What he found was what he had expected. In a letter to Julia Romana, he said: "The bridge, the road, and all the surroundings tell you by their rickety dilapidated & slovenly condition that you are in a country where what we call public spirit is utterly wanting. No side walks, no hand road-bed, no lamp posts, no train fences . . . no signs of taste & culture anywhere. Poor old Virginia, in her best estate bad enough, but now that the iron hoof [of] war has been stamping for months upon her soil, she is indeed desolate & dilapidated."[33]

Like other members of the Sanitary Commission, Howe tended to take the most interest in the conditions of the troops closest to his own home. But that interest began to wane, and by the end of 1862 he had begun to see the commission members as autocratic administrators, more concerned with order and regimentation than with care and charity. Men like the commission's head, the conservative Boston-born, New York patrician Henry W. Bellows and the equally blue-blooded Bostonian Charles Eliot Norton, another member, Howe found were more interested in controlling an impersonal organization than they were in social reform, emancipation, and the humane care of troops and freed slaves. Howe, who looked back to the 1830s, was a reformer, while Bellows and Norton looked to the 1870s and beyond when bureaucratic order would replace perfectionistic hope and social ideals. It is not surprising, then, that by the end of 1862, Howe had lost much of his interest in the work of the Sanitary Commission.[34]

Throughout the year, however, he was bombarded with requests from Northern civilians, many of whom were women, to find positions in the

Union-occupied parts of the Confederacy. In these locations freedmen were in need of personal and social services, as well as education. In August 1862, for example, Charlotte Forten, a black teacher and abolitionist from the North, sought out Howe to secure a position teaching freedmen in the Sea Islands of South Carolina. At first she found Howe to be "cold and hard," but after she told him of her purpose and provided him a letter of introduction from the Quaker poet John Greenleaf Whittier "he was as kind and cordial as c[ou]ld be, and entered with much interest into my wishes."[35]

On the first day of January 1863 Abraham Lincoln announced the Emancipation Proclamation. Three weeks later Howe, along with Wendell Phillips, Moncure Conway, George L. Stearns, and Frank Bird met with President Lincoln at the White House. Delighted by the recent proclamation, the group of Boston reformers tried to persuade Lincoln to appoint John Fremont as military governor over the part of North Carolina in Union hands.[36] Fremont's antislavery credentials, the Boston party argued, made him the best leader of a North Carolina project of reconstruction. Lincoln, who thought less of the general's credentials and more of his earlier unauthorized freeing of slaves under his military jurisdiction, was not persuaded.

From his work on the Sanitary Commission and his efforts for emancipation, Howe came to the attention of the newly appointed secretary of war Edwin M. Stanton. In March Stanton selected Howe, along with the social reformers and abolitionists Robert Dale Owen and James McKaye, to the Freedmen's Inquiry Commission. By April, the commission had opened an office on the corner of Second Avenue and East Ninth Street in New York City, requiring Howe to make frequent trips to New York for commission business. Around that time, Howe wrote Charles Sumner that the Union forces should arm freedmen, giving them the same pay as white soldiers and treating them as equals. In a time when many whites resented being drafted into the army, it only made good sense, Howe claimed, to encourage black men to join the fight for their own freedom.[37] In May the Fifty-Fourth Colored Regiment paraded in Boston before heading south. The place of the free black and the freedman in the armed services and in the newly liberated parts of the South had become a pressing issue. Before the rebellion was brought to an end, 180,000 black men would fight for the Union Army, representing 20 percent of the black adult male population under the age of forty-five.[38]

On 17 May 1863, Howe's youngest child, three-and-a-half-year-old Samuel G. Howe Jr., died. He was the first in his family to be buried in the family's plot on Spruce Street in Mount Auburn Cemetery. The devastation Samuel and Julia felt is reflected in a letter Samuel sent the following September to Mary Mann, who had earlier sent her condolences. He wrote: "Your mention of my lost angel boy opens flood gates of sorrow in my heart. Long as I have lived, I never knew before the real anguish which a human being can have & live. There is no comfort for me but in work which for a while brings oblivion of the past."[39] To deal with the loss, Samuel had increased his efforts on the Freedmen's Inquiry Commission. By the end of the month, he was complaining to Sumner about the uneven work of Owen. In Norfolk, Virginia, while inspecting freedmen settlements, Howe wrote Sumner again, this time about what had increasingly become evident to him.

> The soldiers strip [the freedmen] of valuables & take their money at the outposts. . . . The men are then set to work for the army, & although beyond all question they do as a general thing far more work than white marines, they are promised less wages & the *promise is not kept.*
>
> The [freed] women & children are herded into camps where they generally are ill treated & demoralized by our soldiers. . . .
>
> I would try at drum head Court martial & shoot without delay any man found guilty of driving back refugees or spiriting them of their goods. I would have a complete system of registration by which every man, woman & child coming within our lines should be named, numbered & described, & free papers given them. Those claiming to be man & wife or wishing to be married should be formally married & registered, & the parties given to understand that the man is responsible for the support of his wife & children. I would have a general Superintendent at Wash. With a Bureau & assistant superintendent[s] whenever needed, & all these should report directly to the Sec. of War, & not to the local military authorities. I would have it made sure & certain that every black man employed in any department of the army (& tens of thousands are needed) should be paid regularly, so as to make it *patent* & indubitable & felt throughout slavedom that emancipation means *wages for work*! I believe a system like this, rigorously carried out, in addition to the enrollment arising & *protecting* blacks as soldiers, would in three months do more to disintegrate the slave power & paralyze the rebellion than great victories in the field.

Even in early 1862, Howe had complained to Sumner about the contraband slave (a term that he despised) that he had seen around Alexandria, Virginia, being worked by Union Army troops, locked up in jails at night, but not being paid. For Howe, such actions suggested merely another form of slavery. From his inspection of contraband slaves in Virginia a year later, in 1863, it became even clearer to Howe that former slaves stripped of familiar surroundings and family members were necessarily dependent on Union troops. Rather than exploiting these freed slaves, the troops should employ them. Rather than being a burden to the Union troops, freedmen should become a part of the fighting force.[40]

As 1863 drew to a close, Howe submitted his report, *The Refugees from Slavery in Canada West,* to Secretary of War Henry Stanton. The 110-page report summarized Howe's findings from his visits for the Freedmen's Inquiry Commission in what was then referred to as Canada West, or Lower Ontario. He had visited settlements of former slaves who had escaped on the Underground Railroad and were living in the Canadian cities and towns of Sainte-Catherine, Hamilton, London, Toronto, Chatham, Buxton, Winsor, Malden, and Colchester.

As he developed his report, in August Howe began a correspondence with the Harvard naturalist Louis Agassiz. Howe was interested in the mulatto and especially in the preservation of the mixed-race person's survival in northern climates like that of Canada and, by inference, in the northern states of the United States. Only a few months earlier the *Atlantic Monthly* had published an article arguing that blacks—pure blooded and mulatto—in the South were naturally adapted to that region's warm climate. Once freed, the former slaves would likely remain in the South and would therefore not threaten the "purity [of] the Anglo-Saxon blood."[41] Indeed, developing in the North was a growing position that blacks should be emancipated, but in their freedom, they should not enjoy the same rights and privileges as whites, especially the right to migrate to the North.

In this context, influenced by his correspondence with Agassiz, Howe concluded that the mulatto would not likely survive in the northern regions because the birthrate of mulattos was low. According to Howe, although blacks had become law-abiding and hardworking citizens in Canada, they were naturally destined for southern climates, where they would succeed as citizens without the special help of whites. What the black person needed was freedom, rights, and land. In the proper warm climate, the amalgamation of the races would be unnecessary. Instead, blacks would intermarry, "live in communities by themselves," and "be docile and easily governed by laws, and however given to petty offences, will not be prone to crimes of grave character." Thus, Howe concluded, the mulatto—an evil product of slavery—would "naturally" die out.[42] Howe's views about the "natural" climatic conditions for black men and women was a perspective shared by many antislavery proponents, even Frederick Douglass, who believed that blacks were inclined to warm climates of the South.[43] Howe did not hold, however, that blacks, although freed, should be deprived of the same rights enjoyed by whites.

Howe and the other commissioners sent out two questionnaires that solicited information about the status and abilities of freedmen. The first questionnaire, mailed in August 1863, contained forty-two parts. The com-

missioners sent it principally to public officials in the nonrebellious parts of
the nation. It asked about the freedmen's ability to support themselves, their
views on marriage, and their ability to compete with whites. About a month
later, Howe sent out a much shorter questionnaire to clergy, physicians, and
some elected officials. Like the first questionnaire, this one asked about the
likelihood of contraband slaves' adapting to freedom in a predominantly
white society. The responses the commission received were reflected widely
contrasting opinions. Henry M. Knight, a physician and superintendent of
the Connecticut School for Idiots, for example, wrote: "I am fully impressed
with the conviction that in this region the blacks as a class live as comfortably
as the whites who own no property but depend upon their labor for others for their support. Few colored men in this vicinity own much property,
tho' a few do. . . . I do not believe the race really inferior to whites, if they
may be blessed with the same advantages. But they are *kept down*. In our
public schools the *young* black keeps pace with his fellows who are white, but
as years increase the sympathy (psychical) of childhood is lost. The colored
youth is kept aloof from his mates & must suffer in development."[44] While
correspondence like Knight's reflected positive white opinion about the
adaptability of freedmen, other returned surveys painted a different picture.
For Major James M Pomeroy of the Ninth Kansas Volunteers, for example,
freedmen "are the most worthless vagabonds I ever saw or heard of."[45]

Supporting Owen, but departing from McKaye, Howe held that the
federal government should provide short-term but not long-term assistance
to freedmen. McKaye also argued for the confiscation and redistribution of
land to the newly freed slaves. Howe's more modest approach to social and
economic change was reflected in his involvement in the Freedman's Savings
Bank, where he was a trustee until the bank became insolvent. Although
he did not support the confiscation of rebel land, in several articles from
December 1863 through March 1864 in the *Boston Commonwealth,* Howe
advocated for the redistribution of abandoned land to the freeman as a
vital part of reconstruction.[46] In December 1863, in a letter to Sumner, he
summed up his perspective on how the federal government might construct
a postwar South. He began by reminding Sumner that he had witnessed
the progress of five hundred thousand freedmen and women in Canada,
and in Maryland, Delaware, eastern Virginia, Kentucky, Tennessee and
Missouri. From these observations he concluded: "Though they are a poor
breed physically, they can support themselves & contribute to the material
prosperity of the country." In the Border States, there was little need for federal troop supervision to protect the rights of the newly freed former slaves,
as long as those rights were a matter of the law. In the "Cotton & Sugar
States," however, Howe said, there would be the need for federal troops "for

some time." Howe advocated for full and immediate emancipation. He opposed plans proposed by some politicians that freedmen undergo a form of apprenticeship, which he saw as merely another form of servitude. Like Owen, Howe foresaw that freed slaves would quickly become members of the free economy of the new South. With their political rights protected, freedmen would sell their labor in a free market. In short, the freedmen would become free men, free members of the wage-earning agrarian proletariat. What Howe and many others failed to anticipate was that without long-term federal intervention in the South to protect the rights of black citizens, blacks would not be able to hold onto the rights they secured as the result of emancipation. As history would show, even the Thirteenth, Fourteenth, and Fifteenth Amendments to the U.S. Constitution could not prevent the eventual triumph of Jim Crow.[47]

Family, Friends, and the Institutions during the War Years

Early in the evening of 9 July 1861, Fanny Longfellow was using wax to seal locks she had just cut from her daughters' hair at their Cambridge home. Somehow—it happened so quickly—the match that she had used to melt the wax caught her light summer dress on fire. She ran in panic, fueling the flames, which engulfed her. Henry Longfellow rushed to her, burning himself as he tried to extinguish the flames. In great pain, Fanny Longfellow died the next day. Three days later, the day of her funeral, was also the Longfellows' eighteenth wedding anniversary. Too distraught, Longfellow had attended neither the funeral nor the burial at Mount Auburn Cemetery. Howe had been to the family's house twice, but Longfellow refused all guests. "He still suffers bodily," Howe wrote to Sumner, "but who can measure or understand the mental agony he has to endure! . . .Thus, one after another passes off the stage of the world, the individual actors disappear & are of no account, but the great drama of life goes on & will be fully played out, while we are as nothing. Let us each so live & work that others may be happier & better for what we have done."[48]

And life would go on. With three daughters and a son all in their teens, the Howe household moved from South Boston into Boston in 1862. The population of South Boston had nearly doubled in the past decade to 24,941 residents, and by war's end, it would rise again to 29,363. With the influx of new city dwellers, it was no longer the quaint village it had been twenty years earlier.[49] It had become the site of the Boston House of Correction, the House of Industry (a workhouse for the able-bodied poor), the City Lunatic Asylum, and the House of Reformation for Juvenile Boys. The South Boston docks that had been erected in the 1840s were drawing laborers who filled tenement houses near the bridges going into Boston. By the end of the 1860s, South Boston neighborhoods were made up predominantly of poor and working-class Irish immigrants. Although Howe never expressed the class prejudice that much of his generation of socially elite Bostonians held, he and Julia moved the family to a "better neighborhood" for what they saw as the well-being of their children.[50]

Their new address was 13 Chestnut Street. Laura Howe Richards remembered the Civil War years when the family lived in Boston as a time of constant movement. The population of the city in 1860 was 177,840, up from 43,298 four decades earlier. Men and women of all backgrounds came through the Howe's front door. Samuel's visitors were men concerned with the political activities of the war; Julia's were likely to be literary men and women from her "Brain Club."[51] During the first year of the war, Samuel joined the Saturday Club, made up of literary men and businessmen—Oliver Wendell Holmes Sr., Ralph Waldo Emerson, James Russell Lowell, Nathaniel Hawthorne, Louis Agassiz, and Henry James Sr.—who met at Boston's Parker House once a month for dinner and for humor and light discussion about matters of the day. Florence Howe Hall remembered the club members who visited the Howe home: "They were all middle-aged or elderly men, by no means the heroes of young feminine imagination. Yet their conversation seemed wholly delightful to a girl who loved athletic sports quite as well as reading, perhaps a little better."[52]

Maud Howe recalled a house filled with statuary, paintings Julia had inherited from her father, and engravings of ancient Greek art that hung in Samuel's study.[53] Poles, Austrians, Hungarians, Greeks, and other foreign visitors, like all those who had been coming to the Howe residence since the 1840s, called on Samuel Howe at 13 Chestnut Street for references, temporary shelter, and other favors. Julia Romana and Florence, who had begun to notice David Hall, one of the sons of the family next door, were preoccupied with Back Bay parties. Harry, taking after his father, got into trouble for student pranks, first at the Boston Latin School and then at Harvard University in the mid-sixties. While at Boston Latin he dropped fire buckets out of the Parker House window and was promptly arrested, his sister Laura later wrote, "as an incendiary, and hustle our dear father out of his midnight bed to rescue [him], and pay fines, and what not." At Harry's instigation, two fast-talking fellow students from Harvard came to the Howe house and, announcing to the maid that they had come for a sofa, removed it and carried it down the street and into another house with the cooperation of the unsuspecting maid who answered the door. For some on-campus folly, Harry was suspended for a term during his sophomore year.[54] His father seemed to be forgiving, assuring Julia's sister Louisa, "[Harry] has had the ill luck to be suspended for six months, but not for any immorality or serious offense, but for excess of animal spirit running into wild pranks & mischief."[55] In a letter to Harry's sister Laura, Howe spoke of Harry's "disposition to dandyism," which he called "but a passing blemish which he will soon throw off." But Howe also told Laura: "Harry has come out with very high standing in his class [at Harvard]—second only to one— & hardly second to him. His marks in calculus 97—the maximum being 100. I am much gratified by the development of manly & studious qualities in him."[56]

During the time on Chestnut Street, Maud, the youngest daughter, attended Elizabeth Peabody's kindergarten on Pinckney Street. "We sat on tiny chairs, around a fascinating low table," she remembered, "where we modeled birds' nests in clay and filled the nests with tiny eggs. Another useful art was the weaving of patterns with narrow strips of colored paper. My first lessons in arithmetic were had at the Kindergarten, with the help of a frame strung with red, green, and yellow beads." Later, like her older sisters, Maud attended the Temple Place School led by Henry Williams, who, despite a lump on his forehead and a missing forefinger, had a musical voice "that won the heart of every child."[57]

Howe family activities included daily horseback riding and gathering to hear Samuel read poetry. Since the 1830s, Samuel's principal form of exercise had been a morning horseback ride on his black mare, Breeze. He usually took one of his children with him. All of the Howe children rode horses, for pleasure or transportation. Julia was more likely to employ a carriage. During rainy weather and at night Samuel read poetry in a family circle. Byron, Scott, Burns, and Macaulay were his favorite poets. Maud remembered, "He had a fine voice and read—recited rather, for he knew them by heart—many a stirring poem in the hour of rest he allowed himself after the evening meal."[58]

During the Civil War years, the family spent vacations on a five-acre property Samuel had purchased at Lawton's Valley, near Newport, Rhode Island. Near the house, which Samuel had enlarged, was a stream that led to a waterfall and an old stone mill. Over the years the family added fruit trees and flowers to the garden. Getting to the property was a challenge for the family. The railroad took them only as far as Fall River. From there they traveled the final twelve miles in a carriage that barely held the seven members of the Howe family, along with their cook, nursemaid, and belongings. Julia had spent summers in Newport since her father, Samuel Ward, first brought the family there to escape New York City's cholera epidemic of 1832. In 1836, he had bought a cottage on the corner of Bellevue Avenue and Catherine Street. At Lawton's Valley, Samuel and Julia entertained many guests during the summer months of the war years and thereafter. Julia introduced the new

English practice of serving afternoon tea followed by lively conversation and occasional games. The Howe children remembered morning and afternoon swims in the nearby bay, and they remembered following along with their father as he performed various chores around the place. "He liked to make companions of his children,": Laura remembered, "and was never weary of us 'tagging' at his heels. We followed him about the garden like so many dogs, watching the pruning or grafting which were his special tasks. . . . He loved to play and romp with us. Sometimes he would put on his great fur coat and come into the dining room at dancing time, on all fours, growling horribly, and pursue us into the corners, we shrieking with delighted terror."[59]

In 1865, Samuel sold the property at Lawton's Valley and shortly thereafter purchased a house about a half mile away that the family called Oak Glen. After Fanny Longfellow's death, Henry visited the Howes at their Newport retreats, as did Ralph Waldo and Lidian Emerson, the actors Charlotte Cushman and Edwin Booth, Henry James senior and junior, Elizabeth Peabody, John Andrew, Louis Agassiz (who, the Howe children recalled, put lots of lumps of sugar in his coffee), Oliver Wendell Holmes Sr., James Freeman Clarke, and the young Henry Cabot Lodge. Lodge commented that people rarely lived up to his imagination of them, but Samuel Howe was the exception. "He was a most striking-looking man," Lodge remembered, "hawk-eyed, hawk-nosed, with the expression of wild daring which I expected."[60] But among all the guests who came to Lawton's Valley and Glen Oaks, the favorite of the Howe children was their uncle Sam Ward.

In 1861, Howe purchased a closed carriage that had been made to order for Jefferson Davis but never delivered to him because of the outbreak of war. To the Howe family, it was always the Jeff Davis, as in, "Oh take the Jeff Davis, and you won't get wet." During the war, the Howe daughters, like many other young women in Boston, spent evenings by the fire knitting socks for soldiers and scraping lint and preparing bandages for wounded soldiers. With their mother, they also participated in various fund-raising fairs for war-related charitable institutions, such as the Sanitary Commission and for the National Sailors' Home. One fund-raising event, the Great Fair at the Boston Theater, lasted for ten days. Florence, who was seventeen years old at the time of the fair, recalled, "Every variety of object was sold there—many by means of raffles." Julia, with the help of her oldest two daughters, edited *The Boatswain's Whistle,* the fair's newspaper.[61]

Although no members of the Howe family died in the war, they were affected by deaths among their friends and associates. Laura remembered a stormy afternoon at Lawton's Valley when Margaret McDonald, the matron of the idiot school, appeared to inform Howe that her oldest son, who had served in the Christian Commission, had been taken prisoner by Confederate forces. Although he was released in a few months, he died a year later of consumption. For the rest of her life, McDonald kept a locket of her son's hair in a harp-shaped brooch she always wore and daguerreotypes of him in her room at the idiot school. Florence remembered viewing the funeral corteges that frequently appeared on the streets of Boston and seeing disabled soldiers on visits to Camp Readville outside of Boston. She recalled also that the family's good friend John Andrew, governor during the war, found that he could not attend Sabbath services at the Church of the Disciples because an endless stream of petitioners for war-related relief would disturb his worship.[62]

Not all of the war years, however, were spent in war-related activities. The Howes had moved to Chestnut Street because Samuel and Julia felt that their older children would be socially isolated if they remained in South Boston. A letter Francis Barlow, a young colonel who stayed with the Howes while recuperating from a battle injury sustained at Antietam, wrote to his mother in March 1863 describes the Howe household: "I enjoy it . . . at the Howes & like Mrs. H. very much. She is not only very bright & clever but most amiable & kindhearted & an earnest & good woman. The Dr. is rather a taciturn man but is very cordial. They have six children, the two oldest being very pretty daughters of some 18 & 19 years old."[63]

The older daughters attended dances at their own home and the homes of others, and they took part in the "coming out" rituals of the debutante ball at Papanti's Hall, where young Bostonian elites learned the art of dancing. Florence remembered dancing at one party with Charlie Longfellow, not long before the poet's son ran away to join the Union forces. Because of war shortages, fabric for dresses was precious, and the Howe daughters learned to make them last long and serve multiple purposes. Florence worked as the bookkeeper at the idiot school during the war years to make some money for clothes. The Howes gave frequent parties. Oliver Wendell Holmes, well known in Boston circles for his conversation, was a frequent visitor, especially after Julia started her Brain Club. Ralph Waldo Emerson came for dinner at least once during the war years. "His table talk was fresh, quaint, and delightful," Florence remembered. "Yet he was, on the whole, rather silent than talkative in company." Alexander Hamilton, the son of the Federalist, was a guest of Samuel's. Florence recalled that when William James, who was about the age of the older Howe daughters, visited the Chestnut Street house, he suggested that polygamy might be a good arrangement, to which she had commented at the time, not from the perspective of the woman.[64]

The war brought as little change to the operation of the blind and idiot schools as it did to the routine of the Howe household. Shortly before the war, Howe launched an effort to find domestic positions for some of his recent female graduates. In a letter to prospective employers, he wrote: "They can make themselves very handy & useful in various kinds of house work. They can assist a cook in various ways. They can wash dishes, set tables, & clean them away. They can do chamber work. . . . They would be glad to work for any moderate compensation. If you could have a trial made of one of them in your establishment you would do a kind work & greatly oblige [me]."[65] Also, at the Perkins Institution, Howe continued his policy of boarding out older students who were working in the institution's workshop. In the homes of ordinary citizens, they paid for their room and board from the wages they received. He even insisted that his former students who were now faculty members of the blind school board in the community. He told Sophia Carter, one of his first pupils, who returned in 1857 to teach at the school, that she must find lodging in the community, because, he said, "you could in that way consult your own tastes in matters of diet without causing any trouble in the household here either by causing extra work, or by doing what others would be sure to wish to do also."[66] Howe admitted to the new principal of the Michigan Institution for the Blind and Deaf, Charles L. Palmer, that he had made a mistake early in his career by having pupils live in the same quarters in which they had school. If he had it to do over again, he "would locate [the school] in a populous place." "I would erect a building," he explained, "for two schoolrooms, recitation rooms, music rooms & work shop & that is all. The pupils should board in private families & come to school as other children do."[67]

Howe was proud of the work that his workshop workers produced. To a perspective New York buyer he boasted, "The reputation of our own Shop for good work especially mattresses work is well established, & people buy at our Store not because the goods are made by the Blind but because the work can be relied upon."[68] Some of the manufactured goods—chairs, mattresses, and brooms—had been sent to London for the Great Exhibition of 1851. Many people who paid a penny to enter the exhibition's Crystal Palace saw work of the foremost American school for the blind, and Howe received letters from Europeans who were impressed with the work. Only a few decades earlier, Howe had looked to Europeans for inspiration; now Europeans were inspired by what Howe had accomplished.

Learning a trade continued to be one of Howe's principal goals for the students at the idiot school and especially at the blind school. As he had learned as far back as the 1840s, not all of his graduates could find gainful employment. For this reason, the schools' workshop continued to employ about thirty of the graduates of the two schools. They boarded out in homes usually in South Boston and came to the workshop for their daily work.

Howe insisted that the workshop's merchandise be of the highest quality; yet, he was not beyond appealing to the sympathy of the public to make sales. In 1865, for example, he sent out a letter on behalf of William DeWitt, a blind graduate who had become a salesman for the workshop's products. "The main object of this Institution," Howe wrote, "is to enable the Blind to support themselves by their own labours. In order to do this they will counterbalance the disadvantages growing out of their infirmity & enable them to compete fairly with ordinary workmen." He continued his letter by appealing to the sympathies of DeWitt's potential customers. "As however the object is a public one & as the blind, if left alone must for the most part depend on the public for support it would seem proper that all public & especially State establishments should give them the preference in work which they do as well as others."[69]

Howe felt content too about the growth of education for the blind and the "idiotic" in the United States. In 1857 in a letter to George Combe, whose book *Constitution of Man* Howe had just published in raised letters for blind readers, he boasted: "Our [blind] institutions are sixteen in number, & average fifty pupils. This is a much larger proportion, I think, than exists in any other country. We are now turning our attention to training Schools for Idiotic Children. There are already four large ones."[70]

Having become the nation's leading expert on blindness, Howe often exchanged letters with other leading scientific authorities. To his friend, the Harvard naturalist, Louis Agassiz, he wrote about the unusual case of a blind bird. "There is a common notion, is there not, that animals in the *natural* state, are free from those defects & imperfections of organization such as blindness[,] deafness & the like, which are so common among civilized men?" Howe went on to explain that he had found a young robin at Lawton's Valley that was "perfectly blind," adding: "Not being able to remain & watch the proceedings of the old birds, & feeling sure that the poor blind one must perish if left out over night (as a storm was brewing) I took it to the house. By great care & nursing he has been kept alive until to-day, when he died." Finally Howe got to the point of his curious letter to Agassiz: "On dissecting one side of the head I found no external opening for the eye. There was a cavity where the eye should have been, & the skin was covered with fine down. On removing the skin I found the rudiments of an eye ball on one side. The other I have not opened. I have watched as narrowly as I could the habits of the poor bird with a view to ascertain how far the action of the sense of sight is necessary for training the instinct, & will make a record of them. The object in writing now is to say that if you are curious to see the *subject* it may not be too late to-morrow."[71]

During the war, at the blind school, Thursday was the public's visitation day, and each visitor paid five cents, with the proceeds going for the benefit of indigent pupils. Although the public enthusiasm of the 1840s had diminished by the 1860s, Howe still mildly complained about the curiosity of the public, and Thursdays were always filled with visitors throughout the war.

The practice of cold baths continued at the school, despite the concerns of some parents. In 1872 Howe was accused of cruelty in forcing these baths on his pupils, but twenty of his pupils sent a letter to the formerly Whig and now Republican *Boston Advertiser* supporting cold bathing.[72] In January 1865, three Irish boys assaulted one of Howe's blind pupils; on the advice of a police captain, Howe offered a reward for the apprehension of the boys.[73] Also during the war years, Howe insisted that all pupils return home for school vacations lest they begin to identify the institution as their home. If a pupil had no home in which to return, as he had before the war, Howe would find a guardian or a friend to take in the pupil during the vacation. He sent those for whom a guardian or a friend could not be found to the alms house in their local community or even to one of the newly opened state poor houses.[74]

Before the war was over, Howe began to get requests to educate Union soldiers blinded by battle wounds. Joseph Parsons, for example, "whose eyes were shot out at the second Bull Run Battle," applied for admission to the New England School for the Blind through the efforts of the U.S. Sanitary Commission. Because he was from Maryland, Howe suggested that Parsons apply to the Maryland School for the Blind, but he added that if Parsons were refused admission, he would allow him to attend the New England School. Eventually, Parsons did become a student of the blind school, and Howe assured the Sanitary Commission representative that he was certain Parsons "might learn a trade."[75] Howe also received a request to admit a newly freed slave who was blind, twenty-two-year-old Jonas Carter, from Harper's Ferry, now in West Virginia. He had lost the sight of one of his eyes as the result of a beating from his former owner's overseer, and his other eye was damaged by illness. After working with him in the blind school, Howe pronounced Carter "intelligent but lazy."[76]

Howe continued to receive requests from his former students for help getting employment. He also continued to get such requests from blind adults who had never attended his school, such as Aldisa Parker of Bellowsfalls, Vermont, who wrote him in November 1862. His poor spelling did not get in the way of his request for employment. "Father wrote to you a short time ago and asked you to assist me in geting to work. You said that you would. I have inquired to all stores in the vilage and several others. They think if I get to makeing brooms, I can make good business at it. If you will bee so kind as to send me a mashien and a press, I will do my best, and father thinks we can pay you soon. If it is your request, I will have some one bee responsible for me."[77]

In 1862, when the principal teacher of the blind girls' school resigned, Howe wrote to leading educators to describe the kind of teacher he wanted. His letter reads: "She should be a person of mature age, & good health; she should be of cheerful temper & communicative disposition. A taste for music & a musical voice are very desirable; & so would be some musical attainments, though she will not be called upon to teach music. . . . As the person will have to reside here, & make one of the household, her domestic influence will be considerable, & she should be of a religious disposition, without sectarian or proselytizing zeal." As for her academic skills, "She should have some experience in teaching & be perfectly familiar with the best modes of teaching all the common English branches, including algebra & geometry."[78] Howe's description of this lead female teacher reflected his view of the ideal female worker.

The war years produced national inflation that eventually affected the employees of the blind and idiot schools. On 4 August 1864, Howe received a letter signed by five employees requesting salary increases. They justified the request by the rise in the cost of living caused by the war.[79] By May 1865, with the war just ended Howe sent out a circular to parents, relatives, and local officials of his pupils describing the financial difficulties of the schools and imploring those who could afford it to provide additional funding. Many families and officials wrote back, most to say that they were as cash strapped as were the two schools.

After the Rebellion

In February 1865 shortly before the fighting ceased, Howe led an effort to present a petition before the Massachusetts General Court for a law to prohibit the denial of admission to any theaters and amusement activities on the basis of color or race.[80] In March, along with fifteen other leading Bostonians, he sponsored a call for donations to relieve famine in the South. As his work of the Freedmen's Inquiry Commission revealed, Howe advocated in the *Commonwealth*—a paper supported by the largess of George L. Stearns—what one historian has called an "egalitarian laissez-faire approach."[81] As such, Howe called for governmental assistance to freedmen, but not so much assistance as the freedman might become dependent on it.

On the Fourth of July 1865 at eight in the morning, Howe's effort to honor Horace Mann, which had begun soon after Mann's death in 1859, culminated in the unveiling of a statue of Mann on the grounds of the Massachusetts

Horace Mann statue (1865). Photograph by Sue N. Trent.

State House. Howe had asked Emerson to speak at the dedication ceremony, but Emerson had declined. Instead Howe and Governor Andrew spoke. Howe reminded the audience that Mann had devoted his life to the causes of humanity, and especially to public education. At the end of his address, a Boston school girl, Maggie W. Walker, removed the covering over the statue. Mary Mann and her sisters, Elizabeth Peabody and Sophia Hawthorne, were pleased with Emma Stebbins's sculpture, and Howe was delighted that the monument would compete for attention with the statehouse statue of Daniel Webster, about which he had never had anything but disparaging remarks to make. In attendance were luminaries from across the state and hundreds of children from the Boston Public Schools, many of whom had helped raise funds for the statue. A choir of schoolchildren sang the hymn Julia Ward Howe had composed for the occasion. Howe was gratified that his old friend had at last achieved such a prominent honor.[82]

In October 1865 Governor Andrew appointed Howe chair of the Massachusetts Board of State Charities, on which he had served as a member since December 1864. He would continue to chair the board until 1874. Sanborn, his fellow member of the Secret Six, was secretary. The first board of state charities in the nation, the Massachusetts board reflected the growing state takeover after the Civil War of many charitable institutions previously operated by local governments. Following Massachusetts' example, many states in the two decades after the Civil War created state welfare boards and commissions to bring order to the growing number of charitable organizations and institutions.[83]

A month later, in November, Howe in his new capacity wrote James Freeman Clarke about the need to protect boys and girls who were apprenticed in state reformatories. Once again he made clear his distrust of institutional means to solve social problems along with his awareness that a noninstitutional alternative had to be grounded in appropriate supervision. "You know that we have many hundreds of boys & girls apprenticed out by the several Institutions & still under pupilage," Howe said. It was Howe's contention that in this final stage of their reformation, boys and girls needed careful supervision. Yet, they were receiving just the opposite—too little supervision. Howe had two plans: "the appointment by the State of a *woman* who shall have a good salary, & whose business it shall be by correspondence & by visits to look after the apprentices—boys as well as girls, & to see to it that their masters treat them kindly & wisely, & that they are surrounded by good moral influences . . . [and a] Central Society in Boston with corresponding members in each town of the Commonwealth, & each school district if need be, whose special business should be to look after the apprentices & report monthly to the central society"[84]

Maud Howe often accompanied her father in his capacity as chair of the board of charities on inspection trips to public poorhouses and asylums throughout Massachusetts. "I have slept in almost every poorhouse and insane asylum in the State," she remembered. Howe often made these trips in the evening, when he was least expected. This practice, Maud reported, "gave my father the chance to see the institution in its lying down and getting up, a time when shortcomings are more evident than during hours when trustees and visitors may safely be expected. . . . Tewkesbury Almshouse was a source of a good deal of worry to my father; we were there often and at the Asylum for the Insane at Taunton. While Papa was inspecting buildings and talking with the inmates, I was left with the matron."[85]

In 1866 Howe's distrust for institutional models of charity and care caused him to oppose one of his oldest friends, Longfellow, who, along with several other distinguished Northerners—including William Cullen Bryant, Horace Greeley, Clara Barton, and P. T. Barnum—had petitioned Congress in 1864 for a national organization of homes for disabled Union veterans. As his first report of the Massachusetts Board of State Charities makes clear, Howe felt that institutions for disabled soldiers were in the best interests of neither disabled soldiers nor the public: "Many of our soldiers need homes, but such homes as we ourselves need; and a great institution . . . never was and never can be such a home as our . . . veterans ought to have. . . . Better [to] have 500 maimed veterans stumping about the towns and villages of Massachusetts, living partly on their pension and partly by their work, than shut up in the costliest and best structures that art could plan or money build."[86]

Also in 1866, Howe took the issue of institutionalization to the field in which he was the nation's leading authority—blindness. The State of New York was dedicating a new school for the blind at Batavia. State officials had called on Howe to give the address for the new school's opening. What Howe had to say about the blind must have come as a shock to the officials who invited him to speak. As for the best course of education for the blind, Howe claimed, "Separation and not congregation should be the law of their treatment." Gathering them together (as state officials were preparing to do at Batavia) is a poor way to treat the blind. The goal of treatment and education is self-help, and the outcome of such education, Howe insisted, should be integration into communities. Better to have a central school, Howe argued, but to house the students in the homes of ordinary citizens in the community, much as he was now attempting to do at the Perkins Institution.[87]

As the war was drawing to an end, Howe expressed his views on pressing matters of the time. In February 1865, for example, he wrote Sumner to support his Senate proposal for a progressive federal income tax. "Property must make continual concessions," he said, "if it would claim more respect &

power than inheres in it by natural rights, & among these must be a sliding scale of taxation proportionate to income." Howe acknowledged the social and economic consequences of separately defined worker and owner classes: "I am an ultra in this one thing, to wit, the belief that society never will, & never ought to, rest upon [a] solid & peaceful foundation so long as the labor & drudgery of the world is thrown entirely upon one class, while another class is entirely exempt from it. There is radical injustice in it, & injustice in society is like a rotten timber in the foundations of a house."[88]

While Howe's views on progressive income taxation were ahead of his time, his views on labor were traditional. Since the 1850s he had opposed the ten-hour day, and he opposed worker unions especially if those unions existed to strike collectively for better wages or better working conditions. His views were only reinforced after he developed a close friendship with Francis Bird, a well-to-do paper manufacturer. Bird, like Howe, was firmly antislavery, but Bird held that each individual worker had the right and obligation to enter into a contract for himself with his employer. When government became involved in regulating the free exchange of capital and labor, the law of supply and demand was threatened. Even though Massachusetts was at the time the most industrialized state in the nation and even though he acknowledged the social harm of distinct working and owner classes, Howe in his capacity on the Massachusetts Board of State Charities failed to anticipate the collective needs and concerns of ordinary wage-dependent workers. If there was a failure, Howe continued to insist, it was a failure of the individual, not the economic system. In this respect, his view was similar to that of other abolitionists and antislavery proponents. They, like Howe, supported the redistribution of wealth through a progressive income tax while holding to the belief that an individual should control the terms of his work as a contract between that worker and his or her employer.[89]

The postwar years also gave Howe an opportunity to reconfirm his faith in oral education for deaf people. Since his trip through Prussia in 1832, he had been convinced of the efficacy of teaching deaf students to articulate common speech. Horace Mann, who had witnessed oral methods carried out in Prussian schools for the deaf in 1843, shared his preference for oralism. Howe had long been frustrated that the American School for the Deaf at Hartford had, as he put it in an 1875 letter to the parent of a deaf child, tried articulation, but with little vigor, only "to pronounce it to be a failure." From Howe's perspective, the Hartford educators were prejudiced against oral education and for that reason never gave the method a fair chance. And he acknowledged to the parent, who had asked his opinion, that sectarian differences were also at play. The Hartford school was aligned with orthodox Christianity, he and Mann with Unitarian Christianity.[90] The opening of the

Clarke Institution for the Deaf in Northampton, Massachusetts, founded on oralism, allowed Howe to see his oral methods put into practice. Even before the war, as planners were considering a deaf school for Massachusetts, Howe wrote lawmakers that the new school should avoid congregating large numbers of children together. He received support in his effort from an unexpected source, Amos Smith Jr., the registrar of deeds of the City of Boston. A deaf man educated at the American School for the Deaf at Hartford, Smith had come out in favor of a Massachusetts school for the deaf that rejected what Smith called "one of the great evils of the Hartford Inst, . . . the excess to which they carry out the use of sign language."[91] Although association among the deaf was not in itself a bad thing, Howe claimed, congregating the deaf apart from the hearing would be a mistake. "There is no good and sufficient reason why Deaf Mute Children should be cooped up together any more than ordinary children, certainly none sufficient to counterbalance the great moral disadvantage arising from their being congregated closely together. . . . I am quite sure that there would be great moral and intellectual advantages growing out of the adoption of this principle, that every possible discouragement should be placed in the way of Mutes associating together, and every possible encouragement given to their associating with the hearing."[92] Howe consistently advocated for integration into the main currents of everyday life, whether he was talking about the blind, the "idiotic," delinquent children, or the deaf. For the deaf, to insure this integration, Howe argued forcefully against what he saw as the private language of manual signing. It never occurred to him that among deaf people signing was not only a unique language but also a means of social solidarity.

Despite his new involvement with the board of charities and the education of the deaf, Howe remained principally concerned with his blind and "idiotic" students. In October 1865, a French physician, Alexande Blanchet, wrote to ask him about the state of services in the United States since the end of the war. Howe responded with a long letter. He said he was glad to report that all the blind institutions in the Union states had remained open; indeed, most had increased in their school populations. But in the Rebel states the schools "were broken up & the pupils scattered." Since the restoration of peace, a few Southern schools had opened in Virginia, Tennessee, and Louisiana, but they housed only a few pupils. Howe then explained his now three-decades-old perspective that the education of the blind should take place in a school, not in an asylum. "Into these several Institutions," Howe wrote, "young Blind persons are not only received free of all expenses, but are rather encouraged to come. None of them, however, are considered as asylums for life, but merely as schools for instruction & training during a certain period, the minimum of which is five years—the maximum, seven years." He then went on to describe his ideal curriculum.

> The general idea is to give all children 1st developmental & training of their bodily powers, 2nd the same kind & degree of mental instruction as is given to ordinary children in the Common Schools of the State. In addition of this, a knowledge of the rudiments of vocal & instrumental music in all who have any musical capacity [is given]. 3rd Special instruction in the higher kinds of music to those [who] have special musical talent & such general ability as well warrant the hope that they may become successful teachers of Music, Organists, or Tuners of Piano Fortes. 4th Exercise in some simple handicraft which will develop strength & dexterity, & better prepare them for learning some special trade [is given].

Howe continued his letter to the inquiring Frenchman with his views about the blind in society.

> 1st The subject is beginning to be better understood. Blindness is regarded not as an evil to be forever entailed upon society, but as flowing from a violation of natural laws. That these laws may be known & understood & that the proportion of Blind to the whole population in every generation will increase or diminish according as these laws are obeyed or violated. 2nd That the Blind as a class fall below the average of men in respect to original vital force, that they have less bodily & mental energy, less power of resisting destructive agencies, & shorter duration of life. . . . 3rd That these disadvantages may be counterbalanced in a measure by early training & development of the physical powers, by instruction & improvement of the mental faculties. By the judicious application of capital for the establishment of workshops, in which the Blind shall receive not alms, but so much aid as will counterbalance his natural disadvantage, & enable him to compete with seeing workmen. 4th That by judicious application of aid the majority of the Blind may be lifted out of the dependent class & placed in the Industrial & self supporting class. 5th That it is undesirable to congregate the Blind together in large numbers, & that the period of their being so congregated for the purpose of instruction should be as short as possible. That after being instructed they should be encouraged to settle in their native towns, & not congregated together in cities.

Howe concluded: "In a word, that they should be diffused as widely as possible among the common population. That as in nature there is no such class as the Blind neither should there be in society."[93]

In another letter, this time about the issue of exempting blind people from taxation, Howe insisted that blind people should be treated the same way as sighted people. For too long, he said, the blind have been seen as a separate class of human beings. They might be blind, but they are still human beings. They produce and consume like other human beings. Howe wrote: "We ought to do nothing which tends to segregate them from general society and form them into a class apart—much less should we do anything which holds up the idea that they must have special favors. . . . I think that for the Blind to come before Congress 'in forma pauperis' and ask for exemption from taxation would be an acknowledgement of inferiority which would have a depressing effect upon those who aspire to independence. It would be admitting that they form a special class and are willing to be counted as such whereas they ought to claim rank among ordinary men upon equal terms." Howe remained adamantly opposed to giving special treatment to the blind,, even though he acknowledged that many blind people had low "vital forces."[94]

In March 1870 Howe dismissed Francis J. Campbell, the blind school's principal boys' music teacher over the previous fifteen years. At the time Campbell was completing a tour of Europe partly paid for by the school. In his absence, Howe had hired a teacher identified as Mr. Reeves as a temporary replacement for Campbell. During his tenure, Howe received a petition from eleven male pupils describing their dislike of Campbell's angry tirades and dismissive attitude and asking that Reeves be appointed as their permanent music teacher. Howe honored the boys' request by firing Campbell a few days later. Howe was never more preoccupied with the Perkins Institution than he was during the late 1860s and early 1870.[95]

This preoccupation extended to his effort to establish a college for the blind. Some of his students had gone on to institutions of higher learning— to Harvard, to Dartmouth, to Bowdoin. And certainly some of the blind school's graduates would continue to thrive at New England's best colleges, but many other graduates were not so capable, though they could do college-level work. As Howe envisioned the blind college, its curriculum would center on music, the topic that had been most successful for many of his best graduates, but it would also include instruction in pedagogy, mathematics, and Latin, as well as German, and Italian, two languages that would be important to students of music.[96] Knowing that he needed to find endowed funds for professorships, buildings, and equipment but knowing also that he needed to convince what he perceived to be a public doubtful about the higher education potential of the blind, Howe proposed enrolling four of his most capable blind students "at Harvard or elsewhere." To prepare these boys for college Howe was instructing them in Latin, and he planned shortly to begin a course of Greek. As he had over the years, Howe provided the instruction in the classical languages himself.[97] Oddly enough, the idea of an institution of higher learning just for blind people did not seem to be contradictory for Howe, especially given his opposition to separate institutional structures for disabled people. Howe's desire for a college for the blind, however, never materialized.

Aid for Crete

On 27 January 1866, Howe's older brother, Joseph Neals Howe Jr., died. A successful glassware manufacturer and businessman, Joseph Howe had never had his younger brother's Romantic proclivity for challenging and changing the world. Samuel, who had no concern for great wealth, was an idealistic believer in the perfectibility of humankind. Joseph, in contrast, was a realist who knew how to make money. Besides money making, Joseph's greatest enjoyment was the theater. Often Julia attended plays with her brother-in-law and his wife. Samuel almost never joined them. On occasion, Samuel and Julia's children spent time with their uncle and aunt at their home at Ashburton Place. Maud remembered her uncle as "a tall fair man who wore a high collar, an imposing stock, ruffled shirts, elaborate waistcoats, a handsome fob and seals attached to a great gold warming-pan of a repeater, which rang the hours with a delicate chime." "His house, his dress, everything that was his," she said, "had the stamp of sober wealth. He owned a pew in King's Chapel; his wife and daughters took their exercise in a fine barouche, drawn by two stout horses. The atmosphere of the house at Ashburton Place was as different as possible from our own *ambiente*." Despite the finery of the family, Florence remembered her uncle as "rather mischief loving." It became a family tradition in the 1850s for Samuel and his family to dine with his brother's family for Thanksgiving dinner. The meals were always sumptuous and, to Maud and Florence, the dinner glassware was most impressive.[98]

A month after Joseph's death, Samuel told Sumner: "I am much depressed & sad. My brother's death was a sad blow to me. We did not agree. He was a conservative & illiberal."[99] In his sadness, Howe began to look for a new cause, and before the year was out one appeared. In the summer of 1866 Greeks on the island of Crete were stirring in opposition to Turkish rule. Despite the trauma generated by his own country's devastating civil war, Howe turned away from the troubles of the United States and instead directed his attention to a former but familiar location. It was as if as an old man he might return to the glories of his youth. And besides, with the emancipation of slaves now apparently complete, Howe, like some other abolitionists and antislavery activists, seemed to have lost his interest in what William Dean Howells in the November 1869 issue of the *Atlantic Monthly* labeled the "Negro question."[100]

He was only sixty-five years old and had no doubt that he would make a good U.S. minister to Greece. Few Americans, he firmly believed, were more familiar with the nation. The plight of the Cretans was clear—a Christian people were being enslaved by a cruel Muslim nation. The same month of his brother's death Howe wrote a second letter to Sumner. In it, he mentioned the possibility of a Greek ministerial appointment. Again in April he confessed to Sumner about his desire to return to "the scene of my early labors & adventures."[101] The challenge was getting the approval of Secretary of State William Seward and ultimately the consent of President Andrew Johnson. Howe's well-known friendship with Sumner, who was already beginning to oppose several of the policies of the Johnson administration, did not bode well for Howe's appointment. In May, while in Washington, Julia met with the president and bluntly asked him to appoint her husband to the Greek ministry. Throughout the spring Samuel continued to seek support for the Greek appointment, but Sumner finally acknowledged his pessimism. At last in June Sumner informed Howe that the president was prejudiced against his appointment. Julia learned later that it was Seward who was blocking the selection; yet she and Samuel hoped for a reversal.[102]

By the fall, while helping to found the new Clarke Institution for the Deaf and continuing to work on the Board of State Charities, Howe began communicating with the Cretan Central Committee in Athens. In January 1867 in Boston he gave the first of many speeches in support of the Cretan revolt, and he began a letter-writing campaign to generate financial support for the rebels.[103] Over the next several months, he spoke about the plight of Crete around eastern Massachusetts and in New York City. Large and enthusiastic crowds greeted his talks. He turned to Democrat George Bancroft along with Republican stalwarts like Amos Adams Lawrence, Henry W. Bellows, and Governor John Andrew. By the middle of the month, he informed Sumner in Washington that even without a governmental appointment, "I propose to go out on a mission of my own." In February he wrote George Finlay, his old friend from their time together during the Greek War of Independence. Finlay had settled in Athens with a Greek wife, and Howe was eager to renew contact with a man who took him back to the glories of the 1820s. He informed Finlay that he had raised five thousand dollars for Cretan relief and that he hoped that additional funds would come from a forthcoming concert by the Harvard Musical Association.[104]

On 20 February, Howe wrote Lawrence asking for funds to buy rifles for Crete. Just as he had referred to these rifles during the Bleeding Kansas years as "peace makers," so too did he do so now.[105] Along with Lawrence, Howe worked closely with Hermann J. Warner, a young Boston attorney who had developed an interest in the Cretan cause and would become Howe's

Boston contact after he left for Greece. On 13 March 1867, Howe sailed for England on the Cunard steamer *Asia* with Julia, Julia Romana, and Laura. Florence, in February had become engaged to David Hall, her former next-door neighbor and now a rising young attorney, remained in Boston, as did Maud, who was still in school. In London, Howe wrote Warner that leading Greeks and Greek sympathizers in England had raised fifty thousand dollars for the Cretan cause, and that Greeks in Manchester and Liverpool had acquired a steamer that would attempt to break through the blockade the Turks had imposed on the island. The efforts of Cretan supporters in England made Howe optimistic. "The news," he wrote Warner back in Boston, "from Crete is encouraging—there seems to be little doubt of the result. It is almost certain to be virtual independence from Turkey, and probably entire independence and reunion with the Greek nation."[106]

After spending a few weeks in Paris in April, the family traveled to Rome, where they visited Julia's sister Louisa before going on to Athens. Samuel and Julia Romana went in May, and Julia and Laura joined them in July. (After the death of Thomas Crawford in 1857, Louisa had married the American artist Luther Terry and settled with him in Rome.) Before leaving Rome, Howe visited the thousand-bed Hospital San Spirito for men, which he found "very filthy, foul & fetid, & services mostly by ecclesiastics." He was more impressed with a new city lunatic asylum that used baths and douches to treat patients, an innovation that Howe greatly admired.[107]

Howe and Julia Romana arrived in Athens on 9 May. They stayed with Finlay before moving to more permanent accommodations. Almost immediately after arriving in the capital, Howe met a young patriot, Michael Anagnostopoulos, whom he hired as his secretary, to share the responsibility with Julia Romana. Though at the time Howe could communicate with Anagnostopoulos only in Greek and French, one of the first tasks he gave him was to purchase rifles for the Cretan fighters with the funds Lawrence had provided. "Mr. Anagnostopoulos," Howe assured Lawrence, "will see to shipping the goods which you have so kindly purchased."[108]

Howe was surprised by the large number of refugees from Crete he encountered in Athens, who seemed to have arrived with little more than the clothes they were wearing. Most of the refugees were not registered with any of the Cretan committees that had sprung up in Athens. Howe estimated that there were about twelve thousand Cretan refugees in Greece in need of assistance. Most were subsisting on bread purchased for about five cents a day. Salt, cheese, and cooking oil, like clothing, were almost impossible to obtain. The refugees, he told Warner, were "scattered over Greece in groups of from one to twelve hundred," adding "I have taken measures with the aid of the American missionaries, and of reliable Greeks, to give aid to families who are suffering from sickness or extreme want, and the result has been very satisfactory." He assured Warner that he planned to get assistance to Crete itself but at the moment the Cretan refugees in Athens were his principal concern.[109] In a letter to Maud he described the refugees he had seen on board the blockade runner *Arcadi:* "The poor things had fled from their homes, and hidden themselves among the rocks overhanging the sea, and when the blockade runner came there in the night to land powder and bread for the Greek soldiers, they all scrambled on board and got away. They left everything behind except the clothes on their backs, and were very glad to escape alive. The mothers and young women were very sad and still in fear, and they cuddled down upon the deck upon some old sails which the sailors gave them, but the little children did not know the peril behind and the suffering before them, and they played about the vessel and ran up to us, and seemed as happy as lambs. . . . Poor things! They were already in rags and very dirty, but soon we shall get out some of the nice clothes which the kind American ladies sent to them"[110]

Also of concern to Howe, in Greece, as well as on the island of Crete (as he would soon discover), were bands of outlaws who kidnapped rich or influential people or members of their family and held them for ransom. Howe knew, of course, that banditry had existed in Greece for many years, and these bands had even been used by Greek officials to carry out tasks that police and armies had been unable to handle. He noted that kidnapping was especially problematic outside the cities and on the highways. At the same time, the Klepthes, a particular group of bandits, had traditionally caused trouble for the Turks and had therefore often gained the respect of the Greek peasantry. But with the influx of Cretan refugees, the groups of kidnappers had begun to harass Greek Cretans. Howe feared for the safety of himself and his family as he made plans to distribute relief supplies and visit classical sites around the country. In late June 1867, several groups of bandits were subdued by local authorities and citizens, who decapitated some and had displayed their heads grotesquely and prominently. After that, Howe felt it was safer to move about the country.[111]

By mid-June, despite the blockade, Howe managed to get onto Crete. He told his sister Jennette, that his intention in traveling to the island was "to ascertain accurately the condition of the Christian inhabitants who have fled from their devastated villages into the fortified towns to escape from the fiendish persecution of the irregular soldiers & of the native Turks." The Turkish general Oman Pasha, Howe believed, had starved the Cretan people, subjected them to persecution, and even murdered many of them. Even more than he had indicated in the 1820s, Howe claimed little respect for what he saw as Turkish culture. He wrote: "The people living higgledy piggledy at my right hand are fair specimens of their middle class, of whom I have seen a great many & they are[,] as compared with the Greeks of the same class[,] course, dirty, greedy & brutish. It is a great mistake to suppose that because Mussalmen wash after meals & frequently during the day & take hot baths they are therefore cleanly [*sic*], for the washing is only of the finger ends & the lips; other bathing is a luxury confined mostly to the rich & indulged in only for sensuous gratification, not for cleanliness."[112]

By mid-summer, Howe had concluded that he should distribute relief primarily to Cretans who could work for the relief. As he had done in Greece nearly forty years earlier, he rejected the policy of offering relief without labor. Before long, Howe had set up a cottage industry. He told Warner: "I have organized a system of work for the women and girls, and nearly four hundred are now busily employed at knitting. We supply the thread and yarn, and pay them one drachma a pair for work. The yarn costs fifty leptas a pair, so that our socks cost one and a half drachma. We sell them at this price new, so that our loss is only the small one of commission to sellers, &c. Next week we begin with sewing. I hope to have one thousand women at work within two weeks, and this you will see will be a great gain *moralement!*"[113]

At the end of July, Howe moved his attention from the relief of refugees to arms for the Cretan freedom fighters. It was important, he claimed, "to maintain guerilla war indefinitely." He advised the use of arms and ammunition to lay siege on Episis and Thessaly, and he warned of the likelihood of the outbreak of war between Greece and Turkey. Finally, he advocated for the continued running of the blockade that the Turks had placed around Crete.[114]

Howe's support for the Greek Cretans reflected his and his generation's prejudice about Muslim society. After returning to the United States in the fall of 1867, he wrote a lengthy summary of his position on the matter of Crete, and in it, he spoke of his bias against the Turks. He said: "The Greeks had a religion which, though disfigured by superstition, still preserved the essential features of Christianity, and elevated and strengthened them, while the Turks had a religion [that] degraded and enfeebled them. The Greeks strengthened the ties of family—of kith and kin; the Turks weaken all of theirs. The Greeks sanctify marriage relation by monogamy; the Turks pollute it by polygamy. . . . The Greeks were industrious and thrifty; the Turks, lazy and wasteful."[115]

On 20 July, Julia and her two daughters left what had become an extremely hot Athens and went to Venice. Samuel lingered for another week in the Greek capital, writing letters and making last-minute appeals for aid for the Cretans. In early August, Samuel joined his family in Venice. By 21 August, the Howe family had gone to Geneva, where Samuel delighted in visiting the deaf and dumb asylum, where the oral-articulation method was used. He was impressed with the young (under six years old) deaf children who could speak French. He also visited a prison that he found in good order and well ventilated but that did not maintain separate cells as they claimed. In Paris from late August to the middle of September, Howe arranged for the American Greek Committee to fund Anagnostapoulos's passage to the United States. Back in Athens, the dashing young Greek had fallen in love with Julia Romana. Joining the others in the United States in 1867, Anagostapoulos would shorten his name to Anagnos and assume clerical duties at the Perkins Institution. On 31 December 1870 he married Julia Romana and shortly thereafter become the blind school's assistant superintendent. Howe also toured the Salpetrière, the insane asylum for women, where he took extensive notes. He was surprised by the authorities' attempt to keep the female patients "coquettes" and by the difficulty of visitors like himself gaining permission to visit.[116]

The highlight of Howe's institutional tour in 1867 was his visit to the community of Gheel in Belgium. What he found there and reported in the *Boston Daily Advertiser* on his return home was a method for caring for and treating the insane that was, for him, though counterintuitive, entirely humane. Years earlier Howe had explained his views about congregate asylums in a letter to a colleague. He wrote: "The more I reflect upon the subject the more I see objections in principle & practice to *Asylums*. What right have we to pack off the poor, the old, the Blind into Asylums? They are one of us; our brothers our sisters. They belong in families; they are deprived of the dearest relations of life in being put away in masses in Asylums. Asylums generally are the offspring of a low order of feeling. Their chief recommendation often is that they do *cheaply* what we ought to think only of doing *well*."[117]

Gheel was a community that since the thirteenth century had, under the influence of the Irish-born Saint Dymphna, housed mentally ill people in the private homes of residents. When Howe visited, he found insane people socializing and working alongside of their host family members. The authorities of Gheel had governmental inspectors who periodically visited the insane in their homes. As such, Howe reported, the insane enjoyed far more freedom than a traditionally institutionalized insane person would enjoy, and their insanity was far less pronounced because they were gainfully occupied, and the people they lived with sympathized with their mental and emotional conditions. He noted that Gheel had an infirmary that distressed insane patients could enter, but, he added, the infirmary was almost never full. Most of the mentally ill of Gheel dreaded the infirmary not because it was a bad facility but because they preferred their freedom in the community. Finally, Howe called his American readers' attention to the fact the Gheel system was far less costly than the typical grand institutional system found in the United States. What Howe observed in Gheel that so captivated him was a philosophy of treatment and care to which he had been gravitating to for two decades. At the Perkins Institution he had already begun the process of deinstitutionalization. What the experiment at Gheel demonstrated for Howe was that even people with mental illness could benefit by being freed from the asylum and integrated into normal community structures and relationships. Howe concluded his letter in the *Advertiser* by warning the citizens of Massachusetts to avoid the construction of the large state insane asylum that was currently being planned.[118]

Back Home in Boston

In February 1868 after the Howes returned to Boston, Samuel was delighted that Charles Dickens, who was on his second visit to Boston, had agreed to provide seventeen hundred dollars for the printing of 250 copies of his novel *The Old Curiosity Shop* in raised letters for the blind.[119] On the last day of November, he had joined other members of the Saturday Club to dine with Dickens. Around the same time, the family moved to 19 Boylston Place in Boston, where their neighbors were the Richards family, whose son Henry would marry Laura June 1871. The following November saw a second family wedding at the Boylston Place home. This time Florence married David Hall.

Another marriage—Charles Sumner's 17 October 1866 marriage to twenty-eight-year-old Alice Mason Hooper, a widow of three years with a seven-year-old daughter—had ended first in a separation and in May 1873, in divorce. At the time of their marriage, Howe had referred to Alice as "pretty, lively, [and] spirituelle," but by February 1867, after she began appearing in public with the German nobleman Frederick von Holstein, scandalizing both Washington and Boston, he consoled Sumner by assuring him that most of Boston supported him and would have nothing to do with his cavorting wife. He told Richard Henry Dana that Sumner had "suffered as much as a man could suffer."[120] In Washington during the spring of 1868, the Senate had acquitted President Andrew Johnson after an impeachment trial, to the consternation of both Sumner and Howe (but not Julia's brother, Sam Ward, who actively supported Johnson's brand of reconstruction and vigorously opposed Johnson's removal from office). Howe was quite aware that Sumner's domestic troubles compromised his ability to lead the trial against the president in what he characterized as "these growing reactionary times."[121]

At home, Julia renewed several old activities and began a few new ones.

She continued her involvement in the "Brain Club," sometimes also referred
to as the "Conversation Club." She renewed her devotion to her Unitarian
faith, taking up the role of religious lecturer. And she began to involve herself
in the issue of women's suffrage. Samuel had supported women's rights since
before his marriage to Julia. He had no doubt that women would someday
have the right to vote, to own property independently, and to sue in court.
And as a Bird Club member, he had supported changes to Massachusetts
law that gave greater rights to women to own their own property and to
enter into contracts and that expanded the grounds for divorce to include
extreme cruelty, drunkenness, and the failure of a husband to provide for his
family.[122] But he consistently objected to Julia's speaking appearances, especially in public forums. Julia's diaries and letters to her sisters reveal a great
deal about her suffering because she reported Chev's carping and threatening
behavior. A letter from Samuel to Julia dated 2 October 1868 offers a rare
example of his perspective. He was in South Boston, and he wrote Julia while
she was at Lawton's Valley. Within a week he would join her there. So he
wrote the letter in anticipation of seeing her shortly. It is likely that he also
wrote in anticipation of Julia's taking part as a delegate in two upcoming
events: a convention of Unitarians in New York City later in the month,
and a woman's suffrage meeting at Boston's Horticultural Hall in November.
Lucy Stone had organized the Boston meeting, which Wendell Phillips, William Lloyd Garrison, and James Freeman Clarke were scheduled to attend.

Samuel began his letter by appealing to his own hurt. He wrote: "Your
note of yesterday gives me new pain & sorrow for it almost crushes the hope
I had begun to form that you would yield to my earnest entreaties & to the
considerations of family interests & wishes, & forgo further indulgence in
your passion for public appearance & display." Evidently Julia had written
him to indicate that she planned to make a public appearance—perhaps the
Horticultural Hall women's suffrage meeting in November. Chev proceeded
cautiously: "Pardon me if I find not the exact words." Then he got to his chief
complaint: "I infer from your note that you are again to leave home after so
few days of quiet to participate in two public meetings & probably to take
conspicuous part in one of them at least."

He continued in the letter to appeal to his discomfort, writing: "When I
reflect that only a few days ago I pleaded with you earnestly but tenderly, that
I tried [to] set forth the consequence upon me & the family of another form
of passion, my life long suffering, my blight of heart, my fear of family disgrace, the worst of my domestic happiness & hopes, the occasional inquiry
of doubt about the paternity of offspring; when I imaged other sad effect
upon our family, you seemed to be moved & changed of purpose. I had a
right therefore to hope that you would yield to my request & to the wishes of

the family & make no more engagements for public appearances." For Chev, Julia's public-speaking appearances hurt him, shamed the family, and spread rumors even about the paternity of their children.

He concluded his letter by using kind words, but he also drew on guilt when he "appeals to our dead boy."

> Perhaps it is so. God grant it may be so, & you are now to go out only in consequence of engagements previously formed. But if it is not, if you are determined to persevere, then I beg you would without delay let me know it. Of course I ought to take no harsh or unkind measures to prevent any one from following what they believe to be a call of duty, even though I see its voice drowns other tender & cries, but equally of course I ought to take what measures I can to save the remnant of my life from being so disturbed & distressed that it will be painful to me & useless to others. Perhaps this can be done without in any way acting as a restraint upon your indulgence in any call of fancy or duty. By our old affection, by the memory of our dear dead boy, by the years of heart ache & misery which you acknowledge to have been brought on me by your own indulgence in another form of passion, I entreat you to forego indulgence in this one. But if you cannot, or cannot without feeling of grudge or dislike to your unfortunate husband, then let me know it, plainly & firmly but kindly & that without delay.[123]

It is clear from his letter that Samuel, while hardly harsh or threatening to Julia, was just as disturbed as he had always been by his wife's desire to make public appearances, and especially public speeches.

Why did public speaking by his wife so disturb Howe? Although they had been married for a quarter of a century, Samuel was always troubled by the meaning and purpose Julia found outside of the domestic field. What was said of Amelia Jackson Holmes, the wife of Oliver Wendell Holmes Sr., that she was "devoted wholly to him" could not be said of Julia Ward Howe.[124] Julia was her own woman. Samuel wanted what Holmes had: a domestic wife that saw in him the center of her life. Six years later, in 1874, Howe explained his concerns about Julia's public role in a letter to George Finlay. "Mrs. Howe," he wrote, "grows more and more absorbed in the public work of obtaining woman's suffrage, and like most of her co-workers, shows more zeal than discretion, and in my opinion, does more harm by subordinating domestic duties to supposed public ones. Surely women have the right of suffrage, and will obtain it soon, but zeal in pursuit of it does not justify neglect of domestic relations and occupations, nor attempt to abolish those differences in our political and social sphere and duties, which spring out of difference in the very organization of the sexes."[125] Although he mellowed as he aged and clearly tolerated Julia's growing public persona, Samuel never liked the fact that she did not devote herself exclusively to the domestic sphere.

He had grown up with a mother and sisters who were domestic. Although he could affirm the education of women and even female suffrage, he could never accept the equality of women in the form that Garrisonian abolitionists had proclaimed. Perhaps it was a sense of humor coupled with the fact he began to accept the reality (however grudgingly) that Julia was her own person that in 1871 he told Laura: "Mama is crusading in Phil[adelphia] & adjoining country, & will be absent until Tuesday, I think. She is in sublime health & spirits; indeed her spirits are *fire-proof;* & there is no danger of Purgatory or Inferno, for her; because the devil would not admit her through fear that she would raise a laugh in his warm premises."[126]

CHAPTER EIGHT

Santo Domingo—the Perpetual Summer

Howe had been back in Boston for three months when Charles Sumner on 17 February 1868 wrote him that President Johnson would be nominating Charles Keating Tuckerman as minister to Greece. Sumner was chairman of the Senate Foreign Relations Committee, but despite of his position, his support of Howe for the Greek ministerial position had hurt what little chances Howe had for the appointment he so longed for. A man twenty-six years younger than Howe, Tuckerman was a native of Boston, but he had led the New York School for the Blind since 1856. Howe been passed over for a younger man, who, though he shared Howe's profession, had far less acquaintance with the Greek nation. Howe was hurt. He told Sumner that the lost opportunity was one of the greatest disappointments of his life. Sympathizing with the hurt, Julia wrote a six-stanza poem of grief and affection for her husband.

S. G. H.

The doors of the spirit are circling around him,
The cords of mortality closely have bound him;
The heart beats in anguish that ere could misuse him,
The world hangs suspended in sorrow to lose him.

His heart had a throb from the heart of the master,
A comfort in sorrow, a help in disaster.
When the trumpet of Progress its birth challenge sounded,
He sprang to his feet, and his high pulse bounded.

Farewell, oh farewell! What are meeting and parting?
And sobs that are stifled and tears that are starting?
When the gate of great hope is built up in high heaven
His commission was signed, and his word is given.

The Grecian olives vanish from thy sight,
The wondrous hills, the old heroic soil,
Th' elastic air that fashioned with delight
Thy youthful triumphs, flushed with martial toil.

Oh noble soul! Thy laurel early wreathed
Gathers the Christian rose and lilies fair,
For civic virtue, when the sword was sheathed,
And perfect faith, that bars from every snare.

Let then the modern Embassy float by,
Nor one regret in thy high bosom lurk,
God's mission called thy youth to that soft sky,
Wait His dismissal when thou built His work.[1]

Howe set aside his disappointment and threw himself into old and new crusades. He joined with Boston attorney George T. Angell and businessman William Gray to found the Massachusetts Society for the Prevention of Cruelty to Animals, and he began giving occasional lyceum talks on the need to preserve and protect animals. Howe was especially concerned with the proper handling of horses. He and Julia continued their support for Cretan refugees. In April they worked with Boston women to sponsor a Cretan Fair, which raised nearly twenty-one thousand dollars for the island's relief. During the same month, Howe began publishing *The Cretan,* a newspaper for North Americans about the news and needs of the Cretan islanders. Although the paper appeared irregularly and only ran through June 1869, it provided Howe with a forum to keep the cause of Turkish oppression of Crete before the American public, as small as the interest of that public proved to be as the Turks retained control of the island. In May he continued to commiserate with Sumner about President Johnson's acquittal, writing, "It disgust me to hear men like [Richard Henry] Dana, ladies like Mrs. [Charles W.] Eliot & their surroundings jubilant over the acquittal as they call it (escape as it should be called) of Johnson."[2] In June Samuel and Julia saw Longfellow and his children, still mourning the death of Fanny Longfellow, off for a year-long trip through Europe, and in September Oliver Caswell now back in Jamestown, Rhode Island, wrote Howe a chatty letter in which he shared his plans to travel to South Boston to visit Laura Bridgman and his other old friends at the institution.[3] In November, Brown University awarded its once recalcitrant student an honorary Doctor of Law degree. In a letter to a classmate, Howe wrote that he considered such awards "as trifling relics of darker days," but since the award had already been made without his consent, he would accept it.[4]

At the end of the same month, the New England Woman Suffrage Association was founded with Julia Ward Howe as its first president. When she asked Bronson Alcott about the new association, he warmly supported its founding but warned her not to fail to include men in the association. From her young friend the attorney Hermann J. Warner, now living in Dresden, Julia continued to receive German editions of philosophy and literature. During this period she read more extensively and intently in the writings of Immanuel Kant.[5] On 24 January 1870 the first annual meeting of the Woman Suffrage Association was held at Tremont Temple. Julia presided as its president, and Lucy Stone, as chair of the Executive Committee. Such men as Stone's husband, Henry B. Blackwell, along with William S. Robinson and Charles H. Whipple, were appointed to the Committee on Arrangements. Julia invited Charles Sumner to speak to the gathering, but he declined.

As important as her involvement in the women's suffrage movement had become for Julia, the Franco-Prussian War, which started on 19 July 1870 in Europe turned her attention to the cause of world peace. The war sensitized many Americans, who had just been through their own conflagration, to the necessity of doing something to make world peace possible. In September, Julia published an article in *The Women's Journal,* "An Appeal to Womanhood," in which she linked women's rights and world peace. That linkage would become her signature contribution to feminist thinking of the nineteenth century. Soon she began to plan for the World Congress of Women for Peace, and she called on Sumner—reminding him of his 4 July 1845 speech, "True Grandeur of Nations"—to present a resolution for congressional support. On Friday 23 December the World Congress of Women for Peace convened at the Union League in New York City. By 1873, Julia was thoroughly involved with Lucy Stone in the Women's Peace Movement, along with the Association for the Advancement of Women, and the Women's Temperance Crusade.[6]

On 18 February 1869, Howe wrote the trustees of the blind school that he believed that the time was auspicious to request from the Massachusetts General Court an appropriation for eight family-style homes scattered about South Boston for his female blind pupils. Howe's proposed step toward what today would be called deinstitutionalization was the culmination of his thinking about noninstitutional, family-like environments for the students of the Perkins Institution. The next day, he accompanied a hundred of his blind pupils to the legislature, where before both the Senate and the House of Representatives, they talked with legislators and showed their skills in reading, writing, and handicrafts. For the remainder of the year, Howe worked with the trustees to generate community support for this new direction in living arrangements for his pupils. He also began a process of raising one hundred thousand dollars of private and public funds to apply to the purchase of the new homes. On Wednesday evening, 31 March 1869, for example, blind students presented a "concert and exhibition" at the Huntington Hall in Lowell, and the next day the Harvard Musical Association gave a concert to aid the musical education of the blind at the Perkins Institution. Howe solicited ministers, such as James Freeman Clarke, to announce the concerts from their pulpits. And in May Howe was writing graduates to urge them to contact their legislators about the proposed appropriations for the blind school lodgings and for an expanded musical facility for younger pupils.[7]

Santo Domingo

Three months after Mark Twain read his fiction before a crowd of four thousand people in Boston, and in the same month, March 1870, that Emerson published *Society and Solitude,* the U.S. Senate Foreign Relations Committee issued an unfavorable report on a bill submitted in January to negotiate a treaty to annex Santo Domingo. In reaction to the committee's report, President Ulysses S. Grant on the last day of May reaffirmed his support for the Dominican treaty, despite the Foreign Relations Committee's report.

Between 1866 and 1871 the United States made several efforts to annex Santo Domingo, what is today the Dominican Republic. A principal interest in the island was the desire of both the Johnson and the Grant administrations for a U.S. naval presence in Samana Bay, on the northern end of the island. Occupying the eastern two-thirds of the island that Columbus called Hispaniola, Santo Domingo had received its independence from Haiti in 1844. After years of internal strife between warring factions, Spain occupied Santo Domingo between 1861 and 1865, the years of the American Civil War. With Spain's departure in 1865, U.S. interest in the island grew.

In January 1866, Secretary of State William Seward visited the island to see whether Samana Bay might prove to be a suitable port for U.S. naval ships and equipment. Seward, who believed in manifest destiny, was interested in expanding U.S. interests in the Caribbean. At the same time, two land speculators, both from Massachusetts by way of Texas, William L. Cazneau and Joseph Warren Fabens, were also instrumental in pushing for Santo Domingo's annexation. Working through the State Department in Santo Domingo in the 1850s, they had acquired land on the island and saw the potential for a windfall if the United States were to establish a naval base at Samana Bay.

By December 1868 Seward had persuaded President Johnson to support a treaty for the annexation of Santo Domingo. But congressional hostility to Johnson as he was about to leave office blocked the effort. With Grant in the White House in the spring of 1869, speculators became even more interested in acquiring Santo Domingo. Cazneau and Fabens, along with the new secretary of state Hamilton Fish (the latter, reluctantly) persuaded President Grant to support Dominican annexation. Besides the desire for a naval station in the Caribbean, Grant believed that Santo Domingo might become a place for freedmen in the South to resettle, and it might prove an example of the success of free labor for the slave-owning islands of Puerto Rico and Cuba. Grant's and Fish's motives may have been unadulterated, but Grant's private secretary, Orville Babcock, had self-serving reasons to bring Santo Domingo into the U.S. orbit. Like Cazneau and Fabens, he owned land on the island whose value would inevitably appreciate if the island were annexed.[8]

On 29 November 1869 a treaty of annexation was signed in Santo Domingo by representatives of both the United States and the island nation. The treaty called for the payment by the U.S. Treasury of $1.5 million to assume the country's debt, or if rejected, the lease of Samana Bay at the rate of $150,000 a year for fifty years with the privilege of annexation for $2 million during that period. The treaty followed a plebiscite given with four days' notice and with a promise that opponents of the treaty would be shot or exiled. Not surprisingly the quickly called, rigged plebiscite resulted in a favorable outcome. And the presence of the U.S. naval forces in Samana Bay added weight to President Buenaventura Baez's otherwise shaky government. On 10 January 1870 the treaty was submitted to the U.S. Senate. Charles Sumner, chair of the Senate Foreign Relations Committee, opposed the treaty. Back in Boston his opposition was shared by such long-time abolitionists as William Lloyd Garrison and Wendell Phillips. The final Senate debate on the treaty began 29 June 1870. On 30 June the Senate voted not to ratify the treaty.

Nevertheless, Grant continued to advocate for the treaty. In his second annual message to Congress on 5 December 1870 he renewed his call for the annexation of Santo Domingo. In response to Grant's proposal, on 29 December Sumner gave his famous "Naboth's Vineyard" speech in which he strongly and methodically denounced the efforts to annex Santo Domingo. Sumner argued that the treaty compromised the sovereignty of Haiti, that it would complicate relations with European powers, and that it would involve the United States in exacerbating civil conflict on the island. After resolutions for reconsidering the Dominican treaty had failed in the Senate, Grant on 11 January 1871 appointed a commission to investigate, as Howe recalled, "the physical conditions of that great Island, of its agricultural, mineral and commercial advantages, of the condition of the people and of whatever might shine light upon the important and then interesting subject of annexation."[9] The commissioners included Benjamin F. Wade, as chairman, Andrew D. White, and Samuel G. Howe. Frederick Douglass, now living in Washington, D.C., served as the commission's assistant secretary, and General Franz Sigel was appointed the committee's military adviser. The members of the commission reflected Grant's political acumen and his plans for success. Wade, a former senator from Ohio, was a radical Republican who supported the civil rights of freedmen and women's suffrage; White, president of Cornell University, was young and idealistic; and Howe was Sumner's closest friend. If the appointment of these respected and influential men left any doubt about Grant's good intentions, the presence of Frederick Douglass and Franz Sigel would surely quell critics like Sumner. Or so the president supposed.[10]

On 18 January the party of commissioners, along with their secretaries, and a collection of botanists, zoologists, geologists, and mineralogists, accompanied by reporters from ten of the nation's leading newspapers, left New York for Santo Domingo on the steamer USS *Tennessee*. On board the ship, Howe experienced no seasickness and "promenade[d] the deck [to] the admiration of the whole ship." The passengers enjoyed his tales of Grecian and Prussian adventures.[11] Because they were out of contact with telegraph equipment and were at sea an unusually long time, there was fear—unfounded as it turned out—that the *Tennessee* had wrecked off the coast of Cape Hatteras. Back in Boston, Julia and much of Boston feared the worst, until word arrived that the steamer had arrived safely.

On 21 February 1871, George Washington's birthday, the *Tennessee* landed at Santo Domingo harbor, where a twenty-one gun salute welcomed President Baez on board the ship. The correspondence of the *New York Times* described Baez as "a rather prepossessing man, very polite, very courteous, five feet and a few inches in height, and fifty-five years old." He wore a blue uniform with gold trim. Although he carried no sword, he had a pistol in a gun belt that surrounded his waist. After this initial ceremony, most of party sailed for Azua, while Howe proceeded overland. Almost immediately, the Americans experienced the civil battles that were taking place on the island. They heard rumors that the forces opposed to President Baez and loyal to the guerilla fighter Jose Maria Cabral, with his Dominican and Haitian supporters, were ready to attack Azua at any moment. Howe, having traversed the country on horseback, met the group at Azua a few days later. As he reported to his fellow commissioners, Howe was most impressed with the enthusiastic reception he had received from the Dominican people. He became immediately convinced that both the black and the "Spanish" populations wanted annexation.[12] The next day, the commissioners toured sugar plantations in a large valley about five miles from the town. So taken was Wade by the beauty and good order of the plantations that he declared, "Why when [a] man gets to paradise, he will not appreciate it." Under the guidance of President Baez and his governmental officials, the commissioners were soon convinced that the rebels would destroy any chance for self-government on the island. Only with help from the United States through annexation could Santo Domingo be saved from civil war and destruction, exacerbated by Haitian intrusion.[13]

On 11 March, *Harper's Weekly* ran its lead story on the work of the commissioners. With etchings of each of the three commissioners and a fourth etching of San Domingo City and an altar erected by Columbus, the article painted a picture of a glorious island visited by competent and impartial commissioners who concluded that annexation was in the best interest of both the island nation and the American people.[14] As Howe remembered, "Although I could not properly speaking as [a] commissioner [be] in favor or against annexation, I became thoroughly convinced of its importance, and enthusiastically in favor of it. I resolved then and there to devote my energy to bringing it about. Mr. Wade shared my belief. President White preserved a more cautious mentality, though I believe that he may be considered as an annexationist."[15]

After leaving Santo Domingo, Wade and Howe sailed for Port-au-Prince in Haiti. White would join them in a few days. While they waited for White, Howe toured the city, as did Wade and Frederick Douglass. Not having a President Baez to escort them selectively around the city, they walked about as they pleased and found a population in what they concluded was chaos. The housing was primitive and sometimes nonexistent. There was garbage in the streets and the smells were constantly disturbing. Drunkenness seemed to be ubiquitous, and parties and singing seemed more a way of life than honest hard work. Wade and Howe left Haiti with little respect for either its inhabitants or its government.

On 27 March 1871 Sumner gave a second speech in the Senate opposing Dominican annexation. He argued that U.S. annexation of Santo Domingo would be detrimental to the "African race," to its progress, and to its determination for self-government. Thus, it became clear that Sumner had greater sympathies with the claims of Cabral and his Haitian allies than he did with Baez and his shaky government. The commissioners arrived back from Santo Domingo shortly after Sumner gave his speech, and not long thereafter Howe met with Sumner in Washington. After a protracted discussion, their differences only solidified. Grant submitted the commission's report to Congress on 5 April 1871.[16] The president saw that opposition against annexation remained in the Senate, and therefore he suggested that no action be taken on the commission's report. The report in June was then tabled after a 28–28 tie vote of the Senators.[17] Despite the president's and Secretary of State Fish's support for the treaty, Sumner's influence had led to its defeat.

Howe had no greater friend than Sumner. In August the senator replied to a now lost letter from Howe about the defeated treaty. He began by being straightforward: "I hesitate to write to you of any thing where you & I, usually in such accord, are so far asunder. I cannot see anything in this business as you see it—nothing!" The treaty, Sumner insisted, was based purely on greed—the greed of proslavery rebels like Cazneau and Fabens. President Grant might be talking "humanity" to Howe and his fellow commissioners, but his true purposes were anything but humanitarian. Accompanying greed was imperialism. Besides these matters, Sumner reminded Howe, was the important case of Haiti, a country that Howe regarded as the principal threat to Dominican independence, but that Sumner saw more favorably. He wrote:

> You must pardon my sympathy with the Haytians [*sic*] which dates to my childhood. My father was in Haiti shortly after leaving college, & his stories of the people there are among my earliest memories. He did not describe the people as you do. Then came the embittered discussion about the recognition of their Independence—ending in a Bill drawn by me & carried through the Senate, by which that Independence was recognized. Since then they have been almost my wards. I feel a [paternalism] to them keenly, & when I heard your harsh words about them, when I heard your indifference to their claims & made oaths against even hearing their side, I felt that there was not only a shocking violation of the first principles of justice *andi atterain posteri,* but downright inhumanity.

Finally, Sumner criticized his friend for supporting an action that could lead to civil war, when the goal of U.S. relations with the Dominicans should be to maintain peace. Rather than supporting either Baez or any of the rebel factions, the United States should "put each party on its leg" for democratic elections and democratic civil institutions.[18]

With the defeat of the Dominican treaty and the tabling of the commission's report in the Senate, "The problem of Santo Domingo," according to Harold Schwartz, "was settled for everyone but Samuel Gridley Howe."[19] Over the next nine months, Howe wrote letters to newspapers defending the commission's report and advocating for Dominican annexation. As the weeks and months went on, however, it became apparent that opposition to such a scheme was not confined to Charles Sumner. Opposition came also from such diverse critics as James Redpath, Carl Schurz, and H. J. Ramsdell of the *New York Tribune,* which (unlike the *New York Times*) shared Sumner's opposition to annexation.

At the invitation of President Baez, on 9 February 1872, Howe sailed again from New York for Santo Domingo, this time with Julia, Maud, and four of Maud's cousins and friends, along with Mary Paddock from the blind school. The president continued to have hope for a reversal of the U.S. Senate's decision.[20] Joining the Howes on the island was Henry B. Blackwell, the husband of Julia's friend and colleague Lucy Stone. Blackwell saw the investment in Santo Domingo as partly a matter of reform and partly as a means of making a quick profit.[21] Behind the mission, however, was less Baez's hope than it was the efforts of Fabens and his associates to exploit the Samana Bay for land speculation. Like land developers before and since, Fabens saw in Howe a good "front man" to add legitimacy to what would soon become his con game.

The departure for Santo Domingo began in a winter storm that left the party of travelers cold and miserable. Maud recalled, "Our steamer, the old *Tybee*, was a small crank tub; the twelve days' passage was more uncomfortable than any ocean crossing I have ever made." At the time, the *Tybee* was the only passenger vessel sailing between New York and the Dominican Island. Along with the Howe party was the notorious Fabens himself. The two months' stay on the island was for Maud "among the most delightful of my life." Maud remembered Spanish lessons in the morning, Spanish conversation in the afternoon, and horseback rides on the beach every day at four before dinner. In the evenings, her father read *Don Quixote* to the delight of the assembled party.[22] The family stayed in the Palacio Nacional, where they were at first bothered by fleas, which a thorough washing of floors and articles seemed to eliminate. Soon after their arrival, the Howes decided to sponsor a dance at their residence. Invited to the festivities were townspeople and sailors from a U.S. warship in the harbor. Julia recalled that in the hot climate, the party goers preferred slow "contradanza" to the speedy Virginia reel. And all were disappointed when the Howes stopped the dancing and ended the party at two in the morning.[23]

In the place of a damp and cold Boston winter, the Howes and their company experienced the warmth, beauty, and abundance of Santo Domingo. Samuel wrote his sister Jennette Howe Wales: "We who have been basking in sun shine—enjoying the delicious warmth, bathing in the surf & feasting daily on fresh fruit. We can hardly conceive that any body has been cold. Nothing on earth can surpass the charming beauty of this island in all that regards climate & scenery. It has been perpetual summer, constantly returning sunshine every day & delicious coolness every evening. The thermometer seems to be constantly telling lies. It sometimes ranges as high as 80 to 90 & yet never feels hot. Constantly returning star lit nights with comforting sea breezes & though never feeling cold, yet so fresh that a blanket is not unpleasant."[24]

In his seventieth year, Howe, who suffered from a variety of health problems, found rejuvenation in the heat of the tropical island. For Julia too it was an enchanting place where she could be herself among people who appreciated her for who she was, and especially for her faith, which she began to preach in Dominican Protestant churches, some of which were attended by former slaves from the United States. At the same time, she and Black-well began to submit long letters about the beauty and healing powers of the island to the *Women's Journal.* Julia was struck by the mixed races in Santo Domingo. She wrote, "I could not see that the blacks were looked down upon by the whites, the greater part of whom gave evidence of some admixture of African blood."[25] Back in Boston in early May, Julia would participate in June in the twenty-one-day World Peace Jubilee at Copley Square.

During his stay on the island, Samuel became thoroughly involved in the Samana Bay Company. Formed after the Senate defeat of the Dominican treaty, with the tolerance, if not the complete blessing of President Baez, the Samana Bay Company was a scheme of Fabens and his associates from the New York shipping merchants Spofford, Tileston, and Company to lease the bay from the Dominican government to a group of private American investors headed by the New York firm. Howe agreed to be one of its directors and to take $20,000 worth of stock in the company. In his role as director, the company agreed to pay him $5,000 a year for two years. On Christmas Day 1872 the company was chartered with a capitalization of $800,000. For the rental fee of $150,000, the Dominican government allowed the syndicate to have eminent domain throughout the area in and surrounding the bay. Along with this concession, the Samana Bay Company received the authority to open and manage the port and to develop large tracts of land adjoining the bay. As a special consideration to Howe, the company agreed to establish a system of schools for the children of the general population. Once again, a general (and rigged) plebiscite indicated that the area's population supported the plan by a wide majority. Within days of the government's granting of the company's charter, speculators were investing in the enterprise. As Howe acknowledged in September 1874, long after the fact, "Money was squandered prodigally on fabulous salaries, traveling expenses, and bonuses to officials who accomplished nothing."[26]

Howe's stay on Santo Domingo only confirmed his enthusiasm for the island and his commitment to find a way to link it to the United States, if not through direct annexation, then through commercial relations. When Howe and the family arrived back home in mid-April, he immediately began sending letters to newspapers about the salubrious effects of the island on his own health and about its economic potential for American business interests. At the same time, American and European speculators began to descend on the island. Hoping for quick and large profits, these individuals invested liberally in the Samana Bay Company. But the country's finances were in a shambles, with bonds dating from 1869 coming due in 1872. To deal with the debt the Baez government along with the Samana Bay syndicate fabricated a loan-and-cash scheme that was nothing more than a swindle. Soon thereafter, it became apparent to Howe that he had become a front man for the business interests of unscrupulous men. Even before the Panic of 1873, which began in September with the closing of the Boston Stock Exchange and the failure of several U.S. banks, the Samana Bay Company proved to be an insolvent deception.[27]

In October Howe and Fabens managed to save what little was left of the enterprise by negotiating with the U.S. Navy to lease the Samana Bay as a base for U.S. naval vessels. But internal Dominican political disruptions destroyed what was left of the company. In November, General Ignacio Maria Gonzalez proclaimed a revolutionary new government for the nation. Soon Dominican factions began to coalesce behind him. On 2 January 1874, Baez resigned and fled the country. From Julia Howe's perspective, the overthrow of Baez was the result of "Germans and Jews" in Puerta Plata who feared that the Samana Bay enterprise would thrive at "the expense of their own town."[28]

The relationship between Baez and the Samana Bay Company had made the company's survival possible. Now with the nation under the new leadership of President Gonzalez, the relationship almost immediately became strained. In February, the Gonzalez government demanded the previously agreed-on rent from the company. Unable to raise the necessary payment, the company offered a smaller amount, but the government rejected the offer. In the midst of the impasse, the company directors called on Howe to return to the island to negotiate new terms from the government. At first reluctant to make the long journey, Howe agreed to go with Julia in March 1874 under the assumption that time in the warm climate would be good for his ever-worsening health.

Although the warm climate indeed proved to be good for his health, Howe was unable to persuade the new president to accept any amount less than the $150,000 owed to the country. The company had little money in its treasury, so Howe offered his personal note for $5,000, but Gonzalez remained firm. Soon the president had nullified the contract made under the Baez administration with the company, and the Samana Bay Company was forced to turn over its operation to the government. To Howe's surprise, the local people rejoiced in the streets over the return of the bay to governmental control. Howe was certain that Gonzalez's intransigence was the result of European commercial interests blocking the American presence in the nation.[29]

Samuel and Julia spent a few more weeks in the island nation while Samuel road horses and swam in the ocean waters, and Julia, as she had before, preached in the churches of the region. They stayed in a cottage owned by

Fabens, perched on a hillside overlooking Samana Bay. Both of them retained fond memories of Santo Domingo, for its climate, its people, and its tranquil pace. Howe described it in a letter to his friend Frank Bird: "I linger here to enjoy the delicious climate & recover my health. I am heavier, stronger, hungrier, & more elastic in muscle & mind than I have been during the past ten years. For the most part, every day has been even more balmy & delicious than our summer days. I live in the open air *all* the time, for windows & doors stand open day & night. . . . It is luxury to look around at the gorgeous panorama of hills & mountains of diversified shape & covered by the richest verdure."[30]

On their way back home, they stopped in Washington to have dinner with President Grant and to convey the disappointment they both felt over the loss of the company, and of the island nation. In their absence, while they were still in Santo Domingo, Charles Sumner died on 11 March 1874. It was a heavy blow to both Samuel and Julia, but especially to Samuel. Sumner and he had disagreed over Dominican annexation, but the two men had been close friends for nearly forty years. Mann, Parker, and now Sumner—all were gone. From Oak Glen, Howe wrote to his one remaining old friend, George Finlay in Athens.

As I look back over the past path, I see it crowded with friends and companions in the long distance who become fewer and fewer until one or two weary way-farers are seen, and I am almost alone. It has been my rare good fortune to have known intimately and loved dearly many of the best of men, but only a few are left; you, thank God! among them.

There was Horace Mann, the eminent educator and philanthropist; Theodore Parker, the great religious Reformer and superstitious iconoclast; Charles Sumner, the eloquent orator, the preacher of peace and good will among men, the powerful champion of equal civil rights. All were my well beloved and intimate friends, and all have gone before me. Mann left a successful and promising political career to espouse the cause of popular education, which he made respectable and successful . . . his great love was the cause of education, which he devoted & made respected through our land.

Parker was, in his way, America's Luther; and the moral reformation, which he began, is still forwarded by his writings.

Sumner—dear Charlie, as I was wont to call him—devoted his heart, mind, and estate to the cause of emancipation, of peace, and of civil rights. . . .

All these three, dear friends & intimate associates have departed and left me to derive what benefit I can from recalling our intimate associations, and their daily conversations, in which they poured forth their spirits.[31]

Going Home

Samuel and Julia arrived in New York just in time for the 9 April wedding
of their son, Henry, to Fannie Gay. A few days later they returned to South
Boston, where they enjoyed their two grandchildren, Laura's daughter, Alice
Maud Richards, and Florence's son, Samuel Prescott Hall, both less than two
years old. In a photograph of the period, Howe, now in his seventy-second
year, has Alice draped on his shoulders with her legs around his neck, his old
hands tightly holding her legs, and her gaze set on the photographer. On 9
June, Samuel and Julia attended the grand memorial service in the Boston
Music Hall for Charles Sumner.

Although Howe's health had improved in the weeks in Santo Domingo,
on his return to Boston his physical condition began an inexorable decline. In
August he reported to Finlay that his neuralgia and rheumatism had returned
and persisted, "keeping me confined mostly to the house and in great pain."
He found himself out of breath when he climbed a few short steps, and his
legs began to swell as his heart weakened. Like many men his age, he had to
get up several times during the night because of an enlarged prostate gland.
Headaches and fevers, probably associated with his malaria, continued to be
a source of additional discomfort.

He owned property in South Boston and in Rhode Island, along with
some land he had acquired in Kansas during the Free Soil days of the 1850s.
But he was not a man of great possessions. As he wrote to a man in Kansas
who had offered to name a park for Howe, if he would contribute a thousand
dollars, "I have worked for objects of public charity or beneficence about fifty
years, sometimes without pay, & never for a larger salary than barely paid
any expenses. But for two investments made at timely moments, like that
in Kansas lands, I should now be without any property in my own right."[32]
In his will, Charles Sumner had left each of Howe's four daughters a small
legacy, but as Julia would discover after Samuel's death, there was hardly a
large estate.

During his three trips to Santo Domingo, Howe had turned over more
and more of the responsibilities of the blind and idiot schools to his son-
in-law Michael Anagnos. With his poor health also, he came to depend on
Anagnos for the daily operations of the institutions. By 1871, Anagnos was
identifying himself in correspondence as "resident superintendent." Howe's
daughter Julia Romana was childless and, like her husband, was involved in
the day-to-day activities of the blind school, where she taught classes and
performed other necessary functions in the daily routine of the school. The
public saw Howe as the nation's leading authority on the subject of blindness,
and in the summer of 1872 in Boston, he hosted the third general conven-

tion of superintendents and teachers of blind schools in the United States. More than twenty schools were represented at the convention. The next year in August, when a man from Des Moines, Iowa, wrote him about his fears of his own impending blindness, Howe responded with his ever-optimistic reassurance,

> I am sorry that you are threatened with such a sore privation as loss of sight. I hope that you may find means to escape from it. You do well however to prepare for the worst. Let me assure you that that worst will not be as bad as you now apprehend. It may even prove that blindness will not only not be a permanent source of unhappiness, but on the contrary of happiness. That which seems in the distance a fearful monster may prove to be an angel with blessings on his wings. The faculty of acquiring and imparting knowledge may by proper discipline be enlarged and strengthened. All the principal mental faculties may be quickened. The social affections may become warmer and prove an unfailing source of happiness.[33]

At some point during the 1870s, Howe approved the teaching of the Braille system of reading for his blind students. But he insisted that the system, which was increasingly being employed in the United States since its first widespread use at the Missouri School for the Blind in St. Louis, be used only for communications between blind people in order to save space that raised-letter printing would otherwise take up. It remained important for Howe that his blind pupils continue to learn to read raised letters and to write with block lettering to communicate with the sighted population.

In the 1870s, Howe involved himself in one more fight, this one hardly as heroic as his previous struggles. In 1858 before the outbreak of war, Dempsey Sherrod, a Mississippi blind man and former superintendent of the Mississippi State Institution for the Blind in Jackson, had tried to establish at the Kentucky School for the Blind, a national press for the blind. At the end of the war, he renewed his efforts by touring the country trying to raise money for his projected national press. It is difficult to know why Howe so vehemently opposed Sherrod's efforts. Probably he resented the competition presented to his own press. Yet it is also likely that he saw Sherrod as a bit of an upstart country bumpkin who was using the sympathy he generated before lawmakers to launch an effort that Howe believed was best carried by the Perkins Institution. Perhaps also he disliked the idea of a man from a secessionist state leading a project that he associated with the North. He told Sherrod:

> You have been at work about ten years professedly to print books for the Blind. You have raised thousands of dollars. You have lived upon the fat of the land. You have procured the passage of one of the most extraordinary acts

ever passed by a Legislature—the act by which you and your sister (who is not blind) are quartered for life upon the Mississippi State Institution for the Blind, an act utterly inconsistent with the objects of that institution which is namely for the education of young blind persons.

In all this time, with all this money, you have not given to the Blind a single edition of any book. On the other hand you have done harm to the cause of their education by raising false hopes, by bringing them into disrepute through your life and examples and by keeping honest and earnest laborers out of the field.[34]

Howe spent a decade trying to stop Sherrod from gaining the legislative support he needed to begin his national press for the blind. He was convinced—erroneously as it turned out—that Sherrod was using the legislative appropriation he had received for his own benefit. In letters to national newspapers and at the convention of superintendents for the blind in Indianapolis in 1871, he denounced Sherrod and persuaded most of his fellow superintendents to do the same.

When he was at home, he visited Laura Bridgman usually every day, and when he was away for extended periods, his letters to family members always contained questions about Bridgman's health and happiness. In response to a man in from Vermont who in July 1871 asked about her, Howe wrote: "She has developed considerable character, and although childlike and simple in many of her intellectual ideas, she is an intelligent, virtuous and cheerful woman. . . . She has her little occupations, in which she takes much interest. She finds many persons who can converse with her in the finger language, and loves to gossip with them by the hour. . . . She believes firmly in a future life, and looks hopefully not fearfully for the part which she may play in it." He added that Bridgman usually spent the summers with her mother in Hanover, New Hampshire, and "the winter with us here."[35] When in November 1873, Bridgman's mother expressed her concern for daughter's care after her own death, Howe assured her that because of legacies left on Laura's behalf, she would be cared for at the institution for the remainder of her life should she chose to continue to live there.[36]

Despite a national economic downturn in 1873, Howe raised the salaries of his teachers. Most of his teachers received $300 a year plus room, board, and laundry. Some teachers with greater experience were paid $350, and his lead teacher received $400. The matrons of the blind and idiot schools were paid $500 a year plus room, board, and laundry.[37] Until only a few weeks before his death, Howe continued to walk from Green Peace to the blind school, though he would usually take a carriage to the idiot school for daily inspections. In October 1874 he resigned as chair of the Massachusetts Board of State Charities, and in April 1875 he did not have the strength to deliver a speech he had prepared for the centennial celebrations of the Battles of Lexington and Concord. In his place, Julia Romana read a letter from her ailing father.

He spent the summer and early fall of 1875 at Oak Glen, where he planted his garden and tended to his chickens. He was still able to ride a pony given to him three years earlier by President Baez, but his health remained precarious. He wrote Frank Bird in July that he felt quite sick, adding, "I saw no light or hope for this world & was uneasy & unhappy about the next."[38] Back in South Boston, sometime in the last weeks of November, Julia recorded in her journal that Samuel had acknowledged what appeared to be a marital indiscretion. She recorded her reaction: "I have had some sad revelations from dear Chev, of things about some of my own sex which really astonish me. From these I learn that women are not only sensual but lustful and that men are attracted rather than shocked by that trait. The privacy of offices, or at least their remoteness from domestic visitation, is eagerly made available by these women for the vilest purposes."[39] Her diary entry is at best vague. Is the indiscretion Samuel reported at the end of his life one that involved him, or was he referring the indiscretion of his employees at the blind or idiot schools?

On Christmas day, Howe dined with family and friends. A week later on New York's Day, he told a friend, "They will bury me this month." Four days later he was struck with convulsions followed by unconsciousness. On 9 January 1876 he died peacefully surrounded by his family, intimate staff, and Laura Bridgman "to touch once more the hand that had unlocked the world to her." "She did so weeping bitterly."[40] The next morning, Julia wrote in her journal: "Now, the death of my darling husband makes a new chapture [sic] for me. His remains lie in his room, next to my room, while I write this. These lines I scrawled yesterday, just before I was called to see his exit from this world."

The master to his pupils showed
A little, common-child;
A simple slip of girlhood
Or rambling boy babe wild.

To crown the lovely gospel
And happy doctrine given,
He said: be like this infant
Ye who would enter heaven.

A mother and grandmother,
A widow, long a wife,
I recognize the childhood
That follows me through life.

Now children can be gracious
As babes of heaven now-born;
The life intense within them
Breathing, like day in morn.

But I, a child most forward,
With selfhood ne're subdued,
With ways of strife untoward
And turbulence of mood.

Oh! take me yet, dear Master
Where thy disciples stand;
And set me down before them
With thy instructing hand.

Show them the faulty record,
The willful brow and face,
And tell them this offender
Is conquered by thy grace.[41]

Samuel G. Howe's "exit from this world" on 9 January 1876 marked the beginning of his history, a history that remains important today for all people interested in reform, social change, and the place of disability in the social fabric. Howe's commitment to reform and his belief in the potential of disabled people to thrive remained throughout his life a reflection of his deep belief in the "perfectibility of man." After the Civil War when others of his own generation, and especially of the generation that followed him, turned to a self-seeking materialism, Howe remained true to a vision of human improvement through education and service to others, and through the improvement of social institutions. Of individualism as an outgrowth of humanitarianism, Howe in death became an anachronism in the approaching Gilded Age, when utopian idealism was ridiculed, and greed was lauded as a proper way of life. The new man of the late nineteenth century saw in manliness the rough and readiness of Theodore Roosevelt and the struggle for existence of William Graham Sumner. Born in a time of faith in a rationally ordered universe ordained by a rational and loving Deity, Howe left the world in a time of growing laissez faire confidence when bureaucratic controls increasingly substituted for individual democratic actions, and where Anglo-Saxon hegemony shaped a new brand of restrictive reform over all sorts of "inferior" people. Howe was not a perfect man, but in every age of cynicism and self-centeredness he is a reminder that, despite imperfections, human beings can change the world for the better.

ABBREVIATIONS

BV   Bound volume of letters sent to SGH, housed at HRL

HFP   Howe Family Papers, MS Am 2119, Houghton Library, Harvard University

HL   Houghton Library, Harvard University

HRL   Hayes Research Library, Perkins School for the Blind

JWH   Julia Ward Howe

LB   Letter book of copies of letters sent by SGH, housed at HRL

LJ   *Letters and Journals of Samuel Gridley Howe.* Edited by Laura E. Richards, with notes by F. B. Sanborn. 2 vols. Boston: Dana Estes & Company, 1906–1909.

MHS   Massachusetts Historical Society

SGH   Samuel G. Howe

NOTES

Introduction

1. "Funeral of Dr. Howe," *Boston Daily Globe,* 14 Jan. 1876.

2. Douglas C. Stange, *Patterns of Antislavery among American Unitarians, 1831–1860* (Rutherford, N.J.: Fairleigh Dickinson University Press, 1977), 100–104.

3. "Funeral of Dr. Howe."

4. The description of the service at the Boston Music Hall, including all quotations, is drawn from "Samuel G. Howe," *Boston Daily Globe,* 9 Feb. 1876.

5. Bridgman to Lamson, 30 Jan. 1876, box 3, Lamson Family Papers, MHS.

6. JWH, *Memoir of Dr. Samuel Gridley Howe* (Boston: Albert J. Wright, 1876); Laura H. Richards, *Samuel Gridley Howe* (New York: D. Appleton-Century, 1935); Franklin B. Sanborn, *Dr. S. G. Howe, the Philanthropist* (New York: Funk and Wagnall, 1891).

7. "50 Greatest Sons Picked at Harvard," *New York Times,* 13 Sept. 1936, section N.

8. Hedda Hopper, "Dr. Howe Profile Set as Novel and Picture," *Los Angeles Times,* 15 Apr. 1952.

9. The first crack in SGH's armor appeared in 1956 with the publication of two histories: Harold Schwartz, *Samuel Gridley Howe: Social Reformer* (Cambridge, Mass.: Harvard University Press, 1956); and Louise Tharp, *Three Saints and a Sinner: Julia Ward Howe, Louisa, Annie, and Sam Ward* (Boston: Little, Brown, 1956). Although Schwartz admires SGH's many accomplishments, he portrays SGH as a rigid, often vindictive, and unforgiving "know it all." Tharp in her biography of the Ward siblings depicts SGH as a domineering husband. Using JWH's letters (some of which she cites, though these letters now appear to be lost or to have been available only to her), Tharp portrays JWH's relationship with her husband as unpleasant. The letters recount, for example, SGH's attempts (sometimes successful and sometimes not) to control his wife's public appearances, writings, and assets.

With the emergence of critical social history in the late 1960s and early 1970s, some historians began to question the assumptions behind what many of them saw as the triumphal and "exceptionalistic" versions of U.S. history presented by previous generations. Assuming the doubts Schwartz and Tharp raised about SGH's good character, several of these historians also began to question his motives, especially those associated with his work for reform. The first critic to do so was Michael Katz, who, in *The Irony of Early School Reform* (Boston: Beacon Press, 1968), presents SGH (a minor figure in his book) as part of a group of Massachusetts elites who shaped public education and juvenile delinquency reform in ways that were essentially conservative. SGH's educational reform, in short, was more a matter of class preservation than it was a challenge to dominant class structures. In *The Discovery of the Asylum: Social Order and Disorder in the New Republic* (Boston: Little, Brown, 1971), David Rothman portrays

SGH as a reformer more disturbed by Jacksonian disorder than concerned with fundamental social change. A decade later, SGH's cracked image as a heroic reformer received an especially severe blow with the publication of Harlan Lane's *When the Mind Hears: A History of the Deaf* (New York: Vintage, 1984). Lane argues that SGH was the central and most important advocate for the rise of oralism (the teaching of lip reading and speech) in nineteenth-century deaf education. Lane is uncompromisingly critical of what he sees as SGH's deliberate attempt to deprive deaf people of a valid and reliable language in the form of American Sign Language. In Lane's history, SGH becomes a central villain in a misguided and disastrous social program of oral communication.

Around the time that Lane depicted SGH as a threat to deaf identity, literary and historical critics were rediscovering JWH. In her literary work and her correspondence they found depictions of an often stressful and sometimes unhappy marriage. Their works include Deborah Pickman Clifford, *Mine Eyes Have Seen the Glory: A Biography of Julia Ward Howe* (Boston: Little, Brown, 1979); Mary H. Grant, *Private Woman, Public Person: An Account of the Life of Julia Ward Howe from 1819 to 1868* (Brooklyn, N.Y.: Carlson, 1994); Gary Williams, *Hungry Heart: The Literary Emergence of Julia Ward Howe* (Amherst: University of Massachusetts Press, 1999); and Valarie H. Ziegler, *Diva Julia: The Public Romance and Private Agony of Julia Ward Howe* (Harrisburg, Pa: Trinity Press International, 2003). These critics portray SGH as an impediment to JWH's aspirations, to her social relationships, and even to her identity. Moving beyond Tharp, they explore the contours of the marital problems, depicting SGH—whose heroism had already been challenged by questions about his motives for reform and humanitarian activities—as cruel and mean-spirited in his own home.

The final blow to SGH's once unblemished image came with the publication of three books that examine SGH's treatment of his most famous pupil, the blind and deaf girl Laura Bridgman who in 1837 began her education at the Perkins Institution under SGH's direction: Mary Klages, *Woeful Afflictions: Disability and Sentimentality in Victorian America* (Philadelphia: University of Pennsylvania Press, 1999); Ernest Freeberg, *The Education of Laura Bridgman: First Deaf and Blind Person to Learn Language* (Cambridge, Mass.: Harvard University Press, 2001); and Elizabeth Gitter, *The Imprisoned Guest: Samuel Howe and Laura Bridgman, the Original Deaf-Blind Girl* (New York: Farrar, Straus and Giroux, 2001). Though these authors come from three different academic traditions, they all depict SGH as the central figure in what are ostensibly stories about Bridgman. SGH, they reveal, was less interested in helping Bridgman than in shaping her into his own image of "sentimental affliction" and forming her spiritual awakening to demonstrate a "natural" relationship between God and human beings. According to Freeberg and Gitter, when Bridgman resisted those purposes and developed her own religious sensibilities in 1844, SGH lost interest in her.

10. Palfrey to Bird, 11 Jan. 1876, HFP 1921.

11. My understanding of "manliness" in the nineteenth century has been influenced by Anthony Rotundo, *American Manhood: Transformations in Masculinity from the Revolution to the Modern Era* (New York: Basic Books, 1993). Also, I have considered Mark C. Carnes and Clyde Griffen, eds., *Meanings for Manhood: Constructions of Masculinity in Victorian America* (Chicago: University of Chicago Press, 1990); and Peter Stearns, *Be a Man! Males in Modern Society,* 2nd ed. (New York: Holmes and Meier, 1990).

12. SGH to Longfellow, 15 July 1849, reproduced in JWH, "Dr. Samuel G. Howe," *Cambridge Magazine,* May 1896, 9–14.

13. On the "perfectibility of man," see Abraham S. Lutchin, "The Cult of Curability and the Doctrine of Perfectibility: Social Context of the Nineteenth-Century American Asylum Movement," *History of Psychiatry* 3 (1992): 203–20; Robert D. Richardson Jr., *Emerson: The Mind*

on Fire (Berkeley: University of California Press, 1995), 340–41; John L. Thomas, "Romantic Reform in America, 1815–1865," *American Quarterly* 17 (Winter 1965): 662–68.

14. Thomas F. Harrington, "Samuel Gudley [*sic*] Howe," in *The Harvard Medical School: A History, Narrative, and Documentary, 1782–1905* (New York: Lewis Pub. Co., 1905), 2:753.

1. "A Respectable, If Ordinary Boyhood"

1. *The Manifest Church: Records of the Church in Brattle Square, Boston, 1699–1872* (Boston: Benevolent Fraternity of Churches, 1902), 206; Thomas H. O'Connor, *The Athens of America: Boston 1825–1845* (Amherst: University of Massachusetts Press, 2006), 18. On the family's name change, see Henry B. Peirce, *List of Persons Whose Names Changed in Massachusetts, 1780–1883* (Boston: Wright & Potter, 1885), 16.

2. Samuel K. Lothrop, *A History of the Church in Brattle Street, Boston* (Boston: William Crosby and H. P. Nichols, 1851), 157. See also Conrad Wright, *The Beginnings of Unitarianism in America* (Boston: Starr King Press, 1955), 266.

3. Van Wyck Brooks, *The Flowering of New England, 1815–1865* (Cleveland: World, 1946), 13; Wright, *Beginnings of Unitarianism in America,* 288.

4. Frank O. Gatell, *John Gorham Palfrey and the New England Conscience* (Cambridge, Mass.: Harvard University Press, 1963), 41–42; see also 60; Lothrop, *History of the Church in Brattle Street,* 159–217; Dean Grodzins, *American Heretic: Theodore Parker and Transcendentalism* (Chapel Hill: University of North Carolina Press, 2002), 45.

5. O'Connor, *Athens of America,* 18.

6. "Triumph of Principle," *Independent Chronicle* (Boston), 8 Mar. 1813.

7. "Deaths," *New Hampshire Gazette,* 4 Jan. 1814; "Republican Institution," *National Aegis* (Worcester, Mass.), 17 Mar. 1819.

8. Sean Wilentz, *The Rise of American Democracy: Jefferson to Lincoln* (New York: Norton, 2005), 162.

9. *Boston Patriot,* 26 Feb. 1820, 2. On the cordage business, see Timothy T. Sawyer, *Old Charlestown: Historical, Biographical, Reminiscent* (Boston: J. H. West, 1902), 181.

10. SGH to Mann, [1857], HFP 1474. Although Howe did not date the letter to Mann, its context renders it from 1857.

11. *Boston Public Records, Boston Marriages 1762–1809, from the Record Commissioners Report 101* (1902). On Samuel Gridley's Revolutionary War service, see W. J. Wood, *Battles of the Revolutionary War, 1775–1781* (Cambridge, Mass.: Da Capo Press, 2004), 5–11. On Samuel Gridley's business, see Joseph S. Davis, *Essays in the Earlier History of American Corporations,* vol. 4: *Eighteenth Century Business Corporations in the United States* (Cambridge, Mass.: Harvard University Press, 1917), 263.

12. SGH diary, HFP 1698:101–3.

13. "Deaths," *Boston Patriot,* 19 Mar. 1819; *Manifest Church,* 285.

14. "Triumph of Principle."

15. The story of SGH's childhood game first appeared in JWH, *Memoir of Dr. Samuel Gridley Howe* (Boston: Albert J. Wright, 1876), 3, but Laura Howe Richards repeated the story most often. See, e.g., *LJ,* 1:13–14; Richards, *Two Noble Lives: Samuel Gridley Howe and Julia Ward Howe* (Boston: Dana, Estes, & Co., 1911), 12.

16. SGH, "On Universal Language," in *The Lectures Delivered before the American Institute of Instruction* (Boston: William D. Ticknor, 1842), 58.

17. In recounting the story of SGH's experience at the Boston Latin School in *Memoir,* 3–4, JWH identifies the cruel headmaster as Benjamin Apthorp Gould. Not long after *Memoir*

appeared, the Boston Latin School celebrated its bicentennial anniversary. At the alumni's commemorative dinner, speakers recalled a benevolent Master Gould, and some openly criticized JWH for her disparaging remarks about a headmaster they remembered for his kindness and tolerance. After the episode appeared in the Boston press, a miffed JWH complained to her friend Edward Everett Hale, head of the bicentennial, "I will tell you that the Doctor often spoke to me of Master Gould as a very hard tyrannical man. . . . But what shall we say of the chivalry of the Boston Latin School which attacked with such undeserved enmity and harshness a widow who, in the first year of her affliction, has tried to [do] a service to the public by giving it the most careful and truthful record she was able to give of a truly great and noble man" (JWH to Hale, 11 Nov. 1876, Boston Latin School, 23:174, Boston Public Library). SGH had claimed, JWH remembered, that he entered the school at the beginning of the 1810 academic year when he would have been nine years old. When Hale questioned William Henry Furness, who entered the Latin School in 1812 (the same year SGH's daughter Florence Howe Hall said he entered the school), Furness indicated that he had no memory of SGH at the school (Furness to Hale, 6 Nov. 1876, Boston Latin School, 23:167), and the roll of students who attended the school during the second decade of the nineteenth century does not include the name of SGH (see Boston Latin School Association, *Materials for a Catalogue of the Masters and Scholars Who Have Belonged to the Public Latin School, Boston, Massachusetts from 1635 to 1861* [Boston: Wm. Crosby and H. P. Nichols, 1847], 32–34). The story of his mistreatment by Federalist Latin School authorities may have been a fiction launched by SGH himself and sustained by succeeding biographies. It is even more likely, however, that his attendance was so brief that no record was made of it.

18. Dorus Clarke, "The Necrology: Rev. Joseph Richardson," *New England Genealogical Register* 26 (July 1872): 340; Joseph Richardson, *The American Reader: A Selection of Lessons for Reading and Speaking* (Boston: Lincoln and Edmands, 1810); Charles Brewer, *Reminiscences* (Jamaica Plain, Mass., 1884), 7–8. Brewer gives a good account of his experiences at Richardson's school, and he remembers SGH and Edward Howe as two of his contemporaries at the school. Of Richardson and his wife, Brewer writes, "Both our teacher and his wife were always very kind and pleasant with the scholars, and I left the school after a year and a half well pleased."

19. Quoted in *LJ*, 1:17.

20. "Table Talk" *North American Magazine*, Feb. 1833, 250.

21. Asa Messer, 12 Mar. 1819, President's Letter Book, 1811–1836, Asa Messer Papers, John Hay Library, Brown University. On memories of SGH as a Brown undergraduate, see Editorial, *Louisville Daily Journal*, 4 Nov. 1859. Another anonymous alumnus of SGH's undergraduate days recalled in 1835 that SGH was "a wild, daring, generous fellow." He almost lamented that SGH's "college pranks and freakish feats" were over ("Table Talk").

22. "For Sale, the Following Real Estate," *Berkshire Star*, 6 May 1819; "My Marston and Thayer," *Boston Daily Advertiser*, 7 June 1819.

23. On Joseph Howe's financial problems, see Amos Binney, *Documents Relative to the Investigation, by the Order of the Secretary of the Navy of the Official Conduct of Amos Binney* (Boston: Phelps and Farnham, 1822). On the fire that damaged SGH's business, see *Repertory* (Boston), 16 Nov. 1819, 4. On the effects of the War of 1812 on New England's mercantile enterprises, see O'Connor, *Athens of America*, 12–13.

24. Martha Mitchell, "Asa Messer," *Encyclopedia Brunoniana* (Providence: Brown University Library, 1993), www.brown.edu/Aministration/News_Bureau/Databases/Encyclopedia/search.php?serial=M0280.

25. Jonathan C. Messerli, *Horace Mann: A Biography* (New York: Alfred A. Knopf, 1972),

29–31, 38; William T. Hastings, "Wars of the Greeks at Brown," *New England Quarterly* 5 (July 1932): 533–42. On Brown University during this period, see Walter C. Bronson, *The History of Brown University, 1764–1914* (Providence, R.I.: Brown University, 1914).

26. Editorial, *Louisville Daily Journal,* 4 Nov. 1859. On SGH's membership in the Philendean Society at Brown University, see Bronson, *History of Brown,* 182.

27. "Commencement," *Providence Patriot,* 8 Sept. 1821.

28. SGH to Elijah J. Hamlin, Aug. 1820, Howe 16, loose letters, 1820–40, 26, HRL.

29. Jim Vrabel, *When in Boston: A Time Line and Almanac* (Boston: Northeastern University Press, 2004): 109; Robert D. Richardson Jr., *Emerson: The Mind on Fire* (Berkeley: University of California Press, 1995), 18, 208.

30. Robert Sullivan, *The Disappearance of Dr. Parkman* (Boston: Little, Brown, 1971), 31–34; Helen Thomson, *Murder at Harvard* (Boston: Houghton Mifflin, 1971), 27–31; Eric T. Carlson, "The Unfortunate Dr. Parkman," *American Journal of Psychiatry* 123 (Dec. 1966): 724–28. See also James W. Trent Jr., "Moral Treatment," Disability History Museum, www.disabilitymuseum.org/dhm/edu/essay.html?id=19.

31. On Warren's interest in phrenology, see Anthony A. Walsh, "Phrenology and the Boston Medical Community in the 1830s," *Bulletin of the History of Medicine* 50 (1976): 263–64. Walsh also notes that SGH's teacher, William Ingalls, "gave lectures on the anatomy of the cranium," 268–69.

32. O'Connor, *Athens of America,* 59.

33. See Kenneth M. Ludmerer, *Learning to Heal: The Development of American Medical Education* (New York: Basic Books, 1983).

34. "Commencement at Cambridge," *Salem Gazette,* 7 Sept. 1824.

35. "Commencement at Cambridge," *Salem Gazette,* 7 Sept. 1824; John L. Thomas, "Romantic Reform in America, 1815–1865," *American Quarterly* 17 (Winter 1965): 656–81.

36. On Lafayette's 1824–25 visit of the United States, see Lloyd S. Kramer, *Lafayette in Two Worlds: Public Cultures and Personal Identities in an Age of Revolutions* (Chapel Hill: University of North Carolina Press, 1996); Sylvia Neely, "The Politics of Liberty in the Old World and the New: Lafayette's Return to America in 1824," *Journal of the Early Republic* 6 (1986): 151–71. On the Harvard commencement, see *Salem Gazette,* 7 Sept. 1824, 1. On Mary Peabody's presence at the commencement, see Megan Marshall, *The Peabody Sisters: Three Women Who Ignited American Romanticism* (Boston: Houghton Mifflin, 2005), 141.

37. In the thousands of letters I have read from SGH, I have never found an example when he used or referred to his middle name. He consistently signed letters as either "Samuel G. Howe" or "S. G. Howe." In the same way, his contemporaries never used, or addressed him by, his middle name. The use of "Gridley" began with JWH's 1876 biography of her husband, and her daughters in their various writings about their father sustained a tradition that has continued to the present. I avoid referring to the subject of my biography as "Samuel Gridley Howe" in keeping with his preference.

38. William St. Clair, *That Greece Might Be Free: The Philhellenes in the War of Independence* (London: Oxford University Press, 1972), 150–67. See also Edward M. Earle, "American Interest in the Greek Cause, 1821–1827," *American Historical Review* 33 (Oct. 1927): 44–63; Charles L. Booth, "Let the American Flag Wave in the Aegean: American Responds to the Greek of Independence (1821–1824)" (Ph.D. diss., New York University, 2005); Angelo Repousis, " 'The Cause of the Greeks': Philadelphia and the Greek War of Independence, 1821–1828," *Pennsylvania Magazine of History and Biography* 123 (Oct. 1999): 338–41. On the growth of Hellenism in the United States, see Myer Reinhold, *Classica Americana: The Greek and Roman Heritage in the United States* (Detroit: Wayne State University Press, 1984).

39. SGH to C. C. Felton, 15 Mar. 1855, MS Am 1172, HL, 50. In this letter SGH recounts his experiences in Greece to his friend the Harvard classics professor Cornelius C. Felton.

40. Stephen A. Larrabee, *Hellas Observed: The American Experience of Greece, 1775–1865* (New York: New York University Press, 1957), 41, 301.

41. *Independent Chronicle and Boston Patriot*, 24 Jan. 1824, 1.

42. Henry Mayer, *All on Fire: William Lloyd Garrison and the Abolition of Slavery* (New York: St. Martin's Press, 1998), 28–29, 34–37.

43. Larabee, *Hellas Observed*, 95–147. Gary J. Bass, in *Freedom's Battle: The Origin of Humanitarian Intervention* (New York: Knopf, 2008), 25, describing what he calls the "CNN effect," argues that "mass media is the crucial first step toward humanitarian intervention." During the three years of his medical education (and even before), SGH was exposed to several forms of media information about the blight of Greece. See also Merle Curti, *American Philanthropy Abroad: A History* (New Brunswick, N.J.: Rutgers University Press, 1963).

44. Jonathan P. Miller, letter to the editor, *Boston Atlas*, 13 Oct. 1843, HFP 1907. Jennette Howe's first name is variously spelled Jeanette, Jeannette, and Jennette in family writings. I use "Jennette" because it is the spelling on her tombstone at Mount Auburn Cemetery in Cambridge, Mass.

45. *LJ*, 1:19; Lura Woodside Watkins, *Cambridge Glass, 1818 to 1888: The Story of the New England Glass Company* (Boston: Marshall Jones, 1930), 18, 175–76; George McKearin and Helen McKearin, *American Glass* (New York: Crown, 1941), 334; *Boston Daily Atlas*, 4 Aug. 1854, 2. In his early twenties Joseph Howe was a captain and later a major in the Independent Boston Fusiliers, a local militia that held parades, military drills, and occasional marches to adjacent communities. The Fusiliers' most memorable event was to provide the escort for the Marquis de Lafayette at his triumphal entrance on 30 August 1824 into Boston, five days after his appearance at the Harvard University commencement. See "Miscellany: Commencement at Cambridge," *Boston Commercial Gazette*, 2 Sept. 1824, 26 Feb. 1824; "Commencement at Cambridge," *Connecticut Courant*, 31 Aug. 1824. The only known likeness of Joseph Howe is an 1847 portrait by Charles Loring Elliott at the Hunter Museum in Chattanooga, Tenn. (see http://tnportraits.org/hunter-elliott-howe-joseph.htm). The museum also holds three mid-century landscapes that once graced Howe's home on Ashburton Place. Eugene Tompkins, *The History of the Boston Theatre, 1854–1901* (Boston: Houghton Mifflin, 1908), 68–69, mentions that Howe was a devotee of the theater. SGH to Charles Sumner, 21 Feb. 1866, HFP 1614.

46. Little is known about Edward Compton Howe. He was baptized 13 Feb. 1803. See Richards, *Samuel Gridley Howe*, 4.

47. SGH diary, 28 Mar. 1829, HFP 1698:8–12; *LJ*, 1:364.

48. *LJ*, 1:25.

2. "Greece! Greece!"

1. On the first years of the Greek War of Independence, see Paul C. Pappas, *The United States and the Greek War for Independence, 1821–1828* (New York: Columbia University Press, 1985), 1–11; David Brewer, *The Greek War of Independence: The Struggle for Freedom from Ottoman Oppression and the Birth of the Modern Greek Nation* (Woodstock, N.Y.: Overlook Press, 2001), 26–246; and Gary J. Bass, *Freedom's Battle: The Origin of Humanitarian Intervention* (New York: Knopf, 2008), 51–75.

2. SGH's letter to his father appears in the *Independent Chronicle and Boston Patriot*, 17 Sept. 1825, 1; his letter to William Sampson, in the *Boston Courier*, 14 Sept. 1825, 2. Joseph Jenkes of Fairfax County, Va., read about SGH's exploits in his local newspaper and described them

to George Bucklin of Seekonk, Mass. (Jenkes to Bucklin, 18 Nov. 1825, Student Letters, John Carter Brown Library, Brown University). Both men were Brown alumni and friends of SGH's. SGH's letters were also published in the *Providence Gazette*, 21 Sept. 1825, 1; *Edwardsville [Ill.] Spectator*, 22 Oct. 1825, 2; *Essex Register*, 24 Oct. 1825, 1; *Richmond Enquirer*, 22 Nov. 1825, 1; *Connecticut Courant*, 28 Aug. 1826, 2; *American Mercury*, 9 Jan. 1827, 1; *Baltimore Patriot*, 11 Feb. 1828, 2; *Pittsfield Sun*, 21 Feb. 1828, 3; *Village Register and Norfolk County Advertiser [Mass.]*, 14 May 1829, 1; *Eastern Argus*, 26 June 1829, 2; and *Berkshire [Mass.] Journal*, 19 Nov. 1829, 2.

3. JWH, *Memoir of Dr. Samuel Gridley Howe* (Boston: Albert J. Wright, 1876), 8–9.

4. *LJ*, 1:59–60, 77.

5. *LJ*, 1:51.

6. *LJ*, 1:64, 67–68.

7. *LJ*, 1:74–75.

8. *LJ*, 1:79–80, 84.

9. *LJ*, 1:109.

10. SGH to Charles Follen, 4 Oct. 1836, Follen Manuscripts, Boston Public Library.

11. Of the additional early letters from SGH printed in U.S. newspapers, see *Independent Chronicle and Boston Patriot*, 17 Sept. 1825, 1; *Providence Gazette*, 21 Sept. 1825, 1; *Essex Register*, 24 Oct. 1825, 2; *Essex Register*, 10 Nov. 1825, 2.

12. *LJ*, 1:127.

13. *LJ*, 1:129–30.

14. Florence Howe Hall, "A Modern Hero," *Wide Awake*, Nov. 1890, 345.

15. *LJ*, 1:134–35.

16. *LJ*, 1:136–37.

17. Jonathan P. Miller, letter to the editor, *Boston Atlas*, 13 Oct. 1843, HFP 1907. Accompanying the letter is an envelope postmarked Cambridgeport, Mass., and addressed to Hon. F. W. Bird. The following appears on the cover in JWH's handwriting: "Col. Miller's invaluable letter about dear Chev, mislaid by me when writing my sketch of him. Found by me in this envelope on Dec. 3rd 1896."

18. SGH to Horace Mann, [1857], HFP 1474.

19. *LJ*, 1:157.

20. *LJ*, 1:181.

21. "From Greece," *New Hampshire Sentinel*, 8 Dec. 1826.

22. See e.g., Everett to SGH, 26 Dec. 1826, reel 25, Edward Everett Papers, MHS.

23. *LJ*, 1:209.

24. SGH diary, "Wednesday, July 18—Astros," HRL. For a general description of the distribution of aid to Greece recounted by SGH nearly thirty years later see SGH to C. C. Felton, 15 Mar. 1855, HFP 1172:50.

25. SGH diary, "Napoli, July 19," 22–23, HRL. Note that Richards in her *Letters and Journal* does not print the matter of her father's reporting of the adulterous affair.

26. SGH diary, "Monday, July 23 Monembaria," 30–34, HRL.

27. SGH diary, "Thursday July 26, Palio Kormis," 38–44, HRL. This entry is not included in *LJ*.

28. SGH diary, "Monday, Aug. 20, Napoli [Naplion]," 71–74, HRL. This entry is not included in *LJ*.

29. SGH to C. C. Felton, 15 Mar. 1855.

30. JWH, *Memoir of Dr. Samuel Gridley Howe*, 11–12.

31. SGH diary, "Saturday, Oct 20 Syra," 122–23, "Friday, Oct 26 [from Poros]," 128, "Friday, Nov. 2, Poros," 129, HRL; "Aid to the Greeks," *Farmer's Cabinet*, 1 Mar. 1828, 2. On the Battle

of Navarino, see William St. Clair, *That Greece Might Be Free: The Philhellenes in the War of Independence* (London: Oxford University Press, 1972), 331–33; Stephen A. Larrabee, *Hellas Observed: The American Experience of Greece, 1775–1865* (New York: New York University Press, 1957), 166; Brewer, *The Greek War of Independence*, 325–33.

32. *Baltimore Patriot*, 11 Feb. 1828, 2; *Pittsfield (Mass.) Sun*, 21 Feb. 1828, 3; *Connecticut Courant*, 25 Feb. 1828, 2.

33. *Connecticut Courant*, 25 Feb. 1828, 2.

34. Katherine A. Ware, *The Bower of Taste* (Boston: Dutton and Wentworth, 1828), 184–85, 189; Thomas Pickering, *The Suffering Greeks* (Salem, Mass.: Essex Co., 1828); Edward Everett, "The History of Liberty," in *Orations and Speeches on Various Occasions* (Boston: C. C. Little and J. Brown, 1859), 1:169–70.

35. SGH, *An Historical Sketch of the Greek Revolution* (New York: White, Gallaher & White, 1828), 155. SGH describes Mavrocordatos as "about 38 years of age, rather below the middling height, but perfectly well made. His fine olive complexion looks darker than it really is from the jetty blackness of his hair, which hangs in ringlets about his face, and from his large mustachios and sparkling black eyes. His manners are perfectly easy and gentlemanlike, and though the first impression would be from his extreme politeness and continual smiles that he was a good-natured silly fop, yet one soon sees from the keen inquisitive glances which involuntarily escape him that he is concealing under an almost childish lightness of manner a close and accurate study of his visiter [*sic*]," 50. For other examples of SGH's use of phrenology, see 27–28, 155, 321.

36. Edward Everett, "The Greek Revolution," *North American Review* 29 (July 1829): 138–99. See also "Modern Greece: Review of Dr. Howe's Sketch of the Greek Revolution," *American Baptist Magazine* 9 (1828): 406–11.

37. SGH diary, 23 and 26 Sept., 23 Oct. 1828, HFP 1697:1–6, 9–15.

38. SGH diary, HFP 1697:18–19.

39. For an example of SGH's letters that appeared during 1829 in several newspapers, see a letter dated 3 Nov. 1828 that appear in the *Village Register and Norfolk County Advertiser*, 14 May 1829.

40. SGH diary, 5 Nov. 1828, HFP 1697:25.

41. For a general history of American relief during the Greek War, see Larrabee, *Hellas Observed*, 148–66.

42. "The single column which is standing I shall respect, and shall use every possible precaution to prevent injuring any part of the temple which may be useful or agreeable to have left, being too great an admirer of antiquities to commit any sacrilege upon them." *LJ*, 1:313.

43. *LJ*, 1:310.

44. *LJ*, 1:330.

45. SGH diary, 9 Mar. 1829, HFP 1697:1–4.

46. SGH diary, 12 Mar. 1829, HFP 1697:7–8.

47. SGH diary, 13, 15–16 Apr. 1829, HFP 1697:12–20.

48. SGH diary, 26 Apr. 1829, HFP 1698:32–33.

49. SGH diary, 13 May 1829, HFP 1698:37–38. On the prevalence of malaria, especially in the Peloponnese, see Stephen Minta, *On a Voiceless Shore: Byron in Greece* (New York: Henry Holt, 1998), 22. On JWH's recollection of her husband's malaria, see JWH, *Memoir of Dr. Samuel Gridley Howe*, 10.

50. SGH diary, 21 May 1829, HFP 1698:39.

51. SGH diary, 3 July 1829, HFP 1698:55–56.

52. Everett to Jackson, 22 Apr. 1830, reel 25, Everett Papers. Everett begins his letter by

explaining SGH's work, noting that SGH has been in the country about six years and has learned Greek, that he began as a surgeon and has more recently been distributing aid in the form of supplies and clothing to the Greeks. He then gets to the point of the letter: "It is Dr. Howe's wish to be employed by the gov't of the U. States in Greece. In addition to the evidence of his qualifications furnished in these letters [i.e., copies of SGH's letters that Everett has forwarded to Secretary of State Martin Van Buren, and now to the president], I may add that he possesses very estimable personal abilities and great physical energy. I render this attestation at the request of his friends with the greater pleasure, as I believe as far as he has taken any part in politics, he has been (I know his father has been) on an opposite side from myself."

53. SGH to "Mrs. Joseph N. Howe, Jun.," 26 Aug. 1829, folder 2, record group 20, collection 2085, Yellow House Papers, Maine Historical Society, Portland.

54. Laura H. Richards, *Samuel Gridley Howe* (New York: D. Appleton-Century, 1935), 53.

55. *LJ*, 1:378.

56. SGH diary, 1 Oct. 1830, HFP 1698:100–101.

57. SGH diary, 16 May 1831, HFP 1698:101–3.

3. "The Cadmus of the Blind"

1. For the idea of the self-made American man and the idea of self-improvement, I draw on Daniel Walker Howe, *Making the American Self: Jonathan Edwards to Abraham Lincoln* (Cambridge, Mass.: Harvard University Press, 1997).

2. Everett to Sargeant, 14 Sept. 1831, reel 25, Edward Everett Papers, MHS.

3. SGH diary, 27 Sept. 1830, 1 Oct. 1830 (in Paris), 16 May 1831 (in Philadelphia), HFP 1698:99–103. On Biddle's support for Greece and his connections with Everett, see John Clubbe, *Byron, Sully, and the Power of Portraiture* (Hampshire: Ashgate, 2005), 176. See also *Boston Masonic Mirror*, 6 Nov. 1830, scrapbook of clippings, HRL, in which SGH describes the events he witnessed in Brussels.

4. On SGH's political views at the time, see, e.g., *New Hampshire Sentinel*, 24 June 1831, 3; SGH diary, 16 May 1831. On the emerging Whig party, see Daniel Walker Howe, *What Hath God Wrought: The Transformation of America, 1815–1848* (New York: Oxford University Press, 2007), 583–84.

5. SGH diary, 16 May 1831.

6. Three days later, on 17 July 1831, SGH's older brother, Joseph, whose first wife, Elizabeth Kneeland Harris, had died in September 1829, married Elizabeth Morrill.

7. Photographs and drawings of the "Joseph N. Howe" house in Milton, built by Joseph Howe around 1830 on land inherited by his second wife, Rebecca Thayer Calef, are available at http://lcweb2.loc.gov/pp/hhhtml/hhTitles188.html. See also Albert K. Teele, *The History of Milton, Mass., 1640–1887* (Boston: Press of Rockwell and Churchill, 1887), 186.

8. SGH, "From the MSS of a Traveler in the East, No. I: Death and Burial," *New England Magazine* 1 (July 1831): 40–43; "From the MSS of a Traveler in the East, No. II: Executions," *New England Magazine* 1 (Aug. 1831): 110–12; "From the MSS of a Traveler in the East, No. III: Modern Greek," *New England Magazine* 1 (Sept. 1831): 240–45; "From the MSS of a Traveler in the East, No. IV: Campaigning in the Peloponnesus," *New England Magazine* 1 (Oct. 1831): 290–95; "From the MMS of a Traveler in the East, No V," *New England Magazine* 1 (Nov. 1831): 384–88. Although each article is brief, the five articles are among the most beautifully written accounts that SGH ever produced. They are, in a sense, SGH's "passion flowers." On the history of the *New England Magazine* and SGH's involvement with it, see George Willis Cooke, "The First 'New England Magazine' and Its Editors," *New England Magazine* 22 (Mar.

1897): 103–17; and George E. Woodberry, *Nathaniel Hawthorne* (Boston: Houghton Mifflin, 1902), 25.

9. Kimberly French, *Perkins School for the Blind* (Chicago: Arcadia Press, 2004), 7. See also Joseph L Dowling Jr., "Brown's Cadmuses of the Blind," *Rhode Island Medicine* 78 (Dec. 1995): 363–65; and SGH to Hon. T. G. Cary, 12 May 1848, LB 1848–53:283–85, in which SGH suggests wording for each of the four sides of a monument proposed to honor Fisher after his death. (The monument was built after Fisher's death in 1850). SGH also describes his and Fisher's earliest involvement with the blind: "In 1831, a few days after my return from Europe, while riding with him, the subject of the Education of the Blind came [up] incidentally, & he told me of the difficulties in the way of getting up & organizing an Institution. . . . I proposed to undertake the work, & in ten minutes we agreed upon measures . . . & in less than a week, I was on my way to Europe to procure Teachers, Books, &c." (283–84).

10. Everett to Francis Jeffrey, 19 Aug. 1831, reel 25, Everett Papers; *Boston Advertiser,* 30 Aug. 1831, cited in Harold Schwartz, *Samuel Gridley Howe: Social Reformer* (Cambridge, Mass.: Harvard University Press, 1956), 42. On Nat Turner's raid in the context of the remarkable year 1831, see Louis P. Masur, *1831: Year of Eclipse* (New York: Hill and Wang, 2001), 9–21.

11. *New York Commonwealth Advertiser,* 31 May 1832, SGH writings, box 2, folder 8, HRL. See also Philip B. Kunhardt Jr., Philip B. Kunhardt III, and Peter W. Kunhardt, *P. T. Barnum: America's Greatest Showman* (New York: Alfred Knopf, 1995), 144.

12. A jury finding in the New York Court of Common Pleas, *James W. Hale vs. Samuel G. Howe* occurred on 30 May 1832. A newspaper clipping from an unidentified newspaper about the trial may be found at SGH writings, box 2, folder 10, HRL. As we now know, Hale may have been a displayer of "freaks," but his exhibit of the original "Siamese twins" was authentic.

13. "Answer of Gen. Lafayette," *Daily National Journal* (Washington), 10 Sept. 1831, 2. On the formation of the American Polish Committee in New York, see Jerzy Jan Lerski, *A Polish Chapter in Jacksonian America: The United States and the Polish Exiles of 1831* (Madison: University of Wisconsin Press, 1958), 56–60. On the Parisian connection of Cooper and Lafayette with the Polish refugee relief, see Robert E. Spiller, "Fenimore Cooper and Lafayette: Friends of Polish Freedom." *American Literature* 7 (Mar. 1935): 56–75; and Lloyd S. Kramer, "The Rights of Man: Lafayette and the Polish National Revolution, 1830–1834" *French Historical Studies* 14 (Fall 1986): 521–46.

14. See, e.g., Lafayette to SGH, 7 Jan. 1832, BV 1828–1832.

15. Nathaniel P. Willis, "Jottings," *New York Mirror,* papers about SGH, box 9, HRL. On Willis's observations of his time with SGH in Paris, see "First Impressions of Europe, Number Seven," *New York Mirror,* 25 Feb. 1832, 268; and "First Impressions of Europe from the *New York Mirror,*" *Salem Gazette,* 28 Feb. 1832, 3. See also, on SGH, Willis, *Pencilling by the May: Written During Some Years of Residence and Travel in Europe* (Detroit: Kerr, Doughty and Lapham, 1853), 32, 57, 64, 71, 99, 102, 164; and Willis, *Summer Cruise in the Mediterranean on Board an American Frigate* (New York: Charles Scribner, 1853), xi, 181, 196, 210, 214.

16. Perkins School, *First Annual Report* (1833), 2–14.

17. Willis, "Jottings."

18. Laura Howe Richards dates SGH's arrest as 28 Feb. 1832 (*LJ,* 2:393–95). But the *Augsburg Gazette* places him in Elbing on 1 Mar. 1832 and in Berlin a day later. See "Arrest of Dr. Howe," *Columbian Sentinel,* 2 May 1832, 1. So the date of his arrest is more likely 3 Mar. Though SGH was in prison less than four weeks, between 3 Mar. and 27 Mar., in SGH to Horace Mann, [1857], HFP 1474. he claims to have been in prison for six weeks. See also Henry Barnard, "Samuel Gridley Howe, Memoir," *American Journal of Education* 11 (June 1862): 391–95.

19. Laura H. Richards, *Samuel Gridley Howe* (New York: D. Appleton-Century, 1935), 60–67.

20. SGH to [John Fisher], in "Samuel G. Howe on His Imprisonment in Berlin, 1832," *Bulletin of the New York Public Library* 7 (Feb. 1903): 90–95; SGH to Joseph N. Howe (father), "Prison—Berlin, March 21, 1832," *Boston Weekly Messenger,* n.d., SGH writings, box 2, folder 9, HRL; SGH to William C. Rives, 21 Mar. 1832, HFP 1126. For examples of newspaper reporting of SGH's imprisonment, see *Poulson's American Daily Advertiser* (Philadelphia), 23 Apr. 1832, 1; *New Hampshire Patriot and State Gazette,* 30 Apr. 1832, 1. On Congressional resolutions, *see Rhode Island American and Gazette,* 4 May 1832, 4. See also Lerski, *Polish Chapter,* 51–75; Dean Grodzins, *American Heretic: Theodore Parker and Transcendentalism* (Chapel Hill: University of North Carolina Press, 2002), 38–39.

21. On SGH's illness, see Frank P. Stearns, *Cambridge Sketches* (Philadelphia: J. B. Lippincott, 1905), 226–27. In an early announcement of the blind school, SGH states that the school is "ready to receive pupils from any part of the United States" (*Farmers' Cabinet* [Amherst, N.H.], 26 July 1833, 4).

22. Richards, *Samuel Gridley Howe,* 71.

23. See Berit M. Hattendorf, "Newport's First Woman Portraitist: Jane Stuart," *Newport History* 67, no. 3 (1995): 144–69.

24. Much information about the pupils at the New England School for the Blind and Perkins Institution may be found in *Perkins Institution Roll of Pupils,* HRL. SGH to A. W. Penniman, 22 Jan. 1841, LB 1839–41:308–9.

25. C. W. Cartwright to SGH, 8 Feb. 1836, BV 1836–38:17.

26. James Harris to SGH, 18 Feb. 1837, LB 1836–38:190.

27. Cartwright to SGH, 8 Feb. 1836. For a second example of pupils at the blind school being dismissed from a church, see SGH to Gentlemen of the church of the Rev. Mr. Young, 13 Feb. 1837, BV 1836–38:71–72. Despite his reluctance to admit pupils with epilepsy, in 1840 SGH began to allow students with epilepsy to enter the blind school if the condition was "not in a bad form." See, e.g., SGH to Phineas Barnes of Brunswick, 31 Dec. 1840, SGH to Mr. Read, 4 Jan. 1841, LB 1839–41:292–93, 295–96.

28. SGH to George Jarvis, 2 Sept. 1839, LB 1839–41:91.

29. SGH to Horace Mann, 26 Mar. 1838, LB 1836–38:236–40.

30. SGH to Martha Gold, n.d. [ca. June 1837], SGH to Charles Morrill, n.d. [ca. July 1837], SGH to Joseph B. Morrill [brother of Charles], n.d. [ca. Aug. 1837], SGH to Gold, n.d. [ca. Oct. 1838], LB 1836–38:135–36, 145–48, 150–54, 328–29; Gold to SGH, 18 Oct. 1838 and 4 Apr. 1839, BV 1838–39, box; SGH to Gold, 12 Oct. 1839, LB 1839–41:121–23; SGH to [A. W.]. Penniman, 15 Apr. 1840, LB 1830–41:186–91; Sarah Morrill to SGH, 4 Jan. 1866, BV 1863–67:237; SGH to J. H. Clough, 17 June 1869, LB 1868–70:131.

31. The claim that the sisters were the first pupils at the blind school may have begun with SGH himself. In his 1874 annual report, SGH wrote about the sisters as if they were the first pupils at the school. On SGH's communications with the Carters, see SGH to Mrs. Carter, 17 Oct. 1842, LB 1841–45:333–36; Sophia Carter to SGH, 4 and 8 Oct. 1844, BV 1844–45:113, 114. Even as late as 1857, SGH wrote to Sophia Carter, by then in her thirties and teaching at the institution, urging her to board outside the facility for her independence and the ability to more easily determine her diet (SGH to Sophia P. Carter, Oct. 1857, LB 1853–58:483–84).

32. J. Herrick to SGH, 14 Feb. 1858, BV 1858–60:24.

33. Jacob Doughty to SGH, 28 May 1840, BV 1840–41:63.

34. Frederick Tucker to SGH, 20 May 1842, BV 1842–43:77.

35. Richard B. Holland to SGH, 23 Jan. 1847, BV 1846–47:153.

36. SGH to Chapin,14 Dec. 1842, LB 1841–45:344–48. In the letter, SGH expressed his reluctance to open the workshop:

> It is the hope that the blind would be able to obtain their own livelihood by mechanical employment which has been disappointed. Perhaps this hope was formed too hastily, & without one consideration of the general introduction of machinery, of the subdivision of labor, & of the difficulty of the blind persons working in the shop with seeing persons. There are so many difficulties in the way of employing blind workmen with seeing ones that few persons will do it long. They often employ a blind man hoping that he may earn his wages, but they soon find that in spite of industry, zeal & perseverance, he is comparatively unprofitable; he needs much aid, he is perhaps in the way of others, and they finally consider him rather a burden than a source of profit. In this state of things the blind man soon feels what we should ever teach him to shun [illegible] a sense of dependence.
>
> Those blind persons who set up in business for themselves meet obstacles equally great. They seldom have capital, they cannot purchase stock in large quantities, they cannot hold on to their manufactured articles in order to command the market at the best seasons & are obligated to sell as a loss very often. Do the best he can, the blind man always works at a disadvantage, & should have some indirect aid, not in the way of charity but in the way of combination, just as other men derive advantage from corporation. . . . I am of the opinion that every Institution for the Instruction of the Blind should have a work department attached to it, in which those persons who have finished their course with credit, & have no wealthy friends, may find employment at fixed wages, or may have their rent stock tools etc. furnished to them at the lowest actual cost. Our work department after struggling with difficulties, and incurring some loss, is now doing pretty well, and is in a fair way of having perfect success, that is of paying for board, stock & tools & affording to the workmen a small profit. It has at this moment ten young men and two young women who are at work in the house, and four young men who work away from here, but upon materials furnished by us & for which they pay in articles of their own manufacture. Those in the house are subject only to such rules & regulations as would be established in every well regulated family of workmen or apprentices: they rise at the ringing of the bell, attend prayers, go to work and to bed at the same times, and ask leave, or rather give notice (for leave is never refused) to be absent from work. They have a sitting room by themselves, & associate but little with the scholars.

SGH's optimism about his pupils' employability rose and fell throughout his superintendency. Usually in economic good times when his pupils had an easier time finding work, his perspective reflected optimism. But in bad economic times, such as in 1850, he was more likely to express doubts about their employability.

37. SGH to Patrick Lane, 17 Nov. 1844, LB 1841–45:481–82.

38. SGH to Mr. Chapin, 14 Dec. 1842, LB 1841–45:344–48.

39. Laura E. Richards, *When I Was Your Age* (Boston: Estes and Lauriat, 1894), 59.

40. SGH to R. H. Holland of Nashville, Tenn., 11 Feb. 1847, LB 1845–48:219. For examples of SGH's correspondence about work for his graduated students and the workshop of the Perkins Institution, see Stephen Minot to SGH, 29 Oct. and 27 Nov. 1837, BV 1836–37:325, 338; letters from SGH to Minot, 28 Nov. and 4 Dec. 1837, LB 1836–38:207–9; to "Mr. Ludlow," 10 Feb. 1840, LB 1839–41:154–55; to "Mr. Tower," 13 Apr. 1842, LB 1841–45:255–56; to A[mos A]. Lawrence, n.d., LB 1845–48:252–53 (In this letter, SGH told Lawrence, an industrialist and school donor who had apparently complained about a mattress made for him in the workshop, "Some of our blind people are in tribulation about your mattress & would gladly do the work over ten times rather than give you cause of complaint—you who are the friend of the unfor-

tunate." SGH went on to assure Lawrence that he would personally see to it that the mattress work was done properly.); to Hon. Leavitt Thaxter, 25 Oct. 1847, 284–86; to Malona Erwin, 8 Apr. 1850, to James M. Dunbar, 8 Apr. 1850, to Malona Erwin, 11 Nov. 1850, to Rev. Mr. Foster, 2 Dec. 1850, LB 1848–53:102–3, 192–93, 206–10; to unnamed blind man, 9 July 1852, LB 1848–53: n.p.

41. SGH to R. Elliot, 15 Aug. 1846, LB 1845–48:146–48.

42. SGH to Rev. Mr. [Charles P.] Packard, 29 May 1846, LB 1845–48:124. See also Packard to SGH, 16 May 1846, BV 1846–47:59; Rev. Nathan B. Rogers to SGH, 23 Aug. 1849, BV 1848–49:248; SGH to Rev. Mr. A. Walker, 12 and 21 Aug. 1851, LB 1848–53:316, 318. The best description of Benjamin B. Bowen's early years appears in the preface to his *Daisies and Dew Drops, a Memorial of the Blind* (Lowell, Mass.: A. Watson Printer, 1840), iii–iv. By the early 1850s Bowen had become a Universalist minister. Additional correspondence between Bowen and SGH includes, from Bowen to SGH, 5 [May], 9 June, and 15 June 1838, BV 1838–39:41, 62; 21 July and 30 Sept. 1846, BV 1846–47:73, 101; and SGH to Bowen, 27 Aug. 1846, LB 1845–48: 153–54.

43. SGH to Josiah Quincy, 12 Jan. 1841, BV 1840–41:163.

44. On Smith, see Franklin B. Hough, *American Biographical Notes* (Albany, N.Y.: Joel Munsell, 1875), 366; John Heywood, "Discourse on the Life and Character of Joseph Brown Smith," in *The Golden Sunset; or, The Homeless Blind Girl,* ed. Anne Kane (Baltimore: J. W. Bond, 1867); J. W. [John White] Webster to SGH, "Wed Eveg" [ca. Jan. 1841], BV 1840–41:157. See also SGH to Charles Sumner, 2 Aug. 1843, HFP 1183; "Smith, Joseph Brown—1844," in *Necrology of Alumni of Harvard College, 1851–52 to 1862–63,* ed. Joseph Palmer (Boston: J. Wilson and Son, 1864), 280–82.

45. Benjamin F. Hallett to SGH, 16 Mar. 1833, BV 1828–35.

46. *Salem Gazette,* 12 Feb. 1833, 3; "The Exhibition of the Blind Pupils," *Juvenile Rambler,* 10 Apr. 1833, Perkins Newspaper Notices, 1:22, HRL; letter to the editor, *Eastern Argus,* 10 Feb. 1834, 3.

47. SGH to Rev. Bailey Loring, 9 Sept. 1837, 179, SGH to John Appleton, 23 Nov. 1837, LB 1836–38:179, 205.

48. SGH, "Institution for the Blind," in School Journal, 29 May 1839–25 Apr. 1840, 36–37, 39–41, HRL.

49. SGH to Mr. Perkins, 12 Apr. 1841, LB 1841–43:4.

50. Peter D. Hall, "What Merchants Did with Their Money: Charitable and Testamentary Trusts in Massachusetts, 1780–1880," in *Entrepreneurs: The Boston Business Community, 1700–1850,* ed. Conrad Edick Wright and Kathryn P. Viens (Boston: Massachusetts Historical Society, 1997), 398–99. On Thomas H. Perkins, see Carl Seaburg and Stanley Paterson, *Merchant Prince of Boston, Colonel T. H. Perkins, 1764–1854* (Cambridge, Mass.: Harvard University Press, 1971), 375–80; Edward E. Allen, *The Perkins Institution for the Blind* (Watertown, Mass, 1924), 15–17.

51. *Boston Evening Transcript,* 26 Apr. 1833, 2. On the role of Boston elites in the development of charitable organizations, see Robert F. Dalzell, *Enterprising Elite: The Boston Association and the World They Made* (Cambridge, Mass.: Harvard University Press, 1987), 136; Kathleen D. McCarthy, *American Creed: Philanthropy and the Rise of Civil Society, 1700–1865* (Chicago: University of Chicago Press, 2003), 93–95; Hall, "What the Merchants Did with Their Money," 398–406; Thomas H. O'Connor, *The Athens of America: Boston 1825–1845* (Amherst: University of Massachusetts Press, 2006), 15–17; Ronald Story, *The Forging of an Aristocracy: Harvard and the Boston Upper Class, 1800–1870* (Middleton, Conn.: Wesleyan University Press, 1980), 8–12, 161; Ronald P. Formisano, *The Transformation of Political Culture: Massachusetts Parties,*

1770s–1840s (New York: Oxford University Press, 1983), 289–91. On Perkins's place among Unitarian elites, see Charles Sellers, *The Market Revolution: Jacksonian America, 1815–1846* (New York: Oxford University Press, 1991), 202–3. Conrad Edick Wright, *The Transformation of Charity in Post-Revolutionary New England* (Boston: Northeastern University Press, 1992), 316n9, states, "During the Federalist and Jacksonian periods approximately two-thirds of wealthy Bostonians were Unitarians."

52. Julie Roy Jeffrey, *The Great Silent Army of Abolitionism: Ordinary Women in the Antislavery Movement* (Chapel Hill: University of North Carolina Press, 1998), 107–10; Deborah Bingham Van Broekhoven, *The Devotion of These Women: Rhode Island in the Antislavery Network* (Amherst: University of Massachusetts Press, 2002), 173–97.

53. *Catalogue of Articles to Be Offered for Sale at the Ladies' Fair, Held at Hamilton Hall, in Chestnut St., Salem, Wednesday, April 10, 1833 for the benefit of the New-England Asylum for the Blind,* Perkins Newspaper Notices, 39b, HRL.

54. Megan Marshall, *The Peabody Sisters: Three Women Who Ignited American Romanticism* (Boston: Houghton Mifflin, 2005), 227–31, 262–65, 522; Seaburg and Paterson, *Merchant Prince of Boston,* 380–82.

55. Labiah May Smith to SGH, 20 May 1833, BV 1828–35; Seaburg and Paterson, *Merchant Prince of Boston,* 380–81; *Scenes at the Fair* (Boston: James B. Dow, 1833). See also "Ladies' Fairs," *New England Magazine* 5 (July 1833): 54–59.

56. Throughout the spring of 1833, SGH received letters from people in Rhode Island and Connecticut, as well as Massachusetts, inquiring about exhibitions of pupils at the blind school. See BV 1828–35, letters 30–60, esp. Charles Lawrence to SGH, 23 Mar. 1833, letter 33; see also George Barrett to SGH, 11 Apr. 1833, and Labiah May Smith et. al. to SGH, 20 May 1833. These letters showed that besides the fairs in Salem and Boston, there were several benefit fairs in other towns in Massachusetts and other New England states.

57. On Adams's remark about Jackson, see Edward Pessen, *Jacksonian America* (Urbana: University of Illinois Press, 1985), 180–81. See also David S. Reynolds, *Waking Giant: America in the Age of Jackson* (New York: HarperCollins, 2008), 105; and Joseph Wheelan, *Mr. Adams's Last Crusade: John Quincy Adam's Extraordinary Post-Presidential Life in Congress* (New York: Public Affairs, 2008), 75.

58. "Visit to the Boston Institution for the Blind," *Religious Magazine* 1, no. 3 (1833): 160–67.

59. SGH, "Education of the Blind," *New England Magazine* 4 (Mar. 1833): 177–87; SGH, "Education of the Blind," *North American Review* 37 (July 1833): 20–59. On SGH's editorship of the *New England Magazine* see SGH to Albert G. Greene, 9 Nov. 1834 and 9 July 1835, Greene Collection, Brown Special Collections, John Carter Brown Library, Brown University; and SGH to Longfellow, 28 Sept. 1834, MS. Am 1360, HL, 2867.

60. SGH, "Letter on Slavery," *New England Magazine* 5 (Aug. 1833): 122–29.

61. Henry Mayer, *All on Fire: William Lloyd Garrison and the Abolition of Slavery* (New York: St. Martin's Press, 1998), 135–41.

62. As Masur argues, as a result of Nat Turner's 1831 raids, many Americans, like SGH, were persuaded to support colonization (*1831,* 50).

63. SGH, "Letter to Mrs. Emma Willard [on the education of women in Greece]," *American Ladies Magazine* 7 (Oct. 1834): 459–61. The letter also appears as "Female Education in Greece: Dr. Samuel G. Howe's Letter to Mrs. Phelps," 13 July 1833, unidentified newspaper clipping, Howe letter box 2, folder 4, HRL, and, printed in pamphlet form, as "[Letter to] Mrs. Phelps," in Almira H. L. Phelps, *Address on the Subject of Female Education in Greece* (Troy, N.Y.: Norman Tuttle, 1833), 26–28. On SGH's association with Willard and her teaching methods, see Daniel H. Calhoun, "Eyes for the Jacksonian World: William C. Woodbridge and Emma

Willard," *Journal of the Early Republic* 4 (Spring 1984): 1–26. See also Angelo Repousis, " 'The Trojan Women': Emma Hart Willard and the Troy Society for the Advancement of Female Education in Greece," *Journal of the Early Republic* 24 (Autumn 2004): 445–76.

64. SGH's 1834 arguments about the place of women in society and how women should be educated for this place are remarkably similar to the arguments advanced by Harvey Mansfield in his provocative 2006 book *Manliness* (New Haven, Conn.: Yale University Press). For both SGH and Mansfield, society benefits from, and is even dependent for its stability on, behaviors provided best by womanly, as opposed to manly, ways. SGH was typical of his time in his ideas about the purity of women and his belief that their proper place was in the home and outside of the public forum. See, e.g., the discussion of the General Association of Massachusetts Clergy's censure of the Grimké sisters for speaking in public in the 1830s in McCarthy, *American Creed,* 149.

65. SGH to Mrs. Carter, 17 Oct. 1842, LB 1841–45:333–36.

66. SGH to Catharine Maria Sedgwick, 23 Sept. 1847, LB 1845–48:287–88.

67. Lydia Sigourney to SGH, 4 Oct. 1836, and 20 Apr. 1837, BV 1836–37:114, 222.

68. Marshall, *Peabody Sisters,* 531.

69. Diary of Samuel G. Howe at Sea, 23 Oct. [1828], HFP 1697:9–15. In the same diary entry, SGH shows that along with sexual interest and longing was an ever-present sense of propriety.

70. SGH to J. P. Bigelow [Houghton Library incorrectly identifies the name as T. P. Bigelow] by way of J. K. Mills & J. D. Fisher, 6 May 1840, HFP 1149.

71. SGH to Horace Mann, 6 June 1841, HFP 1155. The passage quoted is part of a letter, with the passage omitted, in *LJ,* 2:107–8.

72. SGH to Mrs. Alfred Stanley, 2 June 1868, LB 1862–68:709.

73. SGH to Longfellow, 28 Sept. 1834. SGH would likely have continued as the editor of the *New England Magazine* had the Board of Trustees of the New England School for the Blind not objected to his assuming the editorship while also superintending the blind school. See SGH to Charles Sumner, [Apr.] 1847, HFP 1284.

74. SGH, "Atheism in New-England," *New-England Magazine* 7 (Dec. 1834): 500–509; SGH, "Atheism in New-England," *New-England Magazine* 8 (Jan. 1835): 53–62. On the Kneeland affair, see Robert E. Burkholder, "Emerson, Kneeland, and the Divinity School Address," *American Literature* 58 (Mar. 1986): 1–4; Henry S. Commager, "The Blasphemy of Abner Kneeland," *New England Quarterly* 8 (Mar. 1935): 29–44; Formisano, *Transformation of Political Culture,* 292–93; Sarah B. Gordon, "Blasphemy and the Law of Religious Liberty in Nineteenth Century America," *American Quarterly* 52 (Dec. 2000): 698–714; Roderick S. French, "Liberation from Man and God in Boston: Abner Kneeland's Free-Thought Campaign, 1830–1839," *American Quarterly* 32 (Summer 1980): 202–21; Leonard W. Levy, "Satan's Last Apostle in Massachusetts," *American Quarterly* 5 (Spring 1953): 16–30; and Christopher Grasso, "Skepticism and American Faith: Infidels, Converts, and Religious Doubt in the Early Nineteenth Century," *Journal of the Early Republic* 22 (Autumn 2002): 465–508. On the connection between Kneeland and Robert Owen and Frances Wright, see Janet Farrell Brodie, *Contraception and Abortion in Nineteenth-Century America* (Ithaca, N.Y.: Cornell University Press, 1994), 136–38; Eric R. Schlereth, "Fits of Political Religion: Stalking Infidelity and the Politics of Moral Reform in Antebellum America," *Early American Studies* (Fall 2007): 288–323.

75. SGH diary, 21 Apr. 1829, HFP 1698:22–23. On the growth of evangelical Protestantism in the period see Reynolds, *Waking Giant,* 123–74. On emerging Unitarianism of the period, see Conrad Wright, *The Beginnings of Unitarianism in America* (Boston: Starr King Press, 1955); Daniel Walker Howe., *The Unitarian Conscience: Harvard Moral Philosophy, 1805–1861* (Cambridge, Mass.: Harvard University Press, 1970); and Reynolds, *Waking Giant,* 124–33. On

missionaries in Greece during the period, see Theodore Saloutos, "American Missionaries in Greece, 1820–1869," *Church History* 24 (June 1955): 152–74. SGH mentions two missionaries: Rev. Josiah Brewer, whom he recognizes as doing good work in Greece, and Rev. Jonas King, whom he clearly dislikes. Both men were evangelical Protestants involved in educational and charitable work during and after the Greek Revolution. King married a Greek woman and lived in Greece for most of the remainder of his life. It is not clear why SGH had such strongly different opinions of the two men. On the two missionaries, see *Annual Report of the Board of Managers of the American Bible Society* (New York: Daniel Fanshaw, 1838), 1:734.

76. SGH to Mr. Dewitt, 9 Oct. 1839, LB 1839–41, letter 897, 115–16.

77. John Quincy Adams is one example of the Unitarians of the period who were committed to Bible reading, Bible study among groups of Christians, and Bible distribution. In 1826 he officially joined the Unitarian congregation of Quincy, Massachusetts. Every morning during his adult life, he read the scriptures for an hour. His goal was to complete the entire Bible in one year. Over the years, he varied his routine by reading the scriptures in French and German along with English. Like SGH and other Unitarians, Adams was especially interested that copies of the printed Bible be widely distributed throughout the nation. Because of the moderately high rate of literacy, especially among Protestant white Americans, Unitarians believed that from the readings of the scriptures, Bible readers would likely come to the rational faith of Unitarians. Adams remained an active member of the American Bible Society, which supported SGH's printing of the Bible for the blind, and he served for a time as its vice president. See Reynolds, *Waking Giant,* 46–47; and Jonathan D. Sassi, *A Republic of Righteousness: The Public Christianity of the Post-Revolutionary New England Clergy* (New York: Oxford University Press, 2002), 177. It is interesting to note that SGH received most of the funding for the printing the Bible from the American Bible Society and the Massachusetts Bible Society. In May 1836, in what was likely his first correspondence with Gerrit Smith, SGH received a check for three hundred dollars for Bible printing for the blind. See Gerrit Smith to William L. Stone, 27 May 1836, BV 1836–37:65.

78. An example of the home-schooled pupils about whom SGH received letters for reading material, see SGH to [unnamed correspondent], 11 May 1838, BV 1836–37, letter 687, 273.

4. A Phrenologist and a Superintendent

1. On Spurzheim, phrenology, and New England medicine, see Anthony A. Walsh, "Phrenology and the Boston Medical Community in the 1830s," *Bulletin of the History of Medicine* 50 (1976): 263–64, and Walsh, "The American Tour of Dr. Spurzheim," *Journal of the History of Medicine and Allied Sciences* 27 (1972): 187–205; Christopher G. White, "Minds Intensely Unsettled: Phrenology, Experience; and the American Pursuit of Spiritual Assurance, 1800–1860," *Religion and American Culture* 16 (Summer 2006): 227–61; and Stephen Tomlinson, *Head Masters: Phrenology, Secular Education, and Nineteenth-Century Social Thought* (Tuscaloosa: University of Alabama Press, 2005), 63. On the general idea of romanticism and social reform, see John L. Thomas, "Romantic Reform in America, 1815–1865," *American Quarterly* 17 (Winter 1965): 656–81; Robert H. Abzug, *Cosmos Crumbling: American Reform and the Religious Imagination* (New York: Oxford University Press, 1994), 167–77. Also see Nahum Capen, *Reminiscences of Dr. Spurzheim and George Combe* (New York: Fowler and Wells, 1881); Charles Colbert, *A Measure of Perfection: Phrenology and the Fine Arts in America* (Chapel Hill: University of North Carolina Press, 1997); John F. Fulton, "The Early Phrenological Societies and Their Journals," *Boston Medical and Surgical Journal* 196 (1927): 398–400; Michael Martin, "Bumps and Brains: The Curious Science of Phrenology, the Wrong Idea at the Right Time" *American History Illustrated* 19, no. 5 (1984): 38–43.

2. Walsh, "Phrenology and the Boston Medical Community," 266–69; Harold Schwartz, "Samuel Gridley Howe as Phrenologist," *American Historical Review* 57 (Apr. 1952): 644–45; Tomlinson, *Head Masters,* 225. Tomlinson incorrectly gives Spurzheim's date of death as 30 Oct. 1832. Obituaries of Spurzheim include "Death of Dr, Spurzheim," and "Remains of Dr. Spurzheim," *Boston Medical and Surgical Journal,* 14 and 21 Nov. 1832. A contemporary review of the last days, death, autopsy, and funeral of Spurzheim, and of formation of the Boston Phrenology Society may be found in Nahum Capen's "Biography of the Author," preface to Johann Gaspar Spurzheim, *Phrenology in Connexion with the Study of Physiognomy* (Boston: March, Capen, and Lyon, 1833), 107–72. See also Park Benjamin, "The Late Dr. Spurzheim," *New England Magazine* 4 (1833): 40–47; Park Benjamin "Phrenology," *New England Magazine* 6 (1834): 467–79. On phrenology in the early republican and antebellum United States, see Robert E. Riegel, "Notes and Suggestions: The Introduction of Phrenology to the United States," *American Historical Review* 39 (Oct. 1933): 73–78; Arthur Wrobel, "Orthodoxy and Respectability in Nineteenth-Century Phrenology," *Journal of Popular Culture* 9 (June 1975): 38–50; John D. Davies, *Phrenology Fad and Science: A Nineteenth-Century American Crusade* (New Haven, Conn.: Yale University Press, 1955); Lisle W. Dalton, "Between in Enlightenment and Public Protestantism: Religion and the American Phrenological Movement" (Ph.D. diss., University of California Santa Barbara).

3. Anne-Marie Taylor, *Young Charles Sumner and the Legacy of the American Enlightenment, 1811–1851* (Amherst: University of Massachusetts Press, 2001), 85.

4. SGH, *A Discourse on the Social Relations of Man Delivered before the Boston Phrenological Society* (Boston: Capen & Lyon, 1837).

5. SGH, "Institution for the Blind," School Journal, 29 May 1839–25 Apr. 1840, HRL.

6. On beliefs about masturbation during the period, see Reynolds, *Waking Giant,* 206–8. See also Thomas W. Laqueur, *Solitary Sex: A Cultural History of Masturbation* (New York: Zone Books, 2004); Jean Stengers and Anne van Neck, *Masturbation: The History of a Great Terror* (New York: Palgrave Macmillan, 2001); Jack Larkins, *The Reshaping of Everyday Life, 1790–1840* (New York: Harper Perennial, 1989), 201–2; Helen Lefkowitz Horowitz, *Rereading Sex: Battles over Sexual Knowledge and Suppression in Nineteenth-Century America* (New York: Knopf, 2002), 92–105.

7. In Sept. and Oct. 1831 while SGH sailed for Europe, Charles Grandison Finney, the father of the Second Great Awakening, delivered a series of sermons at Boston's Park Street Church that inspired a religious revival among Boston's Trinitarians. When SGH wrote about religion a few years later, there is little doubt that the effects of Finney's revival were in the back of his mind. See Louis P. Masur, *1831: Year of Eclipse* (New York: Hill and Wang, 2001), 63–114.

8. Robert D. Richardson Jr., *Emerson: The Mind on Fire* (Berkeley: University of California Press, 1995), 100.

9. Entry for 8 Oct. 1838 in Horace Mann notebook, 3 May 1837–31 Apr. 1843, Horace Mann Papers, 1669–1926, MHS. See also entries for 8 Oct. 1838–13 Aug. 1839. Emerson quoted in Tomlinson, *Head Masters,* 229. The blind nineteenth-century hymnist Fannie Cosby, who entered the New York Institution for the Blind, remembered Combe's visit to that facility. The superintendent, Dr. Silas Jones, who had discouraged her interest in writing poetry, allowed her to continue with her poetry after Combe did a phrenological examination of Crosby and exclaimed, as Crosby recalls: "Why! Here is a poet! Give her every advantage that she can have; let her hear the best books and converse with the best writers; and she will make her mark in the world." Fanny Crosby, *Life Story* (New York: Every Where Pub. Co., 1905), 56–60.

10. N. W. Coffin to SGH, 23 Aug. 1845, and 1 Oct. 1845, BV 1844–45:331.

11. SGH to George Combe, 29 Aug. 1857, LB 1853–58:472–73; SGH to Mann, 17 Feb. 1842,

HFP 1162. (A portion of the letter to Mann is also found *LJ,* 2:120–21, which omits an interesting evaluation by SGH of the character of Edward Jarvis, the Concord physician who at the time was the superintendent of the Asylum for the Insane in Louisville.)

12. SGH to John C. Warren, 17 Sept. 1849, box 22, John Collins Warren Papers, MHS. See also William P. Coues, "The Spurzheim Collection of Phrenological Casts," *Boston Medical and Surgical Journal* 196 (1927): 400–403.

13. On Crockett's visit to Perkins Institution, see *New London Gazette,* 16 Sept. 1835, 2; Abram V. Courtney, *Anecdotes of the Blind* (Boston: Self-Published), 26. For Martineau's impressions of the blind school, see her *Retrospect of Western Travel* (London: Saunders & Otley, 1838), 3: 119–33. For Wines's impressions, see his *Trip to Boston in a Series of Letters to the Editor of the United States Gazette* (Boston: C. C. Little and J. Brown, 1838), 151–91. On Martineau's visit to the United States, see Walter McDougall, *Throes of Democracy: The American Civil War Era, 1829–1877* (New York: HarperCollins, 2008), 26–29.

14. SGH to Mrs. Granger, 25 Feb. 1837, LB 1836–38:75–76; SGH to Mr. [Calvin] Granger, [undated letters from 1837], LB 1836–38:77–81; SGH to Calvin Granger, 7 Mar. 1837, LB 1836–38:81–83; SGH to Mrs. Granger, 30 Aug. 1839, LB 1839–41:89–89.

15. Maud Howe Elliott, *Three Generations* (Boston: Little, Brown, 1923), 5–6. See also a description of the facility in a letter from S. H. Jenks to his daughter, Miss Lucy O. Jenks, Nantucket, 9 Feb. 1840, Laura Bridgman box, HRL. On South Boston in the 1840s, see Oscar Handlin, *Boston's Immigrants, 1790–1880: A Study in Acculturation* (Cambridge, Mass.: Harvard University Press, 1991), 98–99; Joseph Foxcroft Cole, *South Boston, 1859* (Boston: J. F. A. Cole, 1859). For Florence Howe Hall's memories, see Hall, *Memories Grave and Gay* (New York: Harper and Brothers, 1918), 13–15.

16. SGH to Penniman, 23 Apr.1839, LB 1839–41:38–40.

17. In 1840 the population of South Boston was 6,176, while the population of Boston was, 85,475. Within a decade, however, South Boston's population had more than doubled to 13,309. By 1865 with a population of 29,363 it was becoming, like Boston, crowded. On the growth of South Boston, see Handlin, *Boston's Immigrants,* 239.

18. On meals, see SGH to W. R. Faylor, 18 Oct. 1844, LB 1841–45:477–78.

19. School Record Book, 5 Nov. 1846–23 May 1848, HRL.

20. SGH, School Journal, 29 May 1839 to 25 Apr. 1840, 117.

21. SGH, School Journal, 29 May 1839 to 25 Apr. 1840, 130. Of the advantages of his pupils attending concerts, SGH notes:

> There are however some advantages attending these Concerts, with some disadvantage. In a pecuniary point of view there is not much to be desired for the expenses directly & indirectly do not leave much to be paid over to the Treasurer.
>
> They serve however to excite an interest in the public, to cause [them] to keep the cause of the Blind in sight. They by the interest which they excite cause people to talk & think about the blind and often to recall to mind persons who have blind children & perhaps to go to see them & show them the advantages of being educated.
>
> As for the effects upon pupils they are good so far mental excitement of an agreeable kind, change of scene & occupation, & gentle physical exercise go. The greatest objection I see is the inducements which may be held out to the male pupils to form a company with perhaps some of the girls & to go about giving concerts on their own account. (36–37)

See also SGH, School Journal, 5 Nov. 1846–24 May 1848, 20, 48.

22. SGH to W. J. McDonnell, 9 Mar. 1870, LB 1870–71:39–40.

23. Wines, *Trip to Boston,* 157–58.

24. SGH, *School Journal,* 6 July 1839, 47.

25. On the school's general daily schedule, see SGH, School Journal, 29 May 1839–25 Apr. 1840, 36–37, 40–41, 47, and 5 Nov. 1846–24 May 1848, 4; and SGH to L'Abbé Duvas, 16 Sept. 1854, LB 1853–58:127–29. On the daily prayer service, see SGH to D. Hardwell of New York, 18 Feb. 1839, LB 1839–41:14.

26. SGH to Chapin, 14 Feb. 1839, LB 1839–41:156–58.

27. Wines, *Trip to Boston,* 160.

28. On pupils learning skills for practical work, see SGH to R. H. Holland of Nashville, Tenn., 11 Feb. 1847, LB 1845–48:219. His views on such work appear in the same letter:

> Formerly I supposed that it would be easy to find employment for all educated blind persons, that would save them from *too much* phisical [sic] toil (not from all of it, for it is not desirable) but experience has disappointed me, & I now have settled down in the belief that the great majority of blind persons must resign themselves to the task of getting a simple livelihood by working eight or ten hours daily with their hands. This may seem hard & dark at first; but it need not be so always; & if one can feel the just pride & independence & have the means of social enjoyment & devote a few hours every day to his spiritual & intellectual culture, & look upon this life as a transient period of his existence, he may be happy.
>
> We have something like twenty-five blind persons who work in our shop, & they can earn from four to ten dollars per month, besides their board. Their fare is very plain & their life seemingly hard, but it is a better one than they can get elsewhere, & they generally like it.

On educational equipment and academic subjects, see SGH to [William] Chapin, 14 Feb. 1839, LB 1839–41:156–58.

29. SGH, *School Record,* 4 Feb. 1846, 94.

30. On cold bathing, see SGH, School Journal, 29 May 1839–25 Apr. 1840, 39; Winborn Adams for William Chick to SGH, 25 Nov. 1846, BV 1846–47:121; and "The Blind Asylum" [undated letter], *Boston Daily Advertiser,* 2 Apr. 1872, Scrapbook, 7, HRL. In the 1872 reference, twenty-two pupils defend SGH against critics who have called his insistence on cold bathing cruel. On fishing, see SGH, School Journal, 5 Nov. 1846–24 May 1848, 94.

31. SGH to D. Hardwell of New York, 18 Feb. 1839, LB 1839–41:14; SGH to Ambrose Wellington, 24 Apr. 1850, LB 1848–1853:106.

32. SGH to Mr. Ford, 20 June 1842, LB 1841–45:294–96.

33. James R. Mellow, *Nathaniel Hawthorne in His Times* (Baltimore: Johns Hopkins University Press, 1980), 313.

34. SGH to Dorothea Dix, 5 Nov. 1853, LB 1853–58:25–27.

35. SGH to Hon. P[atrick] Sweeney, 7 Mar. 1870, LB 1870–71:27–30. On keeping the Sabbath, SGH writes:

> This institution, from the very commencement, been conducted on the principle of noninterference with any sectarian doctrine: we have, among the pupils, Catholics, as well as Protestants; we have Baptists, Methodists, Orthodox & Unitarians; each enjoys his own opinion without any attempt on the part of the government of the Institution to constrain or persuade him. My views of religion are, that it is a sentiment & not a dogma; I see in every human being a feeling, a sentiment, a part of his nature, which inclines him to worship—to be religious. I endeavor to educate this part of man's nature, as well as the physical & moral part & to do this daily. As for the Sabbath, each one is to observe it in the way that seems to him a religious ordinance should be observed, provided he leaves to others the uninterrupted & peaceful exercise of their opinion. Parents are to choose for their children, & I ask the parent or guardian of every pupil who enters here, what religious denomination they desire their child to worship with, on the Sabbath; whatever place they indicate, the pupil is required to attend regularly.

SGH adds that, although people have proposed bringing pastors of different denominations to the school for Sunday services, he prefers that students leave the institution to attend services in the community. He continues:

> By going out to church they seem at least, to mix with seeing people; & uniting with them in devotional exercises is pleasing to the blind: it gives them exercise in the open air; it gives an occupation to their minds; and an agreeable excitement attends the preparation for church, on the discussion afterwards of what they heard. . . . I think that the complete isolation of the blind, from the seeing community, is attended with unfavorable consequences; I think that it is apt to engender & keep up an *esprit de corps* among them. (SGH to I. Vaughan of Philadelphia, 26 Sept. 1836, LB 1836–38:1–6)

See also SGH to Rev. Mr. Madge, 12 Apr. 1840, LB 1839–41:185; and SGH to "My Friend," 18 Dec. 1850, LB 1848–53:217–18, in which SGH notes to an unnamed parent of one of his pupils that he is reluctant to allow the pupil to acquire church membership without the permission of the parent.

36. JWH, *Memoir of Dr. Samuel Gridley Howe* (Boston: Albert J. Wright, 1876), 34.

37. On the printing of the Bible in raised letters for blind readers, see SGH to Mr. Hyde, Secretary of the American Bible Society, 31 Mar. 1842, and SGH to Miss Chandler, 2 May 1842, LB 1841–45:248–50, 265–66. Despite his Unitarian motives for printing the Bible in raised type for the blind, SGH was willing to join with Trinitarians like Gerrit Smith in the printing enterprise. In 1836 he accepted a three-hundred-dollar donation from Smith. See Smith to Col. William L. Stone, 27 May 1836, BV 1836–37:65. On Unitarian interest in printing and distributing the Christian scriptures in the 1820s and 1830s, see Jonathan D. Sassi, *A Republic of Righteousness: The Public Christianity of the Post-Revolutionary New England Clergy* (New York: Oxford University Press, 2002), 177; Conrad Edick Wright, *The Transformation of Charity in Post-Revolutionary New England* (Boston: Northeastern University Press, 1992), 208.

38. Horace Mann notebook, 3 May 1837–31 Apr. 1843. Concerning SGH's publication of the Christian scriptures, see SGH to Samuel [J.] May, 12 June 1845, LB 1845–48:7–8.

39. For an example to the controversies about printing for the blind, see SGH to Mr. Cox of Edinburgh, 31 July 1841, LB 1845–48:84–86; and SGH, letter to the editor, *N. British Advertiser*, 16 July 1841, LB 1841–45:88–103. In these letters, SGH wrote to refute the Scotsman John Allston, who had made claims against the system of printing that SGH had devised. Allston also questioned the priority of SGH's work.

40. SGH, "Institution for the Blind."

41. M. C. Paddock to SGH, 17 Feb. 1848, BV 1848–49:17.

42. SGH, "Institution for the Blind."

43. SGH to Mr. and Mrs. McDonald. *Correspondence 1848–1858,* Idiot School, Howe Library, Fernald Center, 348.

44. School Record Book, 5 Nov. 1846–23 May 1848.

45. SGH, "Institution for the Blind."

46. SGH to Mr. Esbrin, 27 Jan. 1841, LB 1839–41:310–13.

47. SGH to Rev. Chs. A. Fisher, 29 Mar. 1852, LB 1848–53. For examples of SGH's numerous letters dealing with his pupils' need for clothing and for their vacations, see SGH to Selectmen of Orleans, Cape Cod, 3 Nov. 1836, LB 1836–38:20–21; SGH to Mrs. Chester, 12 Oct. 1841, LB 1841–45:196–97; SGH to Mrs. Eliza L. Coddington, 15 Nov. 1848, LB 1848–53:3.

48. SGH, "Institution for the Blind."

49. During SGH's tenure as superintendent of the Perkins Institution, each of the New England states and the state of South Carolina contracted with the institution for the education of

their indigent blind children. South Carolina continued to send blind pupils to South Boston until the beginning of the Civil War.

50. SGH to Mann, 16 Apr. 1853, HFP 1407; Jonathan C. Messerli, *Horace Mann: A Biography* (New York: Alfred A. Knopf, 1972), 184; *Proceedings of the New England Anti-Slavery Convention Held in Boston on 27th, 28th, and 29th May, 1834* (Boston: Garrison and Knapp, 1834), 14.

51. Child to SGH, 18 July 1835, BV 1828–35:256; SGH to Child, [ca. July 1835], HFP 1117; SGH to Sumner, 17 Jan. [1853], HFP 1399.

52. SGH to Capron, 26 Aug. 1839, LB 1839–41:86–88. See also SGH to American Board of Foreign Missions, 11 Nov. 1839, LB 1839–41:131.

53. In my discussion of Laura Bridgman, I refer to her during her childhood by her first name, Laura, and during her adult years by her surname, Bridgman.

54. Late-twentieth- and twenty-first-century biographers introduced a new generation of readers to the blind girl from Hanover, N.H. Arguing that during Laura Bridgman's first eight years at the Perkins Institution, 1837–45, SGH, her teacher and benefactor, maintained a close relationship with his pupil only to cast her aside after his disappointment with the lost opportunity to manage her religious maturation, these recent biographies have been more about SGH than they have been about Laura Bridgman. See, e.g., by Ernest Freeberg: "'An Object of Peculiar Interest': The Education of Laura Bridgman," *Church History* 61 (June 1992): 191–205, *The Education of Laura Bridgman: First Deaf and Blind Person to Learn Language* (Cambridge, Mass.: Harvard University Press, 2001), and "'More Important Than a Rabble of Common Kings,': Dr. Howe's Education of Laura Bridgman," *History of Education Quarterly* 34 (Fall 1994), 305–27; by Elizabeth G. Gitter: "Charles Dickens and Samuel Gridley Howe," *Dickens Quarterly* 8 (1991): 162–68, *The Imprisoned Guest: Samuel Howe and Laura Bridgman, the Original Deaf-Blind Girl* (New York: Farrar, Straus and Giroux, 2001), and "Laura Bridgman and Little Nell," *Dickens Quarterly* 8 (1991): 75–79; also, Mary Klages, *Woeful Afflictions: Disability and Sentimentality in Victorian America* (Philadelphia: University of Pennsylvania Press, 1999); Cassandra Cleghorn, "Chivalric Sentimentalism: Samuel Gridley Howe and the Case of Laura Bridgman," in *Sentimental Men: Masculinity and the Politics of Affect in American Culture,* ed. Mary Chapman and Glenn Hendler (Berkeley: University of California Press, (1999), 163–80.

SGH's accounts of Laura Bridgman include "Appendix A: To the Trustees [on Laura Bridgman]," in *Ninth Annual Report of the Trustees of the Perkins Institution and Massachusetts Asylum for the Blind* (1841), 23–42; "Appendix A: Director's Report on Laura Bridgman," "Appendix B: Oliver Caswell," "Appendix C: Lucy Reed," and "Appendix D: Julia Brace," in *Tenth Annual Report of the Trustees of the Perkins Institution and Massachusetts Asylum for the Blind* (1842), 29–60; *An Account of Laura Bridgman, of Boston, Mass: A Blind, Deaf, and Dumb Girl* (1843); "Appendix B: Extract from Dr. Howe's Report on Laura Bridgman," in *Eighteenth Annual Report of the Trustees of the Perkins Institution and the Massachusetts Asylum for the Blind* (1850), 47–89; "Laura Bridgman," *Barnard's American Journal of Education* 11 (Dec. 1857), 383–400; and "Laura Bridgman," *American Annals of the Deaf* 20 (1875): 100–110.

Contemporary and early biographies of Laura Bridgman include "Laura Bridgman; the Deaf, Dumb, and Blind Child," *North American Review,* Apr. 1841, 467–86; Mary Swift Lamson, *Life and Education of Laura Dewey Bridgman, the Deaf, Dumb, and Blind Girl* (Boston: New England Pub. Co., 1878); Maud Howe and Florence Howe Hall, *Laura Bridgman: Dr. Howe's Famous Pupil and What He Taught Her* (Boston: Little, Brown, 1903); and Laura H. Richards, *Laura Bridgman: The Story of an Opened Door* (New York: D. Appleton, 1928).

55. Freeberg and Gitter have indicated that Laura Bridgman entered the Perkins Institution on 12 Oct. 1837, but the Perkins School Roll Book, 14, entry no. 93, records the date as 4 Oct.

1837. Hon. James Barrett, "Laura Dewey Bridgeman [*sic*]," *Woodstock (Vt.) Standard,* 27 Jan. 1876, Scrapbook, 75, HRL; SGH to Mussey, [ca. May 1837], LB 1836–38:130–31.

56. Barrett, "Laura Dewey Bridgeman," 75; Christoph Irmscher, *Public Poet, Private Man: Henry Wadsworth Longfellow at 200* (Amherst: University of Massachusetts Press, 2009), 137.

57. SGH to Margaret Teague, 21 Oct. 1837, and SGH to Harriet Ganage, 23 Oct. 1837, LB 1836–38:195–98.

58. SGH to Mr. [Daniel] Bridgman, 8 Nov. and 11 Dec. 1837, and SGH to Mr. and Mrs. [Daniel] Bridgman, 30 Mar. 1838, LB 1836–38:202, 210–11, 241–43.

59. SGH to Sigourney, 20 Apr. 1838, LB 1836–38:255–57; SGH to Beecher, 21 Sept. 1841, LB 1841–45:178–81; Lawrence to Laura Bridgman, 21 June 1851, Laura Bridgman box, HRL. See also Edna Edith Sayers and Diana Gates, "Lydia Huntley Sigourney and the Beginnings of American Deaf Education in Hartford: It Takes a Village," *Sign Language Studies* 8 (Summer 2008): 369–411.

60. On Sophia Peabody's bust of Laura, see Megan Marshall, *The Peabody Sisters: Three Women Who Ignited American Romanticism* (Boston: Houghton Mifflin, 2005), 408, 418. Also see Patricia D. Valenti, *Sophia Peabody Hawthorne: A Life* (Columbia: University of Missouri Press, 2004), 153–54, 163. On Elizabeth Peabody's plans, see Elizabeth P. Peabody to SGH, [ca. 1842], BV 1842–43:2.

61. E. P. Peabody to SGH, [penciled date 16 July 1842], BV 1842–43:102.

62. Thoreau to SGH, 9 Mar. 1841, BV 1840–41:189. The letter reads:

Sir,

I observed in your paper of March 5th an advertisement for an Assistant Teacher in a Public Institution etc. As I expect to be released from my engagement here in a fortnight, I should be glad to hear further of the above—if the vacancy is not already filled.

I was graduated at Cambridge in '37 previous to which date I had had some experience in school keeping—and have since been constantly engaged as an instructor—for the first year, as principal of the Academy here, and for the last two, as superintendent of the classical department alone.

I refer you to Samuel Hoar, Esq., Rev. R. W. Emerson, or Dr. Josiah Bartlett, of this town, or to Prof. Quincy of Harvard University.

Yours respectfully,
Henry D. Thoreau

63. Francis Lieber likely had known SGH since their participation in the Greek War of Independence, and SGH had no doubt continued his friendship with Lieber before his move to South Carolina. Lieber was also well known to SGH's friend Charles Sumner. After SGH's marriage to JWH, Lieber maintained a close relationship with JWH; the two exchanged letters (usually written in German) from 1843 into the 1850s. Of Lieber's comments on Laura Bridgman, see SGH to Lieber, 7 Aug. 1841, LB 1841–45:109–12.

64. Abbott Lawrence to SGH, 18 Dec. 1836 (quoted in text), and John Davis, Daniel Webster, and Henry Clay to SGH, 20 Dec. 1836, BV 1836–37:152, 153.

65. The tour was planned for Howe by Anthony Bowden, who served Howe for twenty-five years as his tour advance man and business agent before becoming the institution's steward. "Service of Fifty-Three Years," *Boston Daily Globe* (1902), 9, on file at HRL. In this interview, Bowden remembers SGH as "odd and philanthropic."

66. SGH to Otis Sutton, 7 July 1841, and SGH to Lieber, 30 Nov. 1841, LB 1841–43:70–73, 221–22.

67. SGH to Charles Sumner, 6 Dec. 1841, HFP 1158 (this letter is also found in *LJ,* 2:109–12); SGH to Mann, 23 and 26 Dec. 1841, HFP 1159. (The 26 Dec. letter is also found in *LJ,* 2:112–15.)

On SGH's speech to the South Carolina legislature, see the report in the *Boston Recorder,* 7 Jan. 1842, in, Howe box 17, papers 1840–59, HRL. After SGH's speech to the South Carolina legislature, the state in 1842 contracted to send some of its blind students to the Perkins Institution for their education. SGH's remarks to Sumner about slavery in the South and its effects on whites were similar to those made by Tocqueville a decade earlier, in 1831. See Masur, *1831,* 43.

68. SGH to Hon. Mr. Smith, Washington, D.C, 29 Mar. 1842, and SGH to Mr. Tower, Pennsylvania, 13 Apr. 1842, LB 1841–45:242–43, 255–56.

69. SGH to Sumner, 1 Feb. 1842, HFP 1161. (Only a small portion of this part of SGH's letter was also reproduced in *LJ,* 2:118–19; Richards excised most of this part of her father's letter probably because, as she saw it, it revealed her father's vanity, an attribute that she consistently tried to suppress.) In the excised portion of the letter, SGH complained about the Ohio superintendent:

> Is this not enough success for one day? And although a very paltry attempt was made by the Superintendent of the Ohio Institution to get the glory for his school or part of it, he can get only what I can not[,] for the glory I have the satisfaction of doing the work & want no more. . . .
>
> They came but lo! Accompanied by the Superintendent of their Institution, a man of very small stature, as Mann says, not projected on a large scale!
>
> Well, he saw I was not going to have two commanders of the expedition, & he told me I should have the entire control of every thing as I had projected the thing & was to pay the expenses of his pupils as well as my own. But after we arrived here and just before the exhibition he came & said he ought to have the examination of his pupils. I said I would not allow any condition to be made. I must do all or nothing but determined to waive every thing for the good of the cause I suggested he could have another exhibition so he gave in, but to day the town is filled with placards about an exhibition of the pupils of the Ohio Institution for the Blind.
>
> But the day is won already. Not a soul must know of our disagreement except you, & you, you dog, are *malque moi* my alter ego.

See also SGH to Smith, 29 Mar. 1842; and SGH to Sumner, 30 Jan. 1841, HFP 1160. (A portion of this letter is also found in *LJ,* 2:116–17.) On the response of local Kentuckians to SGH's 1842 visit to their state, see "Institution for the Blind," *Louisville Daily Journal,* 8 Feb. 1842.

70. Gilderoy W. Griffin, *Studies in Literature* (Baltimore: Henry C. Turnbull, 1870), 11–12.

71. Mary P. Mann, *The Life of Horace Mann* (Boston: Lee and Shepard, 1904), 158–59.

72. SGH to Mann, 17 Feb. 1842.

73. Charles Sumner to Maria Weston Chapman, 30 Nov. 1842, A.9.9.17:125, Boston Public Library; SGH, "Scenes at a Slave Prison," in *Liberty Bell* (Boston: Mass. Anti-Slavery Society, 1843), 175–80. On the *Liberty Bell,* see Debra Gold Hansen, *Strained Sisterhood: Gender and Class in the Boston Female Antislavery Society* (Amherst: University of Massachusetts Press, 1993), 134. SGH's recounting of the slave beating reappeared in 1853 in Harriet Beecher Stowe, *A Key to Uncle Tom's Cabin* (Boston: Jewett & Co., 1853), 34–35. On the "pornography of pain," see Karen Halttunen, "Humanitarianism and the Pornography of Pain in Anglo-American Culture," *American Historical Review* 100 (Apr. 1995): 303–34. On New Orleans as a site for the slave trade, see Josephine F. Pacheo, *The Pearl: A Failed Escape on the Potomac* (Chapel Hill: University of North Carolina Press, 2005), 41–42.

74. Edward F. Payne, *Dickens Days in Boston: A Record of Daily Events* (Boston: Houghton Mifflin, 1927), 61–63, 90. Payne incorrectly claims that SGH met Dickens at the Tremont House on 1 Feb. 1842. On that date, SGH was in Kentucky. See also Amanda Claybaugh, "Toward a New Transatlanticism: Dickens in the United States," *Victorian Studies* 48 (Spring 2006): 450.

75. SGH to Sumner, 1 Feb. 1842, HFP 1161. This letter with the remark about Dickens and other material removed appears in *LJ*, 2:118–19.

76. SGH, "On Universal Language," *The Lectures Delivered before the American Institute of Instruction* (Boston: William D. Ticknor, 1842), 37–83.

5. Private Lives, Public Causes

1. SGH to Mann, 4 Aug. [1847], HFP 1140. The best biography of Horace Mann remains Jonathan C. Messerli, *Horace Mann: A Biography* (New York: Alfred A. Knopf, 1972).

2. Anne-Marie Taylor, *Young Charles Sumner and the Legacy of the American Enlightenment, 1811–1851* (Amherst: University of Massachusetts Press, 2001), 154. See also SGH's undated, written account of his involvement in the Broad Street riots in HFP 2429; and Messerli, *Horace Mann,* 238.

3. Any biography of Sumner must begin with David H. Donald, *Charles Sumner and the Coming of the Civil War* (New York: Knopf, 1960); and Donald, *Charles Sumner and the Rights of Man* (New York: Knopf, 1970). But Donald's interpretation of Sumner as an arrogant and psychologically flawed figure should be balanced with Paul Goodman, "David Donald's Charles Sumner Reconsidered," *New England Quarterly* 37 (Sept. 1964): 373–87; and Gilbert Osofsky, "Cardboard Yankee: How Not to Study the Mind of Charles Sumner," *Reviews in American History* 1 (Dec. 1973): 595–606. Also important to the study of Sumner is Taylor, *Young Charles Sumner.*

4. Quotation from Sumner to Lieber in Franklin B. Sanborn. *Dr. S. G. Howe, the Philanthropist* (New York: Funk and Wagnall, 1891), 121.

5. A recent and innovative biography of Longfellow is Charles C. Calhoun, *Longfellow: A Rediscovered Life* (Boston: Beacon Press, 2004). Less biographical literature exists on Cleveland and Hillard than on the other members of the Five of Clubs. On Cleveland, see George S. Hillard, *A Selection of the Writings of Henry R. Cleveland with a Memoir* (Boston: Freeman and Bolles, 1844). See also Frederick J. Blue, "The Poet and the Reformer, Longfellow, Sumner, and the Bonds of Male Friendship, 1837–1874," *Journal of the Early Republic* 15 (Summer 1995): 273–97; and the brief mention in Van Wyck Brooks, *The Flowering of New England, 1815–1865* (Cleveland: World, 1946), 165. On Hillard and Sumner, see James R. Mellow, *Nathaniel Hawthorne in His Times* (Baltimore, Md.: Johns Hopkins University Press, 1980), 169.

6. Calhoun, *Longfellow,* 134–36. Calhoun incorrectly dates Sumner's first trip to Europe as 1841. On Platonic love among nineteenth-century men, see Mellow, *Nathaniel Hawthorne,* 344–50. On SGH's support of the temperance movement in Boston, see *Boston Atlas,* 8 Oct. 1845, 2; *Boston Atlas,* 3 Oct. 1846, 2. Gary Williams, *Hungry Heart: The Literary Emergence of Julia Ward Howe* (Amherst: University of Massachusetts Press, 1999), 61, 228, suggests that Howe and Sumner had a homoerotic relationship that was likely not realized. This claim reflects a twentieth-century view of homosexuality. Men and women in the antebellum period commonly enjoyed loving Platonic relationships between members of the same sex.

7. Mary H. Grant, *Private Women, Public Person: An Account of the Life of Julia Ward Howe from 1819 to 1868* (Brooklyn, N.Y.: Carlson, 1994), 51.

8. JWH, *Reminiscences, 1819–1899* (Boston: Houghton Mifflin, 1900), 49–50. A sentence in a letter JWH wrote to her sisters suggests that she observed but did not meet SGH in Feb. 1841: "I met the Chevalier there, for the first time, but did not talk to him, as he does not dance, and went away early." JWH to Louisa Ward and Annie Ward, n.d., HFP 382.

9. John Jay Chapman, who knew JWH when he was a young man and she was old, remembered that she had studied Italian with Lorenzo DaPonte, the librettist who had written the

words of the operas *Don Giovanni* and the *Magic Flute* for Mozart. See DeWolfe Howe, *John Jay Chapman* (Boston: Houghton Mifflin, 1937), 196–97; Williams, *Hungary Heart,* 13–23; and Clifford, *Mine Eyes Have Seen the Glory,* 29–51.

10. Grant, *Private Woman, Public Person,* 33, 42.

11. Florence Howe Hall, "The Friendships of Julia Ward Howe: No. 2 Longfellow, Sumner, and Felton," *Housekeeper,* Dec. 1910, 14.

12. SGH to Ward, 1 Jan. 1843, Papers of the Julia Ward Howe Family, 1787–1984, MC272M-133, Schlesinger Library, Harvard University. (Hereafter JWH family papers.)

13. SGH to Ward, 24 Aug. 1842, HFP 1164. See also Kathryn Allamong Jacob, *King of the Lobby: The Life and Times of Sam Ward, Man-about-Washington in the Gilded Age* (Baltimore: Johns Hopkins University Press, 2010), 31–41.

14. Sumner to Lieber, Charles Sumner Papers 3842, MS Am 1, HL; Felton to Ward, 17 July 1842, JWH family papers; Laura E. Richards and Maud Howe Elliott, *Julia Ward Howe, 1819–1910* (Boston: Houghton Mifflin, 1916), 1:73.

15. SGH to Mann, 6 June 1841, HFP 1155.

16. Felton to Sam Ward, 24 Aug 1842, JWH family papers.

17. SGH to Mann, 16 July 1841, HFP 1156.

18. JWH to Annie Ward and Louisa Ward, [ca. winter 1842], HFP 463.

19. SGH to JWH ("Dearest Julia"), [ca. spring 1843], folder 20, record group 20, collection 2085, Yellow House Papers, Maine Historical Society, Portland.

20. SGH to Sumner ("Don Carlos"), [ca. spring 1843], folder 20, record group 20, collection 2085, Yellow House Papers.

21. Longfellow to Ward, 15 Mar. 1843, JWH family papers.

22. JWH to Annie Ward and Louisa Ward, [ca. Jan.–Feb. 1842], HFP 464. See also Charles Francis Adams. *Richard Henry Dana: A Biography* (Boston: Houghton Mifflin, 1891), 1:63.

23. JWH to Annie Ward and Louisa Ward, n.d., HFP 465.

24. *Letters of Henry Wadsworth Longfellow,* ed. Andrew Hilen (Cambridge, Mass.: Harvard University Press, 1966–1982), 2:529–30.

25. Combe to Mann, 31 Mar. 1841, Horace Mann Papers, 1669–1926, MHS; SGH to Finlay, 13 Aug. 1874, HFP 1682. See also SGH to Samuel Ward, 24 Aug. 1842, HFP 1164; Felton to Samuel Ward, 24 Aug. 1842, and Sumner to Samuel Ward, 9 Nov. 1842, JWH family papers. On the Ticknor party, see *Journal of Richard Henry Dana,* ed. Robert F. Lucid (Cambridge, Mass.: Harvard University Press, 1969), 1:131. On Norton's remembrance, see Sara Norton and M. A. DeWolfe Howe, *Letters of C. E. Norton* (Boston: Houghton Mifflin, 1913), 1:22–23. On the Mann wedding and honeymoon plans, see Messerli, *Horace Mann,* 383–85; Megan Marshall, *The Peabody Sisters: Three Women Who Ignited American Romanticism* (Boston: Houghton Mifflin, 2005), 441–47; Mellow, *Nathaniel Hawthorne,* 131. On SGH's hurt leg, see Stephen Tomlinson, *Head Masters: Phrenology, Secular Education, and Nineteenth-Century Social Thought* Tuscaloosa: University of Alabama Press, 2005), 266–67; Laura H. Richards, *Samuel Gridley Howe* (New York: D. Appleton-Century, 1935), 254; Richards and Elliott, *Julia Ward Howe,* 1:78. On SGH's comments to George Finlay about Mann's marriage, see SGH to Finlay, 13 Aug. 1874, HFP 1682.

26. SGH to Sumner, 17 Sept. 1844, HFP 1214.

27. JWH to Eliza Ward Francis, n.d., HFP 466.

28. *Boston Atlas,* May 2, 1843, 2; Horace Mann notebook, 3 May 1837–31 Apr. 1843, Mann Papers.

29. Horace Mann notebook.

30. Horace Mann notebook.

31. JWH, *Memoir of Dr. Samuel Gridley Howe* (Boston: Albert J. Wright, 1876, 26.

32. JWH, *Reminiscences,* 27.

33. SGH to Sumner, 25 May 1843, continued on 2 June 1843, HFP 1178. Houghton Library misdates this letter 26 May 1843.

34. Paul R. Frothingham, *Edward Everett, Orator and Statesman* (Boston: Houghton Mifflin, 1925), 210.

35. *Life and Letters of Francis Lieber,* ed. Thomas S. Perry (Boston: James Osgood, 1882), 176.

36. JWH to Francis, 18 June [1843], HFP 470.

37. Mary Mann to Pickman, 25 May 1843, Mann Papers.

38. SGH to Sumner, 25 May 1843.

39. SGH to Sumner, 2 Aug. 1843, HFP 1183.

40. JWH scrapbook 1843, 21 July 1843, HFP 1108.

41. JWH journal, ca. 1843, 322, MS Am 2214, HL.

42. Fisher to SGH, 15 Oct. 1843, BV 1842–43.

43. SGH to Sumner, 8 Nov. 1843, HFP 1190. The remainder of SGH's letter reads: "No true woman ever considered it a burden to bear her infant within her, to nourish it with her own blood, & to furnish every part of its body from her own flesh. It is not however, as some suppose, the long gestation, the pain & the suffering that cause the mother's love for her child, because her love begins long before she feels any pain, or any inconvenience. Hardly has she become conscious of the existence of her infant when an intense and absorbing love from it fills her bosom. Long before Julia (with blushed & with hesitation) had announced to me her condition had she felt within her heart a flame of affection for her infant, which will never be quenched but with her life. Since then, how much have we rejoiced together. How have we tasted in advance the bliss of parental love. How have we formed plans for its future. How have we felt the power of this new link which rivets our souls together for aye! And she! Oh, how much more than I! I doubt not that most of her day and night dreams are about it. She labours for it every day."

44. SGH to Sumner, 30 Jan. 1844, HFP 1251. Houghton Library misdates this letter 30 Jan. 1846.

45. SGH to Sumner, 2 Feb. 1844, HFP 1197.

46. SGH to Sumner, 28 Dec. 1843 and 17 Jan. 1844, HFP 1193. See also Lauretta Dimmick, "An Altar Erected to Heroic Virtue Itself, Thomas Crawford and His Virginia Washington Monument" *American Art Journal* 23, no. 2 (1991): 4–73.

47. It was a time of births. On 25 Feb. 1844, Horace Mann Jr. was born. A week later, Mary Mann's sister Sophia Hawthorne gave birth to Una Hawthorne. On 12 Mar., Julia Romana Howe was born. See also Combe to JWH, 20, Feb. [1844], Letters to Dr. Howe, 1838–39, HRL.

48. SGH to Sumner, 16 and 20 Mar. 1844, HFP 1201.

49. "Dr. Howe in Greece," *Farmer's Cabinet,* 4 July 1844, 1.

50. George Sumner to SGH, 10 Aug. 1844, BV 1842–43:270. In pencil "1843" is added, but because of the content of the letter, it had to be 1844.

51. SGH to Sumner, 30 June 1844, HFP 1209; SGH to Sumner, 18 Feb. 1844, HFP 1198.

52. SGH to Sumner, 30 June and 31 July 1844, HFP 1209, 1210.

53. "Julia Ward Howe," *Cosmopolitan Art Journal* 2 (Sept. 1858): 187.

54. Schlesinger Library, Harvard University, houses a large collection of Florence Nightingale's letters to SGH and JWH.

55. Felton to Sumner, 4 Sept. 1844, Sumner Papers 2192.

56. Jane H. Pease and William H. Pease, "Whose Right Hand of Fellowship? Pew and Pulpit

in Shaping Church Practice," in *American Unitarianism: 1805–1865,* ed. Conrad Edick Wright (Boston: Massachusetts Historical Society and Northeastern University, 1989), 191.

57. Messerli, *Horace Mann,* 131–32.

58. SGH to Palfrey, 15 June 1842, MS Am 1704, 475, HL.

59. SGH's letter in defense of Dix's findings appears in the 8 and 27 Sept. 1842 editions of the *Boston Daily Advertiser.* Hooker's responses to Howe's charges appear in the 16 and 30 Sept. 1842 *Advertiser.* Among the recent biographies of Dix are David Gollaher, *Voice for the Mad: The Life of Dorothea Dix* (New York: Free Press, 1975); and Dorothy C. Wilson, *Stranger and Traveler: The Story of Dorothea Dix, American Reformer* (Boston: Little, Brown, 1975).

60. SGH to Dix, [ca. 1842], JHW family papers.

61. SGH, "Insanity in Massachusetts," *North American Review* 56 (Jan. 1843), 171–91; SGH to Palfrey, 24 Oct. 1842, MS Am 1704, 475, HL.

62. SGH to Dix, 15 June 1845, MS Am 1838, 357, HL. (Houghton Library misdates this letter 15 June 1849); SGH to Dix, 30 July 1847, JWH family papers; Dix to SGH, 13 July 1848, BV 1848–49; SGH to Dix, 5 Nov. 1853, LB 1853–58; SGH to Andrew, 2 May 1861, MHS.

63. On the link between of Garrisonian abolitionism and the equality of men and women in marriage, see Chris Dixon, *Perfecting the Family: Antislavery Marriages in Nineteenth-Century America* (Amherst: University of Massachusetts Press, 1997).

64. On the controversy of manual versus oral education of the deaf, see Douglas C. Baynton, "'A Silent Exile on This Earth': The Metaphorical Construction of Deafness in the Nineteenth Century," *American Quarterly* 44 (June 1992), 216–43; and Baynton, *Forbidden Signs: American Culture and the Campaign against Sign Language* (Chicago: University of Chicago Press, 1996).

65. Unknown [probably John D. Fisher] to Samuel Sturtevant, 8 Sept. 1844, LB 1841–45:432.

66. SGH to Bridgman, 23 Nov. 1844, Rockville Collection, Schlesinger Library, Harvard University. On Laura Bridgman's conversion to orthodox Christianity in SGH's absence, see Ernest Freeberg, *The Education of Laura Bridgman: First Deaf and Blind Person to Learn Language* (Cambridge, Mass.: Harvard University Press, 2001); and Elizabeth Gitter, *The Imprisoned Guest: Samuel Howe and Laura Bridgman, the Original Deaf-Blind Girl* (New York: Farrar, Straus and Giroux, 2001).

67. SGH to Beecher, 21 Sept. 1841, LB 1841–45:178–81.

68. Freeberg, *Education of Laura Bridgman,* 161–62.

69. *Eighteenth Annual Report of the Trustees of the Perkins Institution and the Massachusetts Asylum for the Blind* (1850), 47.

70. Parnel Wickham, "Conceptions of Idiocy in Massachusetts," *Journal of Social History* 35 (Summer 2002): 935–54. See also James W. Trent Jr., *Inventing the Feeble Mind: A History of Mental Retardation in the United States* (Berkeley: University of California Press, 1994), 12–14. On the North Carolina school, see SGH to Dr. Merillat, 2 Dec. 1844, LB 1841–45:1711; William A. Graham (of the C.C. Literary Board) to SGH, 27 May 1845, BV 1844–45; SGH to Graham [incorrectly addressed as "Gov. Graham"], 7 July 1845, and SGH to Otis Patten, 28 Jan. 1846, LB 1845–46. For correspondence between Woodward and SGH, see Woodward to SGH, 23 Nov. 1844 and 6 Feb. 1845, HFP 2407, 2410; SGH to Woodward, 2 Dec. 1844 and 13 Feb. 1845, LB 1841–45:1712.

71. SGH to Mann, 4 Aug. [1847], HFP 1140.

72. See SGH to Lieber, 7 Aug. 1841, LB 1841–45:2266; Lieber to SGH, 29 Apr. and 26 Sept. 1845, BV 1844–45. See also Lieber, "On the Vocal Sounds of Laura Bridgman," *Smithsonian Contributions in Knowledge* 2, art. 2 (1851): 1–33.

73. SGH to Chapin, 17 June 1846, LB 1845–46.

74. Frank O. Gatell, *John Gorham Palfrey and the New England Conscience* (Cambridge, Mass.: Harvard University Press, 1963), 3.

75. Philip F. Gura, *American Transcendentalism: A History* (New York: Hill and Wang, 2007), 84.

76. Dean Grodzins, *American Heretic: Theodore Parker and Transcendentalism* (Chapel Hill: University of North Carolina Press, 2002), 479.

77. Mann to SGH, 29 Aug. 1845, BV 1844–45:336.

78. Harold Schwartz, *Samuel Gridley Howe: Social Reformer* (Cambridge, Mass.: Harvard University Press, 1956), 129–36.

79. SGH's four letters appear in the 24 and 28 Feb. and 4 and 5 Mar. 1845 issues of the *Boston Daily Advertiser.* See also SGH to Woodward, 2 Dec. 1844 and 13 Feb. 1845, LB 1841–45; Woodward to SGH, 23 Nov. and 15 Dec. 1844, 12 and 16 Feb. 1845, HFP 2407–10.

80. SGH to Julius, 3 Mar. 1840, LB 1839–1841:166–68.

81. SGH to Julius, 3 Mar. 1840, 169; Sumner to SGH, [ca. 26 July 1846; postmarked 27 July 1846], Sumner Papers 3278.

82. Frank Freidel, *Francis Lieber: Nineteenth-Century Liberal* (Gloucester, Mass. Peter Smith, 1968), 208–9.

83. Gollaher, *Voice for the Mad,* 207–8; SGH to Dix, 15 June 1845; SGH to Dix, 30 July 1847, JWH family papers.

84. Sumner to Lawrence, 29 June 1846, box 4, Amos Adams Lawrence Papers, box 4, MHS.

85. SGH. *An Essay on Separate and Congregate Systems of Prison Discipline, Being a Report Made to the Boston Prison Discipline Society* (Boston: W. D. Ticknor 1846).

86. *Weekly Ohio State Journal,* 7 July 1847, 2.

87. SGH, *Report Made to the Legislature of Massachusetts upon Idiocy* (Boston: Coolidge & Wiley, 1848); SGH, "The Causes and Prevention of Idiocy," *Massachusetts Quarterly Review* 1 (June 1848): 329–30; Edward Jarvis, "Reports on Idiocy," *American Journal of Medical Sciences* 17 (Apr. 1849): 421–41. See also Gerald N. Grob, *Edward Jarvis and the Medical World of Nineteenth-Century America* (Knoxville: University of Tennessee Press, 1978), 110–12; and Robert C. Davis, "Social Research in America before the Civil War," *Journal of the History of the Behavioral Sciences* 8 (June 1972): 69–85.

88. Sandra Harbert Petrulionis, *To Set This World Right: The Antislavery Movement in Thoreau's Concord* (Ithaca, N.Y.: Cornell University Press, 2006), 52–53.

89. Felton to Sumner, 7 July 1845, Sumner Papers 2192. See also Charles J. Beirne, "The Theology of Theodore Parker and the War with Mexico," *Essex Institute Historical Collections* 54 (Apr. 1968): 130–37.

90. *School Record Book,* 5 Nov. 1846–24 May 1848, HRL.

91. SGH to S. Fairbanks, 17 Nov. 1848, LB 1848–53:6. On the changing party systems in Massachusetts, see Dale Baum, *The Civil War Party System: The Case of Massachusetts, 1848–1876* (Chapel Hill: University of North Carolina Press, 1984).

92. On Adams's involvement in the antislavery petition movement and the gag rule, see Joseph Wheelan, *Mr. Adams's Last Crusade: John Quincy Adam's Extraordinary Post-Presidential Life in Congress* (New York: Public Affairs, 2008).

93. Albert J. Von Frank, *The Trials of Anthony Burns: Freedom and Slavery in Emerson's Boston* (Cambridge, Mass.: Harvard University Press, 1998), 37–38.

94. *Memoirs of John Quincy Adams,* ed. Charles Francis Adams (Philadelphia: J. B. Lippincott, 1877), 12:274.

95. For SGH's speech, see Sanborn, *Dr. S. G. Howe,* 217–22. See also *Address of the Committee Appointed by a Public Meeting Held at Faneuil Hall, September 24, 1846,* Appendix (Boston:

White & Potter 1846), 2–6; and Thomas Wentworth Higginson, "Dr. Howe's Anti-Slavery Career," in *Contemporaries* (Boston: Houghton Mifflin, 1899), 295–96. Sanborn's assessment of Howe's public speaking abilities is less grandiose than that of Higginson. According to Sanborn, "[Howe] was never very gifted as an orator; had he trained himself to the art of public-speaking, as Phillips did and Dana and Hillard and others of his younger contemporaries; but he had the natural language which flows from the heart and reaches the heart." Sanborn, *Dr. S. G. Howe,* 141.

96. Vigilance Committee Records, Anti-Manhunting League Records, MHS (a single sheet titled "Items for the Meeting" is pasted onto the initial page of the one notebook devoted to the 1846 Vigilance Committee records kept by Nathaniel I. Bowditch). See also Gary Collison, "The Boston Vigilance Committee: A Reconsideration," *Historical Journal of Massachusetts* 12 (1984): 104–16. On Howe's office, see *LJ,* 2:342.

97. Edward Everett to Alexander H. Everett, 30 Oct. 1846, reel 27, Edward Everett Papers, MHS. On SGH's expectation for losing the election, see JWH to Louisa Ward Crawford, 16 Nov. [1846], HFP 529. On Hillard's support for Winthrop, see SGH to Charles Sumner, 9 Nov. 1846, HFP 1279.

98. A. W. McClure, "The Heresy of Love," *Christian Observatory,* Sept. 1847, 292; and McClure "Laura Bridgman," *Christian Observatory,* Mar. 1847, 180–89.

99. SGH to JWH, [ca. 1842], JWH family papers.

100. JWH to Louisa Ward Crawford, 31 Jan. 1846, HFP 519.

101. JWH to Louisa Ward Crawford, 15 Feb. [1846], HFP 520. Houghton Library misdates this letter 16 Feb. [1846].

102. SGH to Sumner, 20 July 1846, HFP 1265.

103. JWH to Louisa Ward Crawford, 24 July 1846, HFP 523.

104. JWH to Annie Ward, [ca. 1846], HFP 513.

105. Sumner to SGH, 30 Sept. 1844, Sumner Papers 3278; SGH to John Ward, 5 July 1845, SGH to Samuel Ward, 12 July 1845, and SGH to John Ward, 4 May 1846, HFP 1237, 1239, 1259.

106. SGH to Ward, 17 Feb. 1846, JWH family papers.

107. Jacob, *King of the Lobby,* 44–46.

108. JWH to Louisa Ward Crawford, 30 May 1846, HFP 522.

109. Maud Howe Elliott, *Three Generations* (Boston: Little, Brown, 1923), 30–32; Florence Howe Hall, *Memories Grave and Gay* (New York: Harper and Brothers, 1918), 21, 40–45; Laura E. Richards, *When I Was Your Age* (Boston: Estes and Lauriat, 1894), 44–45.

110. JWH to SGH, [ca. 1846], HFP 517. SGH wrote May 2 on the cover.

111. JWH to SGH, [ca. Oct. 1846], HFP 448.

112. JWH and Maud Howe, "American Drawing Rooms, The Story of My Boston Drawing Room," *Woman's Home Companion,* Oct. 1910, 7.

113. Hall, *Memories Grave and Gay,* 50–65.

114. Howe and Howe, "American Drawing Rooms," 8.

115. JWH to Annie Ward, 2 Jan. 1846, HFP 518.

116. [Sarah Margaret] Fuller to SGH, 22 Oct. 1845, BV 1844–45. On JWH to her sister Louisa about house guests, see Richards and Elliott, *Julia Ward Howe,* 1:127–28. On JWH's relationship with Margaret Fuller, see Judith Mattson Bean, "Margaret Fuller and Julia Ward Howe: A Woman-to-Woman Influence," in *Margaret Fuller's Cultural Critique: Her Age and Legacy,* ed. Fritz Fleishmann, 00–00 (New York: Peter Lang, 2000).

117. Richards, *When I Was Your Age,* 200.

118. SGH to Sumner, May 1846, HFP 1258. On Jennette Howe Wales's involvement in Boston eleemosynary agencies, see George Adams, *"The Massachusetts Register" for the Year 1853*

(Boston: Damrell and Moore, 1853), 282–83. On Thomas B. Wales, see Charles J. Kennedy, "The Early Business History of Four Massachusetts Railroads," *Bulletin of the Business Historical Society* 25 (Mar. 1951): 52–72.

119. JWH to Louisa Ward Crawford, 30 May 1846, HFP 522.

120. JWH to Crawford, 13 June 1848, HFP 556.

121. JWH to Annie Ward Mailliard, HFP 511. There is no date on this letter, but because JWH notes that it is a time between the birth and baptism of Florence Marion Howe, it was probably written in 1845. Houghton Library misdates it 1846.

6. For Free Soil and Free Men

1. SGH to Lawrence, 27 Dec. 1845, LB 1845–46:64; Lawrence to SGH, [ca. 23 Dec. 1849], BV 1848–49:302. See also John F. Sears, *Sacred Places: American Tourist Attractions in the Nineteenth Century* (New York: Oxford University Press, 1989).

2. Sumner to SGH, [ca. 26 July 1846; postmarked 27 July 1846], Charles Sumner Papers, MS Am 1, 3278, HL; F.L. [Francis Lieber] to SGH, 13 Feb. 1847, BV 1846–47:163; Lieber to SGH, 21 Mar. 1847, BV 1846–47:172; SGH to Longfellow, 8 Nov. 1847, MS Am 1360, 2867, HL.

3. Anthony Kenny, *Arthur Clough: A Poet's Life* (London: Continuum, 2005), 242–50. On Parker's involvement in the antislavery movement of the late 1840s and 1850s, see Michael Fellman, "Theodore Parker and the Abolitionist Role in the 1850s," *Journal of American History* 61 (Dec. 1974): 666–84.

4. David Herbert Donald, *Charles Sumner and the Coming of the Civil War* (New York: Knopf, 1960), 71. A decade earlier, John Quincy Adams gave an even harsher assessment of Emersonian Transcendentalism, calling it "deadly sophistry . . . [that] consists in the alliance of atheism with hypocrisy." Joseph Wheelan, *Mr. Adams's Last Crusade: John Quincy Adams's Extraordinary Post-Presidential Life in Congress* (New York: Public Affairs, 2008), 210.

5. SGH to Samuel Johnston and SGH to J[oshua] C. Drew, 11 June 1847, LB 1845–46:248–49. Howe wrote to Drew: "I am the more particular about it because I like Mr. Parker's preaching very much myself, & often go to hear him; but I know that there is a very strong prejudice against him & that many parents would suppose their children were going to destruction by setting under his teachings. I wish therefore to know your will respecting this matter; & until I hear from you I shall not allow John to go to hear Mr. P." See also Dean Grodzins, *American Heretic: Theodore Parker and Transcendentalism* (Chapel Hill: University of North Carolina Press, 2002); and Henry S, Commager, *Theodore Parker: Yankee Crusader* (Boston: Little, Brown, 1936).

6. SGH to unnamed blind man, 9 July 1852, LB 1848–53.

7. SGH to Scott, 1 July 1847, LB 1845–46:256.

8. *Sixteenth Annual Report of the New England Institution and the Perkins School for the Blind*, 1848. See also "Hereditary Infirmity," *Common School Journal* 10 (1 July 1848): 1–2.

9. SGH to Clarke, 19 Nov. 1847, MS Am 1589, 7, HL; J. Wesley Thomas, "The Conversational Club," *New England Quarterly* 16 (June 1943): 296–98.

10. SGH to Crawford, 5 Apr. 1848, HFP 1291.

11. JWH to Crawford, 18 Apr. 1848, HFP 555.

12. Lieber to SGH, 13 Mar. 1849, BV 1848–49:196.

13. Mann to SGH, Loose Letters, Howe 17, Papers 1840–50, HRL.

14. Stanley Harrold, *Subversives: Antislavery Community in Washington, D.C., 1828–1868* (Baton Rouge: Louisiana State University, 2003), 117; Josephine F. Pacheco, *The "Pearl": A Failed Slave Escape on the Potomac* (Chapel Hill: University of North Carolina Press, 2005)

48–9; Richard C. Rohrs, "Antislavery Politics and the *Pearl* Incident of 1848," *Historian* 56 (Summer 1994): 711–12.

15. Mary Kay Ricks, *Escape on the "Pearl": The Heroic Bid for Freedom on the Underground Railroad* (New York: William Morrow, 2007), 3.

16. SGH to Horace Mann, 28 Apr.1848, quoted in Robert L. Stracker, "Samuel G. Howe to Horace Mann," *New England Quarterly* 16 (Sept. 1943): 479–80.

17. SGH to Sumner, [ca. 7 May 1847], HFP 1287; Jonathan C. Messerli, *Horace Mann: A Biography* (New York: Alfred A. Knopf, 1972), 465, 468.

18. SGH to Mann, 9 June 1848, HFP 1296; Rohrs, "Antislavery Politics," 716–17. In August 1852 by the efforts of then senator Charles Sumner, President Millard Fillmore pardoned both Drayton and Sayres. The two most complete histories of the *Pearl* affair are Pacheco, *"Pearl"* and Ricks, *Escape on the "Pearl"*.

19. Williams to SGH, 14 July 1848, BV 1848–49:92.

20. Anne-Marie Taylor, *Young Charles Sumner and the Legacy of the American Enlightenment, 1811–1851* (Amherst: University of Massachusetts Press, 2001) 272–72; Harold Schwartz, *Samuel Gridley Howe, Social Reformer* (Cambridge, Mass.: Harvard University Press, 1956), 169.

21. SGH to Mann, 8 Aug. 1848, HFP 1297; SGH to Longfellow, 23 Sept. 1848, MS Am 1360, 2867, HL.

22. *New Hampshire Sentinel*, 14 Feb. 1850, 3.

23. Horace Mann to Mary Mann, 20 Feb. 1849, Horace Mann Papers, 1669–1926, MHS.

24. SGH to Horace Mann, 30 July 1840, HFP 1150. Houghton Library follows Richards by dating this letter 1840; the context suggests, however, that it was 1846.

25. George Adams, *"The Massachusetts Register" for the Year 1853* (Boston: Damrell and Moore, 1853), 28.

26. SGH to Mr. and Mrs. Littlefield, 23 July 1849, LB 1848–53:45–49. See also SGH to several families, 7–23 July 1849, LB 1848–53:39–49; and Charles E. Rosenberg, *The Cholera Years: The United States in 1832, 1849, and 1866* (Chicago: University of Chicago Press, 1987).

27. *Salem Gazette*, 29 Sept. 1849, 2.

28. JWH to Annie Ward Mailliard, [ca. March 1850], HFP 598. See also Anne Stokes Alexander, "Laura E. Richards, 1850–1943: A Critical Biography" (Ph.D. diss., Columbia University, 1979).

29. SGH to Sumner, 1 Mar. [1850], HFP 1318.

30. Douglas C. Stange, *Patterns of Antislavery among American Unitarians, 1831–1860* (Rutherford, N.J.: Fairleigh Dickinson University Press, 1977), 38; *Boston Daily Atlas*, 8 May 1852, 2; Albert J. Von Frank, *The Trials of Anthony Burns: Freedom and Slavery in Emerson's Boston* (Cambridge, Mass.: Harvard University Press, 1998), 37–38. Because Congress had already returned Alexandria from the District of Columbia to Virginia. most of the District's former slave trading continued now in Virginia rather than in the District.

31. Messerli, *Horace Mann*, 519–21.

32. Felton to SGH, 9 May 1852, BV 1852–53:77. The remainder of the letter reads:

> Now, when I went to Washington, I passed a few days in Baltimore, on my way. One day, in company here, a very distinguished gentleman, knowing me as a Massachusetts man only, said, "What a singular person Mr. Sumner, the Mass. senator is? After abusing the President like a convicted criminal, he now seeks his acquaintance, and is commonly remarked upon as *his toady*." I defended Sumner, by saying that he doubtless separated the magistrate from the private man, and that he had always been in the habit of associating with the most eminent persons, wherever he was.
>
> But the defense was not admitted: the [illegible] opinion was that, after so grievous an attack on Mr. Fillmore, his frequent visits to him showed the greatest possible insen-

sibility to the proprieties of life. I found the same view universally taken in Washington: and the truth is; my dear Howe, that language of Sumner, if wrong, should have been as publicly retracted as it was first uttered: or, he should never have sought the acquaintance of Mr. Fillmore. Read it, and you cannot help coming to that conclusion yourself.

Now as to myself. The moment I began to differ from Sumner's opinions, he began to use language to me implying either that I was a weakling or a villain. I do not say he meant that, but his language did. Next he began to send newspapers with articles against me into my family. I wrote a short and angry note, requesting him to cease. My language to him, then and on other occasions, was severe, but I never said anything impeaching his honor. One day, however, I was speaking of Calhoun (it was soon after Calhoun's death) and saying how sad it was this so great a man should go down to posterity chiefly as the advocate of Slavery. He turned upon me with great bitterness and said, "Your opinions on slavery are more disgraceful to you, than his were to him." I took my hat and left his office, not trusting myself to reply. The whole tone of his conversation with me implied not only that I was wrong, but disgracefully and criminally wrong: and there was an assumption of superiority in all respects most offensive and insulting. Finally, he wrote me a letter, in which he chose to speak of the "enormity of my conduct" and other language equally outrageous, and inconsistent with friends or any other relations: and then, in express terms, broke off an acquaintance of fifteen or twenty years, which I may venture to say was as useful to him as to me.

But not withstanding this, two or three months after when Kent was in Cambridge, he walked with him to my house. I went out to meet them, an offered Sumner my hand. He received the advance with coldness, and refused to enter my house, but turned without a word even of civility and walked away. Again, at a Phi Beta [Kappa] meeting, I offered him my hand with equal success. I had now done even more than was wholly consistent with self-respect: and came to the conclusion that if our old relations were ever to be restored, it must be by an advance on his part: I could do no more.

When he met my wife afterwards, at a party, he passed her by without a sign of recognition, which he had not done before. Of course this was saying as plainly as anything could, that he meant the breaking off should be entire and final: I so considered it.

When I was in Washington, he passed me by without a sign of recognition too: the first time, I was waiting at the door of the Senate chamber, for a Senator who was going to admit me. Sumner was in the lobby, and entered by the same door, passing me without a look or a word. Of course I expected this: and it was not for me to solicit a renewal of an intercourse that had been so [ ] snapped. But, had he attained the feelings which you suppose, how easy and proper for him, *then* to come forward. But he did not—nor did he on any other occasion of my stay there—three weeks in all. I left Washington not thinking much about it, but convinced that Sumner was still of the same mind as when he wrote his last letter to me.

I must say that my regret has been somewhat diminished by seeing him permit himself [to] become the candidate of such a coalition, and then to accept a deal in the Senate, [ ] by such means. The utter inconsistency of his course, since he entered the Senate, with his speeches before, is another circumstance that has made me review his conduct with a sentiment of distrust. Mr. Fillmore said, when some one spoke to him of Sumner's strange inconsistency in seeking the society at his home, "Mr. Sumner seeks to like me pretty well; at any rate, by coming to my house, he shows *that he did not believe what he said,*" and everybody is making similar remarks; in contrasting his course in the Senate with his violent speeches before he became a member. My opinion is that he is convinced of the wrong and in policy of his former violent course, and is acting and will act in this conviction: but if a thousandth part of this inconsistency has been detected in Winthrop or Webster, these would be [ ] the vituperations with which they would have been loaded.

But I did not mean to go into these public matters. I only wish to recall to your recollection the fact that it was Sumner and not I who ended our relations: and to show you that I have done all and more than all the case required of me, to restore them. He has done nothing, except to send a message through Agassis. Of course, I have no desire to stand on punctilio: but I can never consent again to any intercourse *with any man* who claims the right of charging on me "enormity of conduct" for a difference of opinion. I say nothing of allowing his intimate friend and classmate, to slander my private character in the Commonwealth. Dr. Palfrey, who never was under any obligation of any sort to me, generally defended me: though he allowed the Editor to strike out his well known signature, and the date & place of the communication. I say nothing of these things because these may have been a supposed political necessity. But I have defended Sumner, and Longfellow, under circumstances that could have saved me from all reproach, had abstained. But I have *no policy* to consider, when wrong is to be righted and justice done.

I add to the parcel a copy of the Cambridge Chronicle containing an article on Kossuth's visit—the last part of which (the general reflection) is mine. You will not wholly agree with me her; but partly, you will.

Love to Julia
Ever your friend,
C. C. Felton
P.S. Burn up this letter, when read.

33. Sumner to SGH, 3 Sept. 1850, Sumner Papers 3278.

34. Besides the destruction of the Five of Clubs, the Compromise of 1850 led to the breakup of Howe's and Sumner's relationship with Lieber. Frank Friedel, "Francis Lieber, Charles Sumner, and Slavery," *Journal of Southern History* 9 (Feb. 1943): 75–93. On Sumner's support of Felton at the time of his wife's illness and death, see Taylor, *Young Charles Sumner,* 233.

35. James M. McPherson, *The Struggle for Equality: Abolitionists and the Negro in the Civil War and Reconstruction* (Princeton, N.J.: Princeton University Press), 6–7.

36. SGH to John G. Palfrey, 10 Aug. [1859], MS Am 1704, 475, HL.

37. *Francis William Bird: A Biographical Sketch* (Boston: Privately Printed, 1897), 34–35. See also Donald, *Charles Sumner,* 321–22.

38. Laura E. Richards, *When I Was Your Age* (Boston: Estes and Lauriat, 1894), 182–83.

39. JWH to Louisa Ward Crawford, [ca. May 1850], HFP 599.

40. JWH to Annie Ward Mailliard and Louisa Ward Crawford, [ca. June 1850], HFP 592: 21.

41. SGH to Sumner, 20 and 21 June 1850, HFP 1326 (this letter also appears in *LJ,* 2:312–13, but the description of Miss Hayes is omitted); SGH to Sumner, 27 June 1850, HFP 1327. Recent histories of SGH's work with Laura Bridgman (cited in Chapter 4, n54) have claimed that Howe lost interest in Bridgman after 1844, on Howe's return from his honeymoon and discovery that Bridgman had converted to Trinitarian Christianity. With Bridgman's education completed, Howe was no longer absorbed in daily educational activities with his pupil, though in his absences from the Blind School, he almost always inquired about Bridgman. His interest in her remained steadfast throughout his life, though he left daily companionship to her immediate teachers.

42. Cited in Taylor, *Young Charles Sumner,* 329.

43. Sumner to SGH, 30 July 1850, Sumner Papers 3278. James R. Mellow, *Nathaniel Hawthorne in His Times* (Baltimore, Md.: Johns Hopkins University Press, 1980), 329–30.

44. SGH to Dr. [Hervey] Wilbur, 24 Dec. 1850, LB 1848–53:220–22.

45. SGH to Sumner, 20 Aug. 1850, HFP 1333. This letter also appears in Richards, *JLSGHSH,* 322–23, but SGH's comments about Crawford and George Sumner are omitted.

46. SGH to Sumner, 26 Sept. 1850, HFP 1335.

47. SGH to Byington, 12 Mar. 1846, LB 1845–46:97–100.

48. "Education of Idiots," *Southern Literary Messenger* 15 (February 1849): 65–68; Matilda Freeman Dana, "Idiocy in Massachusetts," *Southern Literary Messenger* 15 (June 1849): 367–70; George B. Emerson, "Dr. Howe's Report on Idiocy." *Christian Examiner and Religious Miscellany,* 15 (Jan. 1851): 103–33.

49. John Greenleaf Whittier, "Instruction of Idiots," *National Era,* 20 June 1850, 1–2. See also Whittier, "Peculiar Institutions of Massachusetts," in *Literary Recreations and Miscellanies* (Boston: Ticknor and Fields, 1854), 20–33.

50. SGH to Longfellow, 5 Dec. 1867, LB 1862–68:579; SGH to Richards, 18 Nov. 1850, LB 1848–53:196. SGH also discusses his community living plan in SGH to Mrs. Hamilton, 18 Nov. 1850, LB 1848–53:197. He discusses Masten in SGH to Overseers of the Poor, Walpole, Mass, 18 June 1850, LB 1848–53:130–31.

> Warren Crane Masten, a pauper of your place having been since Dec. 1848 an inmate of the School for Idiots under the charge of this institution is this day discharged & will be sent to you. All has been done for him that can be done for such a case in such a time. That has been I am sorry to say inadequate to produce any radical change in his condition.
>
> You will see that his countenance & his skin indicate a much better bodily condition than when he came here. His natural functions are more under his own control. He can now observe habits of decency. He is docile & obedient. In all bodily respects there has been great improvement. He will be in a less unhappy condition himself, be a less disagreeable object for others, if care & attention are given him so that he shall not relapse into his former filthy & unhealthy habits.
>
> His mind has become a little less ill-regulated; he can exercise more command over his volition; he can do many things for himself; with a careful & watchful attendant he can do simple work such as picking & wheeling stones, etc. In school he has made a little progress; he knows his letters & simple words.
>
> There is however, I believe some organic cerebral disorder which precludes the hope of any natural change in his unhappy condition. It is from morbid action of the brain & from no willful perverseness that his appetite for food & drink is insatiable. He must be treated with a view to this & considered irresponsible. He may be fed to fullness & given plenty of drink & then he will immediately (if suffered to do as he likes) gorge himself from the swill-pail, & drink from a puddle or from the water closet.
>
> I do not consider him so proper a subject for further continuance in this school, because it is an experimental one & there are other applicants whose claims are stronger than his.

51. Peter R. Knights, *The Plain People of Boston, 1830–1860: A Study of City Growth* (New York: Oxford University Press, 1971), 28.

52. SGH to Thomas R. Howard, Esq., 27 Dec. 1850, LB 1848–53:223–24.

53. Frequent moves like those of the Howe family during the 1850s and 1860s were common in prewar Boston. During the first half of the nineteenth century, in any given year, a quarter of Boston's population moved. Most moves were among different neighborhoods. Jack Larkins, *The Reshaping of Everyday Life, 1790–1840* (New York: Harper Perennial, 1989), 206.

54. Franklin B. Sanborn. *Dr. S. G. Howe, the Philanthropist* (New York: Funk and Wagnall, 1891), 169–70.

55. Anna M. Wallace, *History of the Walter E. Fernald State School* (Waltham, Mass.: Fernald State School, 1940), 10–11.

56. On the growth of institutions for people with intellectual disability, see James W. Trent Jr., *Inventing the Feeble Mind: A History of Mental Retardation in the United States* (Berkeley: University of California Press, 1994).

57. "Idiotic Youth," *Columbus Gazette,* 25 Dec. 1857, 2.

58. SGH to JWH, 27 Oct. [1850], folder 20, record group 20, collection 2085, Yellow House Papers, Maine Historical Society, Portland.

59. Gary Williams, *Hungry Heart: The Literary Emergence of Julia Ward Howe* (Amherst: University of Massachusetts Press, 1999), 117–22, 150–56; Mary H. Grant, *Private Woman, Public Person: An Account of the Life of Julia Ward Howe from 1819 to 1868* (Brooklyn, N.Y.: Carlson, 1994), 97–99.

60. Gary Collison, *Shadrach Minkins: From Fugitive Slave to Citizen* (Cambridge, Mass.: Harvard University Press, 1997), 91–100; Ellen Samuels, "A Complication of Complaints: Untangling Disability, Race, and Gender in William and Ellen Crafts *Running a Thousand Miles for Freedom,*" *MELUS* 31 (Fall 2006): 15–47.

61. Higginson, "Dr. Howe's Anti-Slavery Career," in *Contemporaries* (Boston: Houghton Mifflin, 1899), 297.

62. Stange, *Patterns of Antislavery,* 39.

63. Taylor, *Young Charles Sumner,* 323.

64. JWH to Mailliard, 17 Apr. [1853], HFP 422.

65. SGH to Sumner, 6 Feb. 1852, HFP 1365.

66. SGH to Mann, 7 May [1852], Mann Papers, 1669–1926; *Boston Herald,* 13 Apr. 1853, 4. See also Merle Curti, "The Impact of the Revolutions of 1848 on American Thought," *Proceedings of the American Philosophical Society* 93 (10 June 1949): 209–15; Michael A. Morrison, "American Reactions to European Revolutions, 1848–1852," *Civil War History* 49 (2003): 111–32; Florence Howe Hall, *Memories Grave and Gay* (New York: Harper and Brothers, 1918), 67–68. On Richard Henry Dana's remembrance of his evening with the Kossuths at the Howes, see Charles Francis Adams, *Richard Henry Dana: A Biography* (Boston: Houghton Mifflin, 1891), 1:215–16. On Kossuth in America, see Donald S. Spencer, *Louis Kossuth and Young America: A Study of Sectionalism and Foreign Policy, 1848–1852* (Columbia: University of Missiouri Press, 1977).

67. SGH to Sumner, 28 Dec. 1851, HFP 1361. See also SGH to Sumner, 7 Jan. 1854, HFP 1423.

68. SGH to Sumner, 5 July [1853], HFP 1411. Parts of this letter are also found in *LJ,* 2:391–93.

69. SGH to Hooper, 7 Nov. 1853, HFP 1412.

70. SGH, *A Letter to J. H. Wilkins, H. B. Rogers, and F. B. Fay* (Boston, 1853), 3–36.

71. SGH to Mann, 29 Dec. [1851], HFP 1362. The letter also appears in *LJ,* 2:330. Richards incorrectly dates it 1850.

72. Hawthorne to William Ticknor, *Letters of Nathaniel Hawthorne, 1853–1856,* 177. Sumner to SGH, 15 Jan. 1854, Sumner Papers 3278; Nathaniel P. Willis to SGH, 10 Jan. 1854, HFP 2401; Nathaniel See also Wendy O. Johnson, "Male Sentimentalism through the 'I-s' of Julia Ward Howe's Poetry," *South Atlantic Review* 64 (Fall 1999): 16–35.

73. JWH to Annie Ward Mailliard, [1854], HFP 624, 625.

74. JWH to Louisa Ward Crawford, 23 July 1854, MS Am 2215, 385, HL.

75. Hall, *Memories Grave and Gay,* 130.

76. SGH to Sumner, 10 Jan. 1852, HFP 1364. On the Free Soil movement, see Frederick J. Blue, *The Free Soilers: Third Party Politics, 1848–54* (Urbana: University of Illinois Press, 1973).

77. See Richard Abbott, *Cotton and Capital: Boston Businessmen and Antislavery Reform, 1854–1868* (Amherst: University of Massachusetts Press, 1991).

78. See Eli Thayer, *A History of the Kansas Crusade, Its Friends, and Its Foes* (New York: Harper, 1889).

79. Henry Wilson, *History of the Rise and Fall of the Slave Power in America* (Boston: J. R. Osgood, 1875), 2:436.

80. *Boston Herald,* 27 May 1854, 2.

81. SGH to Parker, 2 June 1854, HFP 1419. On the Anthony Burns capture and trial, see Von Frank, *Trials of Anthony Burns;* and Samuel Shapiro, "The Rendition of Anthony Burns," *Journal of Negro History* 44 (Jan. 1959): 34–51.

82. SGH to Mann, 18 June [1854], HFP 1431.

83. Henry Mayer, *All on Fire: William Lloyd Garrison and the Abolition of Slavery* (New York: St. Martin's Press, 1998), 443–44.

84. Langhorne to SGH, 29 June 1854, BV 1854–55:103.

85. SGH to Langhorne, 14 July 1854, LB 1853–58:112.

86. SGH to Langhorne, 5 Sept. 1856, LB 1853–58:349–51.

87. SGH to Parker, [Nov. 1854], HFP 1421.

88. SGH to Butler, 3 Feb. 1855, HFP 1444.

89. JWH, "The Great Agitation IV: Recollections of the Antislavery Struggle," *Cosmopolitan* 7, no. 3 (July 1889): 284–85.

90. Evan Carton, *Patriotic Treason: John Brown and the Soul of America* (Lincoln: University of Nebraska Press, 2006), 187–93, 197–99, 202–6. See also Michael D. Pierson, "'All Southern Society Is Assailed by the Foulest Charges': Charles Sumner's 'The Crime Against Kansas' and the Escalation of Republican Anti-Slavery Rhetoric," *New England Quarterly* 68 (Dec. 1995): 531–57.

91. SGH to Sumner, 25 May 1856, HFP 1460.

92. *Boston Advertiser,* 25 May 1856, 1.

93. SGH to Agents & Leaders of the [Kansas] Emigrant Train, 1 Aug. 1856, Massachusetts Kansas Aid Committee Manuscripts, MHS.

94. SGH to Lawrence, 22 Dec. 1856, box 10, Amos Adams Lawrence Papers, MHS.

95. Mayer, *All on Fire,* 475.

96. Charles E. Heller, *Portrait of an Abolitionist: A Biography of George Luther Stearns, 1809–1867* (Westport, Conn.: Greenwood Press, 1996), 95–96.

97. SGH to Lawrence, 8 Jan. 1857, box 11, Lawrence Papers. MHS mislabeled this letter 6 Jan. 1857.

98. *Life and Letters of Francis Lieber,* ed. Thomas S. Perry (Boston: James Osgood, 1882), 293.

99. SGH to Kemble, 3 Apr. 1857, LB 1853–58:415–16. Howe thanked Kemble for her visit and added, "I have had a strong desire ever since I heard you read, that the pupils of this Institution should enjoy, likewise, what was to me a rich treat."

100. SGH to Fisher, 1 July 1857, LB 1853–58:108–9.

101. SGH to Julia Romana Howe ("Dudikins"), 9 May [1857], HFP 1304.

102. SGH to Mann, 25 June 1857, HFP 1481.

103. James Freeman Clarke. *Memorial and Biographical Sketches* (Boston: Houghton, Osgood and Co., 1878), 145.

104. On Sanborn's "unpleasant persistence" on Edith Emerson, see Robert D. Richardson Jr., *Emerson: The Mind on Fire* (Berkeley: University of California Press, 1995), 549.

105. Heller, *Portrait of an Abolitionist,* 99.

106. Heller, *Portrait of an Abolitionist,* 96, 99, 100–101.

107. Robert L. Gale, *Richard Henry Dana* (New York: Twayne, 1969), 79–80.

108. SGH to Parker, 17 May 1859, HFP 1512.

109. JWH, *A Trip to Cuba* (Boston: Ticknor and Fields, 1860), 11–12.

110. SGH to Parker, 25 Mar. 1860, HFP 1536.

111. [John Brown] to SGH, 1 Mar. 1859, HFP 75.

112. SGH to Lowell, 14 May [1859], MS Am 1659, 133, HL; Schwartz, *Samuel Gridley Howe,*

233; Jeremiah Chaplin and J. D. Chaplin, *Life of Charles Sumner* (Boston: D. Lothrop, 1874), 23.

113. SGH to Parker, 3 Aug. 1859, HFP 1514.

114. SGH to Palfrey, 3 May 1859, MS Am 1704, 475, HL. Howe used the same description of Webster in a letter to Moncure Conway about the Webster statue: "Among the signs, look at the event we are called upon to celebrate next Saturday: the *erection* of the first statue in the public grounds of Massachusetts to any public man, & that one the man whose last great effort was to debauch the moral sense of the people, & to conquer their prejudice in favour of humanity & justice!" SGH to Conway, 13 Sept. 1859, Letters Received by SGH, MHS.

115. SGH to Sumner, 4 Feb. [1856], HFP 1445. Houghton Library misdates this letter 4 Feb. 1855. The context suggests 1856. The literature on John Brown's activities in Kansas, his association with the "Secret Six," and the raid at Harper's Ferry are chronicled in several recent works: Louis A. De Caro Jr., *"Fire from the Midst of You": A Religious Life of John Brown* (New York: New York University Press, 2002); Stephen B. Oates, *To Purge This Land with Blood: A Biography of John Brown,* 2nd ed. (Amherst: University of Massachusetts Press, 1984); Merrill D. Peterson, *John Brown: The Legend Revisited* (Charlottesville: University of Virginia Press, 2002); David S. Reynolds, *John Brown, Abolitionist* (New York: Knopf, 2005).

7. War, Freedmen, and Crete

1. Philip F. Gura, *American Transcendentalism: A History* (New York: Hill and Wang, 2007), 259.

2. Edward J. Renehan Jr., *The Secret Six: The True Tale of the Men Who Conspired with John Brown* (New York: Crown, 1995), 208–9.

3. Circular, 2 Nov. 1859, box 13, Amos Adams Lawrence Papers, MHS.

4. *New York Herald,* 16 Nov. 1859, 5. The letter is reprinted in Franklin B. Sanborn, *Dr. S. G. Howe, the Philanthropist* (New York: Funk and Wagnall, 1891), 269–70.

5. *New York Herald,* 17 Nov. 1859, 2.

6. David, Gollaher, *Voice for the Mad: The Life of Dorothea Dix* (New York: Free Press, 1975), 386.

7. Joseph Wheelan, *Mr. Adams's Last Crusade: John Quincy Adam's Extraordinary Post-Presidential Life in Congress* (New York: Public Affairs, 2008), 193–94.

8. Douglas R. Edgerton, *Year of Meteors: Stephen Douglas, Abraham Lincoln, and the Election that Brought on the Civil War* (New York: Bloomsbury Press, 2010), 49.

9. *Blue-Eyed Child of Fortune: The Civil War Letters of Colonel Robert Gould Shaw,* ed. Russell Duncan (Athens: University of Georgia Press), 177–78.

10. Charles E. Heller, *Portrait of an Abolitionist: A Biography of George Luther Stearns, 1809–1867* (Westport, Conn.: Greenwood Press, 1996), 106–7; John Stauffer, *The Black Hearts of Men: Radical Abolitionists and the Transformation of Race* (Cambridge, Mass.: Harvard University Press, 2001), 237–45. Tilden G. Edelstein, *Strange Enthusiasm: A Life of Thomas Wentworth Higginson* (New Haven, Conn.: Yale University Press, 1969), claims that although Higginson was the only member of the Secret Six who did not flee the country or burn letters after the John Brown affair, he "never again would . . . admit what he had so jubilantly hailed upon first reading of the attack, when its success seemed possible. He would never again admit that John Brown's actions, and his own words and deeds until Brown's utter defeat, were clearly directed toward 'the most formidable slave insurrection'" (224).

11. T. W. Higginson to SGH, 5 Nov. 1859, MS E.5.1, pt.1, p. 96, Boston Public Library.

12. Gary Collison, *Shadrach Minkins: From Fugitive Slave to Citizen* (Cambridge, Mass.: Harvard University Press, 1997), 211.

13. Henry David Thoreau, "A Plea for Captain John Brown," in *Reform Papers,* ed. Wendell Glick (Princeton, N.J.: Princeton University Press, 1973), 112–15. Also see Gura, *American Transcendentalism,* 260–62.

14. Ralph Waldo Emerson, "Speech at a Meeting to Aid John Brown's Family," in *Emerson's Antislavery Writings,* ed. Len Gougeon and Joel Myerson (New Haven, Conn.: Yale University Press, 1995), 117–20. See also John J. McDonald, "Emerson and John Brown," *New England Quarterly* 44 (Sept. 1971): 377–96.

15. SGH to Sumner, 6 Dec. 1859, HFP 1488 (Houghton Library misdates this letter 6 Dec. 1857). See also Renehan, *Secret Six,* 237.

16. SGH to Sumner, 20 and 26 Dec. 1859, HFP 1521, 1520; Sumner to SGH, 25 Jan. 1860, Charles Sumner Papers, MS Am 1, 3278, HL; "How-e Appropriate," *Vanity Fair,* 21 Jan. 1860, 62.

17. Stearns to SGH, 27 Feb. 1860, Letters Received by SGH, MHS.

18. Thomas to SGH, 15 Mar. 1860, BV 1858–60:315.

19. SGH to Sumner, 5 Apr., 23 May, 1 June 1860, HFP 1537, 1542, 1543.

20. Sam Ward to JWH, 20 Oct. 1860, HFP 2215. Kathryn Allamong Jacob in *King of the Lobby: The Life and Times of Sam Ward, Man about Washington in the Gilded Age* (Baltimore: Johns Hopkins University Press, 2010), 27, is incorrect in her claim that SGH was in Canada in Oct. 1860.

21. SGH to Sumner, 11 and 20 Dec. 1860 and 20 Jan. [1861], HFP 1554, 1555, 1556.

22. SGH to Sumner, 30 Jan. [1861], HFP 1559; SGH to Francis Bird, 30 Jan. [1861], HFP 1558; SGH to Andrew, 13 Apr. 1861, reel 5, John Albion Andrew Papers, MHS; *Boston Daily Advertiser,* 21 Jan. 1861, 1; Adam Goodheart, *1861: The Civil War Awakening* (New York: Knopf, 2011), 178.

23. Harris to SGH, 4 May and 1 June 1861, BV 1861–63:34, 42; SGH to Butler, 4 Aug. 1862, LB 1862–68:86.

24. SGH to Andrew, 7 May 1861, reel 6, Andrew Papers.

25. SGH to Andrew, 17 Aug. 1861, reel 8, Andrew Papers. See also SGH to Sumner, 20 Dec. 1861, HFP 1574.

26. Thomas H. O'Connor, *The Athens of America: Boston 1825–1845* (Amherst: University of Massachusetts Press, 2006), 109–10.

27. James M. McPherson, *The Struggle for Equality: Abolitionists and the Negro in the Civil War and Reconstruction* (Princeton, N.J.: Princeton University Press), 75–79; SGH to Lawrence, 11 Feb. 1863, box 17, Lawrence Papers. On the formation and goals of the Emancipation League, see James M. Stone to Caroline N. Dall, 10 Oct. 1861, reel 3, Caroline Dall Papers, MHS. See also Richard H. Abbott, *Cotton and Capital: Boston Businessmen and Antislavery Reform, 1854–1868* (Amherst: University of Massachusetts Press), 161–62.

28. SGH, *A Letter on the Sanitary Conditions of the Troops in the Neighborhood of Boston, Addressed to His Excellency the Governor of Massachusetts* (Washington, D.C: U.S. Government Printing Office, 1861). On the Sanitary Commission, see Robert H. Bremner, *The Public Good: Philanthropy and Welfare in the Civil War Era* (New York: Knopf, 1980), 35–71.

29. SGH to Sumner, 27 Jan. [1862], HFP 1577.

30. SGH, *A Letter to Mrs. ——, and Other Loyal Women* (Boston: Ticknor & Fields, 1862), 14–16.

31. SGH to Bird, 5 Mar. 1862, HFP 1581. This letter also appears in *LJ,* 2:500–501, but the remarks about McClellan are omitted.

32. SGH to Sumner, 21 Jan. [1862], HFP 1577.

33. SGH to Julia Romana Howe, 9 Dec. 1861, HFP 1573.

34. George M. Frederickson, *The Inner Civil War: Northern Intellectuals and the Crisis of the Union* (Urbana: University of Illinois Press, 1993), 98–112.

35. *The Journals of Charlotte Forten Grimké,* ed. Brenda Stevenson (New York: Oxford University Press, 1988), 375.

36. Heller, *Portrait of an Abolitionist,* 143.

37. SGH's handwritten notes on back of Owen to SGH, 19 Mar. 1863, MS Am 702, 76, HL; SGH to Sumner, 14 Apr. 1863, HFP 1609 (Houghton Library misdates this letter 4 Apr. 1865).

38. Eric Foner, *Reconstruction: America's Unfinished Revolution, 1863–1877* (New York: HarperCollins, 2002), 8.

39. SGH to Mary Mann, 6 Sept. 1863, reel 37, Horace Mann Papers, 1669–1926, MHS. See also Deborah Pickman Clifford, "'The Last Letter to Sammy' by Julia Ward Howe," *Harvard Library Bulletin* 25, no. 1 (1971): 50–62.

40. SGH to Sumner, 27 Jan. [1862] and 11 June 1863, HFP 1577, 1591.

41. E. H. Derby, "Resources of the South," *Atlantic Monthly,* Oct. 1862, 508.

42. SGH, *The Refugees from Slavery in Canada West* (Boston: Wright & Potter, 1864), 104. See SGH to Agassiz, 3 and 18 Aug. 1863, MS Am 1419, 415, 416, HL. In SGH to Sumner, 20 Aug. 1863, HFP 1592, Howe writes: "Letters from Agassiz & others confirm my belief in the non persistence of the Mulattoes anywhere. With the utter abolition of slavery & giving free play to natural laws we shall have an exodus southward & a rapid disappearance by means of nonfertility of this breed, of our mulattoes—a consummation devoutly to be wished for, notwithstanding some brilliant exceptions, it is a very poor breed." See also McPherson, *Struggle for Equality,* 145–46; Foner, *Reconstruction,* 68–69; Sidney Kaplan, "The Miscegenation Issue in the Election of 1864," *Journal of Negro History* 34 (July 1949): 274–343.

43. Stauffer, *Black Hearts of Men,* 280.

44. Knight to SGH, 6 Oct. 1864, Howe Papers, Samuel Gridley Howe Library, Fernald Developmental Center, Waltham, Mass.

45. James M. Pomeroy, "Survey," 3 Sept. 1864, American Freedmen's Inquiry Commission Papers, HL.

46. Foner, *Reconstruction,* 68–69; W. E. B. DuBois and David L. Lewis, *Black Reconstruction in America, 1860–1880* (New York: Free Press, 1998), 599; McPherson, *Struggle for Equality,* 186–87, 252.

47. SGH to Sumner, 19 Dec. 1863, HFP 1597.

48. SGH to Sumner, 14 July 1861, HFP 1583. Houghton Library misdates this letter 1862.

49. Oscar Handlin, *Boston's Immigrants, 1790–1880: A Study in Acculturation* (Cambridge, Mass.: Harvard University Press, 1991), 239.

50. Handlin, *Boston's Immigrants,* 98–99.

51. Laura E. Richards, "My Boston," *Yankee,* July 1937, 6.

52. Florence Howe Hall, letter to the editor, *New York Times Book Review,* 13 Apr. 1919, 192. See also Edward Waldo Emerson, *The Early Years of the Saturday Club, 1855–1870* (Boston: Houghton Mifflin, 1918), 269–76.

53. Maud Howe Elliott, *Three Generations* (Boston: Little, Brown, 1923), 63.

54. Richards, "My Boston," 9–10; Henry Richards, "Henry Marion Howe '69," *Harvard Graduates' Magazine* 31 (Sept. 1922): 56–58.

55. SGH to Terry, 14 Oct. 1866, HFP 1632.

56. SGH to Richards, n.d., folder 20, record group 20, collection 2085, Yellow House Papers, Maine Historical Society, Portland.

57. Elliott, *Three Generations,* 46–47.

58. Elliott, *Three Generations,* 62.

59. Laura E. Richards, *When I Was Your Age* (Boston: Estes and Lauriat, 1894), 62–64, 87, 91.

60. Henry Cabot Lodge, *Early Memories* (New York: Charles Scribner's Sons, 1913), 293–94; Sheldon M. Novick, *Henry James: The Young Master* (New York: Random House, 1996), 116–19; Mary Murphy-Schlichting, "A Summer Salon: Literary and Cultural Circles in Newport, Rhode Island, 1850–1890" (Ph.D. diss., New York University, 1992), 37, 50–53.

61. Maud Howe, handwritten copy of a speech or article, 14 Aug. 1945, folder 28, Maud Howe Elliott Papers and Diaries, Special Collections, John Carter Brown Library, Brown University; Florence Howe Hall. *Memories Grave and Gay* N.Y.: Harper & Brothers, 1918), 142.

62. Richards, *When I Was Your* Age, 184.

63. Christian G. Samito, ed., *"Fear Was Not in Him": The Civil War Letters of Major General Francis C. Barlow, U.S.A.* (New York: Fordham University Press, 2004), 171.

64. Florence Howe Hall, *Memories Grave and Gay* (New York: Harper and Brothers, 1918), 155–77.

65. SGH to "Dear Sir," 21 July 1858, LB 1858–61:95.

66. SGH to Carter, Oct. 1857, LB 1853–58:483–84.

67. SGH to Palmer, 8 Apr. 1850, LB 1848–53:104–5.

68. SGH to J. W. Rainey, 4 May 1854, LB 1853–58:197.

69. SGH to [unstated], [ca. Jan. 1865], LB 1862–68:236.

70. SGH to Combe, 15 Dec. 1857, LB 1853–58:503–5.

71. SGH to Agassiz, 4 June 1856, LB 1853–58:327–28.

72. "The Blind Asylum," *Boston Daily Advertiser,* 2 Apr. 1872, 7:

73. SGH to Capt. Taylor, 17 Jan. 1865, LB 1862–68:234.

74. SGH to Carolus Noyes, 26 Mar. 1861, LB 1853–58:403–4.

75. SGH to Rev. Mr. Knapp, 26 Mar. 1863, LB 1862–68:138. See also Walter S. Gardener to SGH, 22 Oct. 1862, BV 1861–63:232.

76. A. H. Higgs to SGH, 13 and 21 July and 24 Sept. 1866, BV 1863–67:303, 304, 319; F. R. Woodward to SGH, 10 Dec. 1866, BV 1863–67:363.

77. Parker to SGH, 19 Nov. 1862, BV 1863–67:249.

78. SGH to "My Dear Sir," [ca. May, 1862], LB 1862–68:61–62.

79. Perkins Employees to SGH, 5 Aug. 1864, BV 1864–67:72.

80. *Boston Herald,* 16 Feb. 1965, 2.

81. McPherson, *Struggle for Equality,* 186–87.

82. "Dedication of the Statue of Horace Mann," *Boston Herald,* 6 July 1865, 5. See also Elizabeth Milroy, "The Public Career of Emma Stebbins: Work in Bronze," *American Art Journal* 34, no. 1 (1994): 2–14.

83. Jessie Bernard, "The Social Theory of Samuel Gridley Howe," *Sociology and Social Research* 17 (1933): 314–23.

84. SGH to Clarke, 12 Nov. 1865, MS Am 1569,7, HL. See also SGH to Andrew, 26 Feb. 1861, reel 3, Andrew Papers.

85. Elliott, *Three Generations,* 82–83.

86. Quoted in Bremner, *Public Good,* 146–47.

87. SGH, *Ceremonies at Laying the Cornerstone of the New York Institution for the Blind at Batavia* (Boston: Walker, Fuller & Co, 1866), 18–40.

88. SGH to Sumner, 10 Feb. 1865, HFP 1606.

89. Foner, *Reconstruction,* 482–83; Chris Dixon, *Perfecting the Family: Antislavery Marriages in Nineteenth-Century America* (Amherst: University of Massachusetts Press, 1997), 152.

90. SGH to Dear Sir [parent of a deaf daughter], 21 Apr. 1875, HFP 1686.

91. Smith to SGH, 16 Feb. 1858, BV 1858–60:164.

92. SGH to Smith Feb. 1860, LB 1858–61:308–10.

93. SGH to Blanchet, 11 Oct. 1865, LB 1862–65:348–55.

94. SGH to Hartshorn Miller, 11 Jan. 1869, LB 1868–70:69–70.

95. SGH to [each trustee of the Perkins Institution], 20 Feb. 1869, LB 1868–70:80–81; SGH to Lydia Ames, Malden, 16 May 1869, LB 1868–70:114; SGH to Trustees [of the Perkins Institution], 18 Feb. 1869, BV 1869–705:158–59. See also "Concert and Exhibition by the Pupils of the Institution for the Blind in Lowell," Documents Concerning the Reorganization of the Institution for the Blind, box 6, SGH writings, HRL; SGH to Campbell, 18 Mar. [1870], LB 1870–71:52–55.

96. SGH to Thomas Hill, 5 July 1869, LB 1868–70:141–42.

97. SGH to Dr. J. B. Murray, 26 Nov. 1869, LB 1868–70:238–39.

98. Elliott, *Three Generations,* 36–38; Florence Howe Hall to SGH, 4 Apr. 1875, Papers of the Julia Ward Howe Family, 1787–1984, MC272/M-133, Schlesinger Library, Harvard University.

99. SGH to Sumner, 21 Feb. 1866, HFP 1614.

100. William Dean Howells, "Review of *Army Life in a Black Regiment,*" *Atlantic Monthly,* Nov. 1869, 644.

101. SGH to Sumner, 22 Apr. 1866, HFP 1617.

102. JWH to Sumner, 17 June 1866, Sumner Papers 3276.

103. *New York Times,* 21 Jan. 1867, 8.

104. SGH to the Cretan Central Committee at Athens, 21 Dec. 1866, LB 1862–68:401–2.

105. SGH to Lawrence, n.d., box 21, Lawrence Papers. On the back is written, "Dr. S. G. Howe, Feb. 20. 67, about some rifles for Greece."

106. SGH to Warner, 31 Mar. 1867, Letter Book 1864–1869, Herman Jackson Warner Papers, MHS.

107. SGH, "Autograph notes on journey to Greece," 29 Apr. 1867, HFP 1715.

108. SGH to Lawrence, 15 May 1867, box 22, Lawrence Papers. On Michael Anagnostopoulos see Bill Kondellas. *The Educational Philosophy of Michael Anagnostopoulos, 1837–1906: Reflections on Universal Education,* Ph.D. diss., Loyola University Chicago, 2001.

109. SGH to Warner, 13 June 1867, Warner Papers.

110. SGH to Maud Howe, 7 July 1867, HFP 1643.

111. SGH, "Notes on Trip to Argos," 25 and 26 June 1867, HFP 1715. On the interest among Americans in the Cretan rebellion, see Arthur J. May, "Crete and the United States, 1866–1869," *Journal of Modern History* 16 (Dec. 1944): 286–93.

112. SGH to Jennette Howe Wales, 8 July 1867, HFP 1715.

113. SGH to Warner, 6 July 1867, Warner Papers.

114. SGH to Warner, 28 July 1867, Warner Papers.

115. SGH, *The Cretan Refugees and Their American Helpers: A Statement Addressed to the Contributors for the Relief of Cretan Refugees* (Boston: Lee and Shepard, 1868), 8.

116. SGH, "Autograph notes," 1867, HFP 1715.

117. SGH to William Chapin, 20 May 1851, LB 1848–51:289.

118. SGH, "The Lunatics at Gheel," *Boston Daily Advertiser,* 16 Nov. 1867, 2. See also Jackie L. Goldstein and Marc M. L. Godemont, "The Legends and Lessons of Geel," *Community Mental Health Journal* 39, no. 5 (2003): 441–58. Dorothea Dix, among others, had written about the Gheel as early as the late 1840s. See Gollaher, *Voice for the Mad,* 167–68.

119. Dickens to SGH, 3 Feb. 1868, BV 1868–69; SGH to Dickens, 18 Feb. 1868, LB 1862–68:620–22; SGH to Dickens, 9 June 1869, LB 1868–70:126.

120. SGH to Louisa Ward Crawford Terry, 14 Oct. 1866, HFP 1632; SGH to Sumner, 14 Feb. 1868, Sumner Papers 3278; SGH to Dana, quoted in Charles Francis Adams, *Richard Henry Dana: A Biography* (Boston: Houghton Mifflin, 1890), 2:339.

121. SGH to Sumner, 18 May [1868], HFP 1650; SGH to Sumner, 7 Jan. 1868, HFP 1646. On Sam Ward's support for Andrew Johnson during his trial, see Jacob, *King of the Lobby,* 86.

122. Foner, *Reconstruction,* 473.

123. SGH to JWH, [2 Oct. 1868], HFP 1715, vol. 4.

124. G. Edward White, *Justice Oliver Wendell Holmes: Law and the Inner Self* (New York: Oxford University Press, 1993), 13.

125. SGH to Finlay, 13 Aug. 1874, HFP 1682.

126. SGH to Richards, 27 Nov. 1871, folder 2, record group 20, collection 2085, Yellow House Papers.

8. Santo Domingo—the Perpetual Summer

1. JWH, "S.G.H," notebook 9, MS Am 2214, 32, HL. At the end of the handwritten poem, JWH writes: "These lines were written (by me) when dear Chev was disappointed of the mission to Greece, which should indeed have been his, but which became one of the [ ] weights of a political exigency. This was during Grant's first-term. I lost the lines, but found them recently & preserve them here." JWH is mistaken about the time of the poem. It was likely written around the time of the Johnson impeachment trial.

2. SGH to Sumner, 18 May [1868], HFP 1650.

3. Caswell to SGH, 25 Sept. 1868, LB 1868–69:118a.

4. SGH to Albert G. Greene, 27 Oct. 1868, Greene Collection, Howe, 27 Oct. folder, Special Collections, John Carter Brown Library, Brown University.

5. Bronson Alcott to JWH, 22 Aug. 1868, HFP 6; JWH to Warner, 24 Nov. 1868, Letter Book 1864–1869, Herman Jackson Warner Papers, MHS.

6. Andrea Moore Kerr, *Lucy Stone: Speaking Out for Equality* (New Brunswick, N.J.: Rutgers University Press, 1992), 180.

7. SGH to Clarke, 6 May 1868, HFP 1568.

8. Harold T. Pinkett, "Efforts to Annex Santo Domingo to the United States, 1866–1871," *Journal of Negro History* 26 (1941): 14–44. See also Allan Nevins, *Hamilton Fish: The Inner History of the Grant Administration* (New York: Dodd, Mead, 1936), 250–77.

9. SGH to Henry B. Blackwell, 6 Sept. 1874, Howe 16, loose letters, 2, HRL.

10. Jean Edward Smith, *Grant* (New York: Simon & Schuster, 2001), 505–6. On Frederick Douglass's role in the effort to annex Santo Domingo, see Daniel Brantley, "Black Diplomacy and Frederick Douglass' Caribbean Experiences, 1871 and 1889–1891: The Untold History," *Phylon* 45, no. 3 (1984): 201–4.

11. "Life on Board the Tennessee," *New York Times,* 21 Feb. 1871.

12. SGH to Blackwell, 6 Sept. 1874, 4.

13. "A Sail with Baez," *New York Times,* Mar. 17, 1871; "The Commission at Washington," *New York Times,* 29 Mar. 1871.

14. "San Domingo" and "The Commissioners," *Harper's Weekly* 15 (11 Mar. 1871), 209–10.

15. SGH to Blackwell, 6 Sept. 1874, 5.

16. B. F. Wade, A. D. White, and S. G. Howe, *Dominican Republic Report: Report of the Commission of Inquiry to Santo Domingo* (Washington, D.C.: U.S. Government Printing Office, 1871).

17. Pinkett, "Efforts to Annex Santo Domingo," 14–44; Foner, *Reconstruction,* 494–95.

18. Sumner to SGH, 3 Aug. 1871, Charles Sumner Papers, MS Am 1, 3278, HL.

19. Harold Schwartz, *Samuel Gridley Howe: Social Reformer* (Cambridge, Mass.: Harvard University Press, 1956), 309.

20. JWH, *Reminiscences,1819–1899* (Boston: Houghton Mifflin, 1900), 347.

21. Kerr, *Lucy Stone,* 162–63.

22. Maud Howe Elliott, *Three Generations* (Boston: Little, Brown, 1923, 91–105.

23. JWH, *Reminiscences,* 355–56.

24. SGH to Jennette [Wales], 6 Apr. 1872, folder 2, record group 20, collection 2085, Yellow House Papers, Maine Historical Society, Portland.

25. JWH, *Reminiscences,* 349.

26. SGH to Blackwell, 6 Sept. 1874, 6–9.

27. SGH to Blackwell, 6 Sept. 1874, 8–12.

28. JWH, *Reminiscences,* 348.

29. SGH to Blackwell, 6 Sept. 1874, 9–21.

30. SGH to Bird, 9 Apr. 1874, HFP 1677.

31. SGH to Finlay, 13 Aug. 1874, HFP 1682.

32. SGH to Mr. Noyes, 26 July 1871, HFP 1668.

33. SGH to R. J. Funk, 22 Aug. 1873, LB 1871–74:788–89.

34. SGH to Sherrod, 31 Mar. 1870, LB 1870–71:66–67.

35. SGH to H. W. Smith, 18 July 1871, LB 1871–74:37–38.

36. SGH to Mrs. Bridgman, 28 Nov. 1873, LB 1871–74: 842–43.

37. SGH to Thomas Talbot20 Apr. 1873, LB 1871–74:698.

38. SGH to Bird, 20 July 1875, HFP 1690.

39. JWH diary, 1875, HFP 1107.

40. JWH, *Reminiscences,* 368–69.

41. JWH, poem, 10 Jan. 1876, notebook 15, MS Am 2214, 322, HL.

INDEX

JAMES W. TRENT is a professor of sociology and social work at Gordon College in Wenham, Massachusetts. He previously served on the faculty of Southern Illinois University at Edwardsville. His 1994 book, *Inventing the Feeble Mind: A History of Mental Retardation in the United States,* won the Hervey B. Wilbur Award of the American Association on Intellectual and Developmental Disabilities. He is also the coeditor of *Mental Retardation in America: An Historical Reader* (2004). Trent completed his Ph.D. at Brandeis University and holds master's degrees from Duke University and the University of North Carolina at Chapel Hill.